STUDIES IN SCRIPTURE IN EARLY JUDAISM AND CHRISTIANITY

Edited by
Craig A. Evans

Volume 13

Published under
LIBRARY OF SECOND TEMPLE STUDIES

70

formerly the Journal for the Study of the Pseudepigrapha Supplement Series

Editor
Lester L. Grabbe

JEWISH AND CHRISTIAN SCRIPTURE AS ARTIFACT AND CANON

EDITED BY
CRAIG A. EVANS AND H. DANIEL ZACHARIAS

t&t clark

Published by T&T Clark
The Tower Building, 11 York Road, London SE1 7NX
80 Maiden Lane, Ste 704, New York, NY 10038

www.continuumbooks.com

British Library Cataloguing-in-Publication Data
A catalogue record for this book is available from the British Library

ISBN13:978-0-5672-9329-9(paperback)

Typeset by Data Standards Limited, Frome, Somerset, UK
Printed and bound in the UK by the MPG Books Group

CONTENTS

Jewish and Christian Scripture as Artifact and Canon represents the
thirteenth volume to appear in Studies in Scripture in Early Judaism and
Christianity. Two of the previous volumes are monographs, one by
Rebecca Denova on Luke's use of Scripture (SSEJC, 4; JSNTSup, 141)
and the other by Thomas Hatina on Mark's use of Scripture (SSEJC, 8;
JSNTSup, 232). The other ten volumes are collections of studies that have
more or less systematically worked through the Gospels, the letters of
Paul, other Judaeo-Christian bodies of literature from late antiquity, or
have investigated various questions pertaining to biblical understanding in
the period under review. Strong volumes have emerged that have been
well received and reviewed very positively. We record here our thanks and
appreciation to James Sanders, co-founder of the SSEJC series and co-
editor of several of these volumes. Jim was founder and long-time
president of the Ancient Biblical Manuscript Center in Claremont,
California, and for decades has been a leading voice calling for better
understanding of the development and role of sacred Scripture in
communities of faith.

The present collection of studies focuses on the material aspects of
Jewish and Christian Scripture. The contributors explore aspects of
collection and canon, distinctive characteristics of the manuscripts
themselves, scribal conventions, and interesting, even unusual uses of
authoritative writings that in time became recognized as holy Scripture.
We believe these are important dimensions in the scholarly discussion of
the function of Scripture in early Judaism and Christianity. Our work
reflects the growing awareness in recent years of the importance of the
physical and artistic dimension of the books and collections of authoritative literature in the early centuries of Church and Synagogue. The
editors believe this work will advance the discussion in important ways.

As in the previous volumes, the present volume is enriched with
contributions by established scholars, as well as contributions by younger
scholars, whose work is making itself felt in the discipline. The editors
express their deepest thanks to them. The editors also wish to thank

Sharon Leighton for her assistance in editing and formatting several of the papers and Adam Wright for assisting with the preparation of the indexes.

Craig A. Evans
H. Daniel Zacharias
Acadia Divinity College

ABBREVIATIONS

AAUW	American Association of University Women
AB	Anchor Bible (Commentary)
Aeg	*Aegyptus*
AHDRC	Ancient History Documentary Research Centre
AJP	*American Journal of Philology*
AnBib	Analecta biblica
ANET	J. B. Pritchard (ed.), *Ancient Near Eastern Texts*
APF	*Archiv für Papyrusforschung*
ASP	American Studies in Papyrology
ATD	Das Alte Testament Deutsch
BA	*Biblical Archaeologist*
BAGD	Walter Bauer, William F. Arndt, F. William Gingrich and Frederick W. Danker, *A Greek-English Lexicon of the New Testament and Other Early Christian Literature* (Chicago: University of Chicago Press, 2nd edn, 1958)
BASP	*Bulletin of the American Society of Papyrologists*
BETL	Bibliotheca ephemeridum theologicarum lovaniensium
BGPA	*Berichtigungsliste der Griechischen Papyrusurkunden aus Ägypten*. 11 vols
BGU	*Ägyptische Urkunden in den staatlichen Museen zu Berlin: Griechische Urkunden*, vols 1–9 (Berlin: Weidmann, 1895–1937)
Bib	*Biblica*
BICS	*Bulletin of the Institute of Classical Studies* (London)
BICS.SP	Bulletin of the Institute of Classical Studies of the University of London – Supplementary Papers
BJRL	*Bulletin of the John Rylands* Library of Manchester
BKAT	Biblischer Kommentar: Altes Testament
BL	*Bibel und Liturgie*
BN	*Biblische Notizen*
CAH	*Cambridge Ancient History*
CANE	*Civilizations of the Ancient Near East* (ed. J. Sasson; 4 vols; New York, 1995)

CBET	Contributions to Biblical Exegesis and Theology
CBQ	*Catholic Biblical Quarterly*
CE	*Chronique d'Egypte*
CMC	*Cologne Mani Codex*
CP	*Classical Philology*
CPJ	V. A. Tcherikover and A. Fuks (eds), *Corpus Papyrorum Judaicarum* (3 vols; Cambridge: Published for the Magnes Press, Hebrew University, 1957–64)
CPR	*Corpus Papyrorum Raineri.* Volume VII, *Griechische Texte IV* (ed. H. Zilliacus, J. Frösén, P. Hohti, J. Kaimio, M. Kaimio; Vienna, 1979)
ClQ	*Classical Quarterly*
CQ	*Church Quarterly*
CRINT	Compendia rerum iudaicarum ad novum testamentum
DJD	Discoveries in the Judaean Desert
ed.pr.	*editio princeps*
ExpTim	*Expository Times*
FAT	Forschungen zum Alten Testament
FB	Forschung zur Bibel
GCS	Griechischen christlichen Schriftsteller
✓ *GLH*	*Greek Literary Hands, 350 BC – AD 400*
GRBS	*Greek, Roman, and Byzantine Studies*
HBS	Herders Biblische Studien
HE	Ecclesiastical History
HGV	Heidelberger Gesamtverzeichnis der griechischen Papyrusurkunden Ägypten
HSM	Harvard Semitic Monographs
HTR	*Harvard Theological Review*
ICC	International Critical Commentary
IEJ	*Israel Exploration Journal*
JAC	*Jahrbuch für Antike und Christentum*
JARCE	*Journal of the American Research Center in Egypt*
JBL	*Journal of Biblical Literature*
JEA	*Journal of Egyptian Archaeology*
JHNES	Johns Hopkins Near Eastern Studies
JJP	*Journal of Juristic Papyrology*
JJS	*Journal of Jewish Studies*
JQR	*Jewish Quarterly Review*
JRA	*Journal of Roman Archaeology*
JRH	*Journal of Religious History*
JSJSup	*Journal for the Study of Judaism in the Persian, Hellenistic and Roman Period*, Supplements
JSNTSup	*Journal for the Study of the New Testament*, Supplement Series

JSOT	*Journal for the Study of the Old Testament*
JSOTSup	*Journal for the Study of the Old Testament*, Supplement Series
JTS	*Journal of Theological Studies*
KAI	H. Donner and W. Rollig, *Kanaanäische und aramäische Inschriften*
LÄ	*Lexikon der Ägyptologie* (ed. W. Helck, E. Otto, and W. Westendorf; Wiesbaden, 1972)
LCC	*Library of Christian Classics*
LCL	Loeb Classical Library
LDAB	Leuven Database of Ancient Books
MH	*Museum helveticum*
MMAF	*Mémoires publiés par les membres de la mission archéologie française au Caire* (Paris: E. Leroux, 1886–1920)
MPER	Mittheilungen aus der Sammlung der Papyrus Erzherzog Rainer
NA	E. Nestle and K. Aland (eds), *Novum Testamentum Graece*
NCB	New Century Bible
New Docs	*New Documents Illustrating Early Christianity* (North Ryde, NSW: The Ancient History Documentary Research Centre, Macquarie University, 1981–)
NICOT	New International Commentary on the Old Testament
NovT	*Novum Testamentum*
NovTSup	*Novum Testamentum*, Supplements
NPNF [1]	P. Schaff (ed.), *A Selection of the Nicene and Post-Nicene Fathers: First Series* (14 vols; Edinburgh: T. & T. Clark, 1886; repr. Grand Rapids: Eerdmans, 1954–71)
NPNF [2]	P. Schaff and W. Wace (eds), *A Selection of the Nicene and Post-Nicene Fathers: Second Series* (14 vols; Edinburgh: T. & T. Clark, 1890; repr. Grand Rapids: Eerdmans, 1956–79)
NRSV	New Revised Standard Version
NTS	*New Testament Studies*
NTTS	New Testament Tools and Studies
NTTSD	New Testament Tools, Studies and Documents
Numen	*Numen: International Review for the History of Religions*
OLA	Orientalia lovaniensia analecta
OTG	Old Testament Guides
OTP	James H. Charlesworth (ed.), *Old Testament Pseudepigrapha*
PCPhS	*Proceedings of the Cambridge Philological Society*
PGM	K. Preisendanz (ed.), *Papyri graecae magicae: die griechischen Zauberpapyri* (Leipzig-Berlin: B.G. Teubner, 1973) *Reprint*
PSI	G. Vitelli et al. (eds), *Publicazioni della Società italiana per la Ricerca dei Papiri greci e latini in Egitto: Papiri greci e latini*, vols 1–14 (Florence: E. Ariani, 1912–57)
PTS	Patristische Texte und Studien

RevQ	*Revue de Qumran*
RlA	*Reallexikon der Assyriologie*
RSV	Revised Standard Version
SAA	State Archives of Assyria
SAAS	State Archives of Assyria Studies
SB	F. Preisigke et al. (eds), *Sammelbuch Griechischer Urkunden aus Ägypten*
SBLMS	Society of Biblical Literature Monograph Series
SBLSBS	Society of Biblical Literature Sources for Biblical Study
SBLSymS	Society of Biblical Literature Symposium Series
SBLWAW	Society of Biblical Literature Writings from the Ancient World
SD	Studies and Documents
SNTSMS	Society for New Testament Studies Monograph Series
SO	*Symbolae osloenses*
SSEJC	Studies in Scripture in Early Judaism and Christianity
STDJ	Studies on the Texts of the Desert of Judah
StHell	*Studia Hellenistica*
TAD	*Textbook of Aramaic Documents*
TAPA	*Transactions of the American Philological Association*
TD	*Theology Digest*
TENT	Texts and Editions for New Testament Studies
TU	Texte und Untersuchungen
TynBul	*Tyndale Bulletin*
UBS	United Bible Societies
VigChr	*Vigilae christianae*
VT	*Vetus Testamentum*
VTSup	*Vetus Testamentum*, Supplements
WUNT	Wissenschaftliche Untersuchungen zum Neuen Testament
ZAC	*Zeitschrift für antikes Christentum*
ZAH	*Zeitschrift für Althebräistik*
ZAW	*Zeitschrift für die alttestamentliche Wissenschaft*
ZNW	*Zeitschrift für die neutestamentliche Wissenschaft*
ZPE	Zeitschrift für Papyrologie und Epigraphik

LIST OF ILLUSTRATIONS

LIST OF CONTRIBUTORS

Peter Arzt-Grabner, Universitaet Salzburg
Don Barker, Macquarie University
Annette Bourland Huizenga, University of Dubuque Theological
  Seminary
David Chalcraft, University of Derby
Scott D. Charlesworth, University of New England
John Flanagan, Leiden University
Peter M. Head, Tyndale House
Juan Hernández Jr, Bethel University
Larry Hurtado, University of Edinburgh
Eduard Iricinschi, Princeton University
Thomas Kraus, Willibald Gluck Gymnasium
Armin Lange, University of Vienna
Kirsten Nielsen, University of Aarhus
Dorina Miller Parmenter, Spalding University
Stephen Reed, Jamestown College
Marianne Schleicher, University of Aarhus
Gregg Schwendner, Wichita State University
Pamela Shellberg, Marquette University

Introducing Jewish and Christian Scripture as Artifact and Canon

Craig A. Evans and H. Daniel Zacharias

In explaining part of the reason he wrote the recently published *The Earliest Christian Artifacts* Larry Hurtado tells us in his Preface:

> When I was asked about what I was working on during my year-long research leave, and I responded that I was writing a book on the wider historical importance of early Christian manuscripts, the result was usually a blank stare, and a request to illustrate specifically what things I had in mind. They then characteristically were surprised to learn that our earliest manuscripts already attest efforts at punctuation, larger sense-unit demarcation, and a curiously strong preference for the codex, especially for biblical writings. And they were often intrigued that these matters might have interesting implications for familiar historical questions about early Christianity. I have the strong impression that the material discussed in this book is not as well known as it deserves to be among scholars in the field. Thus one of my key aims here is to draw attention to an important body of data that is often overlooked.[1]

We cannot explain the purpose of the present volume any more clearly. Hurtado, one of the contributors to the present volume, hits the nail right on the head. The physical realities of the very literature that biblical scholars study in such depth and with such rigor is to them, surprisingly, *terra incognita* for the most part. To be sure, biblical scholars are aware of scribal errors and glosses, of so-called textual variants, and of tendencies of one sort or another. But for a long time most scholars have had only passing acquaintance with the topics addressed in Hurtado's book and in the present volume. Accordingly, the purpose of the present collection is to bring together several recent studies that break new ground and explore further important areas of investigation that have been introduced in recent years.

---

1 L. W. Hurtado, *The Earliest Christian Artifacts: Manuscript and Christian Origins* (Grand Rapids: Eerdmans, 2006), p. viii.

The pace of investigation into literacy, scribal practice, and the book culture of late antiquity seems to be quickening. Eric Turner, William Harris, Harry Gamble, Kim Haines-Eitzen, Alan Millard, and Gregory Snyder have produced important works that address questions of literacy, writing, and preservation of literature, especially in reference to Christians in the early centuries of the common era.[2] Haines-Eitzen's book is especially relevant for the present volume, for she inquires into the identity of the scribes who copied Christian literature in the second and third centuries and asks how this literature circulated.

The development and use of the ancient book, or codex, continues to be explored, with some very interesting implications.[3] Important studies of specific codices have been undertaken, including some of the early papyrus books (such as P^{45}, P^{66} and P^{75}),[4] as well as the major majuscules of the fourth and fifth centuries (such as א B D and W).[5] Investigations

2   For a selection of studies, see E. G. Turner, *Greek Manuscripts of the Ancient World* (ed. P. J. Parsons; London: Institute of Classical Studies, 2nd edn, 1987); W. V. Harris, *Ancient Literacy* (Cambridge, MA: Harvard University Press, 1989); H. Y. Gamble, *Books and Readers in the Early Church* (New Haven: Yale University Press, 1995); K. Haines-Eitzen, *Guardians of Letters: Literacy, Power, and the Transmitters of Early Christian Literature* (Oxford and London: Oxford University Press, 2000); A. Millard, *Reading and Writing in the Time of Jesus* (New York: New York University Press, 2000); H. G. Snyder, *Teachers and Texts in the Ancient World: Philosophers, Jews and Christians* (Religion in the First Christian Centuries; London and New York: Routledge, 2000). For important collections of studies, see L. V. Rutgers, P. W. van der Horst, H. W. Havelaar and L. Teugels (eds), *The Use of Sacred Books in the Ancient World* (CBET, 22; Leuven: Peeters, 1998); T. J. Kraus and T. Nicklas (eds), *New Testament Manuscripts: Their Texts and Their World* (TENT, 2; Leiden: Brill, 2006). For a study of pre-Masoretic Text Hebrew manuscripts, see E. Tov, *Scribal Practices and Approaches Reflected in the Texts Found in the Judean Desert* (STDJ, 54; Leiden: Brill, 2004).

3   For a selection of studies, see E. G. Turner, *The Typology of the Early Codex* (Philadelphia: University of Pennsylvania Press, 1977); C. H. Roberts and T. C. Skeat, *The Birth of the Codex* (London: Oxford University Press, 1983); A. Grafton and M. Williams, *Christianity and the Transformation of the Book: Origen, Eusebius, and the Library of Caesarea* (London and Cambridge, MA: Harvard University Press, 2006).

4   For a selection of studies, see T. C. Skeat and B. McGing, 'Notes on Chester Beatty Biblical Papyrus I (Gospels and Acts)', *Hermathena* 150 (1991), pp. 21–25 + pl.; T. C. Skeat, 'A Codicological Analysis of the Chester Beatty Papyrus of the Gospels and Acts (P^{45})', *Hermathena* 155 (1993), pp. 27–43; J. N. Birdsall, *The Bodmer Papyrus of the Gospel of John* (London: Tyndale, 1960); G. D. Fee, *Papyrus Bodmer II (P66): Its Textual Relationships and Scribal Characteristics* (Studies and Documents, 34; Salt Lake City: University of Utah, 1968); C. M. Martini, *Il Problema della recensionalità del Codice B alla luce del Papiro Bodmer XIV (P75)* (AnBib, 26; Rome: Biblical Institute Press, 1966). Now especially see J. R. Royse, *Scribal Habits in Early Greek New Testament Papyri* (NTTS, 36; Leiden: Brill, 2008).

5   For a selection of studies, see H. J. M. Milne and T. C. Skeat, *Scribes and Correctors of the Codex Sinaiticus* (London: British Museum, 1938); E. J. Epp, *The Theological Tendency of Codex Bezae Cantabrigiensis in Acts* (SNTSMS, 3; Cambridge: Cambridge University Press, 1966); D. C. Parker, *Codex Bezae: An Early Christian Manuscript and its Text* (Cambridge: Cambridge University Press, 1992); L. W. Hurtado, *Text-Critical Methodology*

such as these have had significant impact on the study of the formation of the Christian biblical canon.[6]

Other studies have focused on a given region or ancient city in which papyri have been recovered. In this regard, some fascinating work on the papyri from Oxyrhynchus has been published in recent years. William Johnson has studied several hundred 'book-rolls' in an effort to understand the production, function and aesthetics of the ancient book. His close analysis of formal and conventional features of the book-rolls not only provides detailed information on the book-roll industry, such as manufacture, design and format, but also raises some intriguing questions and offers provisional answers about the ways in which the use and function of the book-roll among ancient readers may differ from later practice.[7] Alan Bowman and colleagues have edited a collection of studies that take into account, among other things, art, craftsmanship, monuments, architecture, and even the layout of the city itself.[8] Based on a study of approximately 200 Greek papyri Alexander Jones attempts to assess the astrological practices of Oxyrhynchus. His surprising findings reveal the complexity and international character of horoscopes, astrology, and the arithmetic that lies behind them.[9] And finally, we should mention AnneMarie Luijendijk's forthcoming study of Christian life in the city of Oxyrhynchus, as reflected in literary remains that have been

---

and the Pre-Caesarean Text: Codex W in the Gospel of Mark (Studies and Documents, 43; Grand Rapids: Eerdmans, 1981); L. W. Hurtado (ed.), *The Freer Biblical Manuscripts: Fresh Studies of an American Treasure Trove* (SBL Text-Critical Studies, 6; Atlanta: Society of Biblical Literature; Leiden: Brill, 2006). For very helpful bibliographies of scholarly studies of the papyri and majuscules, see K. Aland (ed.), *Repertorium der griechischen christlichen Papyri. I. Biblische Papyri: Altes Testament, Neues Testament, Varia, Apokryphen* (Patristische Texte und Studien, 18; Berlin and New York: de Gruyter, 1976); J. K. Elliott, *A Bibliography of Greek New Testament Manuscripts* (SNTSMS, 109; Cambridge: Cambridge University Press, 2005); D. C. Parker, *An Introduction to the New Testament Manuscripts and their Texts* (Cambridge: Cambridge University Press, 2008).

6 For a selection of studies, see H. Y. Gamble, *The New Testament Canon: Its Making and Meaning* (Philadelphia: Fortress, 1985); B. M. Metzger, *The Canon of the New Testament: Its Origin, Development, and Significance* (New York: Oxford University Press, 1987); L. M. McDonald, *The Biblical Canon: Its Origin, Transmission, and Authority* (Peabody: Hendrickson, 2007). For a very important collection of studies, see L. M. McDonald and J. A. Sanders (eds), *The Canon Debate* (Peabody: Hendrickson, 2002).

7 W. A. Johnson, *Bookrolls and Scribes in Oxyrhynchus* (Toronto: University of Toronto Press, 2004).

8 A. K. Bowman et al. (eds), *Oxyrhynchus: A City and its Texts* (London: Egypt Exploration Society, 2007).

9 A. Jones, *Astronomical Papyri from Oxyrhynchus (P.Oxy. 4133–4300a)* (Memoirs of the American Philosophical Society, 233; Philadelphia: American Philosophical Society, 1999).

unearthed.[10] She is able to sketch the activities of Sotas, third-century bishop of Oxyrhynchus, who corresponds with Christian communities, teaches, and raises money for the production of books. Luijendijk is also able to identify and describe aspects of persecution and Christian responses to it.[11]

This brief introduction points to some of the areas in which new and fascinating work has been undertaken in recent years and in all probability will continue to be undertaken. The studies that have been assembled in the present volume contribute to this ongoing task.

Jewish and Christian Scripture as Artifact and Canon begins with Armin Lange's important study 'Oracle Collection and Canon: A Comparison between Judah and Greece in Persian Times'. Lange compares Greek oracle collections with Israelite oracle collections codified in the prophets, observing that these collections were often recontextualized and reapplied to periods and settings different from their point of origin. A surplus of meaning in these collections is due to the chronological character of the 'diluted' communication that both Israelite literary prophecy and Greek oracle collections try to bridge. Both Greek oracle collections and Jewish prophetic books were reapplied by way of redaction, 'relecture', and interpretation to various new historical contexts and time frames. Both Jewish prophetic books and Greek oracle collections were interpreted by way of atomization of recontextualization to achieve this purpose.

In 'Artifactual and Hermeneutical Use of Scripture in Jewish Tradition' Marianne Schleicher surveys the Jewish tradition to ascertain ways in which Scripture is used in an artifactual way – with rituals for individuals copying Scripture – the way it is stored, and the way it shows how these objects were viewed as vestiges of holiness. Schleicher believes that the hermeneutical use of Scripture, not being mutually exclusive to the artifactual use, enables the individual to utilize Scripture in times where reality contradicted its teaching, or when circumstances caused the reader to seek advice or comfort.

In 'Early Christian Manuscripts as Artifacts' veteran Larry Hurtado surveys manuscripts from the second and third centuries with a focus on those preserved in Egypt. These early Christian artifacts attest the interest in the Old Testament, with the Psalms being the most frequently attested text, and the Gospels of John and Matthew being the dominant Christian writings. The *Shepherd of Hermas* is the third most attested text, making it

---

10   AnneMarie Luijendijk, *Greetings in the Lord: Christian Identity and the Oxyrhynchus Papyri* (Cambridge, MA: Harvard University Press, 2009).

11   For another assessment of the papyri in a given location, see Jaakko Frösèn et al. (eds), *The Petra Papyri*, vols I and III (American Center of Oriental Research Publications, 4–5; Amman: American Center of Oriental Research, 2002, 2007). This work is not complete; further volumes are expected. *4 volumes*

the most popular noncanonical writing before the fourth century. Hurtado points to the Chester Beatty Gospel codex (P^{45}, ca. 250 CE) as our earliest extant empirical instance of the physical linkage of all four canonical Gospels and which represents the earliest artifact for this effort that continued in the church. This artifact, then, provides physical evidence of affirming more than one Gospel, as well as preferring discrete Gospels. P^{46} likewise contains the earliest collection of Pauline writings, a clear confirmation of gathering and circulating Paul's letters together. This also reinforces the early Christian preference for the codex, which is readily known. Our earliest manuscripts also show the *nomina sacra* and the staurogram as our earliest physical evidence of Christian efforts to express their piety visually. Finally, Hurtado notes the indebtedness of Christian scribal practice to Jewish scribal practice over Hellenistic scribal practice.

Stephen Reed's 'Physical Features of Excerpted Torah Texts' investigates how the physical features of some excerpted Torah texts help us better understand the physical usages and functions of the texts themselves. Most excerpted Torah texts, used for phylacteries or Mezuzot, were passages that called upon the reader to meditate on them, study them, teach them to children, or to place them on their arms, foreheads, or houses. These small texts allowed for easy access to favorite passages or those that needed to be used regularly.

In 'Papyrus 967 and the Text of Ezekiel: Parablepsis or an Original Text?' John Flanagan analyzes the importance of Papyrus 967 and its importance for interpreting the original text of Ezekiel, with attention to the ancient versions of Ezek. 36.23-38. After summarizing scholarly contributions on this issue, particularly the work of Johann Lust, Flanagan argues that the differences between Papyrus 967 and the MT/LXX indicate a lack of parablepsis and the existence of an earlier Hebrew text of Ezekiel.

In 'A Fragmentary Psalter from Karanis and its Context' Gregg Schwendner analyzes portions of the Psalter and other texts found at Karanis and the context that gave rise to the texts. Schwendner describes a recently identified Christian papyrus of LXX Psalms 32–33, and places it into its documentary context based on other available texts found at Karanis. The available textual remains are examined in an attempt to grasp the nature of Christianity at Karanis.

In '"He that Dwelleth in the Help of the Highest": Septuagint Psalm 90 and the Iconographic Program on Byzantine Armbands' Thomas Kraus discusses several sixth–seventh-century armbands which were worn as protective amulets, with the majority having a verse or verses from Septuagint Psalm 90, prized for its apotropaic power. Kraus explains that the armband was worn as a sort of effective expression of protection, perhaps in some cases also functioning as a sort of decoration. In any case, it was always visible to others and always determined by its specific purpose and the manifest belief of its wearer in its necessity and efficacy.

Scott Charlesworth's 'Public and Private – Second- and Third-Century Gospel Manuscripts' suggests that the remarkable uniformity in the size of early Gospel codices is evidence for conventional approaches to manuscript production in the second and third centuries. Christians favored a size approximating the Turner Group 9.1 format in the second century, and the Group 8.2 format in the third century. When combined with other conventional approaches to MS production – semi-literary to literary hands and the use of readers' aids to facilitate public reading – there is much support for the proposal that most codices dated up to the early third century were produced in controlled settings (i.e., in small copy centers or scriptoria comprised of at least two trained scribes) for public or liturgical use. In contrast, many third-century Gospel manuscripts (e. g., P[45]) bear the hallmarks of uncontrolled production for private use.

In her intriguing essay 'A Johannine Reading of Oxyrhynchus Papyrus 840' Pamela Shellberg discusses P.Oxy. 840, which she regards as an early text that portrays Johannine traits. The text, which among other things describes ritual immersion that is consistent with archeological findings of *miqwa'ôt* in early Palestine, is strong claim for its antiquity. Shellberg discusses similar theology behind the texts, particularly in regard to the immersion practice. She believes that P.Oxy. 840 can be read as a non-canonical expression of the replacement theology so prominent in the Fourth Gospel.

In 'How Long and Old is the Codex of which P.Oxy. 1353 is a Leaf?' Don Barker discusses P.Oxy. 1353, a manuscript that contains 1 Pet. 5.5-13. Although traditionally dated to the fourth century, Barker argues that the cursive script is better dated to the late second or third century, and may be an example of the Biblical Uncial style. If the production of P. Oxy. 1353 is dated in the third century or possibly even earlier it joins at least two to three other highly calligraphic second- to third-century New Testament manuscripts, P.Oxy. 1780, P.Med. inv. 69.24, and P.Ant. 1.12. The calligraphic nature of these Christian manuscripts along with P.Oxy. 1353 is evidence of early Christian manuscripts being produced by highly trained scribes. Perhaps a wealthy Christian financed these codices for his or her own personal use or for a church, or it may be that a number of members of a church contributed to their production.

Peter Head's 'Letter Carriers in the Ancient Jewish Epistolary Material' investigates ancient Jewish epistolary documents, in order to learn more about the physical delivery of these letters and the role of the letter carrier in the communication between sender and receiver. The period in question (200 BCE–200 CE) offers relatively little evidence with which to work. The letter carrier, usually named in the text, was sometimes authorized to pass on further information by word of mouth which was not found in the letter. From the books of Maccabees, Head finds that letter carriers not only acted as couriers but also set out the terms of peace between leaders. It is clear that letter carriers were often, though not always, more than simple couriers, party to additional information that was essential to the communication between sender and receiver.

In his technical study ' "I Was Intending to Visit You, but . . ." Clauses Explaining Delayed Visits and their Importance in Papyrus Letters and in Paul' Peter Arzt-Grabner discusses numerous papyri examples of letter writers explaining delayed visits, with an eye to how both the explanation and the letter carrier functioned in the process. This study sheds light on how readers of Paul were expected to understand portions of his letters, particularly the letters to the Corinthians and Thessalonians.

Annette Bourland Huizenga's 'Advice to the Bride: Moral Exhortation for Young Wives in Two Ancient Letter Collections' compares the teaching regarding women in the pastoral epistles with some letters attributed to Pythagorean women. Huizenga, following Jerome Quinn, argues for an original sequence of Titus – 1 Timothy – 2 Timothy, which may then establish Titus 2.3-5 as a lens through which to view the moral training for women in the remaining pastoral letters.

In 'Scribal Tendencies in the Apocalypse: Starting the Conversation' Juan Hernández Jr, after surveying past study on the singular readings of the Apocalypse's manuscript tradition, follows E. C. Colwell's method to examine the singular readings of the Apocalypse in Codex Sinaiticus with an aim to understanding the scribal copying patterns in the manuscript. In this fascinating study of one of the most important Greek biblical witnesses Hernández finds 158 significant singular readings, taking the form of additions, omissions, transpositions, various types of scribal harmonizing, and finally, potential theological singular readings.

Eduard Iricinschi's ' "A Thousand Books Will Be Saved": Manichaean Writings and Religious Propaganda in the Roman Empire' concerns itself with the spread of Manichaeism in the Roman Empire. Manichaeism was very much a religion of the book, Iricinschi explains, with Manichaean writings circulating throughout the Roman Empire as instruments of bilingual religious propaganda – texts that were more attractive, in the opinion of some, than their Christian counterparts.

In 'The Danish Hymnbook – Artifact and Text' Kirsten Nielsen discusses a modern example of Christian artifact in the form of the Danish hymnbook. The hymnbook was often regarded as highly as, and perhaps higher, than the Bible itself. New hymnbooks retain the same text so that the same lyrics and tune would be available to all, which helped foster a sense of community. Certain hymns were also associated with particular families, and hymnbooks were common gifts between believers, with the receiver's name being emblazoned on the front. The text of Danish hymns utilize three ways of speaking about God, metaphor, metonymy and parallelism, which are taken from the Bible itself.

David Chalcraft's 'Towards a Sociology of Bible Promise Box Use' offers a sociological study of a modern Christian artifact called a Bible Promise Box. His study of its use primarily stems from the Salvationist tradition, and highlights its use by individuals for individual encouragement and communal encouragement. As such, it has interesting historical roots in antiquity, in which passages of Scripture functioned as talismans and phylacteries. The Promise Box, Chalcraft notes, was often kept in central areas of the house, and even served as a ministry/outreach tool in some.

Our collection of studies concludes with Dorina Miller Parmenter's 'The Bible as Icon: Myths of the Divine Origins of Scripture' in which she discusses how the Bible functions as icon, a material object that facilitates access to its transcendent prototype. Parmenter summarizes some early pre- and parabiblical texts which serve to highlight how heavenly books were perceived. Her argument, which complements Chalcraft's findings, is that the Bible in contemporary Christian circles draws upon this tradition, which has continued in different forms in the Jewish and Christian traditions, so that the physical Bible itself is often representative of God or Christ's presence.

Oracle Collection and Canon: A Comparison between Judah and Greece in Persian Times[1]

Armin Lange

In ancient Israel, a development from aural prophetic utterances to written prophetic books can be observed. Often, even the prophets themselves initiated the textualization of their own prophecies. Prophets like Amos, Isaiah, Jeremiah, and Ezekiel hoped that their message would meet more receptive ears with later audiences. For them, their prophetic utterances spoke not only to their immediate contexts and carried meaning not only for their immediate audiences but applied also to later times. This means that the prophets themselves were aware of a surplus meaning, an ontic plus of meaning, in their prophetic utterances. The prophetic hope for reapplication of their prophecies met very receptive ears in later times. By way of editing and expanding, prophetic collections were reapplied to later times and new meanings were found in them time and again. Based on the resulting prophetic collections, even more prophetic literature was composed. This process has been dubbed as 'literary prophecy' in scholarly literature.[2] The term is an English translation of the German term 'Schriftprophetie'. The reapplication of existing prophetic texts by way of editing and expanding points to an increased acceptance and authority of the prophetic texts in question.

---

1 This article is a revised version of an earlier study on Greek oracle collections and Israelite literary prophecy ('Literary Prophecy and Oracle Collection: A Comparison between Judah and Greece in Persian Times', in *Prophets, Prophecy, and Prophetic Texts in Second Temple Judaism* [eds M. H. Floyd and R. D. Haak; Library of Hebrew Bible/Old Testament Studies, 427; New York and London: T & T Clark, 2006], pp. 248–75). When the editors of this volume approached me, it was my impression that my comparison of classical Greek oracle collections and Israelite literary prophecy has significant implications for the question of canon. Hence, I reworked my earlier study to include a perspective of canonical history. My revision does not include, however, an update concerning the recognition of scholarly literature. For his advice in classical studies, I am deeply indebted to my UNC colleague, Prof. Dr Zlatko Plese. Without his guidance, I would not have been able to write this article.

2 See e.g. the literature quoted in note 4.

Around or after the turn of the era, this process of expanding and rewriting of prophetic texts experienced a first culmination in the creation of the prophetic collection of the TaNaKH.[3]

The recognition that literary prophecy is prophetic in nature is one of the achievements of the last decades of research. Literary prophecy has even been described as a distinctive characteristic of Israelite prophecy.[4] The evidence from the various Ancient Near East (ANE) cultures seems to argue in favor of this hypothesis. But a phenomenon which is similar to Israelite-Jewish literary prophecy can be observed in classical Greece. In Greece's classical period, oracle collections were prominent. These oracle collections were usually attributed to seers of the past as were the prophetic books of the Hebrew Bible. This could mean that literary prophecy was not a characteristic of Jewish prophecy.

But beyond a comparison between Israelite-Jewish literary prophecy and classical Greek oracle collections the evidence from both ancient cultures is significant for the understanding of the canonical history of the Hebrew Bible as well. Both the prophetic collections of Judaism as well as the oracle collections of classical Greece were not only popular but of great religious authority. Hence, a comparison between the two of them helps to better understand the early stages of the canonical process at whose end the Hebrew Bible evolved.

---

3   For my ideas regarding how and when the Hebrew canon developed in its three parts, see 'From Literature to Scripture: The Unity and Plurality of the Hebrew Scriptures in Light of the Qumran Library', in *One Scripture or Many? Canon from Biblical, Theological, and Philosophical Perspectives* (eds Chr. Helmer/Chr. Landmesser; Oxford: Oxford University Press, 2004), pp. 51–107; 'Authoritative Literature and Scripture in the Chronistic Corpus: The Use of כתוב-Formulas in Ezra-Nehemiah and 1–2 Chronicles', in *The Words of a Wise Man's Mouth are Gracious (Qoh 10,12)* (FS. G. Stemberger; ed. M. Perani; Studia Judaica, 32; Berlin and New York: De Gruyter, 2005), pp. 29–52; ' "Nobody Dared to Add to Them, to Take from Them, or to Make Changes" (Josephus, *Ag. Ap.* 1.42): The Textual Standardization of Jewish Scriptures in Light of the Dead Sea Scrolls', in *Flores Florentino: Dead Sea Scrolls and Other Early Jewish Studies in Honour of Florentino García Martínez* (eds A. Hilhort, E. Puech and E. Tigchelaar; JSJSup, 122; Leiden/Boston: Brill, 2007), pp. 105–26; ' "The Law, the Prophets, and the Other Books of the Fathers" (Sir, Prologue): Canonical Lists in Ben Sira and Elsewhere', in *The Book of Ben Sira. Papers of the Third International Conference on the Deuterocanonical Books, Pápa, Hungary, 18–20 May, 2006* (eds G. G. Xeravits and J. Zsengellér; JSJSup; Leiden/Boston: Brill, 2008), forthcoming.

4   J. Jeremias, 'Das Proprium der alttestamentlichen Prophetie', in idem, *Hosea und Amos: Studien zu den Anfängen des Dodekapropheton* (FAT, 13; Tübingen: J. C. B. Mohr [Paul Siebeck], 1996), pp. 20–33; R. G. Kratz, 'Das Neue in der Prophetie des Alten Testaments', in *Prophetie in Israel: Beiträge des Symposiums 'Das Alte Testament und die Kultur der Moderne' anlässlich des 100. Geburtstags Gerhard von Rads (1901–1971) Heidelberg, 18.-21. Oktober 2001* (eds I. Fischer, K. Schmid and H. G. M. Williamson; Altes Testament und Moderne, 11; Münster and London: Lit Verlag, 2003), pp. 1–22 (8–10, 19).

In this essay, I will ask how far Greek oracle collections can be characterized as literary prophecy and how far the similarities between Greek oracle collections and the Israelite-Jewish prophetic collections shed new light on the canonical history of the Hebrew Bible. I will begin by defining some terminology used in this paper (I). Next, I will briefly describe the phenomenon of literary prophecy in the Ancient Near East and in ancient Israel (II). I will then provide a similar sketch of ancient Greek seers and ancient Greek oracle collections (III). By way of conclusions, I will compare Israelite literary prophecy with the ancient Greek oracle collections (IV).

I. *Terminology*

a. *Prophecy*

In principle, two types of divination can be distinguished: deductive and intuitive divination.[5] Deductive divination tries to divine the transcendent and/or the future by way of analyzing material means which can easily be manipulated by the divine world to communicate its intentions. Examples are extispicy (i.e. divining the future by way of analyzing the intestines of sacrificial animals) or lecanomancy (i.e. divination by way of analyzing patterns created by oil when cast into water). Intuitive divination does not use any material means but relies solely on different types of visions and/or auditions. For the reason that it communicates directly with the divine, prophecy does not rely on material means; hence, it must be classified as a type of intuitive divination.[6] Like intuitive divination as such, prophecy is not proper to Israel but can be found all over the Ancient Near East. Therefore, a definition of prophecy needs to include non-Israelite prophecy as well. For this purpose, I rely on the definition of Ancient Near Eastern prophecy provided by M. Weippert:

> Religious revelatory speech can be described as prophecy, if (a) in a cognitive experience (vision, audition, audiovisual experience, dream etc.), a person encounters the revelation of one or more deities and if (b) this person perceives herself/himself as being ordered to transmit what

---

5 For the distinction between deductive and intuitive divination, see e.g. J. Bottéro, *Mesopotamia: Writing, Reasoning, and the Gods* (trans. Z. Bahrani and M. Van De Mieroop; Chicago, IL and London: University of Chicago Press, 1992), pp. 105–07; idem, *Religion in Ancient Mesopotamia* (trans. R. Lavender Fagan; Chicago, IL and London: University of Chicago Press, 2001), 92, pp. 170–85.

6 For the classification of prophecy as a type of divination see e.g. M. Nissinen, *References to Prophecy in Neo-Assyrian Sources* (SAAS, 7; Helsinki: Neo-Assyrian Text Corpus Project, 1998), pp. 6, 167–69.

was revealed in either verbal (prophecy, prophetic word) or non-verbal communication (symbolic act).[7]

According to this definition, prophecy is a process of communication. The prophet receives a message and communicates it to his or her audience. Although prophecy is mostly aural in character (see below), in many cases, the communication of the message to the audience is achieved in written form. Therefore, writing is not alien to Ancient Near Eastern prophecy.[8]

It is now evident that prophecy uses two media to communicate its oracles, speech and text. In view of prophetic texts, the following analysis of ancient sources shows that there are two basic types of prophetic texts, i.e. written prophecy and literary prophecy.

Written prophecy communicates in written form a prophetic utterance over a geographical distance because its addressee, e.g. a king, is too far removed from a prophet to hear the latter's message. Another form of written prophecy serves archival purposes. Prophetic oracles are written down and/or included in extensive collections for purposes of future reference. Depending on the content of the original prophetic utterance, these archived prophecies are later quoted with different functions. For example, royal inscriptions use archived prophecies to support the claim to fame of a king. In other instances, an archived prophecy documents the decisions of a given deity with regard to the ownership of a house, for example. The common point in all forms of written prophecies is that they do not acquire new meanings surpassing the original intention of a given prophecy.

Literary prophecy, on the other hand, is characterized by its acquisition of a surplus of meaning, which surpasses the original meaning of a given prophetic utterance. Literary prophecy communicates prophetic utterances over a chronological distance to future audiences. This entails the reapplication of a prophetic utterance to a later timeframe, i.e. a prophecy is taken from its original context and read instead in a new context (recontextualization). This recontextualization of a given prophecy resolves in a new understanding in light of its interpretation in a new context.

---

7   M. Weippert, 'Prophetie im Alten Orient', in *Neues Bibel Lexikon* 3: 196–200, 197; my translation of Weippert's definition is somewhat paraphrastic. Similar definitions have been given by K. van der Toorn, 'From the Oral to the Written: The Case of Old Babylonian Prophecy', in *Writings and Speech in Israelite and Ancient Near Eastern Prophecy* (eds E. Ben Zvi and M. H. Floyd; SBLSymS, 10; Atlanta, GA: SBL, 2000), pp. 219–34 (219); and by Nissinen, *References to Prophecy*, pp. 6–9; idem, 'Spoken, Written, Quoted, and Invented: Orality and Writtenness in Ancient Near Eastern Prophecy', in *Writings and Speech in Israelite and Ancient Near Eastern Prophecy* (eds E. Ben Zvi and M. H. Floyd; SBLSymS, 10; Atlanta, GA: SBL, 2000), pp. 235–71 (239–40).

8   See Nissinen, 'Spoken, Written, Quoted, and Invented', pp. 240–42.

b. *Canon*

The earliest use of the Greek word κανών as a designation of a list of books is Athanasius' thirty-ninth Easter letter dated to 367 CE. To use the term 'canon' in modern scholarship on ancient Judaism runs thus the danger of cross-cultural misconceptions. Therefore, I use a more nuanced terminology which was introduced into the study of the Hebrew Bible's canonical history by Eugene Ulrich.[9] Ulrich distinguishes between an 'authoritative text', 'that a community, secular or religious, acknowledges to hold authority' and 'a book of scripture' as 'a sacred authoritative text which, in the Jewish or Christian context, the community acknowledges as having authority over the faith and practice of its members'. The term 'canon' refers to 'the established and exclusive list of books that hold supreme authoritative status for a community'. Finally, the term 'canonical process' or canonical history designates the process beginning with the recognition of authoritative texts and ending in an exclusive canonical list of books having binding authority.

II. *Literary Prophecy in the Ancient Near East and in Ancient Israel*

a. *Egypt*

Prophecy is not exclusive to Israel but can be found all over the ancient Near East. The exception to this rule seems to be Ancient Egypt. From Ancient Egypt, neither prophecies nor prophetic texts are known. The only text which is discussed by scholars as prophetic is the so-called '*Prophecy of Neferti*',[10] which influenced later Egyptian apocalyptic texts like the *Potters Oracle*.[11] Nevertheless, according to the definition of prophecy quoted above, the *Prophecy of Neferti* cannot be classified as prophetic. Although the *Prophecy of Neferti* employs visionary style and language,[12] it lacks the element of revelation from the divine sphere: 'the

---

9   E. Ulrich, 'The Canonical Process, Textual Criticism, and Latter Stages in the Composition of the Bible', in *Sha'arei Talmon: Studies in the Bible, Qumran, and the Ancient Near East Presented to Shemaryahu Talmon* (eds M. Fishbane et al.; Winona Lake, IN: Eisenbrauns, 1992), pp. 267–91, esp. 269–76; idem, 'Canon', in *Encyclopedia of the Dead Sea Scrolls* (eds L. H. Schiffman and J. C. VanderKam; Oxford: Oxford University Press, 2000), I, pp. 117–20, esp. p. 117.

10   For characterization of this text as prophetic, see E. Blumenthal, 'Neferti, Prophezeiung des', *LÄ* 4: 379–80 and R. Schlichting, 'Prophetie', *LÄ* 4: 1122–25, (1123).

11   J. Assman, 'Königsdogma und Heilserwartung: Politische und kultische Chaosbeschreibungen in ägyptischen Texten', in *Apocalypticism in the Mediterranean World and the Near East: Proceedings of the International Colloquium on Apocalypticism Uppsala, August 12–17, 1979* (ed. D. Hellholm; 2nd edn enlarged by a supplementary bibliography; Tübingen: J. C. B. Mohr [Paul Siebeck], 1989), pp. 345–77 (360).

12   For the visionary style and language of the *Prophecy of Neferti*, see J. Bergman, 'Introductory Remarks on Apocalypticism in Egypt', in *Apocalypticism in the Mediterranean*

message is predictive but is not attributed to a god's prompting'.[13] Only in late or even Hellenistic times, divinatory practices fitting the above definition of prophecy occur, such as the oracle of Amon in Siwa and apocalyptic texts.[14] The most interesting example is a collection of demotic ostraca from the second century BCE which document incubatory visions by a certain Hor.[15]

b. *Mesopotamia*

Although other forms of divination seem to have been more popular, prophecy is well documented for ancient Mesopotamia. Prophets functioned as a part of the apparatus needed by the gods to reveal their will to humans; foremost among these humans was the king.[16] As an established institution, both in internal and external politics, prophecy was a part of the king's political propaganda. Furthermore, prophetic encouragement for the king was understood as a manifestation of divine support for him.[17] 'Prophecies were regarded as signs of a special and intimate relationship between the gods and the king; a written prophecy could even serve as a *tuppi adê*, an actual document of this divine-royal "covenant" (SAA 9 3.3 ii 27).'[18]

In Mesopotamia, prophecy was mainly aural in character. Because prophecy had an important function in Mesopotamian cultures, it is not surprising that a significant number of recorded prophecies are preserved. Most of them come from two archives. In Mari, in the eighteenth century BCE, dream diviners sent their prophecies to the king in the form of

World and the Near East: Proceedings of the International Colloquium on Apocalypticism Uppsala, August 12–17, 1979 (ed. D. Hellholm; 2nd edn enlarged by a supplementary bibliography; Tübingen: J.C.B. Mohr [Paul Siebeck], 1989), pp. 51–60 (53–54).

13 J. VanderKam, 'Prophecy and Apocalyptics in the Ancient Near East', *CANE* 3: 2083–94 (2084); compare Bergman, 'Introductory Remarks', pp. 53–54; see also H. Goedicke, *The Protocol of Neferyt (The Prophecy of Neferti)* (JHNES; Baltimore, MD, and London: Johns Hopkins University Press, 1977), pp. 3–4 and the literature quoted there.

14 For Egyptian apocalyptic literature, see now A. Blasius and B. U. Schipper (eds), *Apokalyptik und Ägypten: Eine kritische Analyse der relevanten Texte aus dem griechisch-römischen Ägypten* (OLA, 107; Leuven: Peeters, 2002). Cf. also F. Hoffmann, *Ägypten: Kultur und Lebenswelt in griechisch-römischer Zeit: Eine Darstellung nach den demotischen Quellen* (Berlin: Akademie Verlag, 2000), pp. 176–87. For the Amon-Oracle of Siwa, see K. P. Kuhlmann, *Das Ammoneion: Archäologie, Geschichte und Kultpraxis des Orakels von Siwa* (Mainz: Zabern, 1988).

15 For the prophecies of Hor, see Hoffmann, *Ägypten*, pp. 187–94.

16 Nissinen, *References to Prophecy*, p. 164.

17 For the use of prophecy in internal and external political propaganda as well as to support the king, see Nissinen, *References to Prophecy*, pp. 164–65.

18 Nissinen, *References to Prophecy*, pp. 165–66.

letters.[19] And in the seventh century BCE, the library of Ashurbanipal contained a whole collection of cuneiform tablets which preserved prophecies in the names of different deities.[20]

Basically, three different forms of prophetic texts can be distinguished, (1) letters of a god to a king, (2) royal inscriptions, and (3) oracles.[21] In the letter of a god, a prophecy is communicated to the king as if the deity would have written the letter, although the prophecy is delivered through the mouth of a prophet. Often the letters of a god are responses to letters of the king inquiring into the deity's will. In these cases, the letters of a god tend to repeat the language used in the royal inquiry.[22] Using archival materials, such as letters of a god, royal inscriptions sometimes quote prophecies or, in some cases, are phrased based on prophecies without identifying them. In both cases, the intention is to show that the king enjoys the support of the divine. The written oracles are also addressed to the king and are characterized by 'performative Redeformen'.[23] In view of their content, these oracles are mostly positive forecasts. Both in Mari and in the library of Ashurbanipal, collections of such prophecies have been found which resemble the collections of prophetic utterances in the Hebrew Bible (see e.g. SAA 9 nos 1–3, and nos 7–8).[24]

For all forms of written prophecy, the basic motivation to write a prophecy down was a 'zerdehnte Sprechsituation' (diluted communication).[25] A prophecy was spoken in geographical or chronological distance

---

19   An instructive overview can be found in H. B. Huffmon, 'A Company of Prophets: Mari, Assyria, Israel', in *Prophecy in its Ancient Near Eastern Context: Mesopotamian, Biblical, and Arabian Perspectives* (ed. M. Nissinen; SBLSymS, 13; Atlanta, GA: SBL, 2000), pp. 47–70 (48–56). For a detailed recent discussion of the material, see van der Toorn, 'From the Oral to the Written', pp. 219–34. For an edition of the Mari-prophecies, see L. Cagni, *Le profezie de Mari* (Testi del Vicino Oriente antico, 2/2; Brescia: Paideia, 1995); and M. Nissinen, *Prophets and Prophecy in the Ancient Near East* (with contributions by C. L. Seow and R. K. Ritner; SBLWAW, 12; Leiden and Boston, MA: Brill, 2003), pp. 13–95.

20   For the text of the Neo-Assyrian prophecies, see S. Parpola, *Assyrian Prophecies* (SAAS, 9; Helsinki: Helsinki University Press, 1997); and Nissinen, *Prophets and Prophecy*, pp. 97–177. For Mesopotamian oracles and prophecy in general, see M. Nissinen, *References to Prophecy*; and B. Pongratz-Leisten, *Herrschaftswissen in Mesopotamien* (SAAS, 10; Helsinki: Helsinki University Press, 1999). For an instructive overview see M. Nissinen (ed.), *Prophecy in its Ancient Near Eastern Context: Mesopotamian, Biblical, and Arabian Perspectives* (SBLSymS, 13; Atlanta, GA: Society of Biblical Literature, 2000).

21   Pongratz-Leisten, *Herrschaftswissen*, pp. 266–76.

22   Pongratz-Leisten, *Herrschaftswissen*, p. 273.

23   Pongratz-Leisten, *Herrschaftswissen*, p. 270.

24   See Pongratz-Leisten, *Herrschaftswissen*, p. 272; Van der Toorn, 'From the Oral to the Written', pp. 248–51.

25   See Pongratz-Leisten, *Herrschaftswissen*, pp. 267–68. 'Die Notwendigkeit der Verschriftung ergibt sich mit K. Ehlich aus der Situation der "zerdehnten Sprechsituation", die sich dadurch auszeichnet, daß keine Kohärenz von Sprecher und Hörer gegeben ist, und diese "diatope" oder gar diachrone Sprechsituation entweder über

from its targeted audience, mostly the king.[26] Therefore, it needed to be transmitted by a messenger. Sometimes, at some stage in the process of transmission, a prophecy was written down, either by the prophet himself or by a scribe.[27] During this textualization of a prophecy and/or in the process of collecting individual written prophecies, scribes edited and altered the text of a given prophecy.[28] This is especially true when the individual prophecies were compiled into collections of prophetic utterances.[29] In addition to its original use of communicating a prophecy, with two possible exceptions, written prophecies seem to have served mostly archival or propagandistic purposes in Mesopotamia.

For the neo-Assyrian empire, both collections of prophecies and royal inscriptions using prophecies seem to be preserved only from the reigns of Essarhadon and Ashurbanipal.[30] Both kings had especially intense ties to Ishtar, the Assyrian goddess of prophecy, and the ascent to power for both kings met significant difficulties. Their royal inscriptions often quote prophecies (Ashurbanipal Prism A iii 4–7 and Prism B v 46–49), and even non-prophetic passages of these inscriptions are sometimes phrased according to prophecies made earlier to kings (Nin A; Ass A).[31] Supposedly, the scribes responsible for the texts of these inscriptions used the collections of prophecies compiled during the reign of Essarhadon and Ashurbanipal to sanction their rule by way of including prophetic texts into the inscriptions.[32]

In a way that differs from the use of the prophetic books of the Hebrew Bible, there seems to be no evidence in Mesopotamia for a later reapplication of a written prophecy towards a subject matter differing from the original intention of this prophecy. A possible exception to this rule might be two letters dated to the time of Essarhadon (SAA 10 no. 284 recto 4–9 and SAA 10 no. 111 recto 23–26). The general and unspecific

---

das Institut des Boten oder des Textes überwunden werden muß' (Pongratz-Leisten, *Herrschaftswissen*, pp. 267–68). Pongratz-Leisten derives her terminology from an article by K. Ehlich, 'Text und sprachliches Handeln: Die Entstehung von Texten aus dem Bedürfnis der Überlieferung', in *Schrift und Gedächtnis: Beiträge zur Archäologie der literarischen Kommunikation* (eds A. Assmann, J. Assmann and C. Hardmeier; Archäologie der literarischen Kommunikation, 1; Munich: Wilhelm Fink Verlag, 1983), pp. 24–43.

26   Cf. van der Torn, 'From the Oral to the Written', pp. 219–21.

27   See Pongratz-Leisten, *Herrschaftswissen*, pp. 268–69; and Nissinen, 'Spoken, Written, Quoted, and Invented', pp. 244–45, 250–52.

28   Pongratz-Leisten, *Herrschaftswissen*, p. 272; van der Toorn, 'From the Oral to the Written', pp. 228–33; Nissinen, 'Spoken, Written, Quoted, and Invented', pp. 245–46.

29   See van der Toorn, 'From the Oral to the Written', p. 250.

30   Nissinen, *References to Prophecy*, pp. 171–72; van der Toorn 'From the Oral to the Written', pp. 253, 267.

31   van der Toorn, 'From the Oral to the Written', p. 267. For editions of these texts, see Nissinen, *Prophets and Prophecy*, pp. 137–50.

32   van der Toorn, 'From the Oral to the Written', p. 253.

language used in these cases might hint to a later reapplication of individual prophecies taken from a prophetic collection.[33] But still differing from Israelite literary prophecy, this reapplication would have happened during the lifetime of the king to whom the prophecies originally applied. Furthermore, both texts are too fragmentary to allow for a certain interpretation. Another indicator that Mesopotamian written prophecies generally did not transcend their original meaning is the lack of commentaries on written prophecies in the literature of the Mesopotamian cultures. This is all the more significant, as the Mesopotamian cultures did know the genre of commentary. In Mesopotamia, commentaries have been written on different omen lists but also on narrative compositions and even on philological texts. But no commentaries on prophetic texts are preserved.[34] It remains unlikely that Mesopotamian written prophecies transcended 'specific historical situations' and gained 'a generally applicable meaning'.[35]

The discussion of Mesopotamian written prophecies hints already at a distinction of character between Mesopotamian and Israelite prophetic texts. As far as preserved, with two possible exceptions, Mesopotamian written prophecies seem not to have been reapplied to later historical events but have always been restricted to their original context. But for Israelite literary prophecy, this surplus of meaning is typical. This difference in character should also be reflected in the language describing prophetic texts. Therefore, in this article, only prophetic texts which were recontextualized and reapplied to contexts other than their original one are understood as literary prophecy. Prophetic texts and collections which did not transcend their specific historical situations are designated instead as written prophecies.

c. *Syro-Palestine*

In Syro-Palestine, prophecy is not restricted to Israel. In addition to the evidence for Syro-Palestinian literary and written prophecy quoted below, the report of the Egyptian envoy Wen-Amon attests to Phoenician court seers advising the king by means of their visions and/or auditions[36] – an institution which, for later times, is confirmed by an Aramaic inscription (*KAI* 202) discussed below.

Although the evidence is sparse, there can be no doubt that since the ninth century BCE at least, the Syro-Palestinian cultures recorded prophecies in written form. Prominent examples are the Balaam inscrip-

---

33   See Nissinen, 'Spoken, Written, Quoted, and Invented', pp. 262–63
34   See J. Krecher, 'Kommentare', *RlA* 6: 188–91 (188).
35   Against van der Toorn, 'From the Oral to the Written', p. 254.
36   *ANET*[3], pp. 25–29.

tion from Tell Deir Alla (ca. 800 BCE; in the following referred to as DAT)[37] and the so-called Marzeah-papyrus.

The language of the Balaam inscription seems to be archaic in character and suggests a date of its story in the ninth century BCE.[38] As the text of the Balaam inscription is too long to be quoted here, I will briefly describe its content. In combination I, DAT describes how Balaam sees in a vision a council of deities that is determined to bring doom to his people. He then relates this vision to his people. Combination II seems to describe a response of Balaam's audience to this doom prophecy by way of a human sacrifice.[39] As the context in which the DAT inscription was read is lost, there can be no certainty about its character. There are at least 100 years between the paleographic date of the inscription and the dating of the text. Such a discrepancy between story and reading argues a reapplication to a historical situation much different from the one DAT originally addressed. DAT would thus attest to literary prophecy.

The Marzeaḥ papyrus seems to be an autograph of trans-Jordanian, Moabite, or Edomite providence from the mid- or late seventh century BCE.[40] Probably for archival purposes, it records an individual oracle. The Marzeaḥ papyrus thus needs to be classified as written prophecy.

> kh.ᵓmrw.ᵓlhn.lgrᵓ. kl.hmrzḥ.whrḥyn.wh
>
> byt.wyšᶜᵓ.rḥq.mhm.wmlkᵓ.hšlš

Thus says the godhead to Geraᵓ.: 'The *marzēḥ (symposium)*, and the millstones, and the house are thine. As for Yiš ᶜaᵓ, he is without claim on them (lit., is far from them); and Malka is the depositary.'

---

37   For an eighth-century BCE paleographic date of the Balaam inscription, see G. van der Kooij, 'Book and Script at Deir 'Allā', in *The Balaam Text from Tell Deir 'Allā. Proceedings of the International Symposium held at Leiden 21–24 August 1989* (eds J. Hoftijzer and G. van der Kooij; Leiden: Brill, 1991), pp. 239–62, esp. 256–57.

38   See H.-P. Müller, 'Die Sprache der Texte von Tell Deir 'Allā im Kontext der nordwestsemitischen Sprachen – mit einigen Erwägungen zum Zusammenhang der schwachen Verbklasse', *ZAH* 4 (1991): 1–31. Müller describes the language of the DAT inscriptions as 'relativ späten Rest eines nordwestsemitischen Zustands vor der endgültigen Trennung des Aramäischen vom Kanaanäischen, ... wie er sich in einer ritardierenden Randgesellschaft des syrischen Kulturraumes erhalten konnte' (31).

39   See J. A. Hackett, *The Balaam Text from Deir 'Allā* (HSM, 31; Chico, CA: Scholars Press, 1980), pp. 80–85; idem, 'Religious Traditions in Israelite Transjordan', in *Ancient Israelite Religion: Essays in Honor of Frank Moore Cross* (eds P. D. Miller, P. D. Hanson and S. D. McBride; Philadelphia, PA: Fortress, 1987), pp. 125–36 (126).

40   For the Marzeaḥ papyrus, see P. Bordreuil and D. Pardee, 'Le Papyrus du marzeaḥ', *Semitica* 38 (1990): 49–69 pls. VII–X and F. M. Cross, 'A Papyrus Recording a Divine Legal Decision and the Root *rḥq* in Biblical and Near Eastern Legal Usage', in *Text, Temples, and Traditions* (eds M. V. Fox et al.; Winona Lake, IN: Eisenbrauns, 1996), pp. 311–20. For the transcription and translation quoted above, see Cross, 'Papyrus', pp. 311–12. For providence and date of the papyrus see Cross, 'Papyrus', pp. 312–18.

A ninth-century BCE commemorative inscription from Jebel ed-Dala'ah (ancient Rabbat Ammon, the capital of the Ammonite kingdom) preserves a salvation prophecy attributed to the God Milcom. Only fragments from the inscription are preserved. 'Nevertheless, it is evident from the extant portion that the inscription contains an oracle delivered in the name of Milcom, the patron deity of the Ammonites, presumably to the king who erected the commemorative monument of which the inscription is a part. The fragmentary text apparently records a word of divine assurance, no doubt delivered by a human intermediary, for the king's victory over his enemies.'[41] The inscription's use of a prophecy recalls the use of prophecies in neo-Assyrian royal inscriptions.

An Aramaic inscription found on a stele erected by king Zakir of Hamat and Luash describes his victory over an alliance of 17 kings. Zakir's victory was supposedly forecast by a court seer (*KAI* 202 A 11–17):

> (11) But I lifted my hands to Baalshamayn, and Baalshamay[n] answered me, [and] (12) Baalshamayn [said], 'F[e]ar not, for I have made [you] king, [and I who will (14) st]and with [you], and I will deliver you from all [these kings who] (15) have forced a siege against you!' Then Baalshamayn said to m[e ... '(16) a]ll these kings who have forced [a siege against you ... (17)] and this wall whi[ch ...]'[42]

As in the Jebel ed-Dala'ah inscription, the stele of Zakir of Hamat and Luash uses the prophecy of the god Baalshamayn to illustrate the divine support the king enjoyed. In *KAI* 202, the use of prophecy resembles the use of prophecy in neo-Assyrian royal inscriptions. In a way differing from the neo-Assyrian royal inscriptions, neither the Jebel ed-Dala'ah inscription nor *KAI* 202 allow for any conclusions to be drawn concerning collections of prophecies which they might have used as sources to compose their text.

Most of the few Syro-Palestinian attestations to written (Marzeaḥ papyrus, Jebel ed-Dala'ah inscription, *KAI* 202) and literary prophecy (DAT I) reflect the evidence from Mesopotamia. Again, written prophecy is a form of diluted communication ('zerdehnte Sprechsituation'). The few items preserved serve either archival purposes (Marzeaḥ papyrus) or, for reasons of political propaganda, illustrate the divine support which a king enjoys (Jebel ed-Dala'ah inscription and *KAI* 202). In a way differing from Mesopotamia, the distance to be bridged in a diluted communication is more of a chronological than of a geographical nature. But this

---

41 See C.-L. Seow, 'West Semitic Sources', in M. Nissinen, *Prophets and Prophecy in the Ancient Near East* (ed. P. Machinist; Leiden and Boston, MA: 2003), pp. 201–18 (202–03); for the quotation see 202; for the inscription itself see 202–03; for a bibliography on the inscription see 202.

42 Translation according to Seow, 'West Semitic Sources', p. 206.

difference between Mesopotamia and Syro-Palestine should not be overemphasized, because not enough prophetic texts are preserved from Syro-Palestine to allow for any statistical conclusions.

In comparison with the Mesopotamian evidence, the DAT inscription is an untypical form of literary prophecy. It does not bridge a geographical distance between a prophet and his addressee. It does not serve any archival purpose, and it does not bolster divine support for a king's claim to power. On the contrary, it reports a doom prophecy. And if combination II describes a child-sacrifice reacting to this doom prophecy, DAT might commemorate the successful appeasement of the divine. DAT I–II resembles more the literary prophecies collected in the Hebrew Bible than any Mesopotamian text.

d. Literary Prophecy in Ancient Israel and in Ancient Judah
Preserved of Israel's written prophetic tradition are works of prophets, such as Amos, Hosea, Micah, Isaiah, or Jeremiah. From an analysis of their books and from Jer. 36.27-32; 45.1, we know that at least some of these eight- to sixth-century BCE prophets started to collect their own prophetic utterances and edited them. Examples include Isaiah,[43] Jeremiah,[44] and Ezekiel.[45] In the case of other prophetic books, possibly the students and/or followers of the prophets began collecting and editing the prophet's utterances. Examples include Amos, Hosea,[46] and probably Micah.[47] Already these first collections and editions of prophetic messages entailed a reworking and therefore a reinterpretation of the original prophetic oracles.

The common focus of all these prophets is that their messages did not agree with the messages expected by their targeted audiences.[48] As

---

43   For Isaiah as the editor of a kernel of his book, see E. Blum, 'Jesajas prophetisches Testament – Beobachtungen zu Jes 1–11', *ZAW* 108 (1996): 547–68; *ZAW* 109 (1997): 12–29.

44   How far Jeremiah and/or Baruch, his scribe, were involved in editing an early version of the later book of Jeremiah is a question which remains still unanswered. In my opinion, Jer. 36.27-32 reflects such an involvement of the prophet and his scribe.

45   For Ezekiel's editing of his own prophecies, see A. Lange, *Vom prophetischen Wort zur prophetischen Tradition: Studien zur Traditions- und Redaktionsgeschichte innerprophetischer Konflikte in der Hebräischen Bibel* (FAT, 34; Tübingen: Mohr Siebeck, 2002), pp. 131–54.

46   For the redactional and editorial history of the books of Hosea and Amos, see J. Jeremias, *Der Prophet Hosea: Übersetzt und erklärt* (ATD, 24/1; Göttingen: Vandenhoek & Ruprecht, 1983), pp. 18–20; idem, *Der Prophet Amos: Übersetzt und erklärt* (ATD, 24/2; Göttingen: Vandenhoek & Ruprecht, 1995), xix–xxii; idem, *Hosea und Amos: Studien zu den Anfängen des Dodekapropheton* (FAT, 13; Tübingen: J. C. B. Mohr [Paul Siebeck], 1996).

47   For the redactional and editorial history of the book of Micah, see R. Kessler, *Micha: Übersetzt und ausgelegt* (Herders Theologischer Kommentar zum Alten Testament; Freiburg, Basel and Vienna: Herder, 1999), pp. 41–48.

48   Compare the observation of Kratz: 'Die Unheilsbotschaft ist der Grund für die Schriftlichkeit' ('Das Neue in der Prophetie des Alten Testaments', p. 10).

documented in Amos 7.10-17, Amos' message of social criticism and judgment was not welcomed by audiences in the northern kingdom of Israel,[49] and Hosea's monolatric attacks on the polytheistic practices of his contemporaries would not have been accepted graciously by the northern kingdom's Baalistic and polytheistic upper classes either.[50] Micah's defense of the customary rights of the small farmers and his corresponding criticism of the elites in the capital created opposition to his message, which is documented in Mic. 2.6, 11.[51] Isaiah's message, not to call for Assyrian help during the Syro-Ephraimite war as well as his rejection of Hezekiah's rebellion against the Assyrians, marginalized the prophet, who had originally been rather influential.[52] The reaction to Jeremiah's condemning message is well documented in his confession and elsewhere in the book. See e.g. his complaint in Jer. 20.7-12 about his treatment at the hands of his contemporaries or the mockery made of him in Jer. 23.33.[53] Ezekiel might be an exception to this general rejection of the prophets whose messages were transmitted in written form. At least some of the exiles seem to have looked for his advice (see e.g. Ezek. 14.1) and must have listened to his message.[54] But the book of Ezekiel also documents how the prophet was forced to respond to harsh criticism (see e.g. Ezek. 8.12; 12.21-22, 26-27; 18.2, 25, 29).

E. Blum has shown how Isaiah's marginalization and rejection by his contemporaries motivated this prophet to collect and edit his oracles for future audiences who might be more willing to recognize the truth of his message.[55] To me, this seems to be the initial motivation behind collecting the utterances of all the prophets mentioned above. This means that from the beginning of literary prophecy in ancient Israel, literary prophecies aim at posterity and future audiences. Differing from Mesopotamian written prophecy, the idea to be reapplied to the realities and lives of later audiences is inherent in the nature of Israelite literary prophecy. Even more, reapplication seems to have been the main intention of Israelite

---

49   For the historicity of Amos 7.10-17, see e.g. A. G. Auld, *Amos* (OTG; Sheffield: Sheffield Academic Press, 1986), pp. 27–29.

50   For the religious composition of the northern kingdom, see S. Norin, 'Zur Funktion der Soziologie im Studium des Alten Testaments', in *Congress Volume: Oslo 1998* (eds A. Lemaire and M. Sæbø; VTSup, 80; Leiden and Boston: Brill, 2000).

51   See e.g. H. W. Wolf, *Dodekapropheton 4: Micha* (BKAT, 14.3; Neukirchen-Vluyn: Neukirchener Verlag, 1982), pp. 50–51; Kessler, *Micha*, pp. 129–30, 134–35.

52   See e.g. J. Blenkinsopp, *A History of Prophecy in Israel* (2nd edn revised and enlarged; Louisville, KY: Westminster John Knox, 1996), pp. 106–07.

53   See e.g. K. Koch, *Die Profeten II: Babylonisch-persische Zeit* (2nd edn; Urban Taschenbücher, 281; Stuttgart: Kohlhammer, 1988), pp. 39–52; K. Seybold, *Der Prophet Jeremia: Leben und Werk* (Urban Taschenbücher, 416; Stuttgart: Kohlhammer, 1993), pp. 44, 53.

54   See Koch, *Profeten II*, pp. 89–92.

55   Blum, 'Testament', pp. 550–51.

literary prophecy.[56] In other words, in Israel, literary prophecy as a diluted communication ('zerdehnte Sprechsituation') was concerned with the chronological distance between prophet and audience while in Mesopotamia, written prophecy was concerned with a geographical distance between prophet and king.

The Israelite pre-exilic prophets were not disappointed in their hope for future audiences. A good example is the relation between Amos and Isaiah. Already in Isaiah's eyes, at the beginning of literary prophecy, Amos' message of social injustice and judgment was fulfilled by the famous earthquake mentioned in Amos 1.1. Therefore, Isaiah incorporates Amos' message into his own work and is influenced by it (see Isa. 5.25; 9.7-20; 10.1-4).[57] In this way, Isaiah reapplies the judgment that Amos prophesied for the northern kingdom of Israel to the southern kingdom of Judah.

Reapplications of literary prophecies like the incorporation of Amos into the book of Isaiah signal also a heightened authority of the literary prophecy which was reapplied. In the case of Isaiah's use of Amos, there can be little doubt that Isaiah regarded an early version of the book of Amos as a true prophecy of great importance. Hence its reapplication to the southern kingdom by Isaiah. Repeated reapplications would have led to an even larger increase in authority.

The first editions and redactions of prophetic collections initiated an ongoing process of reworking, reapplying and actualizing prophetic books. In the end, both chapter-sized passages (see e.g. Jeremiah 49.7-22; 52) and whole new parts using older prophetic books and other materials were added to individual prophetic books (see e.g. Trito-Isaiah (Isaiah 56–66), Deutero- (Zechariah 9–11) and Trito-Zechariah (Zechariah 12–14)). In addition, even the composition of whole prophetic books was based on older prophetic traditions (see e.g. Joel). Each time a prophetic passage was reworked and/or reapplied its authority would have been increased.

O. H. Steck's work on these literary prophecies marks one of the paradigm shifts in prophetic research. Originally, literary prophecy was labeled as deutero-prophetic[58] and was harshly criticized in scholarly

56   See O. H. Steck, *Die Prophetenbücher und ihr theologisches Zeugnis: Wege der Nachfrage und Fährten zur Antwort* (Tübingen: J. C. B. Mohr [Paul Siebeck], 1996), esp. pp. 149–52. Compare also the remarks of Kratz, who is a student of Steck: 'Dem einmal ergangenen Gotteswort wird eine Eigenmächtigkeit und Langzeitigkeit zugetraut, wie man es bis dahin nicht kannte' ('Das Neue in der Prophetie des Alten Testaments', p. 19).

57   For Amos' influence on Isaiah, see E. Blum, 'Jesaja und der דבר der Amos: Unzeitgemäße Überlegungen zu Jes 5,25; 9,7–20; 10,1–4', *Dielheimer Blätter zum Alten Testament* 28 (1992–1993): 75–95; idem, 'Testament', pp. 13–14.

58   See D. L. Petersen, *Late Israelite Prophecy: Studies in Deutero-Prophetic Literature and in Chronicles* (SBLMS, 23; Missoula, MT: SBL, 1977).

literature as polluting the true prophetic spirit of the original collections.[59] Steck has shown that, regardless of their purely literary character, literary prophecies are to be understood as prophecies in their own right.[60] The future relevance of a given prophetic utterance is already inherent in the original prophecy, and the redactional reworking of prophetic texts is a prophetic process in which new meaning is gained from written prophetic tradition. In a re-lecture of a hypo-text (i.e. the reworked prophetic tradition), new meaning evolves by recontextualizing and reapplying the hypotext to a different timeframe. The new meaning gained is then expressed in the form of a hypertext, which represents the result of a redaction.[61] For example, Amos' original claim, 'I am no prophet' (Amos 7.14), emphasizes his independence from the state's or any other authorities' payroll. Zech. 13.5 adapts Amos' claim for prophets who live in eschatological times. Such a recontextualization results in these prophets denying their occupation for fear of their lives. With each surplus meaning recognized by the hypertext (in my example Zech. 13.5) in the hypotext (Amos 7.14) the fact that the hypotext bears meaning for later times is reemphasized and reconfirmed; i.e., each re-lecture results in an increased authority of the hypotext.

That something is preserved in writing, transmitted, reworked and extended in written form is of no importance when it comes to the question of prophetic character. Not only is new meaning gained by prophetic redactions; texts like Jer. 23.33-40 show that this surplus in meaning is gained by way of revelatory exegesis.[62] Individual elements are isolated from an earlier prophetic oracle and recontextualized into the timeframe of the redactor. By relating them to a new timeframe, the isolated elements gain new meaning. Later applications of the same interpretive techniques can be found in the Qumran pesharim or in the interpretation of Jer. 25.12 in Daniel 9. In the form of new textual elements, the new meaning is inserted into the earlier prophetic oracle. Thus literary prophecy gains its new meanings in a revelatory way and

---

59   See for example B. Duhm's remarks in his Jeremiah-commentary on the parts of the book of Jeremiah, which were labeled C by him and which were later identified as the deuteronomistic Jeremiah-redaction (*Das Buch Jeremia: Erklärt* [Kurzer Hand-Commentar zum Alten Testament, 11; Tübingen and Leipzig: J. C. B. Mohr [P. Siebeck], 1901]).

60   See Steck's argumentation in his monograph *Prophetenbücher*.

61   For the categories of hypotext and hypertext see G. Genette, *Palimpseste: Die Literatur auf zweiter Stufe* (trans. W. Bayer and D. Hornig; Aesthetica, 1683; Frankfurt a.m.: Suhrkamp, 1993), pp. 9–18.

62   For revelatory exegesis as a means of prophetic redaction and literary prophecy see A. Lange, 'Interpretation als Offenbarung: Zum Verhältnis von Schriftauslegung und Offenbarung in apokalyptischer und nichtapokalyptischer Literatur', in *Wisdom and Apocalypticism in the Dead Sea Scrolls and in the Biblical Tradition* (ed. F. Garcia Martinez; BETL, 168; Leuven: Peeters, 2003), pp. 17–33.

then communicates it to its audiences in written form. This agrees well with the definition of prophecy provided by M. Weippert and quoted above.

In postexilic times, literary prophecy became the main form of prophecy practiced in ancient Judah, while aural prophecy was more and more marginalized. This shift from aural to literary would have again increased the authority of the various literary prophecies. In my opinion, there are two reasons for this development. As is documented many times in Israel's prophetic tradition, there is no easy way in the case of contradicting prophetic messages to distinguish between true and false prophecy. The only answer Israel developed in response to this aporia is given in Deuteronomy 18.20-22:

> But any prophet who speaks in the name of other gods, or who presumes to speak in my name a word that I have not commanded the prophet to speak – that prophet shall die. You may say to yourself, 'How can we recognize a word that the Lord has not spoken?' If a prophet speaks in the name of the Lord but the thing does not take place or prove true, it is a word that the Lord has not spoken. The prophet has spoken it presumptuously; do not be frightened by it.[63]

What seems to be a perfect solution, i.e. that true prophecy must come true, is of little help in the actual encounter of aural prophecy. As has been pointed out many times, this type of verification normally requires a long wait.[64] But the pre-exilic prophetic traditions of marginalized prophets like Amos, Hosea, or Jeremiah were readily at hand. Furthermore, the prophets' messages were perceived by exilic and early postexilic audiences to be verified by history. After all, these prophets forecasted doom, and doom was what Israel experienced. For that reason, people turned to prophetic books and preferred these literary prophetic traditions to actual aural prophecy. If the fulfillment criterion is applied to literary prophecies each recontextualization and reapplication of a literary prophecy would reemphasize its truth and hence its authority.

A second reason for the demise of aural prophecy is to be found in the experience of the exile. In their preaching, at least some prophets supported Israel's rebellions against its Babylonian suzerain. Good examples are Hananiah's prophecy about the returning of the temple instruments (Jer. 28.2-4) and the message of the unnamed prophets and diviners in Jer. 27.9-10, 14–15. In Jer. 23.9-32, Jeremiah's polemic against his prophetic opponents seems to point in a similar direction. Therefore, it is no surprise that already a few years after the destruction of Jerusalem

---

63   If not mentioned otherwise, translations of biblical books are taken from the NRSV.

64   See the bibliography in Lange, *Prophetischen Wort*, pp. 174–75 and the literature quoted there in n. 414.

the prophets were blamed for what happened in 587 BCE. Lamentations 2.13-14 and 4.11-13 are two good examples.

> What can I say for you, to what compare you, O daughter of Jerusalem?
> To what can I liken you, that I may comfort you, O virgin daughter of Zion?
> For vast as the sea is your ruin; who can heal you?
> Your prophets have seen for you false and deceptive visions;
> they have not exposed your iniquity to restore your fortunes,
> but have seen oracles for you that are all false and misleading. (Lam. 2.13-14)

> The Lord gave full vent to his wrath; he poured out his hot anger,
> and kindled a fire in Zion than consumed its foundations.
> The kings of the earth did not believe, nor did any of the inhabitants of the world,
> that foe or enemy could enter the gates of Jerusalem.
> It was for the sins of her prophets and the iniquities of her priests,
> who shed the blood of the righteous in the midst of her. (Lam. 4.11-13)

Aural prophecy became more and more marginalized. This marginalization is due to both the impossibility of identifying true prophecy and the involvement of prophets in the events leading to the catastrophe of 587 BCE. Already in the fifth century BCE, Nehemiah was neither surprised that a murder plotted against him by his Samaritan opponents involved hired prophets nor that he is accused of having used prophets for his own propaganda (Neh. 6.1-14). Possibly somewhat later, the author of Zech. 13.2-6 speaks longingly about the eschatological demise of all prophets. Conversely, during this same time period, literary prophecy seems to have become more and more popular. The evidence for this increase is the number of prophetic redactions and compositions preserved from Persian times. The demise of aural prophecy is thus accompanied by an increasing prominence of literary prophecy.

The issues addressed by Israel's literary prophecy were of theological, national and universal character. Three examples may suffice. Jer. 49.7-22 is composed of different references in the book of Jeremiah, and it forecasts the punishment of Edom. Zech. 13.2-6 is concerned with the eschatological demise of prophecy. And Jonah 3.9; 4.2, 11 is concerned with the universality of God's mercy and willingness to forgive.

Compared with each other, prophetic texts from Israel/Judah and the rest of the Ancient Near East (ANE) have a lot in common and at the same time differ significantly from each other. Both in the ANE and in Israel/Judah, prophecy was mostly an aural phenomenon. Both in the ANE and in Israel/Judah, prophecies were written down by prophets and/or scribes. Both in the ANE and in Israel/Judah, the resulting prophetic texts underwent editorial and redactional reworkings. Both in the ANE and in Israel/Judah, prophetic texts are the response to a situation of diluted communication ('zerdehnte Sprechsituation').

But in Mesopotamia and Syro-Palestine, prophetic texts seem not to have been reapplied to later historical situations. These texts were mostly concerned with the reign, deeds and life of one king and they documented divine support for a specific ruler. The diluted communication these texts tried to bridge is mostly geographical in nature. This may be the reason why they remained written prophecy and did not develop into literary prophecy. The only exception to this rule might be the DAT inscription. But as long as we do not know how it was read by its audience, a description of the DAT inscription as literary prophecy must remain speculative.

In Israel/Judah, the situation is different. Several of Israel's prophets were marginalized and rejected due to their critical character and negative attitude towards their audiences. These prophets wrote their messages down in the hope that later audiences might benefit from them. The situation of diluted communication ('zerdehnte Sprechsituation') is thus chronological in character and tries to bridge a distance in time. Israel's/Judah's prophetic texts ask for a later reapplication. When reapplied to later times and contexts, the readers and redactors of Israel's prophetic texts used revelatory exegesis to achieve this reapplication. Israel's/Judah's prophetic texts are thus to be described as literary prophecy.

Another difference between Mesopotamian written prophecy and Israelite literary prophecy is the fact that the latter became part of the biblical canon, i.e. participated in the canonical history of the Hebrew Bible, while the former experienced no such thing. The literary prophecies of ancient Israel became part of the Jewish canon because of the nature of literary prophecy. As the situation of diluted communication ('zerdehnte Sprechsituation') which they address is chronological in nature, i.e. as they aim for future reapplication, Israelite literary prophecies carry the seed of canon. Each time a literary prophecy was reapplied by way of re-lecture or otherwise its truth was reconfirmed and its authority increased. Each reapplication reemphasizes that a given literary prophecy communicates the word of God.

III. *Greek Seers and Oracle Collections*

When comparing ancient Greek oracle collections with Israelite literary prophecy, one encounters a basic problem. In the extant sources, Greek seers and Greek oracle collections are not well documented. In addition, the evidence preserved is not well known to biblical scholars. Therefore, an overview of what is known needs to be given. Due to lack of space, this overview is restricted to the classical (500–323 BCE) and archaic periods (750–500 BCE) – a timeframe which is roughly equivalent to the time when the bulk of Israelite literary prophecy was written. As classical Greek literature might be less known to those who are interested in prophecy and in the canonical history of the Hebrew Bible than the prophetic texts of ancient Israel and Judah, I will quote my sources more extensively in this part of my study. I will begin with a sketch of intuitive divination in ancient Greece before I discuss the oracle collections themselves.

a. *Intuitive Divination in Ancient Greece*

Two forms of intuitive divination produced records in ancient Greece which can be compared with either written prophecy or literary prophecy. The first form is the Greek oracle, such as the oracles of Delphi and the one on the island of Delos.[65] Although these oracles employed forms of deductive divination, intuitive divination was practiced by them, too. For the Delphic oracle, J. S. Morrison describes the procedure as follows:

> The Pythia, a woman past the age of child-bearing, goes down into the *adyton* or inner sanctuary and sits on the tripod as Apollo is said to have done when he first occupied the shrine, while the inquirer who has paid the fee (the *pelanos* ...) remains in the outer room, the *oikos* or *megaron* into which he is also described as going down. The enquirer then sacrifices a goat which is declared acceptable if it shivers on being douched with water. The enquiry is probably written. The Pythia then utters in a state of possession, and the utterance is interpreted and put into hexameter verse by the *prophētēs*.[66]

Numerous inscriptions as well as mentions of utterances of the oracles at e.g. Delphi and Didyma in classical and Hellenistic Greek literature,[67] show that these oracles were recorded in ancient Greece. Although the

---

65 See W. Burkert, *The Orientalizing Revolution: Near Eastern Influence on Greek Culture in the Early Archaic Age* (trans. M. E. Pinder and W. Burkert; Cambridge, MA and London: Harvard University Press, 1992), pp. 81–82; M. L. West, *The East Face of Helicon: West Asiatic Elements in Greek Poetry and Myth* (Oxford: Clarendon, 1997), pp. 49–50; R. Baumgarten, *Heiliges Wort und Heilige Schrift bei den Griechen: Hieroi Logoi und verwandte Erscheinungen* (ScriptOralia, 110; Tübingen: Gunter Narr Verlag, 1998), p. 16.

66 J. S. Morrison, 'The Classical World', in *Oracles and Divination* (eds M. Loewe and C. Blacker; Boulder, CO: Shambhala, 1981), pp. 87–114 (99). For the ancient references see ibid. A comprehensive description of Greek oracles can be found in J. Fontenrose, *The Delphic Oracle: Its Responses and Operations* (Berkeley, CA, Los Angeles, CA and London: University of California Press, 1978), pp. 1–239; Baumgarten, *Heiliges Wort*, pp. 15–38; and in V. Rosenberger, *Griechische Orakel: Eine Kulturgeschichte* (Darmstadt: Wissenschaftliche Buchgesellschaft, 2001).

67 See e.g. the catalogues of Fontenrose, *Delphic Oracle*, pp. 240–416; idem, *Didyma: Apollo's Oracle, Cult, and Companions* (Berkeley, CA, Los Angeles, CA, and London: University of California Press, 1988), pp. 177–246; and T. L. Robinson, *Theological Oracles*

utterances of different oracles were recorded and sometimes even 'published' in inscriptions or quoted by ancient Greek literature, hardly any collection of the utterances of a given oracle existed. Two exceptions to this rule are mentioned by Herodotus. He writes about a collection of Delphic oracles kept in Sparta. This collection seems to have entailed the answers given by the oracle at Delphi to questions posed by the Spartans.[68] Herodotus also hints at the existence of another oracle collection created by the Peisistratide rulers of Athens, which would later have been stolen by Kleomenes of Sparta.[69] Not much is known about how the Athenian and Spartiade oracle collections were used. Otherwise, official state-run oracle collections are only known from Italian cities. The best known examples are the collections of the famous Cumaean sybil in Rome.

The reason why the ancient Greeks did not compile the utterances of their oracles into oracle collections might be found in the character of the oracles themselves. On the one hand, utterances of an oracle like the Delphic one were situational by their very nature. They differ from the utterances of the biblical prophets because they were responses to specific questions and had no bearing on a distant future. Furthermore, unlike a seer or prophet, the ancient Greek oracles existed longer than just one lifespan. There was, therefore, no need to preserve their utterances for posterity. The oracles themselves were always accessible. It seems safe to say that, in general, the recordings of ancient Greek oracles compare with written and not with literary prophecy.

The second form of Greek intuitive divination which is comparable to prophecy is the Greek seer (μάντις).[70] Like the oracles, the *manteis* are mostly known for employing deductive means of divination: 'The male Greek seers were technical specialists, experts on the intestines of sacrificial victims and, especially, the flight of birds.'[71] The exceptions to the rule are the legendary seers of old mentioned by Pausanias.

---

and the Sanctuaries of Claros and Didyma (PhD dissertation; Cambridge, MA.: Harvard University, 1981). An instructive summary about the written documentation of the utterances of Greek oracles can be found in Rosenberger, *Griechische Orakel*, pp. 166–76.

68   See Herodotus VI.57 (translation according to A. D. Godley, *Herodotus: With an English Translation*, vol. 3: *Books V–VII* (LCL, 118; revised and reprinted; Cambridge, MA: Harvard University Press; London: Heinemann, 1963), and the remarks by Fontenrose, *Delphic Oracle*, pp. 164–65, and Baumgarten, *Heiliges Wort*, pp. 61–62.

69   See Herodotus V.90–91 and the ventilations of Fontenrose, *Delphic Oracle*, p. 164; and Baumgarten, *Heiliges Wort*, pp. 60–61.

70   For a more detailed comparison between Greek *manteis* and Israelite Jewish prophets, see my 'Greek Seers and Israelite-Jewish Prophets', *VT* 57 (2007): 461–82.

71   J. N. Bremmer, 'The Status and Symbolic Capital of the Seer', in *The Role of Religion in the Early Greek Polis: Proceedings of the Third International Seminar on Ancient Greek Cult, Organized by the Swedish Institute at Athens, 16–18 October 1992* (ed. R. Hägg; Acta Instituti Atheniensis Regni Sueciae, 8.14; Stockholm: Svenska institutet i Athen, 1996), pp. 97–109 (98).

> Except those whom they say Apollo inspired of old none of the seers uttered oracles, but they were good at explaining dreams and interpreting the flights of birds and the entrails of victims. (Pausanias, *Description of Greece* 1.34.4)[72]

Of these seers only a few names have been preserved. In alphabetic order, we know of Abaris, Bacis, Calchas, Cassandra, Glanis, Helenus, Laius, Lycus, Lysistratus, Mopsus, Musaeus, Orpheus, the Sibyls, Teiresias, and Theoclymenus. Although most descriptions of these figures are mythical in character and refer back to late bronze-age times they seem to reflect a much later reality.[73] How these intuitive Greek seers were perceived is illustrated by the examples of Helenus and Teiresias.

On the one hand, Homer describes Helenus as the wisest of augurs (οἰωνοπόλων ὄχ' ἄριστος; *Iliad* 6.76), i.e. as a diviner who interprets the flight patterns of birds. On the other hand, Homer lets Helenus claim to communicate directly with the gods by way of intuitive divination:

> And Helenus, the dear son of Priam, understood in spirit this plan that had found pleasure with the gods in council; and he came and stood by Hector's side, and spake to him, saying: 'Hector, son of Priam, peer of Zeus in counsel, wouldst thou now in anywise hearken unto me? for I am thy brother. Make the Trojans to sit down, and all the Achaeans, and do thou challenge whoso is best of the Achaeans to do battle with thee man to man in dread combat. Not yet is it thy fate to die and meet thy doom; for thus have I heard the voice of the gods that are for ever.' (*Iliad* 7.44-53)[74]

The example of Helenus fits well Weippert's definition of prophecy. In the *Iliad*, Helenus clearly states that he has the voice of the gods. Homer thus implies that Helenus experienced an audition. Having received this audition, Helenus communicates it to his brother Hector.

But in most references the *mantis* as an intuitive diviner fits Weippert's definition of prophecy only in part. A good example is Teiresias. According to the *Odyssey*, in Hades, Persephone grants Teiresias alone of all deceased reason and knowledge:

> To him even in death Persephone has granted reason, that he alone should have understanding. (*Odyssey* 10.494-495)[75]

---

72 Translation according to W. H. S. Jones, *Pausanias I: Description of Greece Books I and II* (LCL, 93; Cambridge, MA: Harvard University Press, 1998), p. 187.

73 See Baumgarten, *Heiliges Wort*, p. 39.

74 Translation according to A. T. Murray, *Homer: The Iliad I* (LCL, 170; Cambridge, MA: Harvard University Press, 1988), pp. 305, 307.

75 Translation according to A. T. Murray, *Homer: The Odyssey I* (LCL, 104; Cambridge, MA: Harvard University Press, 1984), p. 381.

In a scene which is remarkably close to 1 Sam. 28, Teiresias communicates what he received from Persephone to Odysseus (*Odyssey* 11.90-151).[76] Homer concludes Teiresias' detailed description of how Odysseus can find his way home and how he can communicate with his dead mother in Hades with the remark:[77]

> So saying the spirit of the prince, Teiresias, went back into the house of Hades, when he had spoken according to the divine word (ἐπεὶ κατὰ θέσφατ᾿ ἔλεξεν). (*Odyssey* 11.150-151)[78]

Persephone thus granted Teiresias the cognitive and rational ability which allowed him to receive a divine oracle[79] without interpreting any deductive means and communicate it in turn to Odysseus. Hence, the Teiresias of the *Odyssey* fits Weippert's definition of a prophet well.

However, in the mythic cycles, Teiresias receives his mantic abilities as a gift from the gods in substitution for being blinded.[80] The Hellenistic author Pseudo-Apollodorus refers to different versions of this myth in *Library* 3.6.7. Pseudo-Apollodorus found the earliest version in the writings of Hesiod.[81]

> But Hesiod says that he beheld snakes copulating on Cyllene, and that having wounded them he was turned from a man into a woman, but that on observing the same snakes copulating again, he became a man. Hence, when Hera and Zeus disputed whether the pleasures of love are felt more by women or by men, they referred to him for a decision. He said that if the pleasures of love be reckoned at ten, men enjoy one and women nine. Wherefore Hera blinded him, but Zeus bestowed on him the art of divination (τὴν μαντικήν). (Pseudo-Apollodorus, *Library* 3.6.7)[82]

In this mythical tradition, Teiresias is initially inspired by Zeus. But the gods do not reveal specific knowledge to Teiresias. Instead, Teiresias receives his mantic abilities from a deity as an initial gift to see beyond human perception. Pseudo-Apollodorus uses the word ἡ μαντική ('the divinatory art'), to describe Zeus' gift. In the works of Pseudo-

---

76 For Teiresias in the Nekyia-episode of the Odyssey, see G. Ugolini, *Untersuchungen zur Figur des Sehers Teiresias* (Classica Monacensia, 12; Tübingen: Narr, 1995), pp. 81–91.

77 For the discussion about whether the Nekyia is a later insertion into the Odyssey or not, see A. Heubeck, *A Commentary on Homer's Odyssey 2: Books IX–XVI* (Oxford: Clarendon Press, 1989), pp. 75–77.

78 Text and translation are guided by Murray, *Homer*, pp. 396–97.

79 For this meaning of θέσφατα, cf. Homer, *Odyssey* 11.297 and 13.172.

80 For other versions of this legend, see Ugolini, *Untersuchungen*, pp. 66–78.

81 For this legend, see Ugolini, *Untersuchungen*, pp. 33–65.

82 Text and translation according to J. G. Frazier, *Apollodorus: The Library I* (LCL, 121; Cambridge, MA: Harvard University Press, 1995), pp. 363, 365–67. Instead of 'divination' Frazier translates 'soothsaying'.

Apollodorus, ἡ μαντική designates both deductive and intuitive forms of divination. When he refers to deductive forms of divination, Pseudo-Apollodorus normally describes or names the specific technique of divination (see e.g. *Library* 1.9.11; 3.10.2); however, when he refers to intuitive divination it remains unspecified (see e.g. *Library* 1.4.1; 3.12.5; 3.12.6). This means that in *Library* 3.6.7, Pseudo-Apollodorus describes how Zeus gives Teiresias the art of intuitive divination. This special cognitive gift is more in the character of the second-sight or a sixth sense. Consequently, when Pseudo-Apollodorus or others describe a divination by Teiresias, they mention neither a vision, nor an audition. Teiresias sees and speaks on his own. A good example is another legend about Teiresias' blindness which Pseudo-Apollodorus quotes from an unnamed source. In this legend Teiresias gains even Promethean characteristics by revealing forbidden knowledge to his audience.[83]

> Different stories are told about his blindness and his power of soothsaying. For some say that he was blinded by the gods because he revealed their secrets to men. (Pseudo-Apollodorus, *Library* 3.6.7)[84]

In later versions of the legend of Teiresias' blindness the divinatory gift given to him transforms even into deductive forms of divination. A good example is the legend told by the fifth-century BCE mythographer Pherecydes of Athens:[85]

> But Pherecydes says that he was blinded by Athena; for Chariclo was dear to Athena ... and Teiresias saw the goddess stark naked, and she covered his eyes with her hands, and so rendered him sightless. And when Chariclo asked her to restore his sight, she could not do so, but by cleansing his ears she caused him to understand every note of birds; and she gave him a staff of cornel-wood, wherewith he walked like those who see. (Pseudo-Apollodorus, *Library* 3.6.7)[86]

Regardless of whether Teiresias is described as an intuitive or a deductive diviner, none of the preserved legends speaks of a divine revelation to Teiresias which is communicated by him to his audiences. But without such a divine revelation, the Teiresias figure of Pseudo-Apollodorus' mythical traditions does not fit Weippert's definition of prophecy. Although – sometimes reluctantly – he communicates what he sees to an audience, Teiresias does not receive a message from any deity. Although the descriptions of Helenus and Teiresias in the Homeric epics can be defined as prophecy, the figure of Teiresias as described by Pseudo-Apollodorus is paradigmatic for the inspired seer of ancient Greece.

---

83   See Ugolini, *Untersuchungen*, pp. 80–81.
84   Translation according to Frazier, *Apollodorus*, p. 361.
85   For the Teiresias legend of Pherecydes, see Ugolini, *Untersuchungen*, pp. 66–68.
86   Translation according to Frazier, *Apollodorus*, pp. 361, 363.

Hence, Pseudo-Apollodorus' reading of Teiresias gives us an idea how the ancient Greeks envisioned the seers to whom they ascribed their oracle collections.

   b. *Oracle Collections as Authoritative Texts in Ancient Greece*
Although no collection of the utterances of ancient Greek seers is preserved from archaic or classical times, we know that such collections existed. An impression of how they might have looked can be gained from two later collections, the Jewish collection of the Sibylline Oracles[87] and the Chaldean Oracles, which are only preserved as fragments.[88] The sources suggest that oracle collections were attributed to the following seers: Abaris, Bacis, Glanis, Laios, Lykos, Lysistratus, Musaeus, Orpheus, the Sibyls. At least a significant number of these seers (e.g. Orpheus, Musaeus, Bacis, Glanis, the Sibyls) were legendary figures from a distant past.[89]

   The earliest references to an oracle collection can be found in the writings of Herodotus. He speaks of a collection of the oracles of the famous seer Musaeus[90] that underwent editorial reworking (VII.6).

> With these came Onomacritus, an Athenian oracle-monger, one that had set in order the oracles of Musaeus; with him they had come, being now reconciled to him after their quarrel: for Onomacritus had been banished from Athens by Pisistratus' son Hipparchus, having been caught by Lasus of Hermione in the act of interpolating in the writings of Musaeus an oracle showing that the islands of Lemnos should disappear into the sea.[91]

Herodotus' remarks witness to the great popularity and authority of the Musaeus collection. Furthermore, Onomacritus was commissioned to edit the collection and inserted an oracle into it. This event shows that the Musaeus collection underwent at least one redaction. In this respect, it is comparable with the biblical prophetic books. But different from the redactors of biblical books, Onomacritus suffered severe punishment for his insertion. It seems, however, that Onomacritus' punishment was more a reaction to an anti-Pisistratid aim of his redaction than to the reworking

---

   87   For the Sibylline oracles, see J. J. Collins, 'Sibylline Oracles', *OTP* 1 (1983): 317–472.
   88   For the Chaldean Oracles, see H. Lewy, *Chaldaean Oracles and Theurgy: Mysticism, Magic, and Platonism in the Later Roman Empire* (new edition by M. Tardieu; Paris: Études Augustiniennes, 1978); R. Majercik: *The Chaldean Oracles: Text, Translation, and Commentary* (Studies in Greek and Roman Religion, 5; Leiden: Brill, 1989).
   89   For details, see the overview given by Baumgarten, *Heiliges Wort*, pp. 48–60.
   90   For Musaeus and his collection, see Baumgarten, *Heiliges Wort*, pp. 48–49.
   91   Translation according to A. D. Godley, *Herodotus: With an English Translation*, vol. 3: *Books V–VII* (LCL, 118; revised and reprinted; Cambridge, MA: Harvard University Press; London: Heinemann, 1963), p. 307.

of the Musaeus collection as such.[92] That the Pisistratids felt forced to banish Onomacritus hints nevertheless at a great authority of the Musaeus collection. To call for such a severe punishment, Onomacritus' anti-Pisistratid redaction must have carried the potential of a significant propaganda coup against the Pisistratids, which is only possible if the Musaeus collection was widely respected.

Herodotus also hints at how the Musaeus collection was used. Onomacritus' redactional work was not only editorial in character but reapplied Musaeus' prophecy to his own time in an anti-Pisistratid way. This recontextualization of an earlier prophetic text makes Onomacritus' work comparable to literary prophecy.

Herodotus is not the only ancient author referring to Onomacritus' editorial work. Pausanias (I.22, 7) ascribes most of the Musaeus collection to Onomacritus.[93]

> I have read verses in which Musaeus receives from the North Wind the gift of flight, but, in my opinion, Onomacritus wrote them, and there are no certainly genuine works of Musaeus except a hymn to Demeter written for the Lycomidae.[94]

This quote is taken from Plutarch's treatises, 'The Oracles at Delphi No Longer Given in Verse'. A brief note in this treatise confirms that Onomacritus was indeed a professional in editing and redacting oracles and suggests that his redactional efforts were not restricted to the Musaeus collection.

> Moreover, there was the oft-repeated tale that certain men with a gift for poetry were wont to catch the words spoken, and then weaving about them a fabric of extempore hexameters or other verses or rhythms as 'containers', so to speak, for the oracles. I forbear to mention how much blame men like Onomacritus, Prodicus, and Cinaethon have brought upon themselves from the oracles by foisting upon them a tragic diction and a grandiloquence of which they had no need, nor have I any kindly feeling towards their changes.[95]

The work of Fontenrose shows that Onamacritus' redaction of the Musaeus collection is no exception. According to Fontenrose, internal

---

92   See H. A. Shapiro, 'Oracle-Mongers in Peisistratid Athens', *Kernos* 3 (1990): 335–45, esp. 336–37. The forecast that the islands around Lemnos would disappear under the sea contradicted Athens' own interests in that region.

93   For further literary activities of Onomacritus, see Pausanias VIII.31, 3; VIII.37, 5; IX.35, 5.

94   Translation according to Jones, *Pausanias*, p. 113.

95   *The Oracles at Delphi No Longer Given in Verse*, 407 e. English translation according to F. C. Babbit, *Plutarch's Moralia in Fifteen Volumes*, vol. v: *351 c–438 e* (LCL; Cambridge, MA: Harvard University Press; London: Heinemann, 1962), p. 331. I am indebted to Prof. Dr Zlatko Plese for referring me to this passage.

evidence shows that oracles quoted from the Bacis collection actually came from the oracle at Delphi.[96] A redaction inserted Delphic oracles into the Bacis collection.

How was the character of these redactions understood in classical Greece? To answer this question, it needs to be recognized that Herodotus describes Onomacritus as a χρησμολόγος. Chresmologues, like Onomacritus, were professional diviners who 'possessed a collection or book of oracles that a god or former mantis had reputedly spoken'.[97] As will be seen below, Aristophanes' polemic against the chresmologues shows that the chresmologues applied the oracles of their collections to every situation imaginable when asked by their audiences. In addition, chresmologues were responsible for the interpretation of oracles[98] and sometimes claimed to have received visions or auditions of their own. Chresmologues thus practiced a divinatory recontextualization and reinterpretation of earlier oracles. In this respect, their work is quite comparable with the redactors and tradents responsible for Israelite literary prophecy. The divinatory character of the institution of the chresmologue seems to suggest that the redaction of an oracle collection itself was perceived as an act of prophecy, too.[99] As Onomacritus was one of the many chresmologues active in the fifth century BCE, his redaction of the Musaeus collection was done in the same spirit and needs to be understood as an act of prophecy, too.[100] By using Onamacritus' redaction as an example of ancient Greek chresmologues, we know that ancient Greek oracle collections are comparable to literary and not to written prophecy. The redactions of Greek oracle collections aimed at a reapplication of earlier prophetic texts.

How the chresmologues treated their respective oracle collections is also of interest for questions of canonical history. That chresmologues had oracle collections or a book of oracles which they used for purposes of divination points to the special character and authority of these texts. If the oracle collections themselves were used as divinatory means, it seems as if we observe a phenomenon which might be described as scripture. To be sure, in the preserved evidence, oracle collections are not called holy but if a text becomes a source of divination, in the terminology of Ulrich described above the status of this text can best be described as scriptural. The scriptural dignity of classical Greek oracle collections seems to have developed out of their continuous reapplication to various contexts. In this, classical Greek oracle collections are also comparable to Israelite

---

96   Fontenrose, *Delphic Oracle*, pp. 159–60.
97   Fontenrose, *Delphic Oracle*, p. 153.
98   See Fontenrose, *Delphic Oracle*, p. 153; Baumgarten, *Heiliges Wort*, p. 40.
99   See Baumgarten, *Heiliges Wort*, p. 41.
100   See Fontenrose, *Delphic Oracle*, p. 157.

literary prophecy. Both the scriptural standing of Greek oracle collections and their continuous reapplication can also be observed in other references.

The Musaeus collection is not the only oracle collection mentioned by Herodotus. When writing about the battle of Salamis, Herodotus explicitly quotes a collection of Lysistratus oracles[101] and interprets one of its oracles (Herodotus VIII.96).

> But many of the wrecks were caught by a west wind and carried to the strand in Attica called Colias; so that not only was the rest of the prophecy fulfilled which had been uttered by Bacis and Musaeus concerning that sea-fight, but also that which had been prophesied many years ago by an Athenian oracle-monger named Lysistratus, about the wrecks that were here cast ashore (the import of which prophecy no Greek had noted): 'Also the Colian dames shall roast their barley with oar-blades.'[102]

Herodotus remarks that his interpretation has not been noted by the Greeks. The remark shows that the oracle of Lysistratus originally referred to something else. Only when wreckage was washed on the shores of Colias after the battle of Salamis did Herodotus recontextualize Lysistratus' oracle. The oar-blades refer to the Persian wreckage washed onto the shores of Colias. Herodotus' interpretation of the Lysistratus oracle recalls how earlier oracles were recontextualized, how Israelite literary prophecy was developed and how the Qumran Pesharim interpret their biblical lemmata.[103] That the Lysistratus oracle collection comes to Herodotus' mind when he thinks about the battle of Salamis and that he reads the battle of Salamis in light of this oracle collection points to its special authority.

A little earlier in his report on the battle of Salamis (VIII.77), Herodotus refers to the Bacis oracle collection and its bearing for the fateful battle. Herodotus uses the same hermeneutics in reading the Bacis oracle as with the Lysistratus one. He also regards the Bacis oracle as similarly authoritative as the Lysistratus one.

> But, for oracles, I have no way of gainsaying their truth; for they speak clearly, and I would not essay to overthrow them, when I look into such matter as this:
> 'When that with lines of ships thy sacred coasts they have fencèd,
> Artemis golden-sworded, and thine, sea-washed Cynosura,

---

101   Against Baumgarten, *Heiliges Wort*, pp. 39–40, who understands Lysistratus as a seer making an oracle.

102   Translation according to A. D. Godley, *Herodotus: With an English Translation*, vol. 4: *Books VIII–IX* (LCL, 120; London: Heinemann; New York: G. P. Putnam's Sons, 1924), p. 95.

103   See Lange, 'Interpretation als Offenbarung'.

All in the madness of hope, having ravished the glory of Athens,
Then shall desire full fed, by pride o'erweening engendered,
Raging in dreadful wrath and athirst for the nations' destruction,
Utterly perish and fall; for the justice of heaven shall quench it;
Bronze upon bronze shall clash, and the terrible bidding of Ares
Redden the seas with blood. But Zeus far-seeing, and hallowed
Victory then shall grant that Freedom dawn upon Hellas.'
Looking at such matter and seeing how clear is the utterance of Bacis, I
neither venture myself to gainsay him as touching oracles nor suffer
such gainsaying by others.[104]

Herodotus' references to the oracles of Lysistratus and Bacis[105] attest to
the importance and authority of oracle collections in classical Greece.
They also provide information on how these oracle collections were used.
The historian clearly regards them as being concerned with matters of
international significance, or more precisely, with the Athenian victory
over the Persian fleet at Salamis. Herodotus VIII.77 and 96 are
paradigmatic passages, illustrating how the ancient historian used oracles
and oracle collections. Every time Herodotus quotes or refers to an oracle
collection, its oracles are understood as forecasting matters of international scale, mostly war. In V.90–91, the historian speaks about
Athenian oracles brought to Sparta by Cleomenes. According to
Herodotus, the Spartans' resolve in their conflict with Athens was
hardened by reading these oracles. In another part of his work (VIII.20),
Herodotus interprets a Bacis oracle as forecasting an Athenian attack on
the flocks of the Euboeans. And in IX.43, Herodotus speaks of oracles by
Bacis and Musaeus forecasting a defeat of the Persian army.

On first glimpse, the interpretations of oracle collections which refer to
events of war and international politics recall written prophecies. But the
Greek oracles collected in the respective oracle collections were supposedly delivered hundreds of years before the events of which they spoke
took place. Even if the putative dates were disregarded, they were
certainly not originally addressed to the generals of the Persian and
Peloponnesian wars. With the Greek oracle collections, a reapplication
and recontextualization of earlier prophetic texts to later times can be
observed. Such a reapplication and recontextualization is characteristic
for literary prophecy. As with Israelite literary prophecy, these reapplications led to an ever increasing authority of the Greek oracle collections
which already in classical times had developed a scriptural recognition by
their audiences.

When reading Herodotus, one could think that, in classical Greece,
international conflict and war was the only interpretative key for oracle

104   Translation according to Godley, *Herodotus*, vol. 4, pp. 75, 77.
105   For the Bacis collection, see Baumgarten, *Heiliges Wort*, pp. 50–52.

collections. But the polemical satire of Aristophanes is qualified to correct this one-sided view. Every time Aristophanes mentions oracle collections, he ridicules them. By these overstatements, he attacks actual practices and provides important information about the use of oracle collections in classical Greece.

In several passages of Aristophanes' comedy *The Knights*, one of the protagonists, the Paphlagonian Kleon, 'is in effect a chresmologue who possesses a collection of Bakis' oracles, which helps him to keep Demos under his control (109–143, 195–210, 960–1096). The sausage-seller challenges him with oracles of Glanis, "Bakis' elder brother" (1003–1004), and the two engage in an oracle-reciting contest, in which Glanis' oracles prove superior; for Demos takes the sausage-seller as his steward in place of Kleon.'[106] Although this burlesque certainly exaggerates the use of Greek oracle collections, it nevertheless reflects how these oracle collections were read[107] and the kind of recognition they enjoyed with their audiences.

The repeated reference to the Bacis and Glanis collections by the Paphlagonian Kleon and the sausage-seller reconfirm the observations I made concerning Herodotus' references to the oracle collections. Aristophanes' satire shows that the Bacis and Glanis collections were deemed to be of importance for almost all political as well as day to day decisions. They were used as divinatory means to reach decisions and had thus a scriptural status. A good example is a passage in *The Knights* (1000–1010). Demus, the Paphlagonian (Paph.), and a sausage-seller (S.S.) discuss the relevance of the oracle collections of Bacis and Glanis for every aspect of human life. Aristophanes' satire reflects an opinion which must have been widespread in his time.

Demus. Come, let me see. Whose oracles are these?
Paph. Mine are by Bacis.
Demus. (To S.S.) And by whom are yours?
S.S. Mine are by Glanis, Bakis's elder brother.
Demus. What do they treat of?
Paph. Mine? Of Athens, Pylus,
　　　Of you, of me, of every blessed thing.
Demus (To S.S.) And you; of what treat yours?
S.S. Of Athens, pottage,
　　　Of Lacedaemon, mackerel freshly caught,

---

106 Fontenrose, *Delphic Oracle*, p. 159. For the use of oracle collections in the *Knights*, see also Baumgarten, *Heiliges Wort*, pp. 44–45.
107 See Baumgarten, ibid.

> Of swindling barley-measurers in the mart,
> Of you, of me. That nincompoop be hanged.[108]

As might be observed with ANE written prophecies, the oracle collections are quoted to support a claim to power. But the ANE written prophecies were composed to support the rule of a given king while the oracles of Bacis and Glanis most certainly did not have Demus, the Paphlagonian or the sausage-seller in mind. On the contrary, the Bacis and Glanis collections are recontextualized for this very purpose and reapplied to a timeframe that is later than both their putative and their actual dates. Similarly to Herodotus, Aristophanes' polemic characterizes Greek oracle collections as a kind of highly regarded literary prophecy.

In his comedies, Aristophanes seems to focus his criticism of oracle books in particular on their regular misuse to gain personal and political advantages. His criticism coincides with his pretending that the respective oracles could articulate the divine will about matters of rule and political power. Aristophanes' criticism concerning the oracles' misuse for personal gain is especially evident in *Knights* 960–1150. Lines 1035–1050 are representative:

> **Demus.** Aye, by Poseidon, Glanis, that's far better.
> **Paph.** Nay, listen first, my friend, and then decide.
>   *Woman she is, but a lion*
>   *she'll bear us in Athens holy;*
>   *One who for Demus will fight*
>   *with an army of stinging mosquitoes,*
>   *Fight, as if shielding his whelps;*
>   *whom see thou guard with devotion*
>   *Building a wooden wall*
>   *and an iron fort to secure him.*
>   Do you understand?
> **Demus.** By Apollo, no, not I.
> **Paph.** The God, 'tis plain, would have you keep me safely,
>   For I'm a valiant lion, for your sake.
> **Demus.** What, you Antileon and I never knew it!
> **S.S.** One thing he purposely informs you not,
>   What that oracular wall of wood and iron,
>   Where Loxias bids you keep him safely, is.
> **Demus.** What means the God?
> **S.S.** He means that you're to clap Paphlagon in the five-holded pillory-stocks.
> **Demus.** I shouldn't be surprised if that came true.[109]

---

108 Translation according to B. Bickley Rogers, *Aristophanes: With the English Translation*, vol. 1: *The Acharnians, The Knights, The Clouds, The Wasps* (LCL; London: Heinemann; New York: G. P. Putnam's Sons, 1930), p. 223.

109 Translation according to Bickley Rogers, *Aristophanes*, vol. 1, pp. 225, 227.

It can hardly be imagined that Glanis' oracle collection originally intended the Paphlagonian's personal gain. What is criticized is a wrongful reapplication of Glanis' oracles to a later timeframe. Such a mistake is a bad use of literary prophecy.

In *The Knights* 110–234, Aristophanes' ridicule seems to have a double aim. On the one hand, the governing skills of the elite are compared with the professional skills of a sausage-seller. In the play, the sausage-seller according to an oracle of Bacis is actually supposed to succeed the Paphlagonian as ruler. On the other hand, the play targets chresmologues and their use of oracle collections. A good example is the dialogue between Demosthenes (De.) and the sausage-seller (S.S.) in *The Knights* 190–212:

> **De.** The mischief is that you know anything.
> To be a Demus-leader is not now
> For lettered men, nor yet for honest men,
> But for the base and ignorant. Don't let slip
> The bright occasion which the Gods provide you.
> **S.S.** How goes the oracle?
> **De.** Full of promise good,
> Wrapped up in cunning enigmatic words.
> *Nay, but if once the Eagle,*
> *the black-tanned mandible-curver,*
> *Seize with his beak the Serpent,*
> *the dullard, the drinker of life-blood,*
> *Then shall the sharp sour brine*
> *of the Paphlagon-tribe be extinguished,*
> *Then to the entrail-sellers*
> *shall God great and honour*
> *Render, unless they elect*
> *to continue the sale of the sausage.*
> **S.S.** But what in the world has this to do with me?
> **De.** The black-tanned Eagle that means Paphlagon.
> **S.S.** And what the mandibles?
> **De.** That's self-evident.
> His fingers, crooked to carry off their prey.
> **S.S.** What does the Serpent mean?
> **De.** That's plainer still.
> A serpent's long; a sausage too is long.
> Serpents drink blood, and sausages drink blood.
> The Serpent then, it says, shall overcome
> The black-tanned Eagle, if it's not talked over.
> **S.S.** I like the lines: but how can I, I wonder,
> Contrive to manage Demus's affairs.

This play can be compared with the Ancient Near Eastern use of prophecies. Both support the rule of a given king. Differing from Ancient Near Eastern written prophecy and characteristic for literary prophecy, Aristophanes' ridicule attests to a recontextualization and reapplication of an older oracle to a later timeframe.

The same process of recontextualization and reapplication can also be observed in Aristophanes' attacks on the cavalier attitude with which the oracle collections are reapplied. His attacks use oracle collections as a pretense for purposes of gaining political power or for justifying a change of political power. A good example is the dialogue between Demosthenes (De.) and Nicias (Nic.) in *Knights* 118–143:

> **De.** O you clever fellow you
>   I'll read it; hand it over; you the while
>   Fill me the cup. Let's see: what have we here?
>   O! Prophecies! Give me the cup directly.
> **Nic.** Here! What do they say?
> **De.** Fill me another cup.
> **Nic.** Fill me another? Is that really there?
> **De.** O Bakis!
> **Nic.** Well?
> **De.** Give me the cup directly.
> **Nic.** Bakis seems mighty partial to the cup.
> **De.** O villainous Paphlagon, this it was you feared,
>   This oracle about yourself!
> **Nic.** What is it?
> **De.** Herein is written how himself shall perish.
> **Nic.** How shall he?
> **De.** How? The oracle says straight out,
>   That first of all there comes an oakum-seller
>   Who first shall manage all the State's affairs.
> **Nic.** One something seller; well, what follows, pray?
> **De.** Next after him there comes a sheep-seller.
> **Nic.** Two something-sellers; what's this seller's fortune?
> **De.** He'll hold the reins, till some more villainous rogue
>   Arise than he; and thereupon he'll perish.
>   The follow Paphlagon, our leather-seller,
>   Thief, brawler, roaring as Cycloborus roars.
> **Nic.** The leather-seller, then shall overthrow
>   The sheep-seller?
> **De.** He shall.
> **Nic.** O wretched me,
>   Is there no other something-seller left?
> **De.** There is yet one; a wondrous trade he has.
> **Nic.** What, I beseech you?
> **De.** Shall I tell you?

Nic. Aye.
De. A sausage-seller ousts the leather-seller.[110]

In *Birds* 957–995, Aristophanes criticizes the use of oracle collections – in this case the Bacis collection – as a ruse to gain private advantage while pretending to provide guidance for the sacrificial cult. And characteristic for literary prophecy, a recontextualization and reapplication of an earlier oracle to a later timeframe can be observed. A good example is the conversation between Pisthetaerus (Pei.) and an oracle monger (O.-M.), i.e. chresmologue 957–991:[111]

Oracle-Monger Forbear! touch not the goat awhile.
Pei. Eh. Who are you?
O.-M. A soothsayer.
Pei. You be hanged!
O.-M. O think not lightly friend of things divine;
　　Know, I've an oracle of Bakis, bearing
　　On your Cloudcuckooburies.
Pei. Eh? then why
　　Did you not soothsay that before I founded
　　My city here?
O.-M. The Power within forbade me.
Pei. Well, well, there's nought like hearing what it says.
O.-M. *Nay but if once grey crows*
　　　　and wolves shall be banding together,
　　Out in the midway space,
　　　　twixt Corinth and Sycion, dwelling,—
Pei. But what in the world have I to do with Corinth?
O.-M. Bakis is riddling: Bakis means the Air.
　　First to Pandora offer
　　　　a white-fleeced ram for a victim.
　　Next, who first shall arrive
　　　　my verses prophetic expounding,
　　Give him a brand-new cloak
　　　　and a pair of excellent sandals.
Pei. Are sandals in it?
O.-M. Take the book and see.
　　Give him moreover a cup,
　　　　and fill his hands with the inwards.
Pei. Are inwards in it?
O.-M. Take the book and see.
　　Youth, divinely inspired,
　　　　if thou dost as I did, thou shalt surely
　　Soar in the clouds as an Eagle;

110　Translation according to Bickley Rogers, *Aristophanes*, vol. 1, pp. 135, 137.
111　For this passage, see Baumgarten, *Heiliges Wort*, pp. 42–43.

> *refuse, and thou ne'er shalt become an*
> *Eagle, or even a dove,*
> > *or a woodpecker tapping in the oak-tree.*

Pei. Is it all in it?

O.-M. Take the book and see.

Pei. O how unlike your oracle to mine,
> Which from Apollo's words I copied out;
> *But if a cheat, an impostor,*
> > *presume to appear uninvited,*
> *Troubling the sacred rites,*
> > *and lusting to taste of the inwards,*
> *Hit him betwixt the ribs*
> > *with all your force and your fury.*

O.-M. You're jesting surely.

Pei. Take the book and see.
> *See that ye spare not the rogue,*
> > *though he soar in the clouds as an Eagle,*
> *Yea, be he Lampon himself*
> > *or even the great Diopeithes.*

O.-M. Is all that in it?

Pei. Take the book and see.
> Get out! be off, confound you! (*Striking him*)

O.-M. O! O! O!

Pei. There, run away and soothsay somewhere else.[112]

Aristophanes' critique of the use of the Bacis collection in a cultic context is supported by outside evidence. In his famous magnum opus *The Republic* (364e–365a), Plato criticizes the cultic use of oracle collections, in this case, the use of the Musaeus and Orpheus collections:

> And they produce a bushel of books of Musaeus and Orpheus, the offspring of the Moon and of the Muses, as they affirm, and these books they use in their ritual, and make not only ordinary men but states believe that there really are remissions of sins and purifications for deeds of injustice, by means of sacrifice and pleasant sport for the living, and that there are also special rites for the defunct, which they call functions, that deliver us from evils in that other world, while terrible things await those who have neglected to sacrifice.[113]

Plato's brief mention of the Musaeus and Orpheus collections regrettably does not provide us with any information on how these texts were used in

---

112 Translation according to B. Bickley Rogers, *Aristophanes: With the English Translation*, vol. 2: *The Peace, The Birds, The Frogs* (reprinted; LCL; London: Heinemann; Cambridge, MA: Harvard University Press, 1937), pp. 223, 225, 227.

113 Translation according to P. Shorey, *Plato in Twelve Volumes*, vol. 5: *The Republic*, vol. 1: *Books I–V* (LCL, 237; Cambridge, MA: Harvard University Press; London: Heinemann, 1969), p. 135.

the ritual. The context might suggest that they provided some guidance in the performance of an atonement ritual.[114] If this interpretation is correct, *The Republic* 364e–365a would recall the deuteronomistic understanding of prophets as expounders of religious law. Plato's remarks point also to the popularity of the books in question.

To summarize: In classical Greece, oracle collections were common and widely used. They were attributed, to a certain extent, to seers of the ancient past. The passages preserved from ancient sources seem to indicate a special prominence of oracle collections in the fifth and fourth centuries BCE.[115] This special prominence could have been initiated by the great wars of the fifth century BCE.[116] Oracle collections were mostly used and interpreted by professional diviners, called chresmologues. The oracles were understood to refer to matters of national and international scale as well as to individual concerns. Chresmologues were also responsible for editing and extending the oracle collections in question. As I have shown, the hermeneutics of atomization and recontextualization used by the chresmologues to interpret and rework Greek oracle collections resemble the interpretational strategies used in the interpretation of the biblical prophetic books.[117] In general, like Ancient Near Eastern written prophecy, Greek oracle collections attest to a situation of diluted communication ('zerdehnte Sprechsituation'). In a way differing from Ancient Near Eastern written prophecies, the distance between the prophet and her or his audience bridged by the Greek oracle collections is chronological but not geographical in character. The oracle collections quoted by Aristophanes, Herodotus and Plato were written significantly earlier than the time in which these writers lived. Their use of oracle collections attests to a recontextualization and reapplication of earlier Greek oracle collections. Greek oracle collections are, therefore, to be characterized as literary prophecy.

The references to oracle collections in the works of Herodotus, Aristophanes and Plato might hint at a certain set of oracle collections which were regarded as authoritative in classical Greece and had scriptural status. The collections of Bacis, Glanis, Lysistratus and Musaeus are mentioned repeatedly. The repeated mention of Bacis, Glanis, Lysistratus and Musaeus hints at a prominence of a specific group of oracle collections, but Plato's polemics allow for the conclusion that this group of scriptural collections included even more texts.

The way both Herodotus and Aristophanes describe and treat classical Greek oracle collections shows that they were applied to warfare, politics, and private life. This means that they were deemed as important for all

---

114 Thus Baumgarten, *Heiliges Wort*, p. 118 n. 182.
115 Compare Baumgarten, *Heiliges Wort*, p. 52.
116 Thus Baumgarten, *Heiliges Wort*, p. 49.
117 See Lange, 'Interpretation als Offenbarung', pp. 25–30.

areas of public and private life. Oracle collections were used by chresmologues as sources of divination and enjoyed a scriptural status with the Greek populus.

IV. *Comparison: Israelite Literary Prophecy and Greek Oracle Collections*

The above description of ancient Greek oracle collections shows that, similar to Israelite literary prophecy, Greek oracle collections were recontextualized and reapplied to timeframes later than their place of origin. Both Israelite literary prophecy and Greek oracle collections are literary transmitters responding to a diluted communication ('zerdehnte Sprechsituation') of chronological character. Mesopotamian written prophecy, on the other hand, responds to a diluted communication of geographical character. Thus different from Mesopotamian written prophecy, Greek oracle collections transcend their original contexts and meanings. Similar to Israelite literary prophecy, a surplus of meaning is innate to the Greek oracle collections. In my opinion, this innateness of a surplus of meaning is due to the chronological character of the diluted communication that both Israelite literary prophecy and Greek oracle collections try to bridge. Interestingly enough, both Israelite literary prophecy and Greek oracle collections applied the same interpretive strategies of atomization and recontextualization to earlier oracles in order to access their surplus of meaning.

Despite this basic comparison of hermeneutics, there is no 100 per cent overlap between Israel's literary prophecy and ancient Greek oracle collections. For example, the seers to which the classical Greek oracle collections are applied do not fit Weippert's definition of prophecy. In several respects, however, there are close parallels. Both Greek oracle collections and Israelite literary prophecy enjoyed great prominence and both reached a peak of their prominence at the same time (fifth to fourth centuries BCE). In both cases, this prominence was triggered by a situation of national crisis. In the case of Israelite literary prophecy, its prominence was due to the Babylonian exile and the events of 587 BCE. In the case of the Greek oracle collections, the trigger factor was the wars of the fifth century BCE. Mostly, Israelite literary prophecy and Greek oracle collections attribute their prophecies to figures of the past. In the case of the Greek oracle collections, it is doubtful whether figures like Musaeus, as a student of Orpheus, ever existed; but the existence of Isaiah or Jeremiah, for example, cannot be questioned. Both the biblical prophetic books and the Greek oracle collections underwent redactions and reworkings, sometimes extensively. Even the secondary use of oracles from one prophet by a book attributed to another prophet (see e.g. the use of Amos 7.14 in Zech. 13.5 or the inclusion of Deutero-Isaiah in the book of Isaiah) has a parallel in the inclusion of Delphic oracles into the Bacis collection. In both cases, the process of reworking and editing earlier prophetic texts seems to have been understood as prophetic in character.

It is not known why and when the Greek oracle collections developed. This ignorance differs from our knowledge concerning Israelite literary prophecy. The Greek oracle collections were attributed to seers, who were either figures from the distant past or more recent figures. Nothing is known about a rejection or marginalization of these seers by their respective targeted audiences. The major difference between Greek oracle collections and Israelite literary prophecy is the chresmologue. Although prophetic texts have been reinterpreted and reworked in ancient Israel, there is no hint for ancient Israel at an institutionalized interpreter and owner of prophetic texts. A vague parallel to the chresmologue can be found in the interpretive authority claimed for the Teacher of Righteousness by the Qumran pesharim (1QpHab II.8–10; VII.3–5). And speculatively, it might be asked as to how far the interpretive privilege of the Levites (Deut. 33.10) might correspond to the functions of the chresmologues.

The matters concerning which biblical prophetic books and which Greek oracle collections were interpreted overlap only partially. Both the biblical prophetic books and the Greek oracle collections were applied to universal matters and both were understood as bearing meaning for matters of state. But for ancient Israel, the individual application of oracle collections that Aristophanes criticized is not attested by the extant evidence.

It might be tempting to argue that Greek oracle collections influenced the development of Israelite literary prophecy or that, conversely, Israelite literary prophecy left its mark on classical Greece. But the evidence is not sufficient to make either claim. Another explanation seems to be more probable. When prophetic texts responded to a situation of diluted communication ('zerdehnte Sprechsituation') that was chronological in character, they developed a surplus of meaning, which transcends their historical origins and which is typical for literary prophecy. The potential for literary prophecy seems to be inherent not only in Israelite prophecy but in prophecy as such. Literary prophecy can, therefore, occur in different cultures at the same time. Furthermore, the Demotic Chronicle from Ptolemaic Egypt is an interpretive reapplication of an older astrological oracle.[118]

The potential for future reapplication, i.e. the potential for an ontic plus

---

118   For the Demotic Chronicle see W. Spiegelberg, *Die sogenannte Demotische Chronik: Pap. 215 der Bibliothèque Nationale zu Paris nebst den auf der Rückseite des Papyrus stehenden Texten* (Leipzig: J. C. Hinrichs'sche Buchhandlung, 1914); A. B. Lloyd, 'Nationalist Propaganda in Ptolemaic Egypt', *Historia* 31 (1982): 33–55, esp. 41–45.

in meaning, is inherent in almost all forms of divination. This conclusion raises serious questions concerning the recent claims quoted at the beginning of this article:[119] namely, that literary prophecy is not privileged solely by ancient Israel and is not characteristic for Israelite prophecy. The uniqueness of Israelite prophecy and its particular characteristics are not found in its form or hermeneutic character but in its subject matter.

If Greek oracle collections and Israelite-Jewish literary prophecy did not influence each other but the parallels between them point to a potential of surplus meaning in almost all forms of divination, the comparison between the two of them raises the next question. Why did both Greek oracle collections and Israelite-Jewish literary prophecy gain authoritative status and public acclaim while ANE written prophecies did not? What is the catalyst which set both Israelite-Jewish literary prophecy and ancient Greek oracle collections on the long path to canon?

To answer this question means listing more differences and points of comparison. Different from the prophetic books of Judaism, no canon of Greek oracle collections is known to have ever existed, while the Prophets became part of both the Jewish and the Christian canons. The Greek oracle collections gained scriptural status but have never been understood as holy scriptures. Jewish prophetic books were widely regarded as such since the Hellenistic religious reforms of the years 167–164 BCE[120] but might have held this status in the priestly circles which were responsible for the chronistic literature even earlier.[121] Already in classical times, the redaction of Greek oracle collections was regarded as problematic while no such thing is known for Jewish prophetic books.

Both Greek oracle collections and Jewish prophetic books were reapplied by way of redaction, relecture, and interpretation to various new historical contexts and timeframes. Both Jewish prophetic books and Greek oracle collections were interpreted by way of atomization and recontextualization to achieve this purpose. For the Jewish prophets various ancient commentaries are preserved, which attest to this type of hermeneutics. Examples include the Qumran pesharim. The Greek oracle collections were interpreted in the same way by the chresmologues. No evidence exists, though, that the chresmologues produced commentaries like the pesharim. But the Dervenis papyrus attests to an allegorical commentary of an Orphic poem. Although the Orphic poem in question is not an oracle collection it shows that commentaries on Orphic texts existed. For Hellenistic Egypt, the Demotic Chronicle attests even to a commentary of an Egyptian astrological 'omen list' which achieves its reapplication by way of atomization and recontextualization.

119   See the literature quoted in note 4.
120   See Lange, 'From Literature to Scripture', passim.
121   See Lange, 'Authoritative Literature and Scripture in the Chronistic Corpus', passim.

In terms of literary prophecy as well as in terms of canonical history, the point of comparison between Israelite-Jewish literary prophecy and Greek oracle collections is their reapplication to later historical contexts and timeframes; i.e., what made both Jewish prophetic texts and Greek oracle collections authoritative and gave them even scripture-like status is the use of their ontic interpretive plus by way of redaction and/or interpretation. The comparison between Jewish prophetic books and Greek oracle collections shows that a text can claim religious authority, but what gives him religious authority is his re-lecture and reuse in different contexts beyond his auctorial meaning. The reapplications of Israelite-Jewish prophecies and Greek oracles led to repeated cases in which historical developments reaffirmed the truth of a given prophecy or oracle. These reaffirmations led to increased authority.

Compared with Israelite-Jewish literary prophecy and Greek oracle collections, the ANE written prophecies were certainly religiously authoritative as they communicated messages of various deities. They might even have had the potential for an ontic plus of meaning but they were never reapplied and hence never gained a lasting religious authority. It is not just the potential for an ontic surplus of meaning but later reapplication of religiously authoritative texts which paves the way to canon. Their reapplication to later contexts beyond the auctorial meaning effected an actualization of both Jewish prophetic texts and Greek oracle collections which helped them not only to remain up-to-date and authoritative but to continuously gain in authority.

What puts a text on its way to canon, i.e. the motivator and maybe even one of the initial causes of canonical history, is the repeated interpretive use of its surplus meaning. For the divinatory texts the phenomenon of literary prophecy is hence a key catalyst of their canonical history. This key catalyst is in turn triggered by cultural, religious, social and political crises and developments which required the reapplication of religiously authoritative texts.

The mechanisms of canonical history observed here by way of comparing Israelite-Jewish literary prophecy with Greek oracle collections are not restricted to the canonical histories of divinatory texts. Neither the ontic plus of meaning of texts nor their reapplication to later contexts is a privilege of Greek oracle collections and Israelite-Jewish literary prophecy. On the contrary, an ontic plus of meaning is inherent in every text. And the reapplication of texts to later contexts is widespread in the literary history of the world. Other examples from antiquity include the allegoresis of Homeric epics in the Greco-Roman world or the interpretation of the Mosaic Torah in ancient Judaism. When by repeated reapplication to future historic contexts the ontic plus of meaning is developed in a given text any group of texts walks its first steps on the way to canon.

ARTIFACTUAL AND HERMENEUTICAL USE OF SCRIPTURE IN JEWISH TRADITION

Marianne Schleicher

In Theology and Jewish Studies, scripture has often been equated to canon, and much expertise on the function of canon is presented in the so-called canon debate. Christian and Jewish scholars, being authorities themselves within their respective religious system, have elaborated their views, especially during the last three decades. They agree more or less on the function of canonical texts as a storage place for and a symbol of society's religious norms. Through various agents and symbols, society has used the canon to recall such normativity and thereby to situate itself within a culture and history to which it wishes to belong. Canonical texts offer themselves as means to include or exclude those who are, or are not, considered members of a particular society. Society applies the canon with the purpose of evaluating whether present and potential members remain within the boundaries of whatever it considers to be proper religious doctrines and forms of praxis.[1] These insights of the canon scholars are crucial to any study of scripture and its role in transmitting religious normativity. However, and despite the high quality of the canon debate,[2] it suffers, in my opinion, from an elitist bias that prevents an insight into areas where the authority of the canon scholars has no say. The lay use of scripture, for example, is rarely touched upon, and had one been left with an understanding of scripture as canon, the preponderant part of individual and collective use of scripture would have escaped one's analysis.

Within the discipline of Comparative Religion the concept of scripture

---

1 Cf. Paul Ricoeur, 'The "Sacred" Text and the Community', in *The Critical Study of Sacred Texts* (ed. Wendy Doniger O'Flaherty; Berkeley: Graduate Theological Union, 1979), pp. 271–76.

2 Cf. Lee Martin McDonald and James Sanders (eds), *The Canon Debate* (Peabody: Hendrickson, 2002) and especially Margalit Finkelberg and Guy G. Stroumsa (eds), *Homer, the Bible and Beyond: Literary and Religious Canons in the Ancient World* (Leiden: Brill, 2003).

is hardly ever reflected upon. Miriam Levering's pioneering effort in editing and contributing to the volume *Rethinking Scripture* from 1989 is the exception that confirms the rule that surely scriptures have been studied, analyzed and accordingly recognized as central source material for religious rituals and doctrines. However, it is still a novelty to most scholars of religion to be confronted by such questions as: What is scripture? And: What psychological, social and cultural needs are being met by the use of scripture? As a scholar in Comparative Religion, this analyst therefore argues that her discipline cannot, and neither can Theology and Jewish Studies for that matter, continue to ignore how scripture works in all strata of society.

In 2004 the anthropologist Brian Malley suggested the term 'artifactual' to cover the dominant use of scripture witnessed among Evangelicals, of which most were lay people. He inspired me and others to notice how scripture in this predominantly lay setting works as an artifact whose primary function is to transmit personal and cultural representations in order to help create transitivity between the individual, the community and the religious culture at large.[3] I have blended this inspiration from Malley with the emphasis in Levering's *Rethinking Scripture*, that scripture will always in one way or another contain some kind of revealed, transempirical knowledge[4] that in my opinion cause scripture to usurp the characteristics of holiness in the Ottonian sense of the word. Rudolf Otto defined 'the holy' as the numinousity of a god or a sphere; i.e., the kind of religious power that causes a state of awe and fascination. The holy is awe-inspiring because it transcends everything known and intelligible. In other words, the holy represents 'das Ganz Andere' (the wholly other). At the same time, the holy is fascinating because it induces the hope of possessing and appropriating the numinous to cause a creature feeling in others similar to the one that caused one's own awe.[5] This dimension of the holy should not be ignored when the artifactual use of scripture is subjected to analysis.

---

3 Cf. Brian Malley, *How the Bible Works: An Anthropological Study of Evangelical Biblicism* (Oxford: AltaMira Press, 2004), pp. 41–48, 70–72.

4 Cf. Wilfred Cantwell Smith, 'The Study of Religion and the Study of the Bible', pp. 21, 36, 41–42; Miriam Levering, 'Scripture and its Reception: A Buddhist Case', p. 58; Barbara Holdrege, 'The Bride of Israel: The Ontological Status of Scripture in the Rabbinic and Kabbalistic Traditions', pp. 181–82. All articles in Miriam Levering (ed.), *Rethinking Scripture* (Albany: State University of New York Press, 1989).

5 Cf. Rudolf Otto, *Das Heilige – über das Irrationale in der Idee des Göttlichen und sein Verhältnis zum Rationalen* (Munich: Beck, 1987 [1917]), pp. 8–45. An endless list of scholars have dealt with the concept of holiness and criticized Otto for a Christian bias. However, René Girard has given the Ottonian notion a revival. Under the inspiration of Emile Durkheim, Girard uses Otto's concept of the holy as *tremendum et fascinans* to explain the function of the holy as a matter of preserving society. Within a given society, the holy not only sanctions normativity in times of relative calm and peace. It is accredited for causing

In view of the abovementioned considerations, artifactual use of scripture has as its premise that scripture is first and foremost handled with the caution, fascination and awe that characterize any handling of a holy object. Priority is given to scripture's non-semantic, formal aspects such as binding and embellishment, spelling, recitation, quotation, storage and similar acts of ritual handling that help one recognize this awe-inspiring and fascinating object. The non-semantic aspects transmit an understanding of scripture that is governed, not by its textual content, but by personal and cultural representations. These representations are subsequently and more or less subconsciously transposed into the user's worldview.

The artifactual use of scripture appears to be generally dominating as this article will show. Still, some uses, as they are typically found among religious specialists and artists, display a conscious effort to understand the discourse of scripture without making it conform to personal and cultural representations, which is why I suggest the concept 'hermeneu-tical use of scripture' to supplement the artifactual one. The hermeneutical use approaches scripture as text, which coincides with a philosophically grounded definition of hermeneutics. I shall draw upon and quote Paul Ricoeur's definition. According to Ricoeur, hermeneutics is a matter of connecting

> two discourses, the discourse of the text and the discourse of the interpretation. This connection means that what has to be interpreted in a text is what it says and what it speaks about, i.e., the kind of world which it opens up or discloses; and the final act of 'appropriation' is less the projection of one's own prejudices into the text than the 'fusion of horizons' – to speak like Hans-Georg Gadamer – which occurs when the world of the reader and the world of the text merge into one another. (Ricoeur, 'From Existentialism to the Philosophy of Language', pp. 377–78)

Artifactual use of scripture implies such projection of prejudices, in the philosophical sense of the word, similar to what anthropologists speak of as personal and cultural representations. Hermeneutical use of scripture, however, must have as its vantage point a conscious and sincere effort to understand the discourse of the text that constructs the proposed worldview. As a result, hermeneutical use of scripture rests upon interpretation proper that involves an encouragement to the reader to consider whether the text's proposed religious worldview should be rejected or appropriated. Such rejection and appropriation are matters of

---

societal cohesion against internal and external enemies in crisis, conflict and war despite other obvious causes such as the scapegoat mechanism; cf. René Girard, *Things Hidden Since the Foundation of the World* (Stanford: Stanford University Press, 1987 [1978]), pp. 42–43.

mental transformation, which will help us pursue an understanding of the function that hermeneutical use of scripture activates.

The purpose of this article is to exemplify my distinction between artifactual and hermeneutical uses of scripture and to reflect upon their functions in order to suggest where and why in the pattern of the seemingly dominant artifactual use of scripture do we find examples of hermeneutical use? Examples will be taken from Jewish use of the Torah and the Psalms, both significant and popular collections for beliefs and practices throughout Jewish history from Antiquity until today.[6]

Examples of Artifactual Use of Scripture

When the Jerusalem Temple was destroyed in 70 CE, Jews no longer had access to a sacred place, an *axis mundi*, where contact with the holy could be mediated. The Torah replaced the temple as the centre of cultic activity as it becomes evident in the Mishnaic and Talmudic specifications of how to make and handle the Torah text for liturgical purposes. A sentence in *Mishnah*, 'Pirkey Avot' 1.1 is one among many illustrations of this replacement. It encourages Jews to 'make a fence round the Torah'. Segregating sacred space is a fundamental religious activity in that it marks the boundary between the holy and the profane. When the temple was still standing it was constantly purified; i.e., segregated from profane matters. People officiating within it were equally purified from profanity and the mundane world was fenced out from the temple precincts. When the Mishnaic tractate 'Pirkey Avot' formulates this encouragement in its opening lines, it is hard not to interpret it as an attempt to stress the very holy status of the Torah similar to that of the temple.[7]

In early Rabbinic Judaism specifications are made for the non-semantic formal aspects of the Torah scroll as a holy object that allow for easy recognition and define what is required for a Torah scroll to be perfect and complete. The holy status of the Torah depends on its textual

6   A detailed account of the use of the Torah in Jewish tradition, including the examples brought here, has been given in Marianne Schleicher, 'The Many Faces of the Torah: Reception and Transformation of the Torah in Jewish Communities', in *Religion and Normativity*, vol. 2 (ed. Kirsten Nielsen; Aarhus: Aarhus University Press, forthcoming 2008), while my analysis of the Jewish use of the Psalms has been presented in a Danish article, cf. Marianne Schleicher, 'Religiøs reception og transformation af Salmernes Bog i jødisk tradition', in *Collegium Biblicum* (ed. Bodil Ejrnæs; Copenhagen: Faculty of Theology, 2006), pp. 69–82.

7   In the Middle Ages, the status of the Torah as a holy object – or even sanctuary – is stressed by referring to it as *mikdashyah*; i.e., God's temple; cf. David Stern, 'On Canonization in Rabbinic Judaism', in Finkelberg and Stroumsa (eds), *Homer, the Bible, and Beyond*, p. 233.

passages being written in the Assyrian[8] script, on parchment, and in ink (*Mishnah*, 'Yadayim' 4.5). It furthermore depends on the parchment being made from the skin of a clean animal. The preparations of the hide must be made with the conscious intent of turning it into parchment for the Torah (*bTalmud*, 'Megillah' 19a). The parchment must be prepared on both sides (*bTalmud*, 'Shabbat' 79b) and cut into a square sheet, upon which lines shall be ruled in columns leaving space for margins to surround and protect the holy letters to be written upon them. No vowels or accents are allowed if the scroll shall be fit for public reading. The sheets are then sewed together with threads of dried tendons from clean animals and 'the Scroll of the Law closes at its middle, there being a cylinder at each end' (*bTalmud*, 'Baba Bathra' 14a).

To ensure the material distribution of the Torah, every man must write a Torah scroll for himself (*bTalmud*, 'Sanhedrin' 21b), but if he is unable to write one, he can pay a scribe to do so (*bTalmud*, 'Megillah' 27a). An additional benefit of this specification is that it ensures a bond between scripture and the individual. Concerning the holiness of the Torah scroll, up to two mistakes per sheet are tolerable if corrected and will not subtract from its holy status. However, if there are three – some say four – errors on one sheet, the entire scroll shall be put away in a *genizah*[9] (*bTalmud*, 'Menachot' 29b). Once written, inspected, accepted, and in use for liturgical purposes, the Torah has to be chanted aloud by use of a special melody (*bTalmud*, 'Megillah' 32a), something non-semantic as well.

The many specifications in the *Shulkhan Arukh* for making, handling and reading the Torah in liturgical and study-related settings help maintain the notion of holiness pertaining to the scroll. This legal code from 1564 bases its specifications on the Mishnaic and Talmudic opinions mentioned above, but adds to them by making further meticulous regulations that inform the artifactual use. A scribe – be he professional or lay – had to prepare himself mentally before writing a Torah scroll because of the numinous power of God's holy names in the Torah text. He had to say aloud that 'I have the intent to write the holy name' before doing so. The writing of it was not to be interrupted. If an error occurred in the holy name or transgressed into the margins, the sheet had to be stored away in a *genizah* (*Shulkhan Arukh*, 'Yoreh Deah' 22).

To reflect the awe for the Torah scroll, the Torah scroll is covered by a

8   It is impossible to say if the rabbis knew that the Torah prior to the fifth century BCE was written in paleo-Hebrew letters; cf. Stern, 'On Canonization in Rabbinic Judaism', pp. 234–35.

9   Typically a storeroom in a synagogue in which worn-out, heretical or disgraced scrolls and books are placed to prevent their defective status from affecting the holiness of the ritual in which these objects were otherwise to be used.

mantle in Ashkenazi Jewry while in Sephardic Jewry it is placed in a Torah box. One is not to touch it with dirty hands or take it into impure places. People must stand up when it is carried and cannot sit wherever it is resting. If a Torah scroll is beyond repair and/or unfit for public reading, it must be buried and so must defective accessories of the Torah scroll (*Shulkhan Arukh*, 'Yoreh Deah' 22), known as *keley qodesh*; i.e., holy vessels, typically made in silver except for the two wooden rollers (*ets hayyim*).

The holy accessories include a breastplate (*ephod*) connoting that of the high priest, containing on each side the two pillars Boaz and Jachin of the temple; the Torah pointer (*yad torah*) that prevents the reader of the Torah from touching the holy letters with his impure hand; the Torah crown/crowns (*keter/-im*), evoking messianic hope and God's kingdom, to be placed on top of the rollers; and the bells (*rimmonim*) similar to those carried by the high priest to warn ritually impure people that he was coming and that they would have to stay at a distance. The tradition of making the Torah accessories most likely arose as an opportunity for community members to remember and honor family members by donating such equipment to the local synagogue. In other words, the accessories not only transmit an aura of holiness associated with the Jerusalem Temple and the messianic age, they also serve as a means to create transitivity between the Torah, such associations and individual identities. This function is activated Mondays, Thursdays and Saturdays, and on certain holidays when the Torah scroll is taken out of the cupboard to be recited by representatives and listened to by all who participate in synagogue service.[10]

Transitivity as a central function of artifactual use is established when associations evoked by the artifact transcend the religious sphere and create bonds to individual, collective and cultural representations. It does not only pertain to early or medieval Jewish use of the Torah. On 11 October 2005, I interviewed the former Chief Rabbi of Denmark, Bent Melchior.[11] He related several instances where it was obvious that the importance of creating transitivity was at stake. Melchior was telling me about the unique collection of scrolls in the Danish-Jewish community, when he said:

> In England I had this experience, ... that someone donated a scroll, and
> then a few lines were left undone to enable the members of the

---

10 For more on the accessories, cf. Ismar Elbogen, *Jewish Liturgy: A Comprehensive History* (Philadelphia: Jewish Publication Society, 1993 [1913]), pp. 359–63.

11 I owe my gratitude to former Chief Rabbi Bent Melchior for having read and commented on my transcription of the interview, for agreeing to it in the first place and for allowing me to quote him for scholarly purposes.

community to approach and write a letter – of course under the inspection of the scribe.

It means a lot to the religious identification of each individual within this community that he has contributed to the Torah scroll and thereby becomes linked to it. Melchior, being himself the son of a chief rabbi and probably the most respected minority leader in Denmark ever, has had privileged access all his life to scripture and knows to bring an even stronger example of how transitivity is created. Melchior relates:

> Once someone donated a Torah scroll ... A member of the community went to buy one, and he also donated the equipment for it by an artist named Arje Griegst, who made a [Torah shield] in silver – oh no, actually it is the only gilded one we have. On this shield it says that it was given on the occasion of [the 300 year anniversary of the community] and that this man has given it in memory of my parents [Marcus and Meta Melchior]. Funny how you still make such things! Griegst is a great and skilled artist who has also made jewelry for the Queen and for Royal Copenhagen Porcelain. It was the only one that we took out this Saturday when someone in my family became *bar mitzvah*. I thought it was appropriate to use this shield.

The Torah shield reflects a member's recognition of Melchior's parents. Obviously, Melchior appreciates this recognition and the recognition even grows through associations to Griegst, Queen Margrethe II and Royal Copenhagen Porcelain. Relations are being established, which Melchior is proud of and proud of being able to transmit to his grandson on his *bar mitzvah*. Establishing such relations is a matter of creating transitivity between two distinct generations and between the religious Jewish sphere and national Danish icons.

Melchior continues:

> In there (he points in the direction of his living room) I have a crown for a Torah scroll, which we gave to my father... [We] bought it and had an inscription made for the occasion; and then when dad died, mom insisted that it stayed in our home. So now I have a problem of finding it a place... We have used it now and then in the synagogue when reading the last Torah portion, which is usually an honor given to the rabbi. So I took it to the synagogue to ensure that it was used.

By having a Torah crown in his home, Melchior's mother and later on Melchior himself break the norm of keeping the holy Torah accessories in the synagogue. Melchior does take it to the synagogue for occasional use, but in his own home, the private sphere, Melchior does not know what to do with such a powerful object. One can say that a holy artifact has been conquered despite the adjacent problems of handling it. It is really not a thing to wish for, and certainly not if this artifact is a Torah scroll, as it becomes apparent when I asked this question:

> MS: If you had a Torah scroll made, could you then place it in your own home, or would it have to be kept in the synagogue?

> BM: (Thinks) Well, it could stand in your own home, but then one would have to behave extremely respectable and wear a head cover in the room where it was. Actually, this room would have to be set aside for its mere presence.

The Torah scroll radiates holiness that demands a specific behavior, which is most easily met in a synagogue or a *bet midrash*. However, the apparent wish to link oneself or one's family with the artifact and thereby to draw upon the representations attributed to it seems to supersede the awe for it as a holy object.

There is no independent word for the Hebrew Bible even though it is referred to as TaNaKh – an acronym for its tripartite sections: *Torah* (the Books of Moses), *Nevi'im* (the Prophets) and *Ketuvim* (the Writings). Within the Hebrew Bible there is a hierarchy of holiness which stems from the notion that the Torah contains the direct words of God, the Prophets contain the mediated words of God, whereas the Writings contain human reflection on the two former. Practically, it interferes with how these books are treated when used together. Former Chief Rabbi Bent Melchior and the present Chief Rabbi Bent Lexner, both representatives of the modern Orthodox Jewish community in Copenhagen, Denmark, independently told me that they would never leave a copy of the Prophets or the Writings on top of the Torah. Nevertheless, this hierarchy does not prevent artifactual use of the Prophets or the Writings despite their lower degree of holiness. Therefore, examples will follow of how Jewish tradition is also replete with examples of artifactual use of the Psalms.

In the centuries after the fall of the Jerusalem Temple in 70 CE, various Jewish sects competed to obtain the same degree of religious authority as the Temple priesthood used to have. The rabbis constituted one such faction and portray themselves as the winners of this competition in the rabbinical writings, distributed from 200 CE onwards. The truth is however, as argued by Shaye Cohen, that the rabbis did not consolidate their power until around 600 CE.[12] The Psalms became a weapon in this interim power struggle because they were extremely popular among lay people. Lay people used them in various ways. The Psalms had been used as individual prayers in the Judean countryside and in the Diaspora already in Hellenistic times probably because the wording in itself – i.e., a non-semantic aspect – evoked associations to something established,

---

12 Cf. Shaye Cohen, *From the Maccabees to the Mishnah* (Louisville: Westminster John Knox Press, 2nd edn, 1987), pp. 221–24.

something ritual, that could provide some kind of frame for the individual in his or her need to address God in various situations in life.[13] Around 200 CE, recitation of the Psalms was expected to lead one to a good fate at judgment day,[14] which developed into the notion that Psalmic recitation would have an apotropaic effect on disasters and demons, much in line with Otto's explanation of how one is fascinated with the holy to obtain its ability to cause awe in those who are confronted with it. The physical transmission of the Psalms was ensured by the custom described in *bTalmud*, 'Gittin' 35a to give every newly-wed couple a copy of the Psalms as a wedding gift.

Concerning the activity of the rabbis during the first six centuries after the fall of the temple, the rabbis did not exert their influence within the synagogues, but in the academies and in early rabbinical literature. The editors of the *Mishnah* made use of the Psalms as they wanted to emphasize the necessity of the continued performance of the Passover Ritual. They articulated the halakhic commandment that the recitation of Psalms be transferred from the temple to private homes. During Passover while the temple was still standing, the so-called 'Great Hallel', probably Psalm 36, was recited. After the fall of the temple, it was replaced by an entire cluster of psalms, known as the 'Egyptian Hallel'; i.e. Pss. 113–18.[15] During the new recitation ritual in the private homes, cultural representations of the temple were invoked and helped create transitivity between temple-Judaism and Judaism in its new setting. Yet, the replacement of the 'Great Hallel' with the 'Egyptian Hallel' emphasized the new conditions for the Passover ritual. This artifactual use of the Psalms constitutes an exception to the attitude of the rabbis towards the Psalms, because they were tremendously hesitant towards using the Psalms in this initial phase of rabbinical Judaism. In *bTalmud*, 'Shabbat' 118b the rabbis even forbid the recitation of the 'Egyptian Hallel' outside the Passover week.[16]

The hesitance towards the Psalms of David reflects the general attempt to subordinate the figure of David to that of Moses. According to Clemens Thoma,[17] the rabbis were concerned with the new living

13 Cf. *Mishnah*, Ta'anith 4.2; Stefan Reif, *Judaism and Hebrew Prayer: New Perspectives on Jewish Liturgical History* (Cambridge: Cambridge University Press, 1993), p. 58.
14 Cf. Lawrence Hoffmann, 'Hallels, Midrash, Canon, and Loss: Psalms in Jewish Liturgy', in *Psalms in Community: Jewish and Christian Textual, Liturgical, and Artistic Traditions* (ed. Harold Attridge and Margot Fassler; Atlanta: SBL, 2003), p. 35.
15 Cf. Baruch Bokser, *The Origins of the Seder: The Passover Rite and Early Rabbinic Judaism* (Berkeley: University of California Press, 1984), pp. 14–28.
16 Cf. Clemens Thoma, 'Psalmenfrömmigkeit im Rabbinischen Judentum', in *Liturgie und Dichtung: Ein interdisziplinäres Kompendium I. Historische Präsentation* (ed. Hans Jacob Becker and R. Kaczynski; St. Ottilien: Eos Verlag Erzabtei, 1983), pp. 96–98.
17 Cf. Thoma, 'Psalmenfrömmigkeit im Rabbinischen Judentum', pp. 91–105.

conditions after the fall of the temple. They had an ambition to safeguard the boundaries of Jewish identity and thereby avoid internal strife in the Jewish community. The rabbis wanted to sanction new norms for communal prayer and consolidate other communal rituals. Concerned with the content of Jewish beliefs, they argued for the possibility of atoning sin, of being liberated from suppression, of experiencing the return of the exiled to a rebuilt temple in Jerusalem with priests and Levites in charge of the daily service, and finally they argued for the possibility of the coming of the Messiah. These rabbinic norms had already become or became articulated in the *Amida*, the *Shema*, the *Kiddush* and the *Kaddish*; and the rabbis wanted these texts, not the Psalms, to dominate communal prayer. Thoma explains this by recounting how lay people before the fall of the temple used to contribute to the temple service, otherwise officiated by the temple priesthood alone. Lay people used to sing the Psalms just outside of the temple on Shabbat or on high holidays according to *bTalmud*, 'Sukkot' 55a; 'Rosh haShanah' 31a. After the fall of the temple, lay people felt obligated to ensure the continued lay influence on the worship of God despite its new setting, whereas the rabbis only looked at communal prayer as an interim phenomenon, not as the opportunity of lay people for influence. Yet, to appease the lay people and to consolidate their own power, the rabbis made two concessions to the people's love for the Psalms: The first concession has already been touched upon and was the rabbinic commandment to recite the 'Egyptian Hallel', thus transferring the ritual Passover task of the Levites to every Jew in his or her home all over the Diaspora. This artifactual use is evident from the *Aggadah Shel Pesakh*, the manual for the Passover Ritual.[18] The second concession is witnessed by the rabbis quoting the Psalms. This is particularly evident in the *Siddur*, the Jewish prayerbook, in which more than half of the 150 psalms are quoted in part or in toto.[19] It is also evident from the *Midrash on Psalms*. The *Midrash on Psalms* is a compilation of homilies based on the Psalms and composed by rabbis in Italy probably between 220 and 850.[20] What surprised me when I studied these midrashim on the Psalms was that the biblical text was more or less ignored, only referred to through quotation and as a trigger of associations to topics concerning Jewish living conditions in Italy. Surrounding prayers with quotes from the Psalms or ignoring the textual discourse of the Psalms when conducting a midrash on them are clear examples of artifactual use that seem to have

---

18 Cf. Reif, *Judaism and Hebrew Prayer*, pp. 59, 69; and Bokser, *The Origins of the Seder*, pp. 14–28.

19 Cf. Hoffmann, 'Hallels, Midrash, Canon, and Loss', p. 52.

20 William Braude, *The Midrash on Psalms* I–II (New Haven: Yale University Press, 1987 [1959]).

one overall purpose and that is to legitimize new norms concerning Jewish beliefs and practices in a new setting. This artifactual use made lay people link lay activity, lay influence and rabbinical ways of worshipping God. Consequently, the artifactual use of the Psalms helped the rabbis consolidate their power and promote their version of what Jewish identity ought to be.

Rabbi Nahman of Bratslav, a Jewish mystic and messianic claimant, who lived in the Ukraine around 1800, also applied the Psalms in artifactual ways. Nahman composed a recitation manual, known as *haTikkun haKelali*, meaning 'complete restoration' of the state of the world. In this manual Nahman argues how individual Jews can contribute to the process of redemption, in which Lilith, a female representative of evil, is the main antagonist. Lilith is notoriously known to cause men's nightly emission of semen and, subsequently, to steal it and thereby to conceive legions of demon children. Her demonic pregnancy is a metaphor for the increased level of evil in this world, relaying redemption. Because redemption depended on the defeat of Lilith, Nahman instituted a recitation of ten psalms within a ritual context in 1808. If a man experienced emission of semen, he should instantaneously seek out a *mikveh*, a ritual bath, in which he should then recite the ten psalms. If the man was sick or, for some other reason, prevented from immersing into a *mikveh*, he would still meet the requirements if only he recited the ten psalms in the established order. Recognizing the order of the psalms within the Psalter was more important than anything else.[21] Nahman considered the ten psalms,[22] corresponding to the ten genres of Psalms, apotropaic fetish-like tools to ward off the attacks of Lilith. He believed so because of this somewhat manipulated equation: *Tehillim* = תהלים = $400 + 5 + 30 + 10 + 40 = 485$. *Lilith* = לילית = $(30 + 10 + 30 + 10 + 400) + 5$ for the five letters of the word $= 485$. In this way the recitation of the Psalms became the antidote of Lilith's workings by drawing upon the awe-inducing power of the Psalms. In this artifactual use of the Psalms, the non-semantic aspects are clearly distinguishable and furthermore helped transmit a call for engagement in Nahman's process of redemption, subconsciously promoting and legitimizing his adjacent theology.[23]

In the aforementioned interview with Melchior, I mentioned the idea that the Psalms were supposed to have an apotropaic effect on Lilith,

21 Cf. Nahman of Bratslav, *Rabbi Nachman's Tikun: The Tikun HaKlali* (Jerusalem: The Breslov Research Institute, 1982 [1808]), pp. 14–16, 34–36.

22 These are Psalms 16, 32, 41, 42, 59, 77, 90, 105, 137 and 150. The ten genres are *brecha, ashre, maskil, shir, nitsuach, niggum, tefillah, hodu, mizmor, halleluyah*; cf. Nahman, *Rabbi Nachman's Tikun*, pp. 28–29.

23 Cf. Marianne Schleicher, 'Three Aspects of Scripture in Rabbi Nahman of Bratslav's Use of the Psalms', *Studies in Spirituality* 15 (2005), pp. 1–16. Even though this example reflects an artifactual use of scripture, Nahman was a true master in employing scripture in

which caused Melchior to relate how he was approached by a man who feared for the life of his wife who was in labor. The husband called Melchior to ask him to call some relatives in Israel and ask them to go to the Western Wall to recite the Psalms. At first, Melchior refused, but then he did it anyway. He also went to the husband at the hospital in Copenhagen where the staff saved the life of both mother and child. Melchior finished his account by saying: 'So, I should say that it was fine that they recited *tehillim* down at the *Kothel* in Jerusalem, but it also helped what the doctors did at the hospital (And so he laughs).'

Melchior is completely aware of and has a distance to the superstition implicated by the artifactual use of the Psalms. Yet, he is fascinated with it, partly active and indeed knowledgeable of how to do it, as becomes evident in the following. Melchior mentions *Shir haMa'alot* (Ps 120–134) and of how he himself in the new Danish translation of the *Siddur*, translated them 'Psalms for the Pilgrim'. He says:

> BM: This pertains to gematria [i.e. magic based on the numerical value of the letters], because there were 15 steps at the temple, and there are 15 *Shir haMa'alot*-Psalms. And ... the number 15 recurs again and again in Jewish tradition.
>
> MS: But this is due to the name of God, isn't it?
>
> BM: Indeed. At least it is one explanation. *Yud Hey* = *Yah* = 15. Something which also plays a significant role in the mystical tradition is the priestly blessing. If you count, you will find 15 words in the priestly blessing in Hebrew. You also have many places where you'll find synonyms repeated 15 times in the liturgical text.
>
> MS: Is this interpreted as a praise of God?
>
> BM: (Hesitates) Well, it draws down some kind of blessing.

Finally, there are situations where Melchior's mental orientation seems affected more by the use of the Psalms in a liturgical setting than in their original biblical context. It becomes obvious when he refers to the clusters of Psalms as they appear, not in the Hebrew Bible, but in the *Siddur*. He speaks about the Hallel-psalms, *Shir haMa'alot*, *Pasukey deZimrah* and about which psalms are recited at what times in the synagogue. The order of the Psalms according to ritual praxis dominates over the order in the biblical text and thus severs the Psalms from their original intrabiblical position including the discourse that follows from this intratextuality.

Many other examples of the dominating artifactual use of scripture in Judaism could be mentioned. However, it is now time to turn to the other

---

hermeneutical ways, especially in his tales; cf. Marianne Schleicher, *Intertextuality in the Tales of Rabbi Nahman of Bratslav: A Close Reading of Sippurey Ma'asiyot* (Leiden: Brill, 2007).

kind of use – rare as it may be – of hermeneutical efforts made within religious communities to access the internal discourse of the text. Where and why in the pattern of the dominant artifactual use of scripture do we find examples of hermeneutical use?

Examples of Hermeneutical Use of Scripture

To clarify the hermeneutical use of scripture, I shall begin with the efforts of the early rabbis who tried to meet the biblical encouragement in Deut. 6.6-7; 31.10-13, and Neh. 8.8 to study and explain the Torah. The highest institution for education including Torah exposition and jurisprudence was the rabbinic academy. The rabbinic students studied the entire Hebrew Bible. Together with the Prophets and the Writings, the words of the Torah

> served as the prism, the lens, through which the Rabbinic sages looked at and refracted their conception of the world... [However, the rabbis] knew the Bible as a text they had heard, memorized, and carried around in their heads as a memorized text rather than as one they had read and studied in a scroll and therefore remembered in its spatial context on a writing surface. (Stern, 'On Canonization in Rabbinic Judaism', p. 235)

In other words, the early rabbis used a large amount of their cognitive capacity to memorize the Torah instead of freeing some mental space for critical reflection upon its content.[24] Added to this, the memorized sentences were often quoted out of touch with the intratextual discourses of the Torah to legitimize the early rabbinic theology, which is 'unfortunately' a matter of artifactual use through which the Torah text was only recalled to substantiate or legitimize the postulates of the rabbis. However, it seems that the shift towards hermeneutical use occurred once the rabbis and rabbinical students in the academies engaged in debating and recording especially their legal expositions of the Torah, known as *midrash halakhah*. *Midrash halakhah* designates the activity of verifying the legal praxis by identifying its source in the Torah and by interpreting the Torah as proof of the authenticity of these halakhic midrashim. Rabbi Hillel and Rabbi Ismael collected seven and thirteen rules, respectively, in an apparent effort to safeguard rabbinic Judaism against random interpretation of those legal Torah passages that dealt with everyday life in a setting where the temple was no longer standing and where foreign rule in what was now called Palestine prevented the legal content of the Torah from forming the normative basis. Rabbi Akiva focused not only on the details of the Torah verses, but insisted that 'every passage which stands close to another must

---

24   Cf. Jan Assmann, *Religion and Cultural Memory* (Stanford: Stanford University Press, 2006), pp. 21, 101–21.

be explained and interpreted with reference to its neighbor' (*Sifre*, Num. 131). This attitude reflects a certain interest in understanding the discourse of the Torah text prior to its conscious appropriation in a new historical context. Furthermore, the ideal of keeping as close as possible to the plain meaning – i.e., *peshat* – of a biblical verse came to influence all subsequent midrashic activity through this sentence in *bTalmud*, 'Shabbat' 63a: 'a verse should not lose its literal sense'. Because of this sentence, a *peshat*-oriented exposition came to be considered more valuable than a *derash*-oriented one where meaning was applied to the biblical verse to have it make sense.[25] In other words, it seems that the academies at least encouraged and trained their students in hermeneutical use of scripture.

In the Middle Ages, the Jewish poet Shlomo ibn Gabirol offers excellent examples of a poet's hermeneutical use of scripture. To explain his poetic positioning of alternatives to traditionally rabbinic norms and how his poetry presupposes the hermeneutical use of scripture, I shall include a theory formulated by the Hungarian linguist and psychoanalyst Julia Kristeva. In 1974 she wrote her doctoral thesis on the revolutionary power of poetic language.[26] Poetic language is unique, she says, because the poet creates poetry by revisiting what she calls the semiotic *chora* – a psychic receptacle, in which the signifying process takes place. Here, the inner drives of the individual clash with societal and biological constraints prior to the individual positioning him-/herself through language. This clash does not only take place in pre-oedipal childhood. It constantly takes place in everyone's life; but still, common language does not take account of something so individual; and if common language were all that we had, we would not be able to articulate this clash. Within the world of religions this may illuminate not only the scriptural reuse in poetry where the poet has a unique courage to face and articulate the clash of drives and constraints that are attributed to scripture. Here, the poet's hermeneutical use of scripture becomes a means to point to the exact spots in the scriptural discourse where the constraints originate prior to his positioning of alternatives. Poetry that argues against scripture or points to alternatives within scripture also provides the reader with a potential for repositioning him-/herself at a theological level. The repositioning through poetry is enabled thanks to the mental activity of transference where the reader may associate with any other person – the poet or a literary, biblical character – a potential signifying 'other' whose signification may be appropriated after conscious reflection by the reader as an attractive alternative.[27]

---

25   Cf. David Weiss Halivni, *Peshat and Derash: Plain and Applied Meaning in Rabbinic Exegesis* (Oxford: Oxford University Press, 1991), p. 9.

26   Cf. Julia Kristeva, *La Révolution du langage poétique* (Paris: Editions du Seuil, 1974).

27   For more on the function of religious literature, cf. Schleicher, *Intertextuality in the Tales of Rabbi Nahman of Bratslav*, chapter 1.

Gabirol lived from 1021 to 1070 in Muslim Spain. Living conditions in Muslim Spain were difficult and complex. Despite the fact that Gabirol was under the patronage of Jews employed within the Muslim administration and thus benefited from it, Muslim rule contradicted the dominating textual discourse of the Torah. It is this scriptural discourse that the historical circumstances force Gabirol to reflect upon in this poem:

Open the Gate
Open the gate my beloved –
arise, and open the gate:
my spirit is shaken and I'm afraid.
My mother's maid has been mocking me
and her heart is raised against me,
so the Lord would hear her child's cry.
From the middle of midnight's blackness,
a wild ass pursues me,
as the forest boar has crushed me;
and the end which has long been sealed
only deepens my wound,
and no one guides me – and I am blind.[28]

In this poem, the subject's experience of persecution is clarified through an intertextual reference to the hostile attitude of Hagar and Ishmael toward Isaac in the text of Genesis. The reference to Hagar is established by the expression 'my mother's maid' and the identity of her child as Ishmael is indicated by the term 'wild ass', because in Genesis 16.12 God's angel predicts that Ishmael 'shall be a wild ass of a man: his hand shall be against every man, and every man's hand against him; and he shall dwell in the face of all his brethren'. The two sons of Abraham, the half-brothers Ishmael and Isaac, are considered patriarchs in Islam and Judaism respectively. In this poem the self-reproach of Isaac/the Jew is growing as he realizes that he has not paid attention to the prediction of God's angel that Ishmael/the Muslim will try to take his life. Maybe for this reason and confronted with escape through the gate as his only possibility of survival he appropriates the perception of the religious 'other' of him as blind. Yet, another connotation has been activated that is so typical of Gabirol's courage to argue his case against God. The connotation emerges from the word 'mocking' that in the Hebrew original connotes a mocking laughter. Laughter in the text of Genesis is usually associated with Isaac's mother, Sarah's (disbelief, but) joy at the prospect of giving birth to Isaac (cf. Genesis 18.12), and thereby becoming matriarch of the Jewish people. However, the (mocking) laughter in

---

28   Cf. Shlomo ibn Gabirol, *Selected Poems of Solomon Ibn Gabirol* (trans. Peter Cole; Princeton: Princeton University Press, 2001), p. 120.

Gabirol's poem belongs to the Muslim matriarch Hagar. Hagar mocks Isaac/the Jew and thus legitimizes not only her son's persecution of Isaac, but even God's susceptibility to Ishmael's cry. Laughter, which has been tied to Sarah's hope for Isaac (cf. the Hebrew meaning of his name: 'he shall laugh'), has now been transformed into the mocking laughter of the Muslim directed toward the living Jew, to whom God gave the promise of greatness, but who is nevertheless persecuted and suppressed. Caused by God's apparent disregard for the Jews' need of protection in Muslim Spain, Gabirol posits the question whether God has given the Muslims an opportunity through their mocking laughter to express the point that the Jew is blind to reality. He is blind to reality and naïve to believe in God's promise of greatness to Isaac and his seed now that the descendants of Ishmael are unmistakably the ones elevated to greatness in Muslim Spain, unless of course God decides to intervene, which is ultimately what Gabirol pleads for.

Gabirol also wrote *Keter Malkhut* (the Kingly Crown)[29] which many consider to be the most beautiful poem in Hebrew literature. Here, Gabirol argued that surely he might be punished for sins that he himself had committed, but God's response through exile and persecution was out of proportion to those sins. If God's righteousness, a normative tenet in Judaism, should be defended, Jews had to emphasize God's merciful qualities. Accordingly, Gabirol countered the tendency to view suffering as punishment by juxtaposing the discourse in the book of Job with the discourse in the book of Psalms.

Gabirol, who suffered social isolation because of a painful skin disease and because of his provocative attempts to transform Judaism and thereby ensure its survival in multi-religious Spain, was truly touched by the fate of Job. Yet, as the literary critic Harold Bloom would notice, Gabirol is such a strong poet that he is fully aware of the exact point in the biblical text where his hero Job failed as a poet. Job was stricken with fear when he finally had the chance to argue his case against God in God's very presence (see Job 40.4). Job halted his law suit when he clapped his hand to his mouth and gave up. Subsequently, Gabirol turns to King David, famous for his dialogues with God, hoping to draw upon God's favorite in order to make God respond by arguing the case for every man who experiences suffering, sinful as man may be. The contrasting of Job and David is particularly evident in the 38th song of the hymn, where the central hope-providing message is based on David admitting to his sins, something that Job did not do.

29 In this article I refer to Shlomo ibn Gabirol, *The Kingly Crown: Keter Malkhut* (ed. Andrew Gluck, trans. Bernard Lewis; Notre Dame: University of Notre Dame Press, 2002).

...

If I cannot hope for Thy mercies, who but Thou will have pity on me?

Therefore, 'though Thou kill me, I shall hope in Thee' [Job 13.15],

And if Thou search out my sin, I shall flee from Thee to Thee, and hide myself from Thy wrath in Thy shadow,

I shall hold on to the skirts of Thy mercy until Thou hast pity on me. 'I will not let Thee go, except Thou bless me' [Gen. 32.27]

Remember that of clay Thou didst make me, and with these afflictions didst Thou try me.

Therefore do not visit my acts upon me, nor make me eat the fruits of my deeds ...

What will it profit Thee if worms take me to eat me, 'eat the labour of thine hands' [Ps. 128.2]

(*Keter Malkhut* 38)

Gabirol uses the Psalms to present a different kind of logic than that of classic wisdom. Man would be condemned to suffering if Judaism relied on God's righteous intervention. Furthermore one knows that Job's piety was not sufficient to prevent his suffering. In the book of Job, God demands to be praised for being the creator of the world – and so Gabirol swerves against this claim of God and sets in his argumentative attack right here.[30] Yes, God created the world. And yes, God created man. However, God created man with a good and evil urge; and man cannot by his own free will escape or transcend this premise for existence that inevitably leads to sin. God must take upon himself a responsibility for the sins of man and this responsibility must articulate itself as mercy. Mercy is the suspension of legal thinking and this is what Gabirol pleads for by means of a hermeneutical use of scripture. Of course, there is always something artifactual about quotations, but Gabirol reads and interprets the Jobian discourse prior to his appropriation of the discourse of David. He argues for a transformation of God's righteousness by replacing the Jobian view with the discourse of David, singer of Psalms, to argue the case for mercy. This makes *Keter Malkhut* an example of a hermeneutical use of scripture used at a time where the historical context threatened to reveal the inconsistency of the discourse associated with classic wisdom.[31]

To finish my examples of hermeneutical use of scripture, I shall turn to something that is very hard to evidence in history; i.e., the private hermeneutical use of scripture, which is why I decided to make another

30 On clinamen and swerving, cf. Harold Bloom, *The Anxiety of Influence* (Oxford: Oxford University Press, 1997 [1973]), pp. 14, 18, 29.

31 Cf. Marianne Schleicher, 'The Fate of Job in Jewish Tradition', *Nordisk Judaistik – Scandinavian Jewish Studies* 26 (2008), pp. 5–18.

interview on 9 November 2007 with Melchior, where I asked him under what circumstances individual Jews would use scripture or religious texts as a text, proposing some kind of message to be interpreted and maybe adopted as one's own. He told me how he sometimes receives old prayer books from deceased persons, where it is obvious that the only pages worn in these books are those containing prayers, composed recently in vernacular Danish to be read on special occasions such as the illness of someone beloved. The pages containing prayers in Hebrew had hardly been touched. Here, understanding of the prayer in times of sorrow seems more important than listening to the words in the holy Hebrew language. The private use of scripture outside ritual settings deserves more scholarly attention, but as a vantage point for such imperative surveys I propose that imagined dialogues with God with the prospect of receiving divine comfort and advice in times of crisis could be the objective of such use.

Conclusion

Artifactual use of scripture promotes the non-semantic, formal aspects of scripture that enable the projection of personal and cultural representations onto scripture. These representations are vested with the characteristics of holiness; i.e., awe and fascination, derived from scripture's claim to contain revealed, transempirical knowledge. Powerful as they become, the representations are more or less subconsciously transposed into the user's worldview in settings, often ritual ones, where participation overrides interpretation. The many specifications in Jewish history concerning the making and handling of the Torah, along with the examples of how the Psalms have been similarly treated as objects for projective activities, testify to such use and indicate that establishing and maintaining transitivity is the primary function of artifactual use. This scripture-based transitivity links individuals, collectives, and the overall culture, which is important for mobilizing religious identification in all times.

The hermeneutical use of scripture supplements the dominating artifactual use, and its primary function consists in enabling a conscious dealing with the discourse of scripture in times when e.g. awareness of one's own identity is required, when scriptural discourses contradict reality and demand the positioning of alternatives, or when personal grief makes one look for advice and comfort in what is by most religious people considered divine discourse. In other words, the artifactual and hermeneutical uses have two different functions, but they are not mutually exclusive. They will be activated in turn or simultaneously depending on the psychological, social and cultural needs of the users.

Early Christian Manuscripts as Artifacts

Larry W. Hurtado

My objects in this discussion are to underscore the role of early Christian manuscripts as artifacts, and to urge that they be taken into account in pursuing historical questions about ancient Christianity. I draw heavily upon my recent book, to which I refer those interested in further discussion, and references to the work of others, upon which I gratefully draw.[1] The Christian manuscripts in question are those that can be dated to the second or third century CE, which means that they are among the very earliest physical artifacts of Christianity, some of them likely the very earliest such artifacts extant. Though commonly overlooked beyond the circles of papyrologists and palaeographers, their antiquity surely justifies greater attention to them.

NT scholars are generally aware of early Christian manuscripts, especially early manuscripts of NT texts, and are basically acquainted with their importance in text-critical studies concerned with the textual transmission of these texts, and with establishing a reliable critical edition of the Greek NT. I do not address these matters here, however. Instead, we shall approach manuscripts with a concern for wider historical questions about early Christianity, and we focus more on the physical and visual features of manuscripts rather than the wording of the texts that they contain. Moreover, the scope of manuscripts to be considered extends beyond copies of NT texts, and includes all manuscripts of all literary texts that can fairly safely be identified as either copied by Christians or at least used by Christians. In the interests of the limited space available, I shall restrict attention to a few major phenomena.

---

1 Larry W. Hurtado, *The Earliest Christian Artifacts: Manuscripts and Christian Origins* (Grand Rapids: Eerdmans, 2006).

The Texts Read

Perhaps the most elementary data to observe concern the literary texts that we find in these early manuscripts. The first and broad impression to be taken is that the Christians reflected in these manuscripts enjoyed a diversity of texts, and that reading texts was a constituent feature of early Christianity, a point persuasively made previously a number of years ago by Harry Gamble.[2] In relevant manuscripts of this early period, we have copies of most books of the Hebrew Bible (except for 1–2 Samuel, 1–2 Kings, Ruth, Ezra, Nehemiah, Song of Solomon, and Lamentations), plus Baruch, Tobit, 2 Maccabees, Wisdom of Solomon, and Ben Sirach. We have copies of all NT texts except for 1–2 Timothy and 3 John. In addition, there are copies of at least twenty other identifiable texts, including Christian 'apocryphal' writings, theological tractates, and other sorts of Christian literature, plus another twenty-six or so fragmentary texts that cannot readily be identified.[3]

Moreover, in the body of extant manuscripts, which are all from Egypt simply because ancient manuscripts have survived there better, we have copies of texts that we know were composed in various other places. Aside from the obvious cases of the biblical texts, all of which originated elsewhere, we also have copies of extra-canonical texts whose provenance we know, such as *Shepherd of Hermas* (Rome), Irenaeus' *Against Heresies* (Lyon), and perhaps three distinguishable writings by Melito (Sardis). The texts of these particular authors reflect an impressive geographical reach in interest, and confirm materially the other indications that early Christians were phenomenally engaged in networking with one another, in what Eldon Epp has called 'a brisk "intellectual commerce" and dynamic interchanges of people, literature, books, and letters between Egypt and the vast Mediterranean region'.[4] The vigor of Christian interest in texts is demonstrated if we note that in some cases (e.g., Irenaeus) we have copies of texts from outside Egypt that appear to have been made within a decade or so after their composition.

It is all the more significant that this breadth of readers' interests is reflected in manuscripts that were read, not in some major metropolitan center such as Alexandria, but in much more modest places a hundred

---

2   Harry Y. Gamble, *Books and Readers in the Early Church: A History of Early Christian Texts* (New Haven: Yale University Press, 1995).

3   See Hurtado, *Artifacts*, Appendix 1 (pp. 209–29) for the list of texts with identification of manuscripts in which they are found.

4   Eldon Jay Epp, 'The Significance of the Papyri for Determining the Nature of the New Testament Text in the Second Century: A Dynamic View of Textual Transmission', in *Gospel Traditions in the Second Century: Origins, Recensions, Text, and Transmission*, ed. William L. Petersen (Notre Dame/London: University of Notre Dame Press, 1989), pp. 71–103 (81).

miles or more up the Nile, such as Oxyrhynchus.[5] These manuscripts are material evidence of Christianity's penetration deeply into Egypt in the early centuries, and they also suggest that even in such a provincial town as Oxyrhynchus Christians invested in sharing texts, beliefs, practices, and conventions with believers elsewhere. This impressive circulation of texts trans-locally among Christians demonstrated in these manuscripts in turn suggests that we may be able to treat with some greater confidence the manuscript data from Egypt as indicative also of wider reading tastes and practices and scribal conventions and preferences. To be sure, the earliest manuscripts come from Egypt, and there is a danger in generalizing too much based on artifacts from one locale. But there is in fact some basis for taking seriously the view that these Egyptian manuscripts are instructive of wider Christian manuscript practices.

It is also interesting to note the numbers of copies of each text. Assuming that the comparative numbers of extant copies of texts reflect the comparative numbers of copies circulating in the ancient setting of these copies, we can infer the relative popularity of texts in these Christian circles. Admittedly, this assumption is not beyond question, but I think that it is sufficiently plausible as a working basis. So, what are the numbers?

Perhaps we can begin by noting that these manuscripts clearly reflect Christians interested in the OT. Indeed, the single most frequently attested text is Psalms, with at least sixteen copies.[6] But there are also multiple copies of Genesis (at least eight), Exodus (at least six), Isaiah (six), Leviticus (three), Deuteronomy (two), Esther (two), Proverbs (two), Ecclesiastes (two), Jeremiah (two), Ezekiel (two), Daniel (at least two), and single copies of a number of other OT writings. The presence of some texts such as Psalms or Isaiah will occasion little surprise, as these are the OT texts most heavily cited and alluded to in the NT. But that there are copies of all the Pentateuchal writings, including multiple copies of Leviticus, raises interesting questions about how these texts functioned in early Christian circles, and perhaps points to a significant role of biblical law in shaping their life.[7] This, I think, is a possible topic for further study.

Among texts composed by Christians, the Gospel of John (sixteen copies) and the Gospel of Matthew (twelve copies) clearly are dominant, materially attesting their popularity as also reflected textually in their greater frequency in identifiable citations and allusions in early Christian

5 Peter Parsons, *City of the Sharp-Nosed Fish: Greek Lives in Roman Egypt* (London: Weidenfeld and Nicolson, 2007), gives a fascinating reconstruction of the life of Oxyrhynchus based on the papyri excavated there.

6 This excludes several additional copies of Psalms which, for various reasons, may be of Jewish provenance. For details, see Hurtado, *Artifacts*, pp. 213–14.

7 E.g., did commandments in Leviticus about such things as how to treat slaves and/or about legitimate sexual unions shape their ethics?

writers. Clearly, from the earliest physical evidence, Gospels were widely circulated and used. Moreover, this manuscript evidence is congruent with Charles Hill's recent analysis of the place of the Johannine writings in early Christianity, in which he effectively refutes the common notion that the Gospel of John was favored by Gnostics and suspect among 'proto-orthodox' circles.[8] The presence of so many copies of John in the same locale where there are many copies of OT texts suggests that these copies of John were read by what we can refer to as 'proto-orthodox' Christians.

It is also noteworthy that the manuscript evidence confirms a comparatively less frequent usage of the Gospel of Mark, the only extant copy from before 300 CE remaining in the Chester Beatty Gospel codex (𝔓45). This raises very interesting questions of why and how Mark managed to obtain a place as a canonical Gospel when it appears not to have been particularly frequently copied and used in the second and third centuries. By the way, the validity of the manuscript data is reinforced by the paucity of citations of Mark in Christian writers of the second and third centuries. So, on the common scholarly view of the Synoptic Gospels, Mark was powerfully influential in helping to generate at least two other texts in which Mark was heavily drawn upon (Matthew and Luke), but then appears to have been eclipsed by these latter Gospels in Christian usage in the second century CE. Yet Mark managed somehow to maintain a sufficient regard in Christian circles to be included among the four Gospels that came to be canonical, this regard tangibly reflected in its inclusion with the others in the Chester Beatty Gospel codex ca. 250 CE.

The third most frequently attested Christian text is *Shepherd of Hermas* (eleven copies), among all texts exceeded only by Psalms, John and Matthew.[9] As Carolyn Osiek observed, 'No other noncanonical writing was as popular before the fourth century.'[10] These early papyri provide background for the later inclusion of *Hermas* in Codex Sinaiticus (at the end of the NT) and Athanasius' endorsement of *Hermas* and the *Didache* as well as suitable for reading by catechumens (though, he insisted, not to be included in the NT canon).

On the other hand, for some other texts that are often thought by scholars today to have been popular and perhaps to have functioned as scripture in early Christian circles, the manuscript evidence is not nearly so strong. We have only single copies of some texts, such as the 'Egerton Gospel', the 'Fayum Gospel', and the *Protevangelium of James* (although

8   Charles E. Hill, *The Johannine Corpus in the Early Church* (Oxford: Oxford University Press, 2004).

9   Some twenty-three papyri copies of *Hermas* have been identified, twelve dated fourth century CE and later. See Nick Gonis et al. (eds), *The Oxyrhynchus Papyri, Volume LXIX* (London: Egypt Exploration Society, 2005), p. 1.

10   Carolyn Osiek, *The Shepherd of Hermas* (Hermeneia; Minneapolis: Fortress Press, 1999), p. 1.

this text undeniably went on to enjoy a wide distribution and influence in later centuries). For others, we have a few copies, such as the *Gospel of Thomas* (three), the *Gospel of Mary* (two), and, depending on whether Lührmann's claims for P.Oxy. 2949 and P.Oxy. 4009 can still be accepted, possibly the *Gospel of Peter*.[11] These all certainly evidence some level of interest in these texts, but we do not get an impression of massive interest or widespread usage. To illustrate this with GThomas, it ties for thirteenth place in number of extant copies, along with James, Ephesians, Leviticus, and Acts of Paul, the three copies of GThomas suggesting an interest perhaps approximate to that given to these other writings. On the other hand, obviously the three copies place GThomas ahead of many other texts, for most of which we have only single copies extant, including a number of canonical writings (e.g., Mark)![12]

There are still further observations to be made about the presence and number of copies of particular texts, but space prevents me from pursuing them here. I refer you to my *Artifacts* book (pp. 24–40), and hasten on to other matters.

Text-Collection

In an earlier essay, I urged the importance of text-collection, the association of texts with others, conceptually, functionally and also physically copied together in a given manuscript, as insufficiently

---

11   Dieter Lührmann, 'Pox 2949: EvPt 3–5 in einer Handschrift des 2./3. Jahrhunderts', *ZNW* 72 (1981): 216–26; idem, 'Pox 4009: Ein neues Fragment des Petrusevangeliums?' *NovT* 35 (1993): 390–410. But cf. now T. J. Kraus and T. Nicklas (eds), *Das Petrusevangelium und die Petrusapokalypse: Die griechischen Fragmente mit deutscher und englischer Übersetzung* (GCS, 11; Berlin: de Gruyter, 2004); and esp. Paul Foster, 'Are There any Early Fragments of the So-called *Gospel of Peter?*' *NTS* 52 (2006): 1–28.

12   I list here the literary texts in question in the decreasing order of the numbers of extant copies among Christian manuscripts dated to the second and third centuries CE: Psalms (16), John (16), Matthew (12), Shepherd of Hermas (11), Genesis and Exodus (8 each), Luke and Acts (7 each), Isaiah (6), Revelation (5), Romans and Hebrews (4 each), James, Ephesians, Leviticus, Acts of Paul, GThomas (3 each), 1 Corinthians, Philippians, 1 Thessalonians, 2 Thessalonians, Jude, Irenaeus, Gospel of Mary, Gospel of Peter (?), Deuteronomy, 2 Chronicles, Esther, Proverbs, Ecclesiastes, Sirach, Jeremiah, Ezekiel, Daniel, Minor Prophets, and Tobit (2 each), and a large number of other writings for which we have only one copy from this period (Numbers, Joshua, Judges, Job, Wisdom, Susannah, 2 Maccabees, Mark, 2 Corinthians, Galatians, Colossians, Philemon, Titus, 1 Peter, 2 Peter, 1 John, 2 John, Protevangelium of James, 'Egerton' Gospel, 'Fayum' Gospel, Correspondence of Paul and Corinth, Apocalypse of Peter, Apocryphon of James and Jambres, Apocryphon of Moses, Melito's Paschal Homily, Melito's On Prophecy?, Melito's Paschal Hymn?, Odes of Solomon, Julius Africanus' Cesti, Origen's Gospel Commentaries, a Homily by Origen, Origen's De Principii, Sibylline Oracles, Diatessaron?, Theonas' Against Manichaeans?, and a small number of unidentifiable texts.

observed phenomena that cast some light on the process of the emergent NT canon.[13] The early manuscripts include instances of the physical association of certain texts with one another, and I contend that this probably reflects the view that the texts in question share some common or related subject matter or significance.

The Bodmer and Chester Beatty biblical papyri are, no doubt, the best known early Christian examples. P.Bodmer XIV–XV (𝔓75, ca. 175–225 CE) comprises major remnants of a codex that certainly contained Luke and John, and T. C. Skeat proposed that it originally included Matthew and Mark as well, Luke and John forming one of two component 'gatherings/quires' in the complete codex, Matthew and Mark the other.[14] But the Chester Beatty Gospel codex (𝔓45, ca. 250 CE) is our earliest extant empirical instance of the physical linkage of all four canonical Gospels (in the order Matthew, John, Luke, Mark), and Acts as well, in one codex of 224 pages.[15] It is, however, unlikely that 𝔓45 (ca. 250 CE) was the first instance in which all four Gospels were copied in one volume. There are now good reasons to think that the four Gospels held a growing special significance in Christian groups as early as 120 CE or perhaps even somewhat earlier.[16] Certainly, by the late second century CE, Irenaeus was stoutly defending a closed circle of these four Gospels. (Adv. Haer. 3.11.8). I suspect that the desire to register an exclusive significance of these four Gospels led to efforts to produce codices adequate to contain them all in one book, and that the Chester Beatty Gospels codex is simply our earliest artifact of this effort. In any case, these early papyri are physical evidence of the interesting stance of affirming more than one Gospel, and preferring discrete Gospels too, over against other early Christian options for one Gospel (e.g., Marcion) or for a harmonized Gospel-book (e.g., Tatian).

The inclusion of Acts in 𝔓45 also merits notice, although again I must be brief. In 𝔓74, by contrast, Acts is first in a codex of the Catholic Epistles, acting as the narrative framework/introduction for these texts,

---

13 Larry W. Hurtado, 'The New Testament in the Second Century: Text, Collections and Canon', in *Transmission and Reception: New Testament Text-Critical and Exegetical Studies*, eds J. W. Childers and D. C. Parker (Piscataway, NJ: Gorgias Press, 2006), pp. 3–27.

14 T. C. Skeat, 'The Origin of the Christian Codex', *ZPE* 102 (1994): 263–68 (264), reprinted in T. C. Skeat, *The Collected Biblical Writings of T. C. Skeat*, ed. J. K. Elliott (NovTSup, 113; Leiden: Brill, 2004), pp. 158–92.

15 T. C. Skeat, 'A Codicological Analysis of the Chester Beatty Papyrus of the Gospels and Acts (P45)', *Hermathena* 15 (1993): 27–43, reprinted in Skeat, *Collected*, pp. 141–57, updates the original description in F. G. Kenyon, *The Chester Beatty Biblical Papyri, Fasciculus II: The Gospels and Acts: Text* (London: Walker, 1933).

16 E.g., Martin Hengel, 'The Four Gospels and the One Gospel of Jesus Christ', in *The Earliest Gospels*, ed. Charles Horton (London: T&T Clark International, 2004), pp. 13–26; G. N. Stanton, 'The Fourfold Gospel', *NTS* 43 (1997): 317–46; Theo K. Heckel, *Vom Evangelium des Markus zum viergestaltigen Evangelium* (WUNT, 120; Tübingen: Mohr [Siebeck], 1999).

and this is not a unique positioning of Acts. But the placement of Acts in 𝔓45 is actually much closer to modern scholarly reading of it as the narrative sequel to the story of Jesus in the Gospels. Obviously, in 𝔓45 Acts is still separated from Luke, but my point is that the inclusion of Acts in this manuscript is artifactual indication of a conception of Acts that links it to the Gospels, in contrast to the sort of view of Acts that is reflected in 𝔓74. In short, these and other manuscripts are physical artifacts of early Christian views of the texts.

𝔓46 (the Chester Beatty Pauline codex, ca. 200 CE) is likewise the earliest extant collection of Pauline writings, a clear physical confirmation of the process of gathering and circulating Pauline letter-collections that probably began in the late first century CE.[17] The noteworthy inclusion of Hebrews among Pauline epistles is a direct indication of how at least some early Christians viewed this text, here again this manuscript material evidence of their interpretative stance.

It should also be noted that P.Oxy. 1, the single codex leaf containing a portion of GThomas, certainly derives from a codex in which GThomas was preceded by some other text.[18] This means that in this instance GThomas was apparently linked with that other text in some manner. Unfortunately, we have no direct evidence as to what that other text might have been, or whether still other texts might have been included in the codex as well, following GThomas. Interestingly, in the Nag Hammadi codex containing Coptic GThomas, it was preceded by *Apocryphon of John*, which arguably functioned to set the larger mythic/narrative context in which GThomas was to be read.[19] It is an intriguing question whether

---

17   The earliest textual witness is, of course, 2 Pet. 3.15-16 (dated variously ca. 70–110 CE). Most of 𝔓46 survives, giving us portions or all of writings in the following order: Romans, Hebrews, 1-2 Corinthians, Ephesians, Galatians, Philippians, Colossians, 1 Thessalonians. In addition to the description by F. G. Kenyon, *The Chester Beatty Biblical Papyri, Fasciculus III Supplement Pauline Epistles* (London: Emery Walker, 1936), vii–xxii, see also the magisterial study by Günter Zuntz, *The Text of the Epistles: A Disquisition upon the Corpus Paulinum* (Schweich Lectures 1946; London: Oxford University Press for the British Academy, 1953). For suggestions that there are remnants of Pauline letter-collections in other more fragmentary manuscripts, see Hurtado, *Artifacts*, pp. 39–40.

18   The leaf has the number eleven, indicating that ten leaves probably preceded it in the original codex, far more space than would have been needed for the missing material from GThomas. I discuss the matter further in my essay, 'The Greek Fragments of the Gospel of Thomas as Artifacts: Papyrological Observations on Papyrus Oxyrhynchus 1, Papyrus Oxyrhynchus 654 and Papyrus Oxyrhynchus 655', in *Das Thomasevangelium: Entstehung, Rezeption, Theologie*, ed. Jörg Frey, Enno Edzard Popkes and Jens Schröter (BZNW 157; Berlin and New York: Walter de Gruyter, 2008), 19–32.

19   Codex II contains the following texts in this order: *Apocryphon of John, Gospel of Thomas, Gospel of Philip, Hypostasis of the Archons, On the Origin of the World, Exegesis on the Soul, the Book of Thomas the Contender*. Michael Allen Williams, *Rethinking 'Gnosticism': An Argument for Dismantling a Dubious Category* (Princeton: Princeton University Press, 1996), 241-62, provides an intriguing analysis of the possible significance of

some such connection of GThomas was made with *Apocryphon of John* or some other texts in P.Oxy. 1, and what it might have represented about how GThomas was read ca. 200 CE in Greek.

Roll and Codex

It is, I think, reasonably widely known that early Christians had an unusually strong preference for the codex. Questions about why and what to make of this preference continue to receive differing responses, but it is not my purpose here to attempt persuasive answers.[20] Instead, I shall concentrate on a few uncontroversial phenomena and briefly suggest their importance.

A few quantitative observations will help frame matters. For instance, of all second-century manuscripts logged on the Leuven Database of Ancient Books and identified as either codices or rolls, codices comprise about 6 percent and rolls about 94 percent, whereas among second-century Christian manuscripts about 76 percent are codices.[21] As William Johnson's splendid study of Greek literary rolls shows, the roll was overwhelmingly preferred in the general culture for literary texts for several centuries, only slowly losing ground to the codex significantly after the fourth century CE.[22] But the Christian preference for the codex appears remarkably strong from our earliest evidence, and so requires some explanation.

Before we attempt any, however, it is important to note that the Christian preference for the codex exhibits interesting variation. If we restrict ourselves to those texts that were typically treated as scripture (i.e., read in the worship setting), most obviously the OT writings, but also those Christian texts increasingly treated in the period as part of an emergent NT canon, the preference for the codex is nearly total. Of the approximately 75 manuscripts of OT texts dated to the second/third centuries CE (including several that might be of Jewish provenance), perhaps as many as nine are rolls, about 12 percent. If we remove those quite arguably Jewish manuscripts, rolls comprise about 4–7 percent of

---

the selection and order of texts in the Nag Hammadi codices, his main conclusion being that tractates seen to have been chosen and ordered in these codices as a means of "demonstrating or *establishing* the theological coherence among the works," each writing functioning and interpreted in relation to the other writings in a given codex (261).

20 Again, I refer readers to my extensive discussion in *Artifacts*, pp. 43–93. To consult the Leuven Database of Ancient Books (LDAB), see http://www.trismegistos.org/ldab/. My figures reflect my consultations of the LDAB in November 2005 in writing *Artifacts*.

21 I omit from calculations items identified as 'sheet' or 'fragment'. For further discussion, see Hurtado, *Artifacts*, esp. pp. 47–48.

22 William A. Johnson, *Bookrolls and Scribes in Oxyrhynchus* (Toronto: University of Toronto Press, 2004).

the total. So far as NT texts are concerned, we have none extant on an unused roll among second/third-century manuscripts.[23]

On the other hand, although the codex is dominant generally in this period for all other Christian literary texts as well, there appears to have been a somewhat greater readiness to use rolls for such writings as theological tractates, homilies and liturgical texts, magical texts and some other writings, in comparison to the extremely strong preference for the codex for biblical texts. For instance, of the four earliest copies of *Hermas*, two are codices and one a roll (and another a re-used roll), and both of our copies of Irenaeus' *Against Heresies* are rolls, as are the Dura Europos Gospel Harmony, the so-called 'Fayum Gospel', and a number of other writings. Of the three copies of GThomas, one is a codex, one a roll, and one a re-used roll, and one of the two copies of *Gospel of Mary* is a roll (the other a codex).[24] By my count, of 58 Christian copies of extra-canonical literary texts dated second/third century CE, 18 are rolls (31%, or 34% if we exclude opisthographs). Indeed, for documentary and 'paraliterary' texts (e.g., letters, etc.), Christians continued to use rolls somewhat more freely for a long time, as reflected in the sizeable cache of sixth-century CE carbonized Christian papyri discovered in a church in Petra.[25]

So, in summary, we can see a general Christian preference for the codex, and particularly for those texts treated as scripture, and a somewhat greater readiness to use the roll for other texts. From these general observations, I suggest that we can make at least two further inferences. First, the Christian preference for the codex appears to mean that Christian book-practice was in some ways distinctive, and so differentiated second/third-century Christians from the wider culture of the time. Thus, when scholars engage questions about the emergence of 'Christianity' as an identifiable phenomenon, these manuscripts' data should be considered. Indeed, as I have argued elsewhere, the strong place of the codex in early Christian copying practice may be one of the earliest extant expressions of a distinctively Christian 'material culture'.[26]

Second, in light of the particularly strong preference for the codex for

---

23   This excludes 'opisthographs', re-used rolls. There are a few instances of NT texts written as opisthographs: P13 (Hebrews), P18 (Revelation), P98 (Revelation) and P22 (John).

24   For details on all texts, see Hurtado, *Artifacts*, Appendix 1.

25   The cache comprises 152 rolls containing private papers of a prosperous local family. See Ludwig Koenen, 'The Carbonized Archive from Petra', *Journal of Roman Archaeology* 9 (1996): 177–88; and Jaakko Frösen, *The Petra Papyri* (Amman: American Center of Oriental Research, 2002).

26   L. W. Hurtado, 'The Earliest Evidence of an Emerging Christian Material and Visual Culture: The Codex, the *Nomina Sacra* and the Staurogram', in *Text and Artifact in the Religions of Mediterranean Antiquity: Essays in Honour of Peter Richardson*, ed. S. G. Wilson and Michel Desjardins (Waterloo: Wilfrid Laurier University Press, 2000), pp. 271–88.

copies of texts used as scripture, it appears that copies of texts on rolls signify that they (or at least these particular copies) were not intended to function as scripture, in the sense of being copies prepared to be read out in corporate worship. This is rather self-evident in the case of some texts, such as the theological tractates on rolls, which were never intended to be treated as scripture, but instead functioned for study and teaching purposes. But I contend that it is also true for roll copies of other texts, among which we may note P.Oxy. 655 (GThomas), P.Oxy. 3525 (GMary). In short, I propose that the physical form of copies of texts likely reflects how the texts (or at least those copies) were viewed and how they functioned in the Christian circles from which the copies derive.

Nomina Sacra *and Staurogram*

Another characteristic of early Christian scribal practice was to treat certain words in a special manner, apparently with the intention of setting them off visually from the surrounding text. The way this was done was to write the words in an abbreviated form, and to place a horizontal stroke over the abbreviation, producing what have come to be known as the *nomina sacra*. The phenomenon has received serious attention from time to time, especially recently, and there are a number of disputed matters that cannot be engaged adequately here.[27] Instead, I limit myself to emphasizing two points: that they appear to be a Christian innovation, and their significance as visual phenomena. Indeed, the early Christian preference for the codex and the *nomina sacra* are the two main distinctive features of early Christian scribal practice, such that among papyrologists and palaeographers the combination of these features is sufficient to identify a manuscript, even a fragment of one, as of Christian provenance. The preference for the codex and the *nomina sacra* comprise the earliest extant expressions of an emergent Christian material and visual culture.

Moreover, as with the preference for the codex, the *nomina sacra* practice appears to have its origins amazingly early, so early that both are already conventions in our earliest evidence, fragmentary manuscripts dated to the second century CE. Indeed, it seems likely that we must place the origins at least in the early second century CE and quite plausibly even earlier. It is difficult to account for the apparently rapid diffusion of the practices, for in this period there were no ecclesiastical structures able to exercise the authority to enforce them. In my view, for both the codex and the *nomina sacra* we have to assume that there was some initial Christian usage that was sufficiently influential to generate the widespread conven-

---

27 See Hurtado, *Artifacts*, pp. 95–134, for a full discussion with copious references to other scholars.

tion that is evident in our extant artifacts. Exactly what this was remains somewhat debated, and need not detain us here. However, whatever it was that generated the preference for the codex and also the scribal practice called *nomina sacra*, it was very early and very widely influential.

But I must emphasize that we are dealing with a *convention*, which means a practice disseminated more through social contacts than through some authoritative structure. So, as we should expect, there are interesting variations, even what appear to be experimentations, across the early centuries CE. By about the sixth century CE, we can find some fifteen words treated as *nomina sacra*, all of them part of Christian religious vocabulary.[28] But the evidence is clear that some words were treated as *nomina sacra* earlier and comparatively more consistently than others, and of these the ones that are most consistently written as *nomina sacra* right from our earliest manuscripts are the four words Θεος, Κυριος, Ιησους and Χριστος. If, as most scholars acquainted with the matter believe, the *nomina sacra* originated and continued to function essentially as scribal expressions of early Christian piety, it is significant that key terms for God and Jesus are accorded the same reverential treatment and comprise the earliest words given this treatment.

We should also note that *nomina sacra* are not so often or consistently found in Christian documentary texts and some literary texts, but are more consistently found in Christian copies of biblical texts. That is, as with the codex, the *nomina sacra* seem to have had a particular (but not exclusive) association with Christian copies of texts that functioned as scripture.

Moreover, unlike ancient Jewish scribal treatment of the tetragrammaton, which both set off the divine name from the surrounding text and also signalled that readers were to use a reverential substitution, the *nomina sacra* seem to have been purely *visual* phenomena. I know of no indication that there was any difference in the way the words were read out, or any gesture to be made, such as a bowing of the head. This is why I have pointed to the *nomina sacra* as an expression of the early Christian 'visual culture'. So far as we know, they were purely intended to be seen.

I mention briefly another arresting but considerably less well-known visual phenomenon found in some early Christian manuscripts, the so-called 'staurogram'.[29] This is a monogram-like device formed by

---

28   These comprise the Greek equivalents for the following words: Jesus, God, Lord, Christ, Spirit, Man, son, Father, Cross, David, Mother, Savior, Israel, Jerusalem, and Heaven. For the Greek words and common *nomina sacra* forms of them, see Hurtado, *Artifacts*, p. 134.

29   For further discussion, see Hurtado, *Artifacts*, pp. 135–54; and L. W. Hurtado, 'The Staurogram in Early Christian Manuscripts: The Earliest Visual Reference to the Crucified

superimposing the letter *rho* on the letter *tau*, the earliest instances of this device forming part of a *nomina sacra* treatment of the words σταυρος and σταυροω in several NT manuscripts dated variously ca. 175–250 CE (P75, P66 and P45). Unlike other early 'Christograms' (the *chi-rho*, the *iota-chi* or the *iota-ēta*), each of which alludes to the name 'Jesus' and/or 'Christ', the staurogram is not an abbreviation of, or allusion to any word(s).[30] Instead, it seems to be purely a visual device, which (as previous scholars such as Kurt Aland and Erich Dinkler proposed) most likely is to be taken as a pictographic reference to the crucified Jesus, the *tau* a known early Christian symbol of Jesus' cross (esp. *EpBarn* 9.7-9; Justin, *1 Apol* 55), and the loop of the *rho* probably intended to depict the head of a human figure hanging on a cross.[31] Although usually unknown by historians of early Christian art, these uses of the staurogram are some 200 years earlier than what are commonly regarded as the first visual references to the crucified Jesus. Textual scholars are not the only ones who could benefit from taking greater account of early Christian manuscripts.[32] In sum, the staurogram is a noteworthy scribal device that registers Christian faith visually with specific reference to Jesus' crucifixion; and the staurogram and the *nomina sacra* comprise our earliest physical evidence of Christian efforts to express their piety visually.

Reading and Early Christian Manuscripts

In the final part of this discussion I want to mention several other features of early Christian manuscripts that comprise further artifactual evidence of how they (and the texts they contain) were designed to be used. This has direct bearing on questions about how texts functioned in Christian circles of the period.

We may commence with another notable feature of many early Christian manuscripts, the inclusion of various devices intended to facilitate reading of them. As many will likely know, manuscripts of

---

Jesus?' in *New Testament Manuscripts: Their Text and Their World* (ed. Thomas J. Kraus and Tobias Nicklas; Texts and Editions for New Testament Study, 2; Leiden: Brill, 2006), pp. 207–26.

30 For a representation of early Christograms, see Hurtado, *Artifacts*, p. 154.

31 Kurt Aland, 'Bemerkungen zum Alter und zur Entstehung des Christogramms anhand von Beobachtungen bei P66 und P75' in *Studien zur Überlieferung des Neuen Testaments und seines Textes* (Berlin: De Gruyter, 1967), 173-79; Erich Dinkler, Signum Crucis: *Aufsätze zum Neuen Testament und zur Christlichen Archäologie* (Tübingen: J. C. B. Mohr (Paul Siebeck), 1967), 177-78.

32 Commendably, however, the significance of the staurogram has been noted recently by Robin Margaret Jenson, *Understanding Early Christian Art* (London: Routledge, 2000), p. 138.

literary texts (particularly high-quality copies) were more typically written in *scripta continuo*, with no spaces between words or sense-units, and little or no punctuation. As Colin Roberts observed, 'As a rule [ancient] Greek manuscripts make very few concessions to the reader'.[33] Indeed, William Johnson has proposed cogently that the severe and demanding layout of high-quality literary texts was intended to reflect and cater to the elite readership for whom they were copied.[34] We have cases where a reader of such a high-quality literary text has marked up the manuscript to indicate sense-units and added other marks to aid the reading of the text. But Christian manuscripts often have such readers' aids put in by the original copyist. These include such devices as a double horizontal dot (diaeresis) over an initial *iota* or *upsilon* (to help readers avoid taking the vowel in question as part of the preceding word), occasional breathing marks over aspirated initial vowels, punctuation to mark off sense-units roughly equivalent to our sentences, and spacing and other devices to mark off large sense-units approximating our paragraphs. It also appears that these readers' aids particularly (though not exclusively) characterize copies of texts intended for public reading, that is, texts that functioned as scripture in circles of believers.

In other ways as well, the texts in these Christian manuscripts tend to be laid out with a view to ease the reading of them. They typically have very generous margins and spacing between the lines, and the letters are of good size and usually carefully written, with noticeably fewer lines per page than in comparably-sized manuscripts of pagan literary texts. Christian manuscripts do not typically have the calligraphic elegance of high-quality pagan literary manuscripts, but they exhibit various features that reflect a concern to facilitate the reading (probably the public reading) of the texts that they contain.

I emphasize that this concern is evident in the very earliest Christian manuscripts. In the famous Rylands fragment of GJohn (P52), for example, we can see two clear instances of a diaeresis over an initial *iota* (recto, line 2, and verso, line 2), and slightly wider spaces between certain words (between ουδενα and ινα in recto line 2; between ειπεν and σημαινων in recto line 3; and between κοσμον and ινα in verso line 2), these spaces likely intended to mark sense-units (and signal the reader to make a slight pause).[35] Also, one is immediately struck by the generous size of the script in this manuscript and the spacing between lines.

33   C. H. Roberts, 'Two Biblical Papyri in the John Rylands Library, Manchester', *BJRL* 20 (1936): 227 (241–44). See also E. G. Turner, *Greek Manuscripts of the Ancient World*, ed. P. J. Parsons (2nd rev. edn; London: Institute of Classical Studies, 1987), pp. 7–12.

34   William A. Johnson, 'Toward a Sociology of Reading in Classical Antiquity', *AJP* 121 (2000): 593–627.

35   Interestingly, at both of these points modern printed editions of GJohn often place punctuation. In N/A27, for example, there is a high stop after ουδενα at the end of John

It is worth noting that, although not characteristic of formal copies of pagan literary texts, these sorts of readers' aids are found in Jewish copies of biblical texts, as noted many decades ago by Colin Roberts, and more recently by Emanuel Tov.[36] So, the best guess is that in these matters early Christian scribal practice exhibits the precedent and influence of Jewish scribal practice, especially evident, again, in copies of biblical texts. That is, early Christian manuscripts give physical evidence of the historical connections and indebtedness of emergent Christianity to its Jewish matrix. Indeed, it is very interesting that earliest Christian scribal practice appears to be shaped noticeably more by Jewish copying practices than by those of the larger literary environment of the time.

I have suggested that these readers' aids are more frequent in copies of texts that were intended for public reading. If I am correct (and I confess that a systematic study of the data is still to be completed), then this means that the presence or absence of these phenomena may be one further physical indication of whether a given copy of a text was prepared to be used in corporate worship, that is, treated as scripture in a socially observable sense. Obviously, no one scribal feature is sufficient for making such decisions, but the provision of such readers' aids by copyists may be one feature to be taken into account.

In addition to copies of texts intended for public reading, there are also manuscripts that were clearly prepared for personal use, and we can tell this also from key physical characteristics. For instance, it is widely accepted that 'opisthographs' (re-used rolls, a new text copied on the outer surface) were typically informal copies intended for personal reading and study, rather like cheap editions of literary texts today, such as those intended for students. We have opisthographs of GJohn (P22), Revelation (P18 and P98), *Hermas* (P.Oxy. 4705 and P.Mich. 130), GThomas (P.Oxy. 654), and several other texts, all of which are most likely personal copies of these texts.

Miniature manuscripts are likewise personal copies of texts. It is worth noting, for example, that P.Oxy. 655, one of the three Greek manuscripts of GThomas, is a portion of a roll that was ca. 16 cm in height, and that its columns comprised ca. 30 lines of small but carefully formed script. For comparison, volumes in the Loeb Classical Library are about the same height, and contain approximately the same number of lines per page. So, together with the absence of sense-unit markers and punctu-

---

18.31. For further discussion of P52 and citation of relevant scholars, see L. W. Hurtado, 'P52 (P. Rylands Gk. 457) and the *Nomina Sacra*: Method and Probability', *TynBul* 54 (2003): 1–14.

36 Roberts, 'Two Biblical Papyri', pp. 226–28; Emanuel Tov, *Scribal Practices and Approaches Reflected in the Texts Found in the Judean Desert* (STDJ, 54; Leiden: Brill, 2004), pp. 131–63.

ation, the small sizes of the manuscript and the hand combine to indicate rather strongly that this was a copy of GThomas prepared for personal reading. Likewise, the early third-century codex of GMary measured ca. 9 × 10 cm, obviously another copy of a text prepared for private usage. The same is the case for P78 (preserving Jude 4–5, 7–8), a remnant of a miniature codex of curious dimensions, 5.3 × 2.9 cm (i.e., its width considerably greater than its height).[37]

Collectively, the larger codices kitted out with various readers' aids, the opisthographs, and the rather smaller personal-size manuscripts comprise a rich body of unique physical evidence of the various circumstances and settings in which Christians read their texts. For instance, the manuscripts show that Christians read texts publicly as part of their corporate worship, and that they also read texts personally and for study purposes. Indeed, manuscripts form a considerably larger body of evidence for early Christianity than for any other kind of Roman-era religion, with the exception of ancient Judaism. I urge, therefore, that scholarly inquiries into such matters as early Christian 'textuality', the use and significance of particular texts, the process of canonization, and perhaps other topics as well should give attention to early Christian manuscripts, for they provide us with our earliest artifacts of these activities.

I have already referred to a very informative article by William Johnson in which he provided fascinating glimpses into the 'sociology of reading' in classical antiquity, showing how the typical physical and visual features of ancient literary manuscripts correlate with the social settings in which they were read.[38] The distinctive features of early Christian manuscripts, especially those containing biblical texts, suggest that there may well be distinctive features of the Christian 'sociology of reading', along with likely commonalities with the larger Roman culture. For example, Johnson proposes that the reading of pagan prose literary texts was very commonly done in small social groups and 'so far as we know almost always occurred in elite settings'.[39] But the typical social setting for the reading of Christian literary texts appears to have been the gathered church, which also seems usually to have included a much more diverse and inclusive group beyond the social 'elite'. In any case, to pursue further questions about early Christian reading practices and settings will require close attention to the sorts of manuscript features that I have flagged here.

---

37   It is also possible that this was an amulet, and not a codex. See Tommy Wasserman, 'P78 (P. Oxy. XXXIV 2684): The Epistle of Jude on an Amulet?' in *New Testament Manuscripts: Their Texts and Their World*, eds Thomas J. Kraus and Tobias Nicklas (Leiden: Brill, 2006), pp. 137–60.

38   Johnson, 'Toward a Sociology of Reading in Classical Antiquity'.

39   Ibid, p. 616.

Conclusion

Were archaeologists to unearth identifiable Christian objects from the first three centuries of Christianity, the press would (at least for Andy Warhol's proverbial fifteen minutes!) be abuzz with publicity, and scholars concerned with historical questions about earliest Christianity would feel constrained to familiarize themselves with any such objects. Yet all along we have had an increasing body of physical artifacts of early Christianity that have largely been ignored beyond narrow circles of palaeographers and papyrologists and, to some degree, NT textual critics. This appears to be largely a reflection of an innocent but curious failure to

Physical Features of Excerpted Torah Texts[1]

Stephen Reed

Thousands of fragments have been found near the Dead Sea which provide information concerning scriptural texts used in second temple Judaism. Over 200 biblical texts have been identified among these fragmentary remains. Most attention has been given to the content and text-critical features of such texts. Less attention has been given to their physical characteristics.[2]

Emanuel Tov has assembled much information about these physical features in his work *Scribal Practices and Approaches Reflected in the Texts Found in the Judean Desert*.[3] While he uses this data to provide insights concerning how scribes produced these texts and the forms of the scriptural texts used at that time, he has given less attention to how the physical features of these texts provide information relevant to the usages and functions of particular texts.

The purpose of this paper is to investigate how the physical features of some excerpted biblical texts help us better understand the usages and functions of these texts. Three groups of excerpted texts will be described: *tefillin*, *mezuzot* and other excerpted Exodus and Deuteronomy texts. Such texts were written for different purposes than 'regular' or 'continuous' scriptural texts.

These three groups of texts are connected by a common theme of Torah. Brent Strawn has pointed out that many of the excerpted texts are

---

1 A shorter form of this paper, 'Physical and Visual Features of Dead Sea Scroll Scriptural Texts', was presented with a powerpoint presentation at the SBL Annual Meetings in November 2007 for a session on Scripture as Artifact. I am grateful for the comments and papers of the participants of that session.

2 Larry Hurtado has given attention to such features of Greek texts produced by Christians. Larry Hurtado, *The Earliest Christian Artifacts: Manuscripts and Christian Origins* (Grand Rapids, MI: Eerdmans, 2006).

3 Emanuel Tov, *Scribal Practices and Approaches Reflected in the Texts Found in the Judean Desert* (STDJ, 54; Leiden: Brill, 2004).

from books of the Torah or relate to the theme of Torah.[4] But while Torah is a common theme, this is not just about Torah in general but about specific Torah texts which contain explicit commands for readers to do something physically with these texts – teach them, meditate upon them, write them down. These excerpted texts were produced to assist people to obey these commands.

Differences between Excerpted and Regular Biblical Texts

Not all scholars agree about which of the DSS texts were considered biblical or whether it is anachronistic to use such a term for this literature. Eugene Ulrich, for instance, prefers to use the term 'scripture' and not 'Bible' or 'canon' at this time.[5] For this paper it is sufficient to follow Tov for whom biblical means 'the books contained in the traditional canon of the Hebrew/Aramaic Bible'.[6] There is little question about Torah texts being considered authoritative at this time even if many other texts may also have had this status as well.

Because of the fragmentary remains of many 'biblical' texts at Qumran and the variety of ways that such texts were written, it is often not possible to know for certain whether a particular fragment belongs to a complete scroll, an excerpt of a scriptural text or even a quotation of a text found in a non-biblical scroll. When the size of the writing block can be known, however, it helps one to determine whether a fragment belonged to a complete scroll or a part of a scriptural scroll. Physical features of *tefillin* and *mezuzot* make them quite evident. The nature of some Exodus and/or Deuteronomy fragments is less clear.

Tov makes the general comment that 'little distinction between biblical and nonbiblical literary manuscripts and, more generally, between sacred and nonsacred literary manuscripts is recognizable in scribal conventions or precision in copying'.[7] Biblical texts were not written differently than non-biblical literary texts. Nevertheless, he does identify five 'distinctions

---

4 Brent Strawn, 'Excerpted Manuscripts at Qumran: Their Significance for the Textual History of the Hebrew Bible and the Socio-Religious History of the Qumran Community and its Literature', in *The Bible and the Dead Sea Scrolls: Volume II: Dead Sea Scrolls and the Qumran Community* (ed. J. H. Charlesworth; Waco, TX: Baylor University Press, 2006), p. 155.

5 Eugene Ulrich, 'The Dead Sea Scrolls and Hebrew Scriptural Texts', in *The Bible and the Dead Sea Scrolls: Volume I: Scripture and the Scrolls* (ed. James H. Charlesworth: Waco, TX: Baylor University Press, 2006), p. 98.

6 Emanuel Tov, 'The Biblical Texts from the Judaean Desert – An Overview and Analysis of the Published Texts', in *The Bible as Book: The Hebrew Bible and the Judaean Desert Discoveries* (ed. Edward D. Herbert and Emanuel Tov; London: British Library & Oak Knoll Press, 2002), p. 140.

7 Tov, *Scribal Practices and Approaches*, p. 250.

between biblical and nonbiblical literary manuscripts'.[8] First, a stichographic layout for writing poetry is used almost exclusively for some
biblical poetic texts such as the psalms. Second, biblical texts are found
almost exclusively on leather and only a few on papyrus. Third, a single
waw either in paleo-Hebrew or square script is used three times as a
paragraphing mark only in biblical scrolls. Fourth, biblical scrolls are
written on only one side. Fifth, a *de luxe* format used in some scrolls is
used predominantly in biblical texts.[9] Three of these five features seem
most significant for biblical texts: stichographic layout for poetry, texts
written almost entirely on leather and texts written on only one side of the
leather.

Tov distinguishes between regular biblical texts and excerpted and
abbreviated texts.[10] By 'regular Biblical texts' he means complete copies of
biblical books. The basic pattern was that one biblical book was written
on one side of a scroll made of animal skin. Prose texts were written in
columns with margins left on all sides.[11] Spaces were left between words
and various means of paragraphing were used to designate sections of
texts. Sometimes texts were *de luxe* editions which had wider margins and
were more carefully written.[12]

One of the best preserved manuscripts is the 1QIsa[a] scroll and even if it
is not typical in every respect it is helpful for understanding a complete
scroll of a scriptural book. It is nearly complete with 54 columns and is
7.34 meters (24 ft. 5/16 in.) long.[13] Frank Cross indicates that it was
'composed of seventeen sheets of sheepskin averaging 26.2 cm. (10 5/6 in.)
in height and varying in length, and sewn together with linen thread'.[14]
The average number of lines per column is 28–32 which is a large writing
block according to Tov.[15]

A few scrolls contained more than one book of the Torah. There are six
copies of Torah scrolls which contain joins between Genesis-Exodus,
Exodus-Leviticus and Leviticus-Numbers. Some of these scrolls contained
a large writing block with from fifty to sixty lines.[16] Tov thinks it is

---

8   Ibid., p. 252.
9   Ibid.
10   Tov, 'The Biblical Texts from the Judaean Desert', pp. 146–50.
11   Tov says that these have 'writing blocks that cover the greater part of the surface,
leaving margins on all sides of the inscribed surface'. *Scribal Practices and Approaches*, p. 82.
12   Tov, *Scribal Practices and Approaches*, pp. 125–29.
13   Ibid., p. 76.
14   Frank Cross, 'Introduction' to *Scrolls from Qumran Cave 1: The Great Isaiah Scroll,
The Order of the Community, The Pesher to Habakkuk* (ed. Frank Moore Cross, David Noel
Freedman and James A. Sanders; Jerusalem: Albright Institute and Shrine of Book, 1974),
p. 3.
15   Tov, *Scribal Practices and Approaches*, pp. 87–88.
16   Ibid., p. 75.

possible that some Qumran scrolls might have contained all of the Torah but if they did they would have been 25–30 meters long.[17] He indicates that the fragments of Torah scrolls ranged from the longest writing block of 40–60 lines per column to a medium size one of 24 and 25 lines and the smallest ones of 11 and even 8 lines.[18] He suggests that the average size would have been 20–30 lines per column.

While there is evidence of regular biblical scrolls, there is also evidence of excerpted texts which were produced for special purposes. In a survey of excerpted and abbreviated texts Tov contends that 'The common denominator of these excerpted texts is that they present small or large segments of the biblical text.'[19] Later he says 'Excerpted texts are recognized by the juxtaposition of different biblical texts, either from different books or from the same book.'[20] He suggests that most texts contain excerpts which do not follow the sequence of the biblical text from which they are produced whereas in a few cases (4QExod[d], 4QCant[a], 4QCant[b] and possibly 4QEzek[a]) they follow the sequence of the chapters in the base text.[21] One way of identifying such texts is their small size, making it difficult for an entire book to have been written on one scroll.[22] Tov suggests that they may have been used for liturgical purposes, for personal reading or for ꞁegetical-ideological purposes.[23] He thinks that 'Most excerpted texts were probably made for liturgical purposes.'[24]

Strawn has written a more recent survey of biblical excerpted texts.[25] He proposed five characteristics of these texts. These relate to form – excerpts from one or more base texts; size – often they belong to small scrolls; content – certain key texts are excerpted; text – mixed textual types are used, and the Qumran scribal practice as identified by Tov is also sometimes used. While Strawn mentions phylacteries and *mezuzots* as examples of excerpted texts he does not devote much time to discussing them.

Strawn helpfully distinguishes excerpted texts from the base text which

---

17   Ibid., p. 76.
18   Ibid., p. 98.
19   Emanuel Tov, 'Excerpted and Abbreviated Biblical Texts', *RevQ* 64 (1996): p. 582.
20   Ibid., p. 586.
21   Ibid., p. 597.
22   Ibid., p. 596.
23   Ibid., pp. 585–86, 598.
24   Emanuel Tov, 'Scriptures: Texts' in *Encyclopedia of the Dead Sea Scrolls*, vol. II (ed. Lawrence H. Schiffman and James C. VanderKam; New York: Oxford University Press, 2000), p. 535.
25   Strawn, 'Excerpted Manuscripts at Qumran', pp. 110–20. See also his more recent work in which he reviews some aspects of biblical excerpted texts. Brent Strawn, 'Excerpted "Non-Biblical" Scrolls at Qumran', in *Qumran Studies: New Approaches, New Questions* (ed. Michael Thomas Davis and Brent A. Strawn; Grand Rapids, MI: Eerdmans, 2007), pp. 65–74.

was used to construct it. He indicates in his discussion of the genre that 'The overall *gestalt* is a composition that looks very much like its base text but is not quite the same. It looks more like an epitome, a selection, a pastiche, or catena constructed of or from a base text(s) rather than the base text(s) itself.'[26]

H. Gregory Snyder looks at text-centered groups in the ancient world and considers how and in what ways texts are utilized by teachers in his book *Teachers and Texts in the Ancient World*.[27] He states: 'To different degrees, these groups sought to catalogue and organize their texts, maintain them by textual criticism, epitomize, paraphrase, or expand them, write commentaries upon them, and finally, to study them in private and corporately.'[28] He comments about the purposes of the anthologies found in the Dead Sea Scrolls: 'The forms of these rolls suggest several contexts for use: liturgy, study, private reading, and symbolic uses, where texts are used as talismans.'[29]

Tefillin

Tefillin were small leather boxes containing tiny scriptural texts which were placed on the forehead or arm. There were fragments of 26 found at Qumran (21 from Cave 4 (4Q128–148); 1 from Cave 1 (1Q13); 1 from Cave 5 (5Q8); 1 from Cave 8 (8Q3); 1 from Cave 11 and XQ1–4); 1 found at Murabba'at (Mur 4), and 2 found at Nahal Se'elim (XHev/Se 5 A,B, 34Se 1).[30] According to Martinez 11Q31 Unidentified text probably contained a *tefillin* or *mezuzah*.[31] In addition, '5QPhyl (5Q8) has not been opened'.[32]

Remains of the leather cases which held the scriptural portions and leather thongs which might have been used to attach these cases to the arm/head were also found. Phylactery cases were found in Qumran Caves

---

26   Strawn, 'Excerpted Manuscripts at Qumran', p. 124.

27   H. Gregory Snyder, *Teachers and Texts in the Ancient World: Philosophers, Jews and Christians* (London and New York: Routledge, 2000).

28   Ibid., p. 5.

29   Ibid., p. 149.

30   There is an appendix which includes lists of *tefillin* and *mezuzot* in *The Text from the Judaean Desert: Indices and an Introduction to the Discoveries in the Judaean Desert Series* (ed. E. Tov; DJD XXXIX; Oxford: Clarendon, 2002), pp. 182–83.

31   Reported by Tov, *Scribal Practices and Approaches*, p. 256, n. 314.

32   Ibid.

1,4,5,8 and at Murabba'at. Some were found in archaeological excavations and others were purchased from Bedouin.[33]

According to G. Lankester Harding, two examples of a phylactery case with four compartments for use on the head and remains of four phylactery cases with one compartment for use on the hand were found at Cave 1.[34] J. Carswell says that 'the dozen or more phylacteries from Cave 4 must have been attached to the body in some way, and if they were secured with thongs, some of these thongs may conceivably have belonged to them'.[35] He refers here to thongs found in the Qumran caves.

After the leather scraps were inscribed they were folded and inserted in the phylactery cases. A phylactery case with three compartments was found in Cave 4 but the fragments could only be partially unrolled.[36] Two other cases had phylacteries inside but these could not be unrolled.[37] Yadin purchased a case with four compartments with slips folded inside which he was able to unfold. He determined that three of the slips belonged in their original compartments while the fourth did not.[38] Sometimes folds on the fragments are visible. Morgenstern and Segal indicate that the two fragments of XHev/Se Phylactery were folded together since the same vertical and horizontal fold marks are evident on both fragments.[39] One can see fold marks on some of the photographs of fragments published from Cave 4.[40]

In general, head *tefillin* have four separate slips with a different excerpt on each one whereas arm *tefillin* have one slip with several excerpts on it.[41] Many of those found at Qumran seem to be arm *tefillin* with several excerpts on each one. When only one excerpt is found on a slip, it may be

---

33   For the details see J. T. Milik, 'Introduction' in *Qumrân grotte 4.II: I. Archéologie, II. Tefillin, Mezuzot et Targums (4Q128–4Q157)* (eds R. de Vaux and J. T. Milik; DJD VI; Oxford: Clarendon, 1977), p. 34. For the photograph of the Cave 1 cases see plate I in D. Barthélemy and J. T. Milik, *Qumran Cave 1* (DJD I; Oxford: Clarendon, 1955). Pictures of phylactery cases found in Cave 4 are published on plate VI of DJD VI. There are also pictures of leather thongs found in Cave 8 and Cave 4 on plate V of DJD VI.

34   G. Lankester Harding, 'Introductory, the Discovery, the Excavation, Minor Finds', in DJD I, p. 7.

35   J. Carswell, 'Fastenings on the Qumran Manuscripts', in DJD VI, p. 23.

36   Milik, DJD VI, p. 34.

37   Milik, DJD VI, pp. 34–35.

38   Yigael Yadin, *Tefillin from Qumran (XQPhyl 1–4)* (Jerusalem: Israel Exploration Society, 1969), pp. 11–14.

39   Morgenstern and Segal indicate this while studying XHev/Se Phylactery. M. Morgenstern and M. Segal, 'XHev/Se Phylactery' in *Miscellaneous Texts from the Judaean Desert* (ed. J. Charlesworth et al. in consultation with J. VanderKam and M. Brady; DJD XXXVIII; Oxford: Clarendon, 2000), p. 183.

40   Notable is Phylactery U 4Q148 on pl. XXV of DJD VI.

41   Lawrence Schiffman, 'Phylacteries and Mezuzot', in *Encyclopedia of the Dead Sea Scrolls* (ed. Lawrence H. Schiffman and James C. VanderKam; New York: Oxford University Press, 2000), p. 675.

that this belonged to a head *tefillin*. As an example Phyl D (Deut. 11.13-21), Phyl E (Exod. 13.1-10) and Phyl F (Exod. 13.11-16) were taken from one phylactery case.[42]

The practice of wearing phylacteries is derived from commands in Exod. 13.9; 13.16; Deut. 6.8 and 11.18 which indicate that these texts should be viewed as 'signs on the hand and frontlets between the eyes'.[43] One could interpret this language figuratively, as in a similar instance in Prov. 6.20-22, or literally.[44] Michael Carasik points out that the 'sign' and the 'frontlet' 'represent writing as a symbolic, not a literal, reminder. It is the existence and display of writing that serves to remind, not the reading of its contents.' [45] Even if one could not read the texts, they would still serve as a reminder. One needs to recite them but this could be from memory.

The first evidence of a literal understanding of the commands is found in the Second Temple period. *The Letter of Aristeas* (159), Matthew 23.5 and Josephus (*Jewish Antiquities* 4.213) all refer to physical objects attached to the body. Phylacteries found near the Dead Sea are the first physical examples of such objects. As possible parallels to this practice Weinfeld points out that the high priest wore a frontlet of gold with 'Holy to YHWH' on it (Exod. 28.36-38), and the Egyptian pharaoh had the Uraeus snake on the forehead which was for protection.[46]

Once the decision was made to interpret these texts literally, one needed to determine for each command precisely to what 'these words' (Deut. 6.6), 'my words' (Deut. 11.18), or 'teaching' (Exod. 13.9), referred. Later the prescribed texts were Exod. 13.1-10; Exod. 13.11-16; Deut. 6.4-9; and Deut. 11.13-21 but some of the Qumran texts contained additional texts such as the Decalogue. Milik indicates that the largest extent for pericopes included the following: Exod. 12.43–13.16; Deut. 5.1–6.9; 10.12–11.21 and sometimes Deuteronomy 32.[47] Some of the additional texts found at Qumran preceded the later standardized passages: Deut. 5.1–6.3 (including the Decalogue) preceded 6.4-9; Deut. 10.12–11.12 preceded 11.13-21 and Exod. 12.43-51 preceded 13.1-10, 11-16.[48]

Michael Fishbane indicated that the Decalogue may have been included because it is introduced with 'these words' in Exod. 20.1.[49] The

42   Milik, DJD VI, pp. 34–35, 56.

43   Michael Fishbane, 'Interpretation of Mikra at Qumran', in *Mikra: Text, Translation, Reading and Interpretation of the Hebrew Bible in Ancient Judaism* (ed. Martin Jan Mulder; Philadelphia: Fortress, 1988), p. 352.

44   Moshe Weinfeld, *Deuteronomy 1–11* (New York: Doubleday, 1991), pp. 341–42.

45   Michael Carasik, *Theologies of the Mind in Biblical Israel* (New York: Peter Lang, 2006), p. 66.

46   Weinfeld, *Deuteronomy 1–11*, pp. 342, 343.

47   Milik, DJD VI, p. 38.

48   Tov mentions this (*Scribal Practices and Approaches*, p. 270).

49   Michael Fishbane, 'Interpretation of Mikra at Qumran', p. 352.

combination of the *Shema* with the Decalogue is also known in the Nash Papyrus. Moshe Greenberg has drawn attention to the note in the Talmud that during Second Temple times 'they recited the Decalogue, the *Shema*, etc.' [50] It seems doubtful if these texts were recited in the temple for the same reason that they were worn on their bodies. It is more likely that this was done in obedience to other commands such as the need to meditate upon these texts and teach them to their children.

Moshe Weinfeld referred to these four texts as catechetical passages; three of them explain Passover, Mazzoth and firstborn rituals while the fourth in Deuteronomy is not linked to a ritual. Mention of teaching children is found in each of these texts (Exod. 13.8; 13.14; Deut. 6.7; 11.19). These four texts share common features such as the instruction of teaching children, practicing these commands, and keeping them as signs at all times. The verb used for teaching of children is different in Deut. 6.7 than in the other texts. George Brooke has pointed out the variant reading between Deut. 5.1 and 5.2 in Phylactery G which places emphasis upon teaching children.[51] The term for teaching was found in MT 5.1 but what is found in Phylactery G at a different place is 'teaching them to your children' which may reflect the reading of Deut. 11.19 as noted by Milik and Brooke.[52] Mention of 'teaching children' already in Deut. 5.1 establishes that the Decalogue should also be included with the other catechetical passages.

In one case Deuteronomy 32 is found in a *tefillin*. Elsewhere this text is written in poetic form. After Moses recited the words of the song (Deuteronomy 32) to the people he tells them that they are to take to heart 'these words' and teach them to their children so that they will practice these words (Deut. 32.45-46). The language here is similar to the other four catechetical passages and it is not surprising that this text would be included with them. Weinfeld cites texts which indicate that Deuteronomy 32 was 'known as a liturgical text used to be recited by the Levites in the Temple on the sabbath'.[53]

While the first three slips that Yadin published were rectangular in shape and writing was only on one side, many of the Cave 4 *tefillin* (and slip 4 of XQPhyl published by Yadin) were written on both sides of scraps

50 Moshe Greenberg, quoted in Michael Fishbane, 'Interpretation of Mikra at Qumran', p. 352, n. 32.
51 George Brooke, 'Deuteronomy 5–6 in the Phylacteries from Qumran Cave 4', in *Emanuel: Studies in Hebrew Bible, Septuagint, and Dead Sea Scrolls in Honor of Emanuel Tov* (ed. Shalom M. Paul, Robert A. Kraft, Lawrence H. Schiffman and Weston W. Fields, with the assistance of Eva Ben-David; VT Sup, 94; Leiden: Brill, 2003), p. 68.
52 Brooke, 'Deuteronomy 5–6 in the Phylacteries from Qumran Cave 4', p. 68 and Milik, DJD VI, p. 58.
53 M. Weinfeld, 'Grace after Meals in Qumran', *JBL* 111 (1992): p. 428.

of various sizes and shapes.[54] Almost every space of these tiny scraps is filled with letters. These texts are examples of *scriptura continua* or continuous writing with no spaces left between words.[55] Such a practice is rare in the Dead Sea Scrolls as spaces are usually left between words and margins are left surrounding written texts. Three spaces were left between different scriptural excerpts in all Cave 4 examples while open sections were used in MurPhyl and 8QPhyl.[56]

Milik tells about how these texts were written. After writing a text on the recto side, the scribe would turn the fragment over, rotate it 90 degrees and write on the verso. Sometimes the scribe did not calculate how much space it would take on the verso. In two cases the scribe wrote the first part of the text on the verso of a fragment and then wrote the end of the text above this text (Phyl B and Phyl R).[57] On the verso of 4Q144 Phyl R the scribe started part way down the fragment and wrote five lines of 13.7-10a, then returned to the top of the fragment and continued the end of verse 10 in one line above verses 7–10 but with a small space between this line (end of verse 10) and 7–10.

In the most unusual case (4Q137 Phylactery J) after the scribe filled up the recto he wrote on the verso and turned the fragment 180 degrees twice before finishing the text. The scribe started writing part way down the fragment, wrote 5.24-28 in about 22 lines, rotated the fragment 180 degrees and wrote five lines of 5.29-32 at the other end of the fragment, then rotated the fragment again 180 degrees and wrote 6.2-3 right below 5.29-32 in the center of the fragment. This results in the sequence on this side appearing to be 5.29-32 at the top, 6.2-3 in the middle with empty spaces and 5.24-28 at the bottom.

Another curious text is Phylactery N 4Q141 which has Deut. 32.14-20 written on most of the fragment but then 32.32-33 is written perpendicular to the other text on the left hand side in what Milik refers to as a kind of 'window' near the left border.[58] Scribes went to considerable trouble to write texts on sometimes irregularly shaped fragments.

Tefillin are written in very tiny letters and are quite difficult to read with the naked eye. Milik says in general that the size of letters for the phylacteries was less than a millimeter on the recto and slightly more than a millimeter on the verso.[59] Yadin indicates that the sizes of the letters of XQPhyl are about .5–.7 mm.[60] Tov gives a variety of sizes for letters of

---

54   Yadin, *Tefillin from Qumran*.
55   Tov, *Scribal Practices and Approaches*, p. 131.
56   Ibid., p. 257.
57   Milik, DJD VI, p. 36.
58   Ibid., p. 72.
59   Ibid., p. 36.
60   Yadin, *Tefillin from Qumran*, p. 21.

biblical texts: 'regular sized letters of 4QChr (0.2–0.3cm)' 'petite letters of 4QEzr[a] (0.1–0.15cm)' and large letters of 4QDan[e] (0.4–0.5 cm).[61]

Modern-day scholars can enlarge photographs of these fragments to study them. Milik indicates that he had infrared photographs in normal size and three fold enlargements but that he preferred using a high powered magnifying glass on the originals for his transcriptions.[62] Morgenstern and Segal indicate that while studying XHev/Se Phylactery it was difficult to decipher the texts partly because of the 'minuscule' proportions and the fact that such fragments had been folded. They utilized four fold enlargements to do their work.[63] Another reason such texts were difficult to read was because the skin on which they were written was very thin and the writing can be seen from the opposite side which makes it difficult to read either side.

Often when such documents are published, enlarged photographs are used. Unfortunately, often there is no indication of scale in the published photographs in DJD volumes so this is not evident to the reader. D. Barthélemy does mention that the phylactery published in DJD 1 was double sized.[64] Milik mentions that the Cave 4 phylacteries and mezuzah G were enlarged three times, the other mezuzot two times while the leather cases were natural size.[65] In DJD III there is a note on 8Q4 Mezouza that the photograph has been enlarged twice.[66] In DJD II, notes on the photographs of Mur 4 Phylactery and Mur 5 Mezuzot indicated that these fragments were shown in both natural size and enlarged three times.[67] There were no notes near the published photographs in DJD VI about enlargements.

In spite of the minuscule writing of these texts, considerable attention has been given to the specific wording of these texts. Tov has concluded that some of these texts reflect what he has called 'the Qumran practice' (4QPhyl A, B, G-I, J-K, L-N, O, P and Q) and some do not (4QPhyl C, D, E, F, H, R, S).[68] While these texts have often been considered a special category of excerpted texts, Brooke raises the possibility that they should be considered as examples of 'rewritten or reworked forms of scripture'.[69] He points out examples of scribal lapses, harmonizations, abbreviations, vocabulary differences and matters of content which can also be found in

---

61 Tov, *Scribal Practices and Approaches*, p. 17.

62 Milk, DJD VI, p. 33.

63 M. Morgenstern and M. Segal 'XHev/Se Phylactery' in DJD XXXVIII, p. 183.

64 Barthélemy and Milik, DJD I, p. 74.

65 Milik, DJD VI, p. 74.

66 M. Baillet, J. T. Milik and R. de Vaux, *Les 'petites grottes' de Qumrân* (DJD III; 2 vols; Oxford: Clarendon, 1962).

67 P. Benoit, J. T. Milik and R. de Vaux, *Les grottes de Murabba'at: Volume II: Planches* (DJD II; Oxford: Clarendon, 1961), plates XXIII, XXIV.

68 These are listed in Brooke, 'Deuteronomy 5–6', p. 56.

69 Ibid., p. 69.

'rewritten Bibles'. Yet some of these same features can also be found in other copies of biblical books at Qumran. The textual characteristics of these texts have often been considered harmonistic by scholars. Tov notes that 'The juxtaposition of these passages in its turn may have influenced biblical MSS, especially because of the great importance of the phylacteries in daily life.'[70] While scholars may have been suspicious of using them for text-critical work, some of their textual variants could be due to the fact that they were produced from memory.[71] Such texts were not produced primarily to be read for their content.

Milik already noted that there were two different groups of *tefillin* found at Qumran. One group reflects later rabbinic instructions for their production and another group does not.[72] Tov notes that these two groups can be distinguished by 'content, textual character, and scribal habits'.[73] He is particularly interested in noting which *tefillin* are written in his 'Qumran scribal practice' and which are not. Because of the fragmentary nature of some of these texts, it is not certain to which group they might belong but some are more certain. Assumedly this reflects two different groups of people using two different systems for producing these texts. Later rabbinic texts will affirm one of these traditions and not the other as authoritative.

List of tefillin *which seem to reflect rabbinic standards*[74]

4Q130 Phyl C	Exod. 13.1-16; Deut. 6.4-9; 11.13-21
4Q131 Phyl D	Deut. 11.13-21
4Q132 Phyl E	Exod. 13.1-10
4Q133 Phyl F	Exod. 13.11-16 + unidentified piece
4Q145 Phyl R	Recto: Exod. 13.1-7 Verso: Exod. 13.7-10
4Q146 Phyl S	Deut. 11.19-21
XHev/Se Phylactery	Fragment 1: Exod. 13.1-16; Deut. 6.4-9; 11.13-17 Fragment 2: Deut. 11.17-21
34Se 1 Phylactery	Fragment a: Exod. 13.2-10 Fragment b: Exod. 13.11-16
Mur 4 Phylactery	Fragment 1: Exod. 13.1-10; 13.11-16; Deut. 11.13-21 Fragment 2: Deut. 6.4-9

---

70 Emanuel Tov, 'The Nature and Background of Harmonizations in Biblical Manuscripts', *JSOT* 31 (1985): p. 19.

71 This is mentioned by Emanuel Tov, *Textual Criticism of the Hebrew Bible* (Minneapolis: Fortress, 1992), p. 119.

72 Milik, DJD VI, pp. 38–39.

73 Tov, *Scribal Practices and Approaches*, p. 271.

74 Contents of these texts are largely from Milik, DJD VI.

List of tefillin *which do not seem to reflect rabbinic standards*[75]

4Q128 Phyl A	Recto: Deut. 5.1-14; 5.27–6.3; 10.12–11.17
	Verso: Deut. 11.18-21; Exod. 12.43–13.7
4Q129 Phyl B	Recto: Deut. 5.1–6.5 Verso: Exod. 13.9-16
4Q134 Phyl G	Recto: Deut. 5.1-21 Verso: Exod. 13.11-12
4Q136 Phyl I	Recto: Deut. 11.13-21; Exod. 12.43–13.10
	Verso: Deut. 6.6-7 (?)
4Q137 Phyl J	Recto: Deut. 5.1-24 Verso: Deut. 5.24-32; 6.2-3
4Q138 Phyl K	Recto: Deut. 10.12–11.7
	Verso: Deut. 11.7-12
4Q139 Phyl L	Deut. 5.7-24
4Q140 Phyl M	Recto: Exod. 12.44–13.10
	Verso: Deut. 5.33–6.5
4Q141 Phyl N	Deut. 32.14-20, 32–33
4Q142 Phyl O	Recto: Deut. 5.1-16 Verso: Deut. 6.7-9
4Q143 Phyl P	Recto: Deut. 10.22–11.3
	Verso: Deut. 11.18-21
4Q144 Phyl Q	Recto: Deut. 11.4-18 Verso: Exod. 13.4-9
XQPhyl	Slip 1: Exod. 12.43-51; Exod. 13.1-10; Deut. 10.12-19
	Slip 2: Deut. 5.22-33; Deut. 6.1-3; Deut. 6.4-9
	Slip 3: Deut. 5.1-21; Exod. 13.11-16
	Slip 4: Exod. 13.1-10?

The first group of *tefillin* contains only pericopes which are later authorized in rabbinic texts. The one anomaly is 4Q145 Phyl R which has writing on both sides of a fragment. This practice was not acceptable according to later standards. The second group of *tefillin* has certain texts which are not authorized in later rabbinic texts. In this group many of the texts have writing on both the recto and verso sides.

In the first group the later canonical order of Exodus followed by Deuteronomy is found in 4Q130 Phyl C, XHev/Se Phylactery, Mur 4 Phylactery. In Mur 4, however, Deut. 11.13-21 precedes Deut. 6.4-9. Milik notes that the sections of Exodus in Phyl D, Phyl E, Phyl F followed the ones of Deuteronomy in Phyl D. These three slips came from the same phylactery case.[76] In the second group one has a variety of different orders: Exodus on the recto and Deuteronomy on the verso (Phyl M), Exodus followed by Deuteronomy on one side (slip 1 of XQPhyl), some

---

75   Contents of these texts are largely from Milik, DJD VI.
76   Milik, DJD VI, p. 56.

have Deuteronomy on the recto and Exodus on the verso (Phyl B, G, Q), one has Deuteronomy followed by Exodus on one side (slip 3 of XQPhyl), one has Deuteronomy followed by Exodus on the recto and Deuteronomy on the verso (Phyl I), one has Deuteronomy on the recto and verso and Exodus following Deuteronomy on the verso (Phyl A), some have only Deuteronomy on both the recto and verso (Phyl J, K, O, P) or only Deuteronomy on one side alone (Phyl L, N; slip 2 of XQPhyl), possibly Exodus alone on slip 4 of XQPhyl.

Such variability may raise questions about whether we have only two different systems or rather a certain variability of order of the excerpted texts. Furthermore, one might also wonder if it was considered obligatory at these early times to include all of the portions. Milik thought it was not necessary to write out all of the pericopes in their entirety or to include all of the pericopes.[77] While the fragmentary nature of these texts makes definitive statements problematic, it appears that there was considerable variation in the particular selection of texts to be included in any particular *tefillin* and in how the texts were formatted upon the leather pieces used.

Sometimes different excerpts are separated from one another because they are on different fragments. Sometimes different excerpts are separated from one another because individual excerpts are found on the recto and verso sides of a fragment. At other times there are two or more excerpts that are placed on the same side of a fragment. In such cases they are usually separated from one another in one way or another. Tov says that all of the Cave 4 phylacteries used 'three letter-spaces to separate the sections'.[78] As an example one can note Phylactery C in which one finds spaces in lines 8, 15, 19 to separate the four excerpts.[79] Mur Phyl leaves a blank line between each excerpt and these are found in line 41 (following Exod. 13.1-10) and line 75 (following Exod. 13.11-16).[80] A blank line separates excerpts in 8QPhyl and the first line of the next excerpt is indented.[81] While such methods of separating excerpts are also used to indicate various sense units in other texts from the Dead Sea Scrolls, since the usage of spacing is so rare in these particular texts, it means that the scribes wanted to separate these excerpts physically to show the end of one excerpt and the beginning of another one.

After the portions were placed into the phylactery cases, according to Schiffman, 'the leather compartment is stitched closed'.[82] That would

77   Ibid., p. 38.
78   Tov, *Scribal Practices and Approaches*, p. 257.
79   Milik, DJD VI, p. 55.
80   Milik, DJD II, pp. 81–85.
81   Tov, *Scribal Practices and Approaches*, p. 257.
82   Lawrence Schiffman, *Reclaiming the Dead Sea Scrolls* (New York: Doubleday, 1995), p. 307.

make accessing these texts difficult. While those who used such phylacteries could have taken out the scriptural portions and consulted them, this seems doubtful.

Mezuzot

Mezuzot were containers for scriptural portions which were placed on the gates and doorposts of houses. These texts were produced to show obedience to the commands of Deut. 6.9 and 11.20 'write them on the doorposts of your house and on your gates' (NRSV). Deut. 6.4-9 and 11.13-21 became standard texts at later times, but the Qumran texts also contained additional passages such as the Decalogue (Exod. 20.1-14 and Deut. 5.6-18).[83] *The Letter of Aristeas* 158 and Josephus (*Jewish Antiquities* 4.213) mention the practice of placing *mezuzot* on doorposts.[84] There were nine of these found near the Dead Sea – eight at Qumran (seven at Cave 4 (4Q149–155), one at Cave 8 (8Q4)) and one at Murabba'at.[85] Weinfeld draws attention to the more than a dozen stone plaques of Samaritan origin found with the Decalogue on them that were placed near entranceways.[86] Milik mentions the use of the Decalogue on doors of houses and synagogues.[87]

List of mezuzot *and contents*

4Q149 Mez A	Exod. 20.7-12
4Q150 Mez. B	Deut. 6.5-6; 10.14–11.2
4Q151 Mez C	Deut. 5.27–6.9; 10.12-20
4Q152 Mez D	Deut. 6.5-7
4Q153 Mez E	Deut. 11.17-18
4Q154 Mez F	Exod. 13.1-4
4Q155 Mez G	Exod. 13.11-16
8Q4 Mezuza	Deut. 10.12–11.1
Mur 5 Mezuza?	cannot be deciphered

In many cases, fragments include only one excerpted text (4Q149 Mez A, 4Q152 Mez D, 4Q153 Mez E, 4Q154 Mez F, 4Q155 Mez G). In only two cases are there two excerpted texts on one fragment (4Q150 Mez B, 4Q151 Mez C). In Mez C there is another fragment with evidence of writing but the text cannot be identified. The transition from Deut. 6.6 to 10.14 has

---

83   Ibid., p. 31.
84   Schiffman, 'Phylacteries and Mezuzot'.
85   Tov, 'Categorized List of the "Biblical Texts"', DJD XXXIX, p. 183.
86   Weinfeld, *Deuteronomy 1–11*, p. 343.
87   Milik, DJD VI, p. 80.

not been preserved in Mez B nor the transition from Deut. 6.9 to Deut. 10.12 in Mez C.[88]

When 8Q Mez was found it was rolled up with the beginning in the interior.[89] No *mezuzah* has been found in a case or wrapping but there was a piece of parchment which was folded three times which could have served as a wrapper for such a text.[90] At Murabba'at a leather envelope contained both a *tefillin* as well as a leather piece with a list of Greek names on it (Mur 4 and Mur 95).[91] Presumably the texts placed within the *mezuzot* could be consulted and read but they probably remained inside a case of some sort.

It is sometimes difficult to tell whether particular texts are from phylacteries or *mezuzot* because they share similar features including contents. Milik suggests uncertainty about Phylactery S, Phylactery U and Mezuzah G.[92] He indicates two features which help distinguish them. Phylacteries are written on thinner parchment than normal texts whereas *mezuzot* are written on the same kinds of skin as ordinary manuscripts.[93] *Mezuzot* resemble phylacteries by the dimensions of inscribed pieces, the small size of letters, the type of writing and other paleographic details such as the absence of dry lines to guide the writing.[94] Tov adds two other differences: *mezuzot* are written only on one side whereas the phylacteries often are written on both sides and the '*mezuzot* are written on neatly shaped pieces of leather, while *tefillin* were usually written on leather of ragged shapes'.[95] *Mezuzot* have margins whereas *tefillin* do not.

While in general the letters of the *mezuzot* are larger than those of the phylacteries, there is not a great difference.[96] According to Tov's categories for letter sizes, the *mezuzot* would range from petite to regular.[97] The letters of the *mezuzot* were quite small and these texts are generally published with enlarged photographs.[98] According to M. Baillet 8Q4 Mezouza was +/− 1 mm.[99] According to Milik one has the following

88   Ibid., p. 81.

89   M. Baillet, 'Mezouza' in Baillet, Milik and de Vaux, DJD III, p. 158.

90   Milik, DJD VI, p. 35.

91   Ibid., pp. 80, 227.

92   Ibid., pp. 36, 78, 84.

93   Ibid., p. 36.

94   Ibid., p. 36.

95   Tov, *Scribal Practices and Approaches*, p. 258.

96   At one point Tov seems to overstate the differences when he says 'The letters in *mezuzot* are of regular size, while the letters in *tefillin* are minute.' Tov, *Scribal Practices and Approaches*, p. 258.

97   See Tov, *Scribal Practices and Approaches*, p. 17.

98   The Cave 4 phylacteries and *mezuzah* G were enlarged three times and the other *mezuzot* two times in the published photographs. Milik, DJD VI, p. 74; see also Baillet, DJD III, p. 158.

99   Baillet, 'Mezouza', p. 158.

sizes of Mezuzot: Mez A (2 mm), Mez B (1.5 mm), Mez C (1.1 mm), Mez D (2 mm), Mez E (1.5 mm), Mez F (2.5 mm), Mez G (less than 1 mm).[100] Tov gives a variety of sizes for letters of biblical texts: 'regular sized letters of 4QChr (0.2–0.3cm)' 'petite letters of 4QEzr^a (0.1–0.15 cm)' and 'large letters of 4QDan^e (0.4–0.5 cm)'.[101] It would have been easier to read the writing on the *mezuzot* than the *tefillin*. Yet after the texts were placed within a case of some sort, it is doubtful if they were used for reading.

Usages of tefillin *and* mezuzot

Those who used *tefillin* and *mezuzot* were doing so out of obedience to specific commands. These texts show evidence of Torah piety that devotes attention to specific Torah texts. One is to place these Torah texts on one's forehead, forearm and one's gateposts. These texts had to be written small enough that they could be used for these physical purposes. While leather pieces had texts on them, these texts did not need to be easily legible.

Tefillin cases, leather thongs and other leather pieces are artifacts used to contain or attach scriptural portions. Scriptural portions are hidden inside these cases so it is the cases and thongs which are visible to the user and to others. The written texts were not meant to be read or consulted. They came to have a purely symbolic function. They had become artifacts. Their users may have memorized the texts so the written texts were not necessary for consultation or study.

Wearing of *tefillin* and placing *mezuzot* on gates and doors of houses would have served as identity markers for Jewish practitioners or particular groups of Jewish believers. Such practices would have set them apart from others – at least from Gentiles if not other Jewish groups. A hint of this is suggested in Matt. 23.5 where Jesus criticizes Pharisees who wear broad phylacteries as a show of religiosity.

Phylacteries were later used in private prayer and probably were used similarly during the Second Temple period. While George Brooke refers to their broadly liturgical purpose he notes that 'Some scholars have also considered that within the context of private prayer the use of phylacteries is apotropaic.'[102] Weinfeld thought that when these selected texts were worn on the body they were used for apotropaic purposes. He notes examples of wearing amulets with writing on them which were 'apotropaic in nature (offering protection from evil)'.[103] He also mentions that the *Shema* or Decalogue was written on bracelets or frontlets to show religious affiliation.

---

100   Milik, DJD VI, pp. 80–84.
101   Tov, *Scribal Practices and Approaches*, p. 17.
102   Brooke, 'Deuteronomy 5–6', p. 59.
103   Weinfeld, *Deuteronomy 1–11*, p. 342.

Some texts at Qumran indicate the belief in demons, and some prayers such as 4Q510–511 have been described as having apotropaic functions. The prose note of 11QPs[a] mentions that David composed four psalms for the stricken which probably related to those affected by demons.[104] 11QPsAp[a] (11Q11) appears to be a collection of four psalms, including Psalm 91, that was used against demons. Van der Ploeg suggested that this collection is the one mentioned in the prose note.[105]

The Greek term *phylaktērion* ('phylactery' used in Matt. 23.5) suggests 'safeguard, means of protection'.[106] This text probably refers to *tefillin*. Danker indicates that 'In some circles devices were used as amulets protecting against demon influences.'[107] Tigay says '... there is no lack of evidence that *tefillin* were ascribed apotropaic properties and used as such'.[108] *Mezuzot* attached to the doorposts of houses could have been understood to provide protection as well.

Tefillin and *mezuzot* would have been much easier to produce than whole scrolls and therefore would have been more affordable for most people. *Tefillin* and *mezuzot* may have been the only personal portions of scripture that many people had.[109] While the precise usage of these texts at this time is not known, assumedly individual copies of *mezuzot* would be necessary for each home, and individual *tefillin* may have been necessary for each person using them. Whereas communities might share scrolls for many purposes, this would not have been the case with *tefillin* and *mezuzot*.

Deuteronomy and Exodus Excerpted Texts

It may be that other excerpted texts, like the *tefillin* and *mezuzot*, were produced in obedience to particular biblical commands. Julie Duncan argues that some Deuteronomy and Exodus texts are excerpted texts because they contain the same text selections as found in phylacteries and *mezuzot* such as the Decalogue, Deuteronomy 10 and 11, Exodus 12 and

---

104   James Sanders, *The Psalms Scroll of Qumran Cave 11* (DJD IV; Oxford: Clarendon, 1965), p. 93.

105   As reported in Peter Flint, *Dead Sea Psalms Scroll and the Book of Psalms* (STDJ 17; Leiden: Brill, 1997), p. 43.

106   Frederick William Danker (ed.), *A Greek-English Lexicon of the New Testament and other Early Christian Literature* (Chicago: University of Chicago Press, 3rd edn, 2000), p. 1068.

107   Ibid.

108   Jeffrey H. Tigay, 'On the Term Phylacteries', *Harvard Theological Review* 72 (1979): p. 51.

109   See Schiffman, 'Phylacteries and Mezuzot', pp. 674–77.

13 and Deuteronomy 32.[110] While these texts are fragmentary, there is evidence that they do not belong to complete scrolls. Several of these texts belong to small scrolls. 4QDeut^q preserves the end of a scroll with Deut. 32.37-43 which does not have Deuteronomy 33–34 after this portion. 4QDeut^n contains Deut. 8.5-10; Deut. 5.1–6.1 in that order. Exodus and Deuteronomy fragments found in 4QDeut^j are similar to those found in phylacteries and *mezuzot*.[111]

Text	Contents	Special features
4QExod^d	Exod. 13.15-16; 15.1	Text goes from 13.16 to 15.1 without intervening text
4QExod^e	Exod. 13.3-5 alone	Margins above and below this text
4Deut^q	Deut. 32.9-10?, 37-43[112]	stichometric arrangement, does not include Deut. 33–34
4QDeut^n	Deut. 8.5-10; Deut. 5.1–6.1	Unusual order, first column is not full
4Q Deut^j	Deut. 5.1-11, 13–15, 21-33; 6.1-3; 8.5-10; 11.6-10, 12, 13; 11.21? + Exod. 12.43-51; 13.1-5; Deut. 32.7-8[113]	Mixture of Deuteronomy and Exodus texts on the same scroll
4QDeut^{kl}	Deut. 5.28-32; 11.6-13; 32.17-18, 22-23, 25-27[114]	Scattered texts which correspond with those in *tefillin* and m*ezuzot*

These excerpted Exodus and Deuteronomy texts are by no means a homogeneous collection. Since the texts are now quite fragmentary it is impossible to know for certain what may have been contained in complete texts. One can describe what remains. In two cases one has one excerpted text from one book (4QExod^e (Exod. 13.3-5); 4QDeut^q (Deut. 32.37-43)). In three cases there are two or more excerpts from the same book

110 Julie Duncan, 'Excerpted Texts of Deuteronomy at Qumran', *Revue de Qumran* 18/69 (1997): p. 44.

111 Duncan, 'Excerpted Texts of Deuteronomy at Qumran', pp. 44–47.

112 Patrick Skehan and Eugene Ulrich, '4QDeut^q', in *Qumran Cave 4.IX: Deuteronomy, Joshua, Judges, Kings* (eds E. Ulrich, F. M. Cross, et al.; DJD XIV; Oxford: Clarendon, 1995; reprinted 1999), p. 137.

113 Duncan, '4QDeut^j', in DJD XIV, p. 76.

114 Duncan, '4QDeut^{kl}', in DJD XIV, p. 93.

(4QExod[d], 4QDeut[n], 4QDeut[k1]). In one case one has a collection of excerpts from Exodus and Deuteronomy (4QDeut[j]).

In collections of excerpted texts, individual excerpts are often separated from one another in various ways when evidence exists. 4QDeut[k1] contains separate fragments of Deuteronomy 5, 11 and 32 with no fragments which contain portions from more than one excerpt. In 4Q15 Exod[d] one has three lines of Exod. 13.15-16 followed by possibly two lines of Exod. 15.1. Judith Sanderson suggests in her reconstruction that there would have been an empty space (*vacat*) at the end of line three and that Exod. 15.1 begins on the right side of the column of the next line. She refers to this empty space as a 'major interval'.[115]

4QDeut[n] is odd because there are two excerpted Deuteronomy texts with Deut. 8.5-10 preceding Deut. 5.1–6.1. Six successive columns contain Deut. 5.1–6.1 on a small scroll. Another page of a scroll with stitching on both sides contains Deut. 8.5-10 on one column. Since there was stitching on both sides, one assumes that there were other texts preceding it and following it. When the text was originally found the sheet with Deut. 8.5-10 was attached on the right hand side of the short scroll of Deuteronomy 5.1–6.1. During restoration the piece was detached.[116]

What is also unusual is that the width of the column of Deut. 8.5-10 is much wider (col. I – 9.5 cm wide) than the width of later columns (col. II – 5.3 cm wide, col. III – 6.0 cm wide, col. IV – 6.4 cm wide, col. V – 7.1 cm wide).[117] While there were twelve inscribed lines on each of six successive columns of Deut. 5.1–6.1, only seven lines are used on the column with Deut. 8.5-10 and there is an empty line left between lines four and five. At least four blank lines are left without writing on the first column as compared to the later columns.

While spacing is sometimes left between excerpts, this is a very large empty space. When more than one book is found on one scroll, usually no more than three empty lines are left between compositions.[118] Column I appears to be a kind of patch which was added secondarily. While White makes a compelling case that this text is more like a collection of excerpted texts (as suggested by H. Stegemann) and not 'a biblical manuscript which was damaged at 8.5-10 and was repaired incorrectly' (as suggested by John Strugnell), physical features of the text make one

115 Judith Sanderson, '4QExod[d]', in *Qumran Cave 4.VII: Genesis to Numbers* (ed. E. Ulrich, F. M. Cross, et al.; DJD XII; Oxford: Clarendon, 1994; reprinted 1999), p. 128.

116 Sidnie White Crawford, '4QDeut[n]', in *Qumran Cave 4.IX: Deuteronomy, Joshua, Judges, Kings* (eds E. Ulrich, F. M. Cross, et al.; DJD XIV; Oxford: Clarendon, 1995; reprinted 1999), p. 117.

117 Ibid.

118 Tov, *Scribal Practices and Approaches*, pp. 165–66.

wonder about the precise nature of this text.[119] Tov suggests that 'This sheet was prepared originally for a larger scroll, and was subsequently adapted to the needs of 4QDeut^n'.[120]

While the selection of both Exodus and Deuteronomy texts in 4QDeut^j is similar to those found in *tefillin* and *mezuzot*, there are no clear joins of excerpted texts. Duncan reconstructs the fragments into twelve columns and arranges them with Deuteronomy texts first followed by Exodus texts but the evidence for this is less than compelling. There may have been a small interval between Deut. 5.33 and Deut. 6.1 on column IV.[121] Deut. 8.5-10 is found on one column (col. V) and top and bottom margins are visible. Since there are generally 14 lines per column in this scroll it seems likely as Duncan suggests that at least two whole lines were left blank and most of another line as well at the bottom of the column.[122] This sheet appears to be similar to the initial column of 4QDeut^n which contains the same pericope. Duncan suggests that column IX as she has reconstructed it may have a line of Deut. 11.21 with a *vacat* after it and Exod. 12.43 on the next line.[123] Phylactery A and Phylactery I have an excerpt ending in Deut. 11.21 followed by an excerpt beginning with Exod. 12.43. Only one word, however, has been preserved of Deut. 11.21 in 4QDeut^j. Duncan's reconstruction suggests that there may have been other short intervals in the text which indicate sense divisions but these do not relate to separating excerpts of the text.

The new text found in these excerpted texts, not found in other *tefillin* or *mezuzot* from Qumran, is Deut. 8.5-10 which is found in 4QDeut^n and 4QDeut^j . This text was found on one whole column in both of these manuscripts.[124] Duncan draws attention to the Nash Papyrus which contains the Decalogue as well as the *Shema* on one page.[125] The Nash Papyrus preserves a hybrid form of the Decalogue which draws upon both Deuteronomy 5 and Exodus 20. The forms of the Decalogue in some phylacteries and some Deuteronomy texts exhibit similar harmonistic features. Sidnie White has drawn attention to the harmonizing tendencies of the Decalogue in 4QDeut^n.[126] Weinfeld has noted that the *Shema* in

---

119   Sidnie Ann White, '4QDt^n: Biblical Manuscript or Excerpted Text?' in *Of Scribes and Scrolls: Studies on the Hebrew Bible, Intertestamental Judaism and Christian Origins* presented to John Strugnell on the occasion of his sixtieth birthday (ed. Harold W. Attridge, John J. Collins, Thomas H. Tobin; Lanham: University Press of America, 1990), pp. 14–17.

120   Tov, *Scribal Practices and Approaches*, p. 60.

121   Duncan, '4QDeut^j', in DJD XIV, p. 84.

122   Ibid., p. 85.

123   Ibid., p. 88.

124   Ibid., p. 79.

125   Duncan, 'Excerpted Texts of Deuteronomy at Qumran', p. 44.

126   Sidnie White, 'The All Souls Deuteronomy and the Decalogue', *JBL* 90 (1990): pp. 193–206.

Deut. 8.5-10 becomes the basis for the rabbinic tradition about the blessing after meals.[127]

Duncan thinks that two Exodus documents may also be excerpted texts. 4QExod^d contains Exod. 13.15-16 followed immediately by 15.1 and 4QExod^e contains Exod. 13.3-5 alone.[128] Even though Exodus 15, the Song of the Sea, was not found in other collections, Duncan thinks that the presence of this poetic text is not unusual since another poetic text, Deuteronomy 32, the Song of Moses, was also found in 4QPhyl N. Sanderson thinks that 4QExod^d may have been a liturgical scroll.[129] She also thinks that 4QExod^e may have been a liturgical scroll because of the small size of the column and because of its inclusion of instructions for the festival of unleavened bread.[130]

Duncan notes material features of the Deuteronomy texts. They all have short column heights that are much shorter than standard biblical texts. She notes that 'The excerpted manuscripts all attest a column height of fourteen lines or less: 4QDeut^q, 11 lines, 4QDeut^j, 14 lines; and 4QDeut^n, 12–14 lines.'[131] 4QExod^e has a column length of 8 lines.[132] This is small since, as Tov says, 'Probably the average scroll of a single book of the Torah contained 20–30 lines.'[133] Stephen Pfann refers to 'portable scrolls intended to be carried during feasts or carried for a distance concealed (e.g. in a purse or belt)'.[134]

Snyder comments on the small size of the Deuteronomy scrolls (4QDeut^j, 4QDeut^k, 4QDeut^q). He notes 'All these texts are of small dimensions and would be easy to transport. 4QDeut^n, for example, measures a mere 7 cm in height. A scroll of this size would reside easily in a pocket without being crushed. Such a scroll would also be convenient to handle, easy to roll and unroll.'[135]

Duncan comments about the formatting of certain texts. 4QDeut^j and 4QDeut^n begin the top of a column with chapter 5 verse 1 of the Decalogue, there is a single column which is reserved for Deut. 8.5-10 in

---

127   M. Weinfeld, 'Grace after Meals in Qumran', *JBL* 111 (1992): p. 429.

128   Duncan, 'Excerpted Texts of Deuteronomy at Qumran', pp. 61–62.

129   Sanderson, '4QExod^d', DJD XII, p. 127.

130   Sanderson, '4QExod^e', DJD XII, p. 130.

131   Duncan, 'Excerpted Texts of Deuteronomy at Qumran', p. 49.

132   Sanderson, '4QExod^e', DJD XII, p. 128.

133   Tov, 'Biblical Texts from the Judaean Desert', p. 143.

134   Stephen Pfann, 'Words of the Maskil to all the Sons of the Dawn', in *Qumran Cave 4.XV: Sapiential Texts, Part 1* (ed. T. Elgvin et al., in consultation with J. A. Fitzmyer; DJD XX; Oxford: Clarendon, 1997), p. 7. In footnote 17 he says 'Most portable scrolls were owned by individuals and were intended to be carried about and read during certain feasts. Typically these scrolls contained 7–10 (and not more than 15) lines.'

135   Snyder, *Teachers and Texts in the Ancient World*, p. 149.

4QDeut^n and 4QDeut^j, and the same segment in Deut. 11, which takes up about a column, is found in 4QDeut^j and 4QDeut^{k1}.[136]

Duncan suggests that these texts seem to have a liturgical or devotional function because they contain the same excerpted texts as the *tefillin* and *mezuzot*.[137] She notes that the *tefillin* and *mezuzot* may have had a 'more symbolic as opposed to a more practical function', however. Unlike the *tefillin* and *mezuzot*, these more legible texts were better suited to be read, studied and taught to others. These texts included instructions not only for people to wear them on their heads and forearms and place them on the doorposts of their houses but also to meditate upon them and teach them to their children. Unlike complete scrolls the small size of these excerpted texts made them readily portable and accessible for regular and repeated usage by individuals. Their artifactual qualities enhanced their usages.

Another possibility is that selections of such texts were written down to aid those who were constructing *tefillin* and *mezuzot*. While scribes may have produced such texts from memory, it may have been necessary to consult the base texts sometimes. It would have been simpler if the selected texts had been brought together first and then used for the production of copies of *tefillin* and *mezuzot* rather than hunting through regular copies of Exodus and Deuteronomy. Brooke suggests 'Perhaps these manuscripts represented a group of texts containing the source material from which a phylactery could be copied.'[138]

Concluding Comments

While regular biblical scrolls would have been well suited for reading and studying a whole book, there were times when people needed more accessible texts for particular purposes. Regular biblical scrolls were not divided into chapters and verses which allowed easy access to particular texts. If one wanted to access selected texts on a regular basis, regular biblical books were difficult to use and were probably not readily available for each individual.

Some excerpted texts allowed favorite texts and passages to be easily available. It would have been possible for individuals to more easily possess for themselves some of these excerpted texts. Such individuals did not always need access to complete biblical scrolls but they did need

---

136   Duncan, 'Excerpted Texts of Deuteronomy at Qumran', p. 50.

137   Ibid.

138   George Brooke, 'Torah in the Qumran Scrolls', in *Bibel in jüdischer und christlicher Tradition. Festschrift für Johann Maier zum 60. Geburtstag* (ed. H. Merklein, K. Muller and Günter Stemberger; Frankfurt am Main: Verlag Anton Hain, 1993), pp. 109–10.

regular access to some texts which they were commanded to recite and use daily.

The tiny size of phylacteries made it possible to attach these texts physically to the body. *Mezuzot* texts could be slightly larger and still be placed upon doorposts of homes. They did not need to be consulted or read because their owners probably had memorized them. They were produced to show obedience to specific biblical commands found within the texts. For Torah observant Jews, these commands which came from God ought to be obeyed.

Other Deuteronomy and Exodus texts contained similar pericopes to those found in phylacteries and *mezuzot*. Often such scrolls are small, making them easily accessible and portable. The letters of such texts are larger and easier to read than those of phylacteries and *mezuzot*. They are more conducive to study and teaching. They might have been used as master copies to produce phylacteries and *mezuzot*.

The excerpted texts that have been discussed in this essay are all Torah texts. Specific Torah texts call upon their readers to meditate upon them, study them, teach them to their children and to place them on their arms, foreheads and houses. It is not all Torah texts which are excerpted but particularly those that have instructions within them for explicit usages of such texts. The physical features of these excerpted texts fit well with the specialized usages of these texts.

PAPYRUS 967 AND THE TEXT OF EZEKIEL: PARABLEPSIS OR AN ORIGINAL TEXT?

John Flanagan

The most important textual problem in the book of Ezekiel pertains to Papyrus 967 and its significance for establishing the original text of Ezekiel. This paper will seek to analyze the importance of Papyrus 967 for interpreting the original text of Ezekiel. Attention will be given to a columnmetric synopsis of the ancient versions of Ezek. 36.23-38. I will briefly summarize and evaluate scholarly contributions to the problem with particular attention given to the work of Johan Lust. I will seek to argue that the MT does in fact offer a representative of Ezek. 36.23-38 that is just as viable as that of Papyrus 967.

I.

G. A. Cooke noted in his ICC commentary, 'In the Hebrew Bible perhaps no book, except 1 and 2 Samuel, has suffered more injury to its text than Ezekiel.'[1] Indeed the textual problems in Ezekiel are particularly difficult with reference to the differences between the MT and the LXX. These difficulties are highlighted by the problem of Papyrus 967. Papyrus 967 dates from the second to third century AD, making the document the oldest known witness to the Greek translation of Ezekiel.[2] The papyrus is part of the John H. Scheide collection of biblical papyri consisting of 21 leaves from an ancient codex. The codex consists of 122 pages of Ezekiel. Two important features are the omission of Ezek. 36.23-30 in the papyrus as well as rearrangement of chapters 36–39. This puzzle is only more

---

1 G. A. Cooke, *A Critical and Exegetical Commentary on the Book of Ezekiel* (ICC; Edinburgh: T & T Clark, 1936), p. xl.

2 A. C. Johnson, H. S. Gehman and E. H. Kase, Jr., *The John H. Scheide Biblical Papyri: Ezekiel* (Princeton: Princeton University Press, 1938), pp. 5–10.

enigmatic in that the Old Latin translation preserved in *Codex Wirceburgensis* also lacks these exact same verses.[3]

II.

The proposed solutions by the scholarly community have been varied. Long before the actual discovery of Papyrus 967, H. St. J. Thackeray proposed that Ezek. 36.16-38 came from another version much like that of Theodotion. He claimed the early verses were used as an anthology of expressions within the Jewish synagogues.[4] Thackeray argued that the Greek translation of Ezekiel stemmed from two authors and was divided into three parts. Parts I (Ezek. 1–27) and III (40–48) were translated by the same individual, while part II (Ezek. 28–39) was the work of a different translator. He observed that the Greek of the first and third sections share similar vocabulary and also employ some of the same stylistic phrases.[5] He also observed that the prepositions were different between parts one and three and that of section two. In Thackeray's opinion the style of verses 23–38 differ materially from that of the other two postulated authors of the LXX. He therefore suggested its use within the Jewish religion and claimed it was borrowed from Theodotion.

The discovery of Papyrus 967 with its omission of Ezek. 36.23–38 has forced scholars to look at the issue much more closely. The divergent views have ranged from criticism and support of the papyrus to relative indifference concerning the matter. In one of the first articles dealing with Papyrus 967, Floyd V. Filson argued that the omission was due to *homoioteleuton*, also known as *parablepsis*. Filson argued that Papyrus 967 did not support Thackeray's theory in any of its three forms. Neither did the arguments support the originality of the codex.[6] Filson's view that Papyrus 967 suffered from *homoioteleuton* is due to the fact that the manuscript ends 36.23 with the following words: καὶ γνώσεται τὰ ἔθνη ὅτι ἐγώ εἰμι Κύριος. The LXX text ends 36.38 with the words: καὶ γνώσεται τὰ ἐγὼ Κύριος. Filson argued that the scribe simply skipped from the last part of 36.23 onto 36.38. Filson further supported his case stating that Papyrus 967 breaks off in the middle of a verse. The manuscript omits 36.23b-38. The part of the verse which it does contain

---

3   Pierre-Maurice Bogaert, 'Le témoignage de la Vetus Latina dans l'etude de la tradition des Septante Ezéchiel et Daniel dans le Papyrus 967', *Biblica* 59 (1978): 387–92.

4   H. St. J. Thackeray, 'Notes and Studies: The Greek Translators of Ezekiel', *JTS* 4 (1903): 408.

5   Ibid., pp. 398–403.

6   Floyd V. Filson. 'The Omission of Ezekiel 12.26-28 and 36.23b-38 in Codex 967', *JBL* 62 (1943): 27–32.

ends with words identical to the ending in verse 38.[7] This position has been supported recently by J. W. Wevers who states, 'G. Pap. 967 omits from the end of the recognition formula [in v. 23] to the end of verse 38 by *parablepsis*, both parts ending in: "know that I am Yahweh" '.[8]

Another early view was postulated by William A. Irwin. He argued that the section was not present in either original Greek or Hebrew manuscripts. His theory was that the section was simply inserted into an enlarged version of Ezekiel over time.[9] The editor of the Scheide Papyri, A. C. Johnson, proposed that Ezek. 36.23-38 was originally present in the section but was later omitted by *parablepsis*. The error was discovered and the text was corrected using a version by Theodotion. This would then explain the passage occurring in all LXX manuscripts except Papyrus 967.[10] However, this hypothesis is not unanimous among the editors of the Scheide Papyri. Another editor, Edmund H. Kase Jr., proposed that the section was never in the LXX and is simply an insertion. Therefore Papyrus 967, according to Kase, is the only original testimony to the LXX.[11]

William A. Irwin in his book, *The Problem of Ezekiel*, views 36.23b-38 as an insertion into the original text, dating it within the period from the translation of the LXX to the copying of Papyrus 967.[12] He argues therefore that the passage is in fact the latest in the book of Ezekiel as well as the entire Hebrew Bible. Irwin claims that Filson's emphasis on the fact that Papyrus 967 breaks off at the middle of 23 is misplaced, arguing that the Hebrew text itself suggests a balance of the verse as an addition.[13]

Emanuel Tov has acknowledged the uniqueness of Papyrus 967, noting that 'it is certainly not impossible that the short text of the papyrus represents the original Greek translation, based on a shorter Hebrew text'.[14] Tov views the papyrus as representing a pre-hexaplaric text, lacking the changes towards the MT, which have been inserted in the Hexapla in the third century. Tov concludes:

> This late intrusion in the Hebrew book of Ezekiel was subsequently also added in the Greek textual tradition. Thus the pre-hexaplaric witnesses such as the Chester Beatty papyrus reflect the short original text, while

---

7 Ibid., p. 31.

8 J. W. Wevers, *Ezekiel* (NCB; London: Nelson, 1978), p. 273.

9 William A. Irwin, *The Prophets and their Times* (Chicago: University of Chicago Press, 1941), p. 203.

10 Johnson, Gehman and Kase, *Ezekiel*, pp. 7–10.

11 Ibid., p. 10.

12 William A. Irwin, *The Problem of Ezekiel: An Inductive Study* (Chicago: University of Chicago Press, 1943), p. 63.

13 Ibid., p. 63.

14 Emmanuel Tov, *The Text-Critical Use of the Septuagint in Biblical Research* (Jerusalem: Simor, 1981), p. 304.

the expanded text is found in the post-hexaplaric Greek sources. If the evidence of the Chester Beatty papyrus and the Old Latin can indeed be trusted, the Old Greek translation lacked a section which is secondary in the Hebrew text of Ezekiel and this information is essential for our understanding of the literary growth of the book.[15]

The importance commentators have placed upon the problem has varied from work to work. The commentary by Walther Eichrodt does not even make mention of the problem while the work of H. F. Fuhs makes mention of it in passing. Zimmerli provides arguments for a late date of the section in the MT, while denying any significance to the problem of Papyrus 967 for the textual criticism of the Hebrew Old Testament.[16] A closer investigation into his hypothesis will follow in section IV. Renowned Jewish scholar Moshe Greenberg has staunchly defended the originality of the Masoretic text. Greenberg sees no evidence for redactional activity in the book of Ezekiel.[17] He claims that the Masada Hebrew text of Ezekiel, dated to the first century AD contains clear remains of vv. 24–34, all identical to the MT.[18] If Greenberg's dating of the Masada text is accepted, it is earlier than all the extant versional witnesses, including Papyrus 967.

M. V. Sporttorno has proposed a unique explanation for the absence of 36.23-38 in Papyrus 967. He has argued that a codex page from the papyrus was lost either by frequent use or by haplography.[19] Leslie Allen has echoed this sentiment noting the structural importance of v. 27a within the redactional framework of the ensuing chapter. Allen views v. 27a as being deliberately repeated in 37.14a, and v. 27b in 37.14b.[20] Allen concludes stating, 'It is probable that we are to envisage two separate phenomena, redactional amplification within the Hebrew text and

---

15   Emmanuel Tov, 'Recensional Differences between the MT and LXX of Ezekiel', *Ephermerides theologicae lovanienses* 62 (1986): 100–01.

16   Walther Zimmerli, *A Commentary on the Book of the Prophet Ezekiel: Chapters 25–48*, trans. Ronald E. Clements (Hermeneia; Philadelphia: Fortress Press, 1983), p. 243.

17   Moshe Greenberg, 'What are Valid Criteria for Determining Inauthentic Matter in Ezekiel?' in *Ezekiel and his Book: Textual and Literary Criticism and their Interrelation*, ed. Johan Lust (Leuven: Leuven University Press, 1986), pp. 248–54.

18   Moshe Greenberg, *Ezekiel 21–37: A New Translation with Introduction and Commentary* (AB, 22A; Garden City: Doubleday, 1997), pp. 739–40. For a detailed examination of the Qumran scrolls of the book of Ezekiel see also Mladen Popović, 'The Authoritativeness of Ezekiel and Pseudo-Ezekiel in the Dead Sea Scrolls and Beyond', a paper delivered at the Groningen Qumran Institute Symposium 2008, April 28–29, revised version to be published in M. Popović, *Authoritative Scriptures in Ancient Judaism: Proceedings of the Groningen Qumran Institute Symposium, 28–29 April 2008* (JSJSup; Leiden: Brill), forthcoming.

19   M. V. Sporttorno. 'La omission de Ez. 36.23b-38 y la transposicion de capitulos en el papiro 967', *Emerita* 50 (1981): 93–99.

20   Leslie C. Allen, *Ezekiel 20–48* (WBC, 29; Dallas: Word, 1990), p. 177.

coincidental omission of a wider block of material in the Greek tradition.'[21] E. J. Revell has postulated that both the MT and Papyrus 967 have a common origin due to the paragraphing of the Greek manuscript. He has argued that the paragraphing of 967 is clearly related to the *petuhot* and *setumot* divisions of the Hebrew Bible. Revell acknowledges that 967 and the MT are not of the same tradition but that the two systems do in fact share a common origin. Revell concludes:

> The MT tradition was used in Fouad pap. 266, a Jewish text, and a tradition related to that of the Septuagint text brought, to some extent, into conformity with the standardized Hebrew text. It would seem, then, that the use of paragraphing related to that of MT does have some connection, if not with the textual tradition in which it was used, then at least with the outlook of those who used the text.[22]

III.

Scholarship within the last fifty years has produced more debate concerning the issue. At the center of the studies concerning Papyrus 967 has been Johan Lust at the Katholieke Universiteit Leuven. Lust has devoted the majority of his life to Septuagint studies, with a particular emphasis upon the book of Ezekiel. Lust has published many articles pertaining to the problem of Papyrus 967 and its relevance for the text of Ezekiel. In order to fully understand and appreciate Lust's thesis we shall devote considerable attention to examining the primary article Lust has written.

Lust's article, 'Ezekiel 36–40 in the Oldest Greek Manuscript', serves as the fundamental presentation of his views concerning Papyrus 967. Lust begins his article by arguing against the hypothesis held by Filson and Wevers, mainly the occurrence of *parablepsis* caused by *homoioteleuton*. Lust lists the following arguments against this view:

1. A long omission of 1451 letters is very unusual since the longest omission through *parablepsis* in the papyrus appears to be 266 letters.
2. If the omission had been caused by a single *homoioteleuton*, then the next verse should have been 37.1. However, the scribe jumps to 38.1, putting chapter 37 after chapters 38–39.
3. The omission of 36.23c-38 and the transposition of chapter 37 is also attested in the *Codex Wirceburgensis*.[23]

21 Ibid., p. 177.
22 E. J. Revell, 'A Note on Papyrus 967' in *Studia Papylogica* 15 (1976): 136.
23 Johan Lust, 'Ezekiel 36–40 in the Oldest Greek Manuscript', *CBQ* 43 (1981): 520.

110   *Jewish and Christian Scripture as Artifact and Canon*

Lust continues his thesis by noting the unique style and terminology of the actual passage of 36.23c-38. H. St. J. Thackeray had already noted the differences between this passage and the rest of the LXX text, claiming that the LXX was borrowed from another version resembling that of Theodotion. Lust argues that these special features also pertain to the Hebrew text itself. First, there are numerous *hapax legomena* throughout the passage. The pericope in question, according to Lust, has the character of an anthology because most of the expressions are found elsewhere in Ezekiel. Several examples of this situation will suffice.

Verse 28 includes the longer form of the personal pronoun אָנֹכִי whereas everywhere else in the book it includes the shorter form אֲנִי. Lust notes how this passage is especially reliant upon the work of Jeremiah. Verse 28 reads '. . . the land which I gave to your fathers'. This is a favorite expression in the book of Jeremiah. The closest parallel within Ezekiel is 37.25.[24] The rare adjective חָרֵב is used in Ezekiel 36.35, 38. It is also attested in Jeremiah 33.10, 12. In the view of Lust, this signifies the late redactional nature of both this passage in Ezekiel and that of Deutero-Jeremiah. There are also numerous other peculiarities such as the occurrence of the plural of טֻמְאָה in verses 25 and 29. Elsewhere in Ezekiel (22.15; 24.13; 36.27; 39.24) the term is rendered in the singular. Lust concludes, 'The redactor probably tried too hard to be faithful to Ezekiel's style, knowing that the prophet often used plural forms when rendering abstract notions but overlooking the fact that he never did so in this context.'[25]

Next, Lust observes a series of expressions, which show a literary connection between 36.23c-38 and some other pluses of the MT absent from both the LXX and the *Vetus Latina*. First, in 34.31 the MT has אָדָם אַתֶּם 'you are men', in addition to 'you are my sheep, the sheep of my pasture'. The addition, 'you are men', is absent from both the LXX and the *Vetus Latina Codex Sangallensis*. This is quite similar to the phrase כְּצֹאן אָדָם 'like a flock of men'. Second, the notion of increase, expressed by רָבָה in 36.29, 30, and 37, is also found in 36.10-11 and 37.26 in the MT. In both cases the LXX and the *Vetus Latina* have shorter forms. Finally, Ezek. 34.13 is much longer in the MT than in the LXX and *Vetus Latina*. The pluses appear to introduce vv. 25 and 239 in chapter 36. Lust concludes that Ezekiel 26.23c-38 is probably a late redactional addition to the MT.[26]

The final argument proposed by Lust for the originality of Papyrus 967 concerns the ordering of the chapters 36–40 and the literary link between chapters 36 and 37. According to Lust, Ezekiel 36.23c-38 is an anthology

---

24   Ibid., p. 522.
25   Ibid., p. 523.
26   Ibid., pp. 524–25.

of expressions, which are found elsewhere in Ezekiel and Jeremiah. Furthermore, the omission of the passage in Papyrus 967 signifies that the passage was composed as a link between chapters 36 and 37. If the passage had been within Papyrus 967 it would have been followed by chapters 38–39 according to the ordering of the MS. The passage would have not suited the literary context. None of these in 36.23c-38 prepares for the material in chapters 38–39. Lust concludes:

> This leads us to the conclusion that the original LXX was probably based on a Hebrew text where chapter 36 was followed by chapters 38–39 and then by chapter 37. In this ordering of the book there was no place for 36.23c-38. The pericope was composed for another, probably later, Hebrew text with a different order. This Hebrew text became the accepted MT. In a revision of the LXX, the Greek version was adapted to the new Hebrew text. This required a special translation of 36.23c-38, since this section had not yet been taken up in the earlier version. This explains why this passage betrays the hand of a translator different from the ones responsible for the other chapters. The revision in question is most likely attributable to the so-called Asiatic school.[27]

Most of the other pertinent literature by Lust dealing with the problem simply reiterates the argument espoused in his 1981 article.[28] In fact it can be said that all of Lust's publications with regard to the omission of Ezek. 36.23c-38 are restatements of this earlier article. Therefore we shall now seek to observe some of the primary critiques of his thesis.

One of the most important critiques of Lust's hypothesis has been in the work of Daniel I. Block. In his commentary on Ezekiel, Block offers seven factors which caution against Lust's thesis.[29] First, the appearance of the recognition formula within the oracle rather than at the end is not uncommon in Ezekiel (28.22; 35.12; 37.13; 38.23; 39.28). Second, the unique style of the passage does not require one to find a different author from the rest of the book. The change in style may simply be a literary strategy in order to give emphasis to the subject matter.

Third, one must realize that the LXX evidence is not conclusive. Block notes how this omission is only preserved in one Greek manuscript and an obscure Latin text. An original reading would have surely been preserved among a variety of textual witnesses and versions.[30] Block states, 'In any case, those responsible for the transmission of the LXX recognized the

---

27   Ibid., p. 528.

28   See especially Johan Lust, 'Major Divergences between the LXX and MT in Ezekiel', in *The Earliest Text of the Hebrew Bible: The Relationship between the Masoretic Text and the Hebrew Base of the Septuagint Reconsidered*, ed. Adrian Schenker (Atlanta: SBL, 2003).

29   Daniel I. Block, *The Book of Ezekiel Chapters 25–48* (NICOT; Grand Rapids: Eerdmans, 1998), pp. 340–42.

30   See Appendices II and III.

gap and filled it in with a reading that bears remarkable resemblance to Theodotion's text-form.'[31]

Fourth, Block claims that Lust's proposal runs counter to the evidence of recent form-critical scholarship. Lust disregards v. 23c as a secondary correction even though this recognition formula is quite evident in other passages within Ezekiel (5.13; 6.13; 12.15; 30.8; 33.29; 34.27; 38.16; 39.28).

Fifth, if one assumes Lust's hypothesis to be correct the remaining section of verses 16-23b appears to be fragmentary. By removing vv. 23c-38 the text is left with a two-part pronouncement which makes little sense by itself. Most of Ezekiel's restoration oracles average twenty-seven verses. Without the inclusion of 23c-38 the remaining oracle consists of only eight verses with little thematic development.

Sixth, Block notes how Lust's reconstruction of the LXX is extremely speculative. Block states:

> Indeed, one could argue with equal if not greater force that the growth of apocalypticism in the late intertestamental period stimulated the rearrangement of oracles in this text-form, so that the resurrection of the dead is seen as the final eschatological event prior to the reestablishment of a spiritual Israel, rather than simply a metaphor for the restoration of the nation from exile.[32]

This sentiment is echoed in Moshe Greenberg's commentary in which he argues that a reconstruction of a Hebrew *Vorlage* on the basis of the LXX is a highly subjective task.[33]

Finally, Block views Lust's understanding of Ezek. 36.23c-38 functioning as an editorial bridge between 36.16-23b and chapter 37 as unconvincing. Block argues that the ties between vv. 23c-32 and 16-23b present a sound case for unitary treatment. The arrangement of 36.23c-38 and chapter 37 follows a typical Ezekielian pattern of raising a subject, only to drop it immediately and then return to it for fuller development in a later oracle.[34] Block concludes, 'Accordingly, the editors of MT intend 37.1-14 as an explication of 36.27. 37.15-28 not only portrays a reversal of 36.16-23 but also expands on 34.23-31.'[35]

Other scholars have also followed Block in arguing against Lust's hypothesis. S. Ohnesorge has argued that it is hard to believe that such a lengthy passage could find itself as an addition to the work in such a late

---

31   Block, *The Book of Ezekiel Chapters 25–48*, p. 340.

32   Ibid., p. 341.

33   Moshe Greenberg, *Ezekiel 1–20: A New Translation with Introduction and Commentary* (AB, 22A; Garden City: Doubleday, 1983), pp. 19–20.

34   Block, *The Book of Ezekiel Chapters 25–48*, p. 342.

35   Ibid., p. 342.

stage within the history of the book.[36] In a recent article, Michaël N. van der Meer has also called Lust's view into question.[37] Van der Meer has argued that from a linguistic and literary-critical standpoint there is no reason to regard the passage missing from Papyrus 967 as being a later addition to the text of Ezekiel. Van der Meer adopts his methodology from that of Mark Rooker who regards the language of the book of Ezekiel as a transitional stage between early, pre-exilic biblical Hebrew and that of late, post-exilic Hebrew.[38] By utilizing Rooker's criteria of linguistic contrast and distribution, Van der Meer seeks to assess the diachronical questions regarding the textual problem of Ezek. 36.23c-38. He presents seven unique cases in order to argue his thesis.

First, van der Meer points out the problem between the presence of the longer and shorter form of the first person pronoun. Van der Meer notes that both forms are used interchangeably throughout early biblical writings. The author claims:

> The linguistic variation would have been a strong argument in favor of the secondary character of Ezekiel 36.23b-38, had the longer form been the dominant one in Ezekiel, and the shorter the sole exception attested in Ezekiel 36.28. The reverse, however, is the case, which would rather suggest that this passage is older than the remainder of the book.[39]

Second, van der Meer analyzes the alleged late biblical Hebrew expression וְעָשִׂיתִי אֵת אֲשֶׁר. While the relative pronoun שׁ is a product of late biblical Hebrew, van der Meer argues that the construction used in Ezek. 36.27 with אֵת אֲשֶׁר as introduction to an object clause is common both in Ezekiel and early biblical compositions.[40]

Next, van der Meer turns his attention to phrases that are atypical of Ezekiel but characteristic of the book of Jeremiah. The author examines the word מַעֲלָל which occurs only once in the book of Ezekiel (Ezek. 36.17), while the feminine word עֲלִילָה occurs frequently. The situation is reversed in Jeremiah with the form מַעֲלָל occuring at least 17 times. Van der Meer concludes that the lexeme cannot hold any weight for being characteristic of Deuteronomic phraseology. The phrase in Ezek. 36.31

---

36 S. Ohnesorge, *Jahwe gestalt Sein Volk Neu: Zur Sicht der Zukunft Israels nac Ez 11,14–21; 20,1–44; 36, 16–38; 37, 1–14.15-28* (FB, 64; Wurzburg: Echter, 1991), pp. 207–82.

37 M. N. van der Meer, 'A New Spirit in an Old Corpus? Text-critical, Literary-critical and Linguistic Observations regarding Ezekiel 36.16-36', in *The New Things: Eschatology in Old Testament Prophecy. Festschrift for Henk Leene* (Maastricht: Amsterdamse Cahiers voor Exegese van de Bijbel en zijn Tradities, 2002), pp. 147–58.

38 Mark F. Rooker, *Biblical Hebrew in Transition: The Language of the Book of Ezekiel* (Sheffield: JSOT Press, 1990), pp. 55–64.

39 Van der Meer, 'A New Spirit in an Old Corpus?', p. 153.

40 Ibid., p. 153.

therefore has no literary-critical value *contra* Lust. Van der Meer concludes:

> The absence of the passage in the earliest recoverable stage of the transmission of the Greek version may be due to the loss of a folio. Textual and literary criticism do not overlap in this case... Inter-textual relations with the Deuteronomistic sections of the book of Jeremiah do not necessarily point to a literary dependence of the passage in Ezekiel from these deutero-jeremianic strata, but can also be explained *vice-versa* or alternatively as relatively independent formulations of expectations in the time of the exile. The eschatological ideas expressed in Ezekiel 36.23-38 need therefore not be dated to a late post-exilic or even Maccabean period, but fit the exilic or early post-exilic period.[41]

Recently, Lust has responded to these criticisms, particularly to the issues raised by Block.[42] First, Lust addresses Block's first objection concerning the recognition formula. Although Lust agrees with Block that the formula can and does occur within the oracle at times in Ezekiel, Lust argues that it still does not build a clear case for *parablepsis*.

Next, Lust argues against the possibility that the length of omission and the theological content preclude a scribal lapse. Lust states that the accidental loss of a leaf or more does not take into account the different order of the chapters in Papyrus 967 and *codex Wirceburgensis*. The author states, *contra* Block, that the Latin codex is not an obscure text, yet he fails to explain how this is so.

The possibility of Ezek. 36.23b-38 being original leaves the preceding passage (Ezek. 36.16-23) lacking coherence according to Block. Lust argues that although the passage is indeed short it may still gather explanation through the following oracles announcing the battle against Gog. Lust continues by countering Block's claim that 36.23b-38 does not function as a bridge to the surrounding material. Lust states, 'Once the editorial character of the section is admitted, to a large extent on the basis of an objective philological argumentation, it is perfectly reasonable to recognize a bridge function in this composition.'[43]

Lust's view will continue to produce healthy debate among scholars as to the origin of the text. However, if one accepts Lust's proposal, does that actually signify an original text for the MT or simply a detailed indication of the history of the LXX? It is to this matter that we now turn.

---

41   Ibid., pp. 157–58.
42   Johan Lust, 'Textual Criticism of the Old and New Testaments: Stepbrothers?' in *New Testament Textual Criticism and Exegesis: Festschrift J. Delobel* (Leuven: Leuven University Press, 2002), pp. 15–31.
43   Lust, 'Textual Criticism of the Old and New Testaments', p. 30.

IV.

Earlier in our discussion we mentioned how Zimmerli argued that the existence of Papyrus 967 had little bearing on the textual history of the Hebrew Bible. There is no doubt that the papyrus poses a textual problem. The omission as an act of *parablepsis* is neither convincing nor feasible. The same may be said of the possibility of a leaf or page being lost. Even the most irresponsible scribe would never have let such a thing happen. Yet one must ask, if Lust is granted these propositions, does it really carry significance for the textual history of the Hebrew Bible? It is at this junction in our thought that Zimmerli appears to be correct. Papyrus 967 appears to be a problem for the textual history of the LXX, not the textual history of the Hebrew Bible. Indeed, Papyrus 967 has posed numerous problems for the textual reconstruction of the LXX as noted by Ziegler.[44] He saw the text as pre-Hexaplaric and representing the earliest form of the LXX. However, one must then venture into the broader ocean of debate concerning the relationship of the LXX with the MT. Zimmerli states:

> Now the text-critical examination led to the conclusion that the whole passage v. 23b-38 seems to be missing in the old textual witness Papyrus 967. Thus the question arises whether v. 23b is not the beginning of a section which was still absent from the Hebrew original of Papyrus 967 and which therefore represents a later component of the book of Ezekiel... There is still the fact that the section which ends with v. 23b gives, on its own, a fragmentary impression. The real material exposition of Yahweh's proving that his name is holy is missing from it. There is the additional fact that the end of the section vv. 22–32 comes back to the beginning (v. 32a = v. 22a). A similar framework was found already in 20.1-31, so it is not unique. This might advise against breaking up vv. 22–32 and instead regarding it as an original unit. The possible absence of the passage from Papyrus 967 and the peculiar character of the translation of it would then be a problem from the history of the LXX, but not of MT.[45]

Second, a detailed syntactical comparison of the MT with the LXX yields favorable results for the originality of the MT. A comparison of the ancient versions also produces a verdict in favor of the MT over Papyrus 967. There are simply no other manuscripts other than the papyrus and the *Codex Wirceburgensis* which testify to another reading of the text. To

---

44   Joseph Ziegler, 'Die Bedeutung des Chester Beatty-Scheide Papyrus 967 fur die Textuberlieferung der ezechiel-Septuaginta', *ZAW* 61 (1945–48): 76–94.

45   Zimmerli, *A Commentary on the Book of the Prophet Ezekiel: Chapters 25–48*, p. 245. See also the original German edition W. Zimmerli, *Ezechiel 2. Teilband, Ezechiel 25–48* (BKAT 13/2; Neukirchen-Vluyn: Neukirchener, 1969), pp. 870–71, 873.

adopt such a reading and emendation of the MT would be unprecedented in the science of textual criticism. The evidence is simply not there to warrant the adoption of an earlier original text within Papyrus 967.

Finally the problem of Papyrus 967 is best explained as a problem of internal transmission within the Greek. The importance of the papyrus is not so much in its relevance to the MT but its relation to Septuagint studies. Indeed much more work must be done and the constant desire to discover more manuscripts is forever in our hopes, but the present facts rule the day. To argue for the plausibility of Papyrus 967 on literary grounds is to mix textual and literary criticism into one unit of investigation. The admonition of Natalio Fernández Marcos is particularly relevant for our case: 'If these phenomena, or some of them occurred in the period of literary growth of the biblical book before its final edition was concluded, they have to be analysed by using methods of literary criticism but not the criteria of text criticism.'[46]

Conclusion

This paper has attempted to examine the various theories concerning Papyrus 967 and its use for establishing the original text of Ezekiel. Particular attention has been given to the work of Johan Lust and his theory that Papyrus 967 represents an original text earlier than what we have within the MT. I have especially alluded to the work of Daniel I. Block to serve as a foil for Lust's view. Ultimately, I have concluded that no one can know for sure at the present time what text is the basis for Papyrus 967 or if indeed there ever was one. I have argued along with Zimmerli's proposal that Papyrus 967 is ultimately an issue for the complicated development of the LXX rather than the MT. This proposition seems best given the strong external evidence of the ancient versions, including the LXX itself, in favor of the MT reading of Ezekiel 36.23b-38. The omission within Papyrus 967 appears to be a problem of internal transmission within the Greek as well as a link within the vast and complicated textual history of the Septuagint itself.

---

46 Natalio Fernández Marcos, *The Septuagint in Context: Introduction to the Greek Versions of the Bible* (Leiden: Brill Publishing, 2001), 82.

A FRAGMENTARY PSALTER FROM KARANIS AND ITS CONTEXT*

Gregg Schwendner

Pic's p 312

When the Archive of Aurelius Isidorus (P.Cair.Isid.) was published in 1960, its contents seemed able to tell 'us nothing about his religious inclinations at a time of extreme crisis in the religious thought of Egypt and the Empire'.[1] This appraisal changed with the publication of P.Col.VII 171, a petition by Isidorus in the year 324 AD recording how two Christians, a deacon and a monk, came to his aid during an altercation near his home in Karanis.[2] Only a few of the papyri of this archive were excavated;[3] most

Columbia

---

*   See Appendix for map and figures relating to this chapter.

1   P.Cair.Isid., 17. References to editions of ostraca and papyri are made according to the *Checklist of Editions of Greek, Latin, Demotic, and Coptic Papyri, Ostraca, and Tablets* at http://scriptorium.lib.duke.edu/papyrus/texts/clist.html. For literary papyri, the reader is referred to the LDAB (Leuven Database of Ancient Books) at http://www.trismegistos.org/ldab/. I also provide Mertens-Pack numbers for classical literature, and Van Haelst's numbers for Christian texts (J. Van Haelst, *Catalogue des papyrus littéraires juifs et chrétiens* [Paris: Publications de la sorbonne, 1976]). Reference is also made to mich.apis, that is the *Advanced Papyrological Information System*, at http://www.columbia.edu/cu/lweb/projects/digital/apis/search/. Locations excavated at Karanis (Kom Aushim) and items found there are designated by their excavation label number, which refers to the volume and section of the Record of Objects e.g.: 28 C87K B refers to Volume 1928 of the Record of Objects, the section covering excavation unit C87K (the courtyard of house C87), item B.

I read this paper at the SBL in 2005 (Philadelphia) in the 'Papyrology and Early Christian Backgrounds' section, thanks to D. G. Martinez. Thanks also to D. Rathbone, who read an early version of it, and to P. J. Parsons and M. W. Haslam for discussing some details of the script with me by email. Thanks especially to Prof. T. Gagos of the University of Michigan for permission to publish this papyrus, and to D. Wilburn and T. Szymanski for their help in obtaining digital photographs of it. This paper draws on research I did during a Tytus summer fellowship in 2003. I wish to thank Prof. G. Cohen, P. van Minnen, and the Dept. of Classics at the University of Cincinnati and the staff of the Burnam Classical Library for this support.

2   E. A. Judge, 'The Earliest Use of Monachos for ›Monk‹ (*P. Coll. Youtie* 77) and the Origins of Monasticism', *JAC* 20 (1977): 72–89; *New Docs*: 1 (1981) 124 ff.

3   The exclusion of P.Mich. IX 573 (AD 316), found in house C27, by K. Geens is too arbitrary (p. 10 n. 7), since it assumes that no material belonging to the archive was left behind by the 'unofficial excavators' (http://www.trismegistos.org/arch/archives/pdf/34.pdf). This papyrus was found in house C27, adjacent to dump 242*.

were sold on the antiquities market between 1923 and 1925. We can now learn much more about Aur. Isidorus' neighbors, and those of his father, than was realized 50 years ago by applying the Gagos-van Minnen 'house-to-house' method to the entire neighborhood where the archive was probably found.[4] This method enables us to contextualize literary finds, like the present papyrus (P.Mich. inv.5475.c), more completely by putting all excavated texts together in their archaeological findspots, i.e. by not abstracting literary material from documentary or school texts.[5] These documents were excavated by the University of Michigan and published as O.Mich. I–IV, and P.Mich.VI and VIII before the publication of P. Cair.Isid., and therefore none of the abundant prosopographical correlations between the excavated texts and the Archive were made in the edd. prr. The focus of this paper is a recently identified Christian papyrus excavated at Karanis and how it fits into its documentary context.

Papyrus

This fragment of a codex leaf of LXX Psalms 32–33 is too small to judge the overall dimensions of the page accurately. Between the last line of the recto and the first of the verso, 25–26 lines are lost, so each page could have contained about 40 lines, a written area of about 20 cm in height. The lines are written stichically, i.e. one poetic *stichos* per line, corresponding to the line-divisions in the LXX. This would have produced some lines that were quite long, more than 40 letters, or about 20 cm. If this ratio of *stichoi* per page was observed throughout, the entire Psalter could have taken up c. 125 pages.

Nomina sacra appear once, verso 7 κ̅υ̅ and were used elsewhere as well, to judge from the comparative line lengths: verso 1. κ̅ς̅] 3. κ̅υ̅] 6. κ̅υ̅]. *Vacats* are observable at the line-end of verso 2 and 3.

The possible textual variants are the omission of διάψαλμα at the beginning of Ps. 33.12. The papyrus supports maintaining the same verse as one stichos, rather than dividing it into two.

---

4 I infer that the archive was found in a dump such as 242*, rather than in a house, since dumps preserved papyri much better than living-contexts, where they tended to become badly mutilated.

For the bibliography, see P. van Minnen, 'House-to-House Enquiries: An Interdisciplinary Approach to Roman Karanis', *ZPE* 100 (1994): 237–49; G. W. Schwendner, 'Literature and Literacy at Roman Karanis: Maps of Reading' in J. Frösén, T. Purola and E. Salmenkivi, eds, *Proceedings of the 24th International Congress of Papyrology, Helsinki 1st–7th August 2004* (Commentationes Humanarum Litterarum, 122.1; Helsinki: Societas Scientarum Fennica, 2007), pp. 991–1006, and http://www.umich.edu/~kelseydb/Exhibits/Karanis83/ KaranisExcavation/Bib2.html#Full (1997).

5 I have concentrated for the most part on the textual data from the site for practical reasons and because of the limits of my own expertise.

The hand is an early form of the Biblical Majuscule.[6] The uniformity and boxlike form of the letter-sizes, the absence of serifs, the angularity of *alpha*, and the bilinearity of *ypsilon* are typical of this style of uncial writing. There is also a modest, if inconsistent, contrast between thick and thin strokes, as in the thin left and thick right sides of *alpha* and its thin crossbar, the thin loop of *phi*, in contrast to the thick hasta, and in any curved letter, where the shape of the pen made the stroke thinner when running horizontally and thicker vertically, *epsilon* and *beta* being the clearest examples. A similar effect is achieved by the descender of *xi*.

Several features show the scribe to be inexperienced, not fully able to control the pen to produce the required letter shapes elegantly or consistently: e.g. the oval, somewhat squashed *theta* and *omicron*, and the lack of uniformity in the size of the *omicron*; the way letters do not always sit squarely, but tilt forward (*lambda*) or backwards (*beta*). One might also look at the lack of uniformity in thick/thin contrasting strokes, especially in *alpha*. The letters are written slowly and are distinct from one another. The overall effect is a highly legible, if not calligraphic, script. The third-century date seems to support Cavallo's theory of the development of the biblical majuscule script.

In general, the letters are square, and there is little or no overlap between letters *Pi* is box-like; its horizontal extends only a little. The horizontal of *eta* descends slightly from left to right. Angular letters are *alpha*, *delta*, *kappa*, *lambda*. The apex of *alpha*, *delta*, and *lambda* projects to varying degrees. *Epsilon* and *sigma* are round; *omicron* and *theta* are oval. *Psi* and *phi*, and *ypsilon* extend below or above the line less dramatically than is typical in this style. The right loop of *phi* is wedge shaped.

Only a few early examples of this style of writing can be provided with a *terminus ante quem*. These are: P.Ryl. I 16 (before 255–56 AD), P.Oxy. 661 (second-century document on back, date assigned palaeographically), P. Oxy. 20 (second-century document on back, date assigned palaeographically), and NT P[64] ± P[67],[7] reused in the binding of a third-century codex of Philo.[8]

The date of the Karanis Psalter is constrained by the apparent use of apostrophe to separate two stops (verso 6) ελατ'τ[ωθησονται (see note),

---

6   A good recent collection of early examples is given in P. W. Comfort, *Encountering the* ✓ *Manuscripts* (Nashville: Boardman and Holman, 2006), pp. 110–13. The classic work on this script is G. Cavallo, *Ricerce sulla Maiuscola Biblica* (Firenze: Le Monnier, 1967).

7   Whether or not P4 was a part of the same codex is controversial. P. W. Comfort, 'New Reconstructions and Identifications of New Testament Papyri', *NovT* 41, Fasc. 3 (July 1999): 214–30, argues in favor; see also P. M. Head, 'The Date of the Magdalen Papyrus of Matthew (P.Magd. 17 = P64): A Response to C.P. Thiede', *TynBul* 46 (1995): 251–85.

8   *Quis Rerum Divinarum Heres Sit; De Sacrificiis Abelis et Caini, MMAF* 9.2 (1893): 151–21 (LDAB 3541, Mertens-Pack 1345, Van Haelst 0695). On the date, see E. G. Turner, *The Typology of the Early Codex* (Philadelphia: University of Pennsylvania Press, 1977), p. 113.

which would be unusual before the third century. Palaeographically, it resembles other examples assigned to the third century rather than the fourth. Compare e.g. P.Oxy. XXVIII 2498.[9] Its immediate archaeological context favors a date early in the third century, and would not exclude one in the late second century, as we shall see. Hurtado lists 21 other papyri of the Psalms from the second–third centuries.[10]

This edition is collated against the text of A. Rahlfs, *Psalmi cum Odis*[3] (Septuaginta: Vetus Testamentum Graecum v. 10, Göttingen 1979).

LXX: Psalms 32–33 (33–34)

RECTO: ↓ PSALMS 32.11-18 (frr. 1–2)   P.MICH. INV. 5475.B (Cairo)
fr.1 4.6 cm × 3 cm   *Record of Objects*: 1928 C87 K item A
fr.2 4 cm × 3 cm   third century AD

— — —

	[η δε βουλη του κ̄ῡ ει]ς τ̣[ον αιωνα μενει]	
r° 2	[λογισμοι τη]ς κα[ρδιας αυτου εις γενεαν και γενεαν]	32.11
	[μακαριον το] εθνος ο[υ εστιν κ̄ς̄ ο θ̄ς̄ αυτου]	32.12
r° 4	[λαος ον εξελ]εξατο ε[ις κληρονομιαν εαυτω]	
	[εξ ουρανου ε]πεβλεψ[εν ο κ̄ς̄]	32.13
r° 6	[ειδεν τους υιο]υ̣ς των [ανθρωπων]	
	[εξ ετοιμου] κατοικ[ητριου αυτου]	32.14
r° 8	[επεβλεψεν επι παντας τους κατοικουντας την γην]	
	[ο π]λασα[ς κατα μονας τας καρδιας αυτων]	32.15
r° 10	[ο σ]υνει[ω]ν̣ [εις παντα τα εργα αυτων]	
	[ου] σωζε[τ]α̣[ι βασιλευς δια πολλην δυναμιν]	32.16
r° 12	[κα]ι γιγα[ς ου σωθησεται εν πληθει ισχυος αυτου]	
	[ψε]υδης [ι]π̣[πος εις σωτηριαν]	32.17
r° 14	[εν] δε πληθ[ει δυναμεως αυτου ου σωθησεται]	
	[ιδ]ο̣υ οι ο̣[φθαλμοι κ̄ῡ επι τους φοβουμενους αυτον]	32.18

— — —

Verso → fr. 1 only

PSALM 33.9-13

— — —

	[γευσασθε και ιδετε οτι χρηστος ο κ(υριο)]ς̣[	33.9
v° 2	[μακαριος ανηρ ο̣ς ελπιζει επ αυτ]ο̣ν *(vac.)* [	
	[φοβηθητε τον κ̄ῡ οι αγιοι αυ]του *(vac.)* [	33.10
v° 4	[οτι ουκ εστιν υστερημα τοις] φοβου[μενοις αυτον]	
	[πλουσιοι επτωχευσαν και ε]πειν̣ασαν	33.11

---

9   Hesiod, *Ehoiai*. The greatest similarity is in its overall appearance, its square letters, angular letters (except kappa, the arms of which are not angular, and alpha, which has a loop rather than an angular left half).

10   L. Hurtado, *The Earliest Christian Artifacts* (Grand Rapids, MI and Cambridge: Eerdmans, 2006), pp. 213–14, nos. 41–62, where the present papyrus is listed as no. 51.

v° 6   [οι δε εκζητουυντες τον κ̄ν̄ ο]υκ ελατ᾽τ[ωθησονται
             παντος αγαθου]
         [δευτε τεκνα ακουσατε μου] φοβον κ̄[ῡ διδαξω υμας]   33.12
v° 8   [τις εστιν ανθρωπος ο θε]λων ζωην   33.13

— — —

NOTES

R° 5   ε]πεβλεψ[εν the papyrus after *psi* is stripped.

R° 6   παντος has perhaps been omitted; in any case, the paradosis (πάντας τοὺς υἱους τῶν ἀνθρώπων) is too long for the space available in lacuna.

R° 7   κατοικ[ητριου The fiber on which the initial kappa is written is skewed to the left on the photo.

R° 10   [ο σ]υνει[ω]ν read συνιων with B U corr.. Most MSS. read συνιεις.

R° 14   πληθ[ει After *pi* are indistinct traces consistent with ληθ[

V° 1   κ(υριο)]ς only traces consistent with the bottom of sigma remain on the papyrus, but the use of the abbreviated form of the *nomen sacrum* better explains the spacing of lines 1–3. The last letter of V° 1 *sigma* should be more or less above the last letter of V° 2 *nu*.

V° 6   ελατ᾽τ[ωθησονται From the photograph, there appears to be an apostrophe between two stops, which is common only from 200 AD onwards; cf. F. Gignac, *A Grammar of the Greek Papyri of the Roman and Byzantine Periods*, vol. I, *Phonology* I (Testi e documenti per lo studio dell'antichità, 55; Milan), pp. 161–64; and E. G. Turner, *Greek Manuscripts of the Ancient World* (BICS Supplement 46; London: Institute of Classical studies, 2nd edn, 1987), pp. 11 and 108. This needs to be confirmed on the original. The two *taus* seem to be spaced so as to accommodate the putative apostrophe, but uniformity being the signal failing of this scribe, this cannot be a conclusive argument.

V° 7   κ̄[ῡ The stroke above the kappa is just visible, partly hidden beneath a fold in the papyrus.

[δευτε τεκνα ακουσατε μου] φοβον κ̄[ῡ διδαξω υμας] Most MSS. divide this verse into two *stichi*, and this is colometry used by Rahlfs; Sinaiticus, the Sahidic Coptic Version, Rahlf's Western text family (R', 32 ff.), and Alexandrian family (A', pp. 70–71).

The papyrus omits διαψαλμα, to judge from the spacing. This verse (11. b) is one of the longest in the Psalm; the scribe of P.Bodmer IX writes the παντος αγαθου δι[αψαλμα above the line to accommodate its length. For the omission of this term in the manuscript tradition, see A. Pietersma, *Two Manuscripts of the Greek Psalter in the Chester Beatty Library, Dublin* (Analecta Biblica, 77; Rome: Editrice Pontificio Istituto biblica, 1973), p. 39.

Context[11]

This house (C87) produced some of the earliest dated texts from this sector of the site, all of which were found, dumped rather than stored, in the courtyard of a very small house. All have the same excavation label: 1928 C87 K *item* A.

1 Aug./Sept. 207 AD, a slave registration (P.Mich. IX 546 revised as *SB* V 7563, mich.apis 2472);

2 Before 212 AD, a declaration of a Roman soldier's property (P. Mich. IX 542, mich.apis 2467)

3 2 July, 237 AD, a petition complaining of the assignment of liturgies (P.Mich. IX 529 revised as *SB* XII 10797, mich.apis 2469 and 2470)

4 253–56 AD, a list of pack animals (*SB* XXIV 15884, mich.apis 2479)

5 265–66 AD, a receipt for delivery in kind (*SB* XXIV 15878, mich. apis 2476)

6 271–72[12] official correspondence (? *SB* XXII 15777, mich.apis 2477)

7 II–III AD an uncertain document (*SB* XXIV 15889, mich.apis 2475)

8 III AD an account (*SB* XXII, 15771, mich.apis 2478).

A note of caution is obligatory here. Beside the published texts from Karanis one must bear in mind the very many unpublished (difficult, fragmentary) texts whose eventual publication could change the apparent certainty of the list above.

In addition to the published documents, two identified Greek literary fragments must be taken into account:

10 Demosthenes, *In Aristocratem* (C87 K item A), assigned to the second century palaeographically.[13]

11 Callimachus *Aetia* book 1 (C87 K item A), second–third AD, assigned palaeographically.

There are at least four additional fragments that appear to be literary, or subliterary, found in the same location: structure C87 K. All appear to be written in second–third AD hands.

Literary texts dated palaeographically to the second and third centuries are not uncommon in the northeast sector of the *kôm*, where documents

---

11 This section is derived from my study of the published texts, *A Reader's Guide to Karanis*, in prep.

12 217–76 AD ed.pr., mich.apis; refined by A. Martin, 'P.Mich. inv. 5478a et le préfet d' Égypte Statilius', *Latomus* 59 (2000): 399–402, accepted by *HGV*. (Heidelberger Gesamtverzeichnis der griechischen Papyrusurkunden Ägypten: http://www.rzuser.uni-heidelberg.de/~gv0/Einfuehrung.html.)

13 E. Mullett Husselman, 'Two Literary Papyri from Karanis. I. Isocrates, *Pros Demonikon* 33–34. II. Demosthenes, *Kat' Aristokratous* 166–72', *TAPA* 76 (1945): 120–25; Mertens-Pack 0316, LDAB 655, P.Mich. inv. 5472 (Record of Objects 1928 C87 K *item* B) + 5475a (upper left). This fragment (5475a) was not connected to the inv.no. 5472 at the time of its publcation.

are more typically dated to the third or fourth centuries. To take the most proximate example, a copy of Hesiod, *Works and Days*[14] dated in the ed. pr. to the first or second centuries AD was found in house C55 (see Figure 15). A cache of ostraca was also found in this house that can almost all be related prosopographically to the Aur. Isidorus archive.[15] A hoard of coins from the reigns of Aurelian (270–75 AD) and Vaballathus (270–72 AD) was also found.[16] In another house in the same small insula C87, C54, one text, dated to 299 AD was found.[17] From the surrounding structures, and the northeast sector of *kôm* altogether at this level, the majority of datable texts can be connected to the *floruit* of Aur. Isidorus, c.290–324.

Other examples of literary papyri found in this part of Karanis among documentary texts with third–fourth century dates are:[18]

1   c. 100 AD:[19] Apion, or Apollonius Sophistes, *Homeric Lexicon* (C65*),[20] LDAB 295;
2   I–II AD: *Alexander Romance* (C63),[21] LDAB 3862;
3   I–II AD: Isocrates, *Ad Demonicum* (242*),[22] LDAB 2477;
4   II AD: Homer, *Iliad* 2 (C63),[23]
5   II–III AD: Homer, *Iliad* (230),[24] LDAB 1816;

---

14   LDAB 1178, Mertens-Pack 0489.2; M. L.West, 'Three Papyri of Hesiod', *BASP* 3 (1966): 65–8.

15   O. Mich. I 602, 603 (prosopographical links with *P.Cair.Isid.*), 604, 605, 662, a school exercise 'Palmyrenes', 502, 302 AD, 606 (naming, int.al., Ptolemaios son of Sabinus, who occurs again in 490, 301 AD, 607, 608, 609, 610).

16   R. A. Haatvedt and E. E. Peterson, *Coins from Karanis: The University of Michigan Excavations 1924–1935* (Ann Arbor: Kelsey Museum of Archaeology, 1964), Hoard 8.

17   O.Mich. I 469 (O.Mich. inv. 9061), (19)27 C54 D *item* D.

18   For specific arguments about the layers and their dating according to the excavated texts from this section of the site, see G. W. Schwendner (note 4 above), pp. 991–1006. For the above list, see pp. 1003–4.

19   M. Haslam, 'The Homer Lexicon of Apollonius Sophista: II. Identity and Transmission', *CP* 89 (1994): 112 n. 15, assigns it (cogently) to the 'middle of the first century, or somewhat later'. Renner, ed.pr., dates for the second century.

20   C65* brought to light several ostraca from the archive of Manes son of Maron (see W. H. M. Liesker and K. A. Worp, 'Datings in Third Century Michigan Ostraca', *ZPE* 88 [1991]: 185–86), which dates to the mid- to late third century: O.Mich. I 160, 369, 379, and 458.

21   C63 is a large, official building; published dated/datable documents range from 182 AD (O. Neugebauer and H.Van Hoesen, *Greek Horoscopes* no. 182) through the third century AD.

22   242* is a dump below house 242 (see Schwendner, above n. 4, pp. 994–5); dated/ datable documents have been published from 215–216 (*SB* XXII 15784) to 311 (O.Mich. I 522).

23   G. W. Schwendner, *Literary and Non-Literary Papyri from the University of Michigan Collection* (diss., Mich. 1988), no. 2, 4–8. Part of this text was found in 219*, a dump located in the street outside the main door of C63; a third fragment has been identified in the Aberdeen collection. See Schwendner (above n. 4), p. 997.

24   No other texts have been published from house 230.

6   III AD: Homer, *Odyssey* (C68),[25] LDAB 1981.

Old books in Greek continued in use during the third and fourth centuries at Karanis, but new ones are rare in the third and lacking altogether. Literary hands are dated with stylistic, not historical, accuracy and it may be that what appeared to be second AD hands set only in the context of other book hands may be re-dated seen in the light of their documentary contexts. It would help if we had some accurate notion of how long a book on papyrus was likely to remain in use.

Here we have only a few guideposts. Sheets of papyrus were often re-used for unrelated documents or other texts, usually on the back. When both sides are datable, although generally the texts are within the same generation,[26] the upper limit for re-use is about 100 years. Literary texts with dated documents on the back, such as P.Ryl. I 16 and P.Ryl. II 236 (dated 256 AD) can be dated within 25–100 years of one another. Turner put the case for an upper limit of 100 years, Cavallo 220–25.[27]

The decline in new-book production/ownership in Karanis coincides with the abolition of the position of village scribe, or *komogrammateus*, in the mid-third century.[28] The village scribe, or at least his clerks,[29] were probably the local book copyists, and may also have been schoolteachers. Without paid professional scribes in the village, new books in Greek became scarcer in the third century, then disappeared altogether during the fourth.[30]

Based on the published dated documents, the Karanis *Psalms* codex, or at least one damaged page from it, would seem to have been deposited between the reigns of Caracalla and Aurelian, that is, between 207 and 272 AD. The precision of these dates is of course misleading, and a vaguer, more humanistic frame of reference would better reflect the nature of the evidence: during the *floruit* of Isidorus' father, Ptolemaios (mentioned in

---

25   C68 has palaeographically datable texts from the first or second century (O.Mich. II 963, 814, III 1002) to as late as 289 AD (O.Mich. III 1060, with F. Reiter, 'Vorschläge zu Lesung und Deutung einiger Transportbescheinigungen', *ZPE* 134 (2001): 204).

26   E. G. Turner, 'Recto and Verso', *JEA* 40 (1954): 102–6, esp. p. 106 nn. 3–4. Cf. *PSI* VIII 921.

27   E. G. Turner, 'Writing Material for Businessmen', *BASP* 15 (1978): 167–9; G. Cavallo (see above, n. 6).

28   The last attestation of this office is in 245 AD. R. S. Bagnall, *Reading Papyri, Writing Ancient History* (London and New York: Routledge, 1995), p. 50; J. D. Thomas, 'The Introduction of the Dekaprotoi and Comarchs into Egypt in the Third Century', *ZPE* 19 (1975): 111–19.

29   The village scribe was sometimes hardly able to write himself, as in the famous case of Petaus: H. C. Youtie, '*Pétaus, fils de Pétaus, ou le scribe qui ne savait pas écrire*', *CE* 41 (1966): 127–43 = *Scriptiunculae* I (Amsterdam), 25–33.

30   R. S. Bagnall, *Egypt in Late Antiquity* (Princeton: Princeton University Press, 1993), p. 316, links the decline in literary texts in documentary assemblages to the movement of wealthy landowners off the land and into the metropolis.

texts between 267 and 283 AD, certainly dead by 298 AD), or his paternal grandfather, Pankratios, rather than during the time of Isidorus himself. If the texts were collected and discarded at the same time, which may be so, it might be connected to the uncertain period between 271 AD, when the name of Vaballathus, Zenobia's son, starts to appear on coins and in regnal formulae on texts, until June 272 AD, when Roman sovereignty over Egypt was re-established.[31] This is reflected by one of the datable published texts from the neighboring structure, C67: P.Bingen 113 (272– 73), a very interesting, but fragmentary petition from a newly recruited legionary at the time of Aurelian's Palmyrene campaigns. See also *SB* XXII 1577 (no. 6 in the documents from above C87 above), and O.Mich. I 662[32] (house C55), a school text spelling out the word *Palmyrenes*.

Why a Psalter, rather than, say, one of the Gospels? The writing of the Karanis Psalter is very legible, and this, in combination with its stichic format, would have made it suitable for recitations or as an exemplar. Psalmody played a key role in Christian worship amongst monks in the fourth century,[33] and no doubt had a part in lay worship as well. No churches have ever been identified in Karanis, although a possible candidate was briefly described by Hogarth.[34]

We know too that the Psalms played a role in early Christian education. Four leaves of a papyrus notebook written in Cribiore's 'Zero-grade' hand (i.e. someone just learning to write) has copied verses from Psalm 32.[35] Furthermore, we can infer that there was a classroom somewhere nearby house C87 from the following: the literary finds in houses C87 and C55 discussed above (just across a narrow lane from one another); the school exercises found in house C55, and wax tablets in house C67,[36] sharing an adjoining wall to the east of C87. This sort of clustering of items associated with education is unusual in Karanis. Two other locations show a similar pattern: B224[37] and possibly C63, a house that played some role in the village government, similar to the probable *komogrammateion*, house 5006.

31   A. Watson, *Aurelian and the Third Century* (New York: Routledge, 1999), pp. 67 ff., *CAH* XII.2, 514 ff.

32   R. Cribiore, *Writing, Teachers, and Students in Graeco-Roman Egypt* (American Studies in Papyrology, 36; Atlanta: Scholars Press, 1996), cat. no. 142.

33   L. Dysinger, *Psalmody and Prayer in the Writings of Evagrius Ponticus* (Oxford: Oxford University Press, 2005).

34   'Low down on the northern slope, we made a trial in February, and found well-built houses, but apparently of very late period. One was adorned with extremely rude frescoes of Coptic saints. No papyrus rewarded our efforts ....' *P.Fayum Towns*, p. 28.

35   Cribiore no. 388 and 403 (above, n. 32); H. Marrou, *A History of Education in Antiquity* (Madison: University of Wisconsin Press, 1982), p. 331, and the sources there cited.

36   Kelsey Museum acc. no. 6282, 6278; see Schwendner (above, n. 4), 1005, map. 6 no. 3.

37   A. Loftus, 'A New Fragment of the Theramenes Papyrus (P. Mich. 5796b)', *ZPE* 133 (2000): 11–20.

The only other Christian text excavated at Karanis is a fragmentary leaf from a codex containing Job 30.21-30 in Coptic.[38] Dated conservatively by its editor to the IV/V AD, it has been re-dated to c. 300 AD because of its context, since nothing from the area where it was found dates to later than 325.[39] Even the earlier date would make this the latest literary text excavated at Karanis.

Some Christian artifacts were also found at the site: wooden pendant crosses, a wall painting, *dipinti* on amphorae, one lamp inscription, and some African red slipware with Christian imagery. The wooden crosses[40] are of uncertain date: accession no. 4846, 25–339 D *item* H (no texts); no. 7561, 28–165*A *item* I;[41] no. 7562, 28-C42 J *item* KI;[42] no. 7564, 28–109 F**item* M; no. 7566, 28-B131 *item* S. As noted, two of these crosses can be tenuously linked to dated texts, but one must be careful not to overstate the value of such a correlation. There is no real stratigraphy for the Karanis material, so one cannot distinguish between layers of deposition.[43] Discarded items found together can be dated 70 years apart (C87 K item A, see above) or more. There is little evidence for dating the houses above dumps like 165*. The few instances of published texts from such houses date from mid–late fourth.[44] This gives us a general impression of when dumps such as 165* were sealed by new houses, but not more than that. Similarly, the loose correlation of text and object from the same findspot gives us only an impression as to the object's date, but one that cannot be confirmed.

The 'Christian symbol' on the wall of C45 B looks like an ankh-cross

38   G. M. Browne, *Michigan Coptic Texts* 2 (*Pap.Castr* VII, 1979), P.Mich. inv. 5421, House 28-B168 L *item* B.

39   P. van Minnen 'The roots of Egyptian Christianity', *APF* 40 (1994): 72.

40   Kelsey Museum acc. no. 7561: see H. Maguire, E. Maguire and M. Duncan-Flowers, *Art and Holy Powers in the Early Christian House* (Illinois Byzantine Studies, 2; Urbana: University of Illinois Press, 1989), no. 94 p. 169. An assemblage of Christian objects, including wooden pendant crosses, are illustrated in E. Gazda, *Karanis: An Egyptian Town in Roman Times* (Ann Arbor: University of Michigan Press, 1983), fig. 75.

41   See Maguire et al. (above n. 40), pl. 94, with the date fourth–fifth century. Because O.Mich. I 531 (undated) is a receipt bearing his name, the date range for this dump can be correlated with the Archive of Ouenaphris (Gonaphris), dating from 299–339 AD.

42   There is one published text, O.Mich. I 506 (29 Jan., 303 AD).

43   For an example of the stratigraphy of a dump where ostraca were found, see J. Bingen, 'Dumping of Ostraca at Mons Claudianus', in D. M. Bailey, *Archaeological Research in Roman Egypt: The Proceedings of the Seventeenth Classical Colloquium of the Department of Greek and Roman Antiquities*, British Museum, *held on 1–4 December, 1993* (Journal of Roman Archaeology Supplement, 19; Ann Arbor: University of Michigan Press, 1996), pp. 29–38.

44   House 102: L. C. Youtie, 'A Sale of Wheat in Advance: P.Mich. Inv. 3036', *ZPE* 24 (1977): 140–42 = *SB* XIV 12109, 377 AD; house 113, texts from which date between 299 (O. Mich. I 470) and 346 AD (O.Mich. I 199).

(crux ansata),[45] the inference being that Christians once lived in or used this house. Many amphorae found at Karanis are reported by Pollard to have a shoulder dipinto 'χμγ'.[46] One terracotta lamp bears the inscription: εἷς θεὸς ὁ βοηθῶν 'there is one God who helps'.[47]

The most impressive Christian finds from Karanis are the African Red Slipware dishes, a cache of which was found in house C53[48] and in various rooms of C42,[49] and elsewhere as well. Dated by Johnson to 3–4 AD, in keeping with dated finds from the area, they have recently been re-dated to c. 500 AD by N. Pollard, more in keeping with the current chronology of the ARS types involved.[50] Without careful attention to stratigraphy, singularly missing from Michigan excavation, it cannot be excluded that C53 and C42 were re-used during the fifth century.

inventory of identifiable people

A Prosopography of Possibly Christian Names from Excavated Karanis

More than 20 years ago, R. S. Bagnall tried to quantify the rate of Christian conversion over time by identifying Christian names in lists of tax payers starting with P.Cair.Isid. 9 (309 AD) with 122 legible names.[51] Of these, two are

A. Isidorus

45 E. Mullett Husselman, *The Topography and Architecture of Karanis, Egypt* (Ann Arbor: University of Michigan Press, 1979), pl. 25. On the dubious relationship between the ankh-cross and the staurogram, see Hurtado, pp. 143–44 (n. 10 above).

46 N. Pollard, 'The Chronology and Economic Condition of Late Roman Karanis: An Archaeological Reassessment', *JARCE* 35 (1998): 155.

47 L. Shier, *Terracotta Lamps from Karanis, Egypt* (Kelsey Museum Studies in Archaeology no. 3; Ann Arbor: University of Michigan Press, 1978) cat. 284, p. 109 (Kelsey Museum accession no. 22439, a surface find). The drawing (pl. 4) incorrectly shows an upside-down omega. The final *nu* seems to have been incised in three unconnected strokes. Thanks to Prof. Terry Wilfong for sending a digital photograph of this lamp, and his help deciphering the final letter. This leaves the question of the possibly Christian iconography of frog lamps, of which a number were found at Karanis.

48 B. Johnson, *Pottery from Roman Karanis* (Kelsey Museum Studies in Archaeology no. 7; Ann Arbor: University of Michigan Press, 1981) for C53 K: cat. nos. 234, 235, 239, 240, 245. Cat no. 239 = Kelsey Accession 2.0024, illustrated in plate 60 in Maguire et al. (above n. 40), dated there to the fifth century; cat. 245 = Kelsey accession 7167, plate 61, ibidem, with the date 'sixth century'.

There is one published text from C53: *SB* XXII 15841, written for indiction 14. The editor suggests 340 or 355 AD as suitable dates. The receipt is the same type and hand as the 'Sons of Ptollas/Toulla' archive from dump 158* (see n. 83 below for a discussion of its possible date).

49 B. Johnson (see above n. 48), cat. 232, 247, 249. One dated text has been published from C42, see above n. 42.

50 Pollard (see above, n. 46) 152–53. For the findspots one must refer to B. Johnson, *Pottery from Karanis* (Ann Arbor: University of Michigan Press, 1981).

51 R. S. Bagnall, 'Religious Conversion and Onomastic Change in Early Byzantine Egypt', *BASP* 19 (1982): 105–24; *Egypt in Late Antiquity* (Princeton: Princeton University Press, 1993), p. 201; using names as a heuristic device for determining conversion remains

possibly Christian, although one of the two he readily conceded was problematic, a rate then of 1.6 percent or 0.8 percent. Bagnall's results have remained very influential, and it is therefore worth examining these and other possibly Christian names from excavated Karanis prosopographically.

One of the two names mentioned by Bagnall as possibly Christian in P. Cair.Isid. 9 must be eliminated from consideration: Apollos, son of Apollonius.[52] Although Apollos is a hypocorastic form of a pagan theophoric (Apollodorus, e.g.), it was also the name of the Egyptian Apostle, an Alexandrian Jew mentioned in Acts 18, and a common name in Byzantine Egypt.[53] It was also in use in Roman Karanis: three distinct persons of that name are recorded in the Karanis Tax Rolls of 171/72, and 172/73 AD.[54] The name continued to be used in the third and fourth centuries; there is no way to distinguish whether this Apollos is a family name or Christian.

Five individuals named Paul (Paulos)[55] occur in texts excavated at Karanis that can be linked to the Archive of Aurelius Isiodorus; two should be linked to the generations following, and two have no firm date.

1   **Paulos**, son of Isidoros (O.Mich. II 850, house C403; O.Mich. III 1049, house/granary C123; O.Mich. I 347, house 5095; O.Mich. I 585, house 5008)[56] occurs in several texts from the Archive.[57] In one text, his son Isidoros son of Paulos appears (P.Cair.Isid. 61.12, 323 AD). There is no way to know if this is the same Paulos who reports in 10.210, or who writes for Isidorus, son of Ptolemaios (the owner of the archive) in 78.20 (324 AD) and for his wife in 77.30 (320 AD).

---

controversial: see E. Wipszycka's response, 'La valeur de l'onomastique pour l'histoire de la christianisation de l'Egypte. A propos d'une étude de R. S. Bagnall', *ZPE* 62 (1986): 173–81; G. Horsley, 'Name Change as an Indication of Religious Conversion in Antiquity', *Numen* 34 (1987): 1–17, and *New Docs.* 8, p. 211, with Bagnall's reply in 'Conversion and Onomastics: A Reply', *ZPE* 69 (1987): 243–50, and further discussion in *Reading Papyri, Writing History*, pp. 85–89.

52   Apollos, son of Apollonios, occurs outside P.Cair.Isid. in O.Mich. II.851.5 and O. Mich. I 614. A second Apollos, son of B[is listed in *SB* XXII 15893; a third in O.Mich. I 610 (son of Pankrates), O.Mich. I 575; a fourth in O.Mich. I 101 (son of Apollo).

53   There are over 80 occurrences in J. Diethart, *Prosopographia Arsinoitica*, vol .1. S VI– VIII (Wien: Kommission bei Verlag Brüder Hollinek, 1981), s.v.

54   Apollos son of Aksall( ) (Askalas?). P.Mich. IV 223.1901, **224**.2220; the son of Mysthes and Thaseis, **223**.226, 695, 1080 etc. (see P.Mich. IV. 2, p. 153); the son of Ptolemais, **224**.1600.

55   There are over 100 instances of the name in Diethart (see above, n. 53); it also occurs in Coptic Text (Hasitzka s.v., n. 67 below).

56   Paul (O.Mich. II 941), without a patronymic, is listed with a certain Amoules and Abaous, both of whom recur in O.Mich. I 347 together with Paulos son of Isidorus. It would be a fair inference, therefore, that Paul in O.Mich. II 941 was the son of Isidorus. Patronyms are frequently omitted in lists of liturgists at Karanis.

57   P.Cair.Isid. 9.234 etc.

2   Paulos, son of Senas (O.Mich. I 106)[58] can be linked to P.Cair.Isid.
    by prosopography, since Ptollas son of Sarapion (a rather prom-
    inent farmer) occurs in both (320 AD).[59] In fact, of the 20 names with
    patronyms listed on this ostracon, 15 also are found in P.Cair.Isid.[60]
3   Paulos, father of Chaeremon (O.Mich. I 594.5 house B103, III–IV
    AD) is listed along with (*int.al*) Ptolemaios, son of Panesates,[61] who
    occurs again in P.Cair.Isid. 10.127 and 125.15. An obvious
    interpretation would be that Paulos belongs to the preceding
    generation, and that his son, Chaeremon, is a contemporary of
    Isidorus. But since this Charemon is only tethered in an indirect way
    to the time of P.Cair.Isid., the point cannot be pressed very far.
4   Paulos son of ? (Probos?) O.Mich. III 1090.8 (house C86);[62]
5   Paulos (O.Mich. I 1020) signs a delivery of chaff on behalf of Ptollas
    son of Apollonios, who is Aurelius Ptollas from P.Cair.Isid. 9.121,
    232 etc. This may be the same as the Paulos who signs in P.Cair.Isid.
    78.20 (324 AD), since writing ability was restricted even amongst the
    liturgical class in Karanis at this time.

One further Paulos, son of Alexandros (P.Col. VII 134.21) can be
connected to the *floruit* of Aur. Isidorus, to judge from the prosopographical connections between this text and his Archive.[63]

Of a further four occurrences of the name, three certainly, and one
probably, date after Aur. Isiodorus' death (we last hear from him in 324
AD):

7   Paulos the overseer (son of NN) (house 5006, *SB* XXII 15830)
    receives instructions from the land owner, Elias, who occurs in P.
    Cair.Isid. and in documents from the subsequent generation (see
    below).
8   Paulos son of Patermouthis (*SB* XXII 15602), dated in the edition to
    c. 334–5 CE.

---

58   CA12 + CS20, inv. 9085, E-10 SW, Map 12. A third Paul, son of Tanis, is also named
on another ostracon, O.Mich. I 592 (with BL VII) a list of names, one of whom is also named
in the P.Cair.Isid. 9.140, 10.4, 14.118, 17.147 etc.: Sotas son of Apollonius. Tanis should
probably be corrected to Senas.
59   O.Mich. I 106.8, P.Cair.Isid. 9.121 and 232 etc.
60   Besides Ptollas, these are: Patas son of Apynchis, Serenos son of Ptolemaios,
Pankratios son of Ptolemaios, Palemon son of Ptolemaios, Aunes son of Poleion, Kastor son
of Neas, Paesis son of Ptolemaios, Paianis son of Aphelis, Sarapion son of Makrinos, Neilos
son of Kasianos, Heron son of Ammonas, Heras son of Kastor, and Ptoleamios son of
Melas.
61   *BL* 8, 290.
62   Ouenaphris, son of Aion is in the same list (O.Mich. III 1090.5), who is listed again in
O.Mich. I 342.6 with Aion son of Papeeis (O.Mich. I 342.1) who occurs in P.Cair.Isid. 6.315,
9.68 and 179, 10.127, 12.9, 17.15, 22.9; likewise Atisis, son of Païanos.
63   P.Col. VII 134 introduction.

9   Paulos (son of NN) *SB* XIV 12109 (house 102) dated in the ed.pr. to 377 CE.
10   Paulos son of Ptolemaios (O.Mich. I 624.3–4, house 4006). In line two of the same text, Horion son of Valerius (Oualerios) is listed, who occurs also in P.Col. VII 167.7 (373 AD).

This leaves only a few occurrences of the name that have no relatively firm date.

11   Paulos the arche(phodos?) T. Gagos – P. J. Sijpestein, 'Towards an Explanation of the Typology of the So-Called "Orders to Arrest"', *BASP* 33 (1996): 91–92 (michigan.apis 2482); on the back is an order for arrest, both dated by the edd. to the IV CE.
12   Aur. Paulos (*SB* VI 9241, III AD, dump 158*) agrees that he will restore the house of Aur. Melas whenever he returns to Karanis. Melas is too common a name in Karanis to be of much help.[64]

The distribution of the name Paulos in Roman Karanis shows a stark contrast. Before 212 AD, there are no occurrences, as against 12 in the third–fourth centuries. Six of these can be linked to the Archive of Aurelius Isidorus. Of the remaining six, the four that can be dated at all come later than 324 AD. Two cannot be given a firm date, and so it may be earlier or later than P.Cair.Isid. The only Paulos who could prima facie be linked to the *floruit* of Aur. Isidorus' father, Ptolemaios (who is named in documents between 267 and 290) is no. 3, Paulos the father of Chaeremon, although even this cannot be said to be more than a bare possibility.

Subsequent to the *Constitutio Antoniniana* (212 AD), adding a Roman element to one's name became a regular practice, by, e.g., adding 'Aurelios' as a praenomen. 'Paulos' would have added a Roman veneer to the sons of an Isidorus ('gift of Isis'), or a Ptolemaios. But note that in Rome and Carthage, the name Paulos was a common name in pagan, Jewish and Christian burial contexts.[65] Most telling is Dionysios of Alexandria, quoted by Eusebius,[66] who attests the popularity of the names Peter and Paul among children of believers in Egypt during the third century. It was also a common name in Coptic.[67] So the situation is ambiguous. At a time when Christian persecutions must have been a vivid

---

64   There is an Aurelius Melas in P.Cair.Isid. 97.5 (308 AD), and another in P.Col. VII 153.55 and 166.7 (both 345–46 AD).
65   I. Kajanto, *Onomastic Studies in the Early Christian Inscriptions of Rome and Carthage* (Acta Instituti Romani Finlandiae II.3; Rome, 1963), pp. 91, 96.
66   Euseb. 7.25.13, cited by M. Choat, *Belief and Cult in the Fourth Century Papyri* (Turnhout: Brepols, 2006), p. 51.
67   M. Hasitzka, *Namen in koptischen dokumentarischen Texten* (Papyrussammlung der Österreichischen Nationalbibliothek 2007: http://www.onb.ac.at/files/kopt_namen.pdf), s.v.

memory, this ambiguity would have given parents (or catachumens adopting new names) some degree of comfort.

Elias, son of Melas, occurs in two texts: O.Mich. I 598,[68] an undated list of names found in C35[69] (along with 22 other texts), and in a list of names P.Cair.Isid. 20, dated later than 314 AD. In the latter, the regnal year is doubtfully read ('year 5'), and the editors suggest, on the basis of prosopography, that most of the names are 'at least one generation removed' from those named between the years 300–315 AD. A later date is supported prosopographically.[70] The name is an unusual one for this date, and is unambiguously Christian,[71] as Elias 'Elijah' does not seem to have been used by Jews.[72]

The most secure Christian names at Karanis occur in a complaint by Aur. Isidorus that he was assaulted by several other villagers in 324 AD until being rescued by a deacon named Antoninos and a monk named Isak.[73] We do not know whether this monk and deacon lived in the village, but it is at least instructive to know the names of two men who were indisputably Christians in Karanis, and to compare them with their namesakes in the village.

Antoninos is a less common name at Karanis than Antonios, but there are several instances. It is uncommon in Byzantine texts.[74]

1 Antoninos, father of Achillas, Tapaïs and Theonas in P.Cair.Isid. 6.98 etc., 9.64 etc., O.Mich. II 930.2 (313 AD), P.Mich. VI 376.32.
2 The son of Antoninos O.Mich. III 933.2.
3 The son of NN, O.Mich. I 419.5 (298 AD), 444.5 (293 AD).
4 A fourth, Antoninos son of Isidorus O.Mich. II 1006.7 (270 AD), is probably too early to be our deacon.

---

68 With *BL* 7 290.
69 Granary and Dovecote, E-10 SW (see Figure 15).
70 Atisis, son of Abok, who occurs again in the Karanis papyri in the collection of Columbia University (P.Col. VII 130.36) dated to 334–35 AD (these papyri in general belong to the generation after Aur. Isidorus 324–360 AD). The name Elias occurs 6 times in P.Col. VII 188.13 (320 AD), 152.42, 29 (343–44 AD), 158.20, 23, 28, 31 (344 AD), 163.8 (348 AD); P. NYU 5.12, 19, 6.4, 11.8, 99, 108.
71 There are just over 100 instances in Diethart (n. 53 above).
72 Tal Ilan, *Lexicon of Jewish Names in Late Antiquity, Pt.1 Palestine 300 BCE – 200 CE* (Tübingen: Mohr Siebeck, 2002), pp. 5, 63. A DDbDP (s.v. Ηλιας) search yielded 628 hits, only one of which antedates P.Cair.Isid. 20: P.Laur. III 98, III AD Theadelphia. Furthermore, this name does not occur in control texts such as the Josephus *BJ*, or in papyri from Roman Palestine (P.Babatha), nor in texts from Dura-Europos in Syria. It does occur in a few inscriptions: LGPN III.A s.v.: *CIJ* 628, III AD tombstone from Calabria.
73 P.Col. VII 171.14-14 (ed.pr. P.Coll.Youtie II 77), E. A. Judge (see above n. 2). There are just over 40 instances of this name in Diethart (n. 53 above) and it was also common enough in Coptic (see Hasitzka, n. 67 above).
74 No instances in Diethart (n. 53 above) and only two in Coptic texts (see Hasitzka, n. 67 above).

The name Isak occurs in the following decades,[75] between 336 and 342 AD, as the son of Ision: O.Mich. I 206 (house 5016, 336 AD) and O.Mich. I 216 (house 5020, 342 AD, or 326 BL VII).[76] Although Isak may also be considered a Jewish name,[77] the context makes this unlikely. There was only one Jewish family in the second-century tax rolls from Karanis,[78] and no discernible Jewish community in the third–fourth centuries.

One other ostracon[79] was found nearby house C87 which deserves to be mentioned here. It appears to bear a writing exercise, the first five letters of the Greek alphabet in inverse order ΕΔΓΒΑ preceded by the name ΑΝΤΟΝΙ. The lack of a Greek case ending on the name may be an indication that the language of the writer or perhaps the language of writing is Coptic rather than Greek, depending on whether the spelling is taken as intentionally Coptic, or simply bilingual interference. Antonios is a rather common Roman name at Karanis, too common to make any correlation with its later Christian counterpart.

Aurelius Ioannes, who appears in a document from P.Cair.Isid. 114.2, 115.5 (304 and 306 AD), is literate and appears to have been a gymnasiarch. The name could indicate a Jewish origin, despite the apparent incongruity of a Jewish gymnasiarch.[80] But it is also attested as a Christian name in Egypt during the third century.[81]

Two Karanids named John[82] are known from excavated texts. They may or may not be identical, as a patronymic is recorded for only one. Ioannes, father of Hol, occurs in an unequivocally Christian context (*SB* VI 9436 a,

---

75   Isak is a common name in Coptic: Hasitzka 2007, s.v. (n. 67 above).

76   See Bagnall-Lewis' discussion in P.Col. VII p. 69, along with numerous occurrences of the same person.

77   O.Mich. I 206 is *CPJ* III 480.

78   *CPJ* II 460; *The Cambridge History of Judaism* (Cambridge: Cambridge University Press, 1984) vol. I, p. 63.

79   Found in Street CS70, ed.pr. O.Mich. I 659; republished as *SB* XIV 11457; *BL* XI, 213, Cribiore (see above n. 32), 186–187, no. 57, with pl. IV.

80   Aurelius Joannes is included in *CPJ* III 474 a–b, and by C. Haas, *Late Antique Alexandria* (Baltimore and London: Johns Hopkins University, 1997), p. 121. At a somewhat later date, we know that Jews belonging to the curial or bouleutic class could be obliged to undertake civic duties even if this clashed with religious beliefs: cf. *Theodosian Codex* 16.8.2, *The Cambridge History of Judaism*, p. 159). T. Rajak, *The Jewish Dialogue with Greece and Rome* (Leiden: Brill, 2002), p. 369, notes but accepts the singularity of a Jewish gymnasiarch, as does the ed.pr. See Choat's discussion of the name (n. 66 above), p. 91.

81   Eusebius *HE* 7.25.14, quoting Dionysius of Alexandria.

82   A very common name in the Byzantine period, with 240 instances in Diethart (n. 53 above).

158*):[83] a staurogram and the symbol χμγ stand at the top of the document.

A third Ioannes is known from a tax list (P.Mich. VI 379) as Ἰωάννης ὁ πρεσβύτερος 'John the elder'. In the fourth century, the term *presbyteros* is generally taken to imply a church-related position, rather than, say, a village-elder.[84] This text is dated by the editors palaeographically to the mid-fourth century, and by the late P. J. Sijpesteijn to the fifth.[85] In the context of the other textual finds from this dump (158*), the fourth-century date is preferable (see n. 83).

So much, I think, is enough to substantiate, or at least illuminate, Bagnall's claim for a small but quantifiable Christian community at Karanis during the time of Aur. Isidorus and after. But it still leaves us a little in the dark as to the possible third-century users of the Karanis Psalter. We must also bear in mind that these names represent primarily the liturgical class at Karanis. We have no way of knowing how great the ratio of liturgists : landless peasants might have been, to say nothing of slaves.

Karanis ceases to be a rich source of written evidence within two generations of the last dated text from Aur. Isidorus' archive (6 June, 324). The precipitous decline in the number of datable texts reflects an overall fall in dated texts from the whole nome after 360. Viewed in isolation, the decline of dated texts from Karanis has seemed to indicate a decline in its population, presaging its eventual abandonment sometime in the mid-fifth century.[86] But compared to figures for the entire nome, an alternative interpretation may explain the catastrophic decline in both. Almost all the dated texts from the late third to mid-fourth century Karanis have to do with the liturgical system. They are lists of liturgists, receipts for tax payments in kind, their transportation and delivery. When these sorts of texts are subtracted, very little remains. The decline in dated texts during the reign of Theodosius I (379–395) may seem to indicate a collapse of the liturgical system in rural areas like the Fayyum. Although

83   Dated texts from this sub-A level dump site are from 309 (*SB* 15837 + 838) 312 (P. Mich. XII 652), 341 (*SB* XXII 15845). The only published text from a house in this area dates to 377 (*SB* XIV 12109). One of the receipts (*SB* XXII 15841) was found outside the dump, in house C53, an area from which a large number of texts were found, all dating from the first half of the fourth century. On the question of whether such Christian symbols were ever used in documents before the fifth century, see J. Gascou, P.Sorb. II p. 46, with M. Choat's remarks (n. 66 above), p. 116 n. 524. Given the context of *SB* VI 9436, and the use of Christian symbols at the beginning of the fourth-century P.Kellis IV, Gascou's redating is questionable.

84   Choat (n. 66 above), pp. 57–68.

85   P. J. Sijpesteijn, '*Naulepleon*: A Ghost Word?' *ZPE* 64 (1986): 117.

86   This was the conclusion of the excavators and P. van Minnen, 'Deserted Villages: Two Late Antique Town Sites in Egypt', *BASP* 32 (1995): 41–56. J. G. Keenan's replies in 'Deserted Villages: From the Ancient to the Medieval Fayyūm', *BASP* 40 (2003): 119–39.

numbers of dated texts continued at a constant, if lower, level in and
around metropoleis like Hermopolis and Oxyrhynchus, the numbers of
dated texts remains flat in the Arsinoite throughout the fifth century.

Years	Dated texts from all Egypt	From Arsinoite[87] % of texts from all Egypt		Karanis % of Arsinoite totals	
306–323	702	230	32%	147 (gross)	64%
Constantine I (in Egypt) 324–337	396	111	28%	67	60%
Constantius 337–360	601	231	28%	149[88]	64%
364–75	136	17	12%	9[89]	52%
379–397	121	9	.7%	1[90]	
408–450	228	6	.26%	1[91]	

Magic and Christianity

One magical text was found at Karanis from this area: P.Mich.Koenen
786, a fever amulet edited by Wm. Brahsear, found in the dump over
which house 242 was built (242*).[92] The Fayum was always a malarial
place: large amounts of standing water (the largest being the nearby Birket

87   I have counted as individual texts receipts recorded on single roll, as P.Mich. XII 648.

88   27 texts (18% of the total from Karanis from the reign of Constantine II) have an
uncertain or questionable date. Of these, two have suggested alternate dates from the reign of
Constantine I or before: P.NYU I 2 347–48, 332–33 or 377–78; O.Mich. I 195: 341–42, 307–8,
326–27. *BGU* II 608 342 or mid-fifth AD. Eighteen of these come from an archive of the sons
of Ptollas/Toullas (P.Mich. VI 409–416). All come from a dump below house 158 (designated
158*). One other in the same hand *SB* XXII 15841 = ed.pr. P. J. Sijpesteijn, 'Varia
Papyrologica IV', *ZPE* 108 (1995): 219 was found in house C53, not far from C87, and with
much the same dating profile.

89   P.Col. VII 187 is uncertain.

90   *SB* XXII 15798.

91   P.Haun. III 58.

92   For the location of this dumpsite, see Figure 15. The note in the ed.pr., p. 78 n. 13, is
confused on this point. The 'P' in the excavation label refers to the item no., not a room. The
label 28 242* -P refers to *Karanis Record of Objects 1928 (Season 1928–29)* 102*-242*, B108-
B172, CS23-CS130. The page recording the finds from 242*, including P.Mich.inv. 5302,
explains 242* thus: 'Area between C47 and C65'. Item P, P.Mich.inv. 5302 (the items

al-Qarun) and the hot climate meant mosquitoes were numerous and malaria was endemic, as shown by comparative work on the subject by W. Scheidel.[93] Amulets to help heal those stricken by the fevers that typify this, and other diseases, are numerous. What is interesting about the Karanis fever amulet is that we can connect it to a particular social-historical context. No text from this dump dates later than 325 AD. The charm is written in the same sort of rapid cursive hand that characterizes most of the documentary texts from this part of the site (called *Verschleifung* 'slurred' by papyrologists). The scribe, moreover, knew of the Christian scribal practices (if he was not himself a Christian), since he uses a *nomen sacrum*:

lines 4–7: οὗτοι αἱ δυνα|μεραὶ τοῦ θ̄ῡ καὶ δυναμ<ε>ις τῆς θεραπ<ε>ίας | θεράπευσον Σαραπίωνα ὃν ἔτεκεν Ἀ|λλοῦς ἀπὸ παντὸς ῥιγοπυρέτου τριταίου κτλ.

It is possible that one of the persons named in the charm is known from the Archive: Allous, the mother of Sarapion, is the hypocarastic form of the name Kyrillous. This form of the name is not a common one in the village or in the Fayum generally; indeed, we can only connect it to the formal version Kyrillous because she figures in two documents concerning the division of property inherited from her mother (P.Cair.Isid. 104.4 and 105), the first written on 20 Nov., 296 AD and the second three days later (23 Nov., 296). In Bagnall and Lewis's reconstruction of her life,[94] she was probably born c. 280 AD, and married at a young age (13) to a certain Abous (perhaps the son of Pekysis, as in O.Mich. I 577), producing a son, Antiouros, around 293 AD; a second marriage to a certain Heras (son of NN) produced three children. Altogether, she can be documented between the years 296 and 316 AD. Sarapion, the child the fever charm is meant to protect, is not otherwise known.

What is significant for the history of Christianity in the village is that the scribe uses a *nomen sacrum* θ̄ῡ for God in the sentence: 'These are the potentates of God and the power of healing.' The use of *nomen sacrum* in an otherwise pagan magical text presents us with a small conundrum: does its use indicate Christian belief either on the part of the spell's practitioner or his client (Allous)? Or should we rather say the magician was aware enough of Christian scribal practices to make use of them himself? Or yet, that he merely copied the form of the spell he found in his exemplar, and thought no more about it?

---

registered in the Record of Objects are itemized by letters of the alphabet A-Z, letter plus Roman numeral, A I-Z I, then A II-Z II and so on. Items found in house 242 are recorded in the *Record of Objects 1927*.

93 *Death on the Nile* (Mnemosyne Suppl., 228; Leiden: Brill, 2001), pp. 76–88.
94 P.Col. VII, 4–9.

C. H. Roberts's view that the use of *nomina sacra* in magical texts unequivocally indicated a Christian origin or milieu seems untenable when one examines closely the examples of its use in *PGM*. Some of these refer to particular Egyptian gods, such as Anoubis (*PGM* VII 331), although others are inspecific enough to be taken as references to the one god of Christian theology.[95]

95   P.Yale II 130 = Suppl.Mag. I 84; C.H. Roberts, *Manuscript, Society and Belief in Early Christian Egypt* (Oxford: Oxford University Press, 1979), p. 82, et al. take the *nomen sacrum* to be an indication of Christian origin/milieu. But cf. the use of *nomina sacra* in *PGM* VII (P.Lond. I, P. 83ff.): e.g. 331 φανης μοι κ(υρι)ε Ανουβι; 583 εστιν γαρ δυναμεως ονομα του μεγαλου θ(εο)υ. See Choat (n. 66 above), pp. 123–24 and n. 568.

'HE THAT DWELLETH IN THE HELP OF THE HIGHEST': SEPTUAGINT PSALM 90 AND THE ICONOGRAPHIC PROGRAM ON BYZANTINE ARMBANDS[1]

Thomas J. Kraus

1. *Introduction*

The usual and traditional way of editing a newly discovered archaeological artifact is as follows: the object is described in its entirety, the text preserved on it is critically transcribed and reconstructed, and its socio-historical background is (at least briefly) explained. In case of the presence of images, signs, and/or symbols on an object, these are explained in regard to the text or, vice versa, the text in regard to the images, signs, and/or symbols. Thus, the focus is on the text in the first case and on the non-textual elements in the latter. Based on a profound and individual investigation into both text and images (and signs and symbols), the interaction between textual and iconographic elements in both directions, however, is only rarely taken into account. In addition, the material can equally be of importance for a full explanation of the socio-cultural setting an artifact belongs to. Consequently, this triad of text, iconography (if present at all), and material, together with their interrelation and interaction, can be a major leap forward towards a more in-depth and a more complete understanding of archaeological artifacts.[2]

This is more true the more a text itself becomes an artifact or, in a much narrower sense, when scripture (= text) is presented and treated as an

---

1 Based on a paper delivered during the 'Scripture as Artifact Consultation' in the course of the SBL Annual Meeting in San Diego Scripture (18 Nov. 2007).

2 Recently interest in such interrelations and interactions appears to have grown. Cf., for instance, S. Goldhill and R. Osborne (eds), *Art and Text in Ancient Greek Culture* (Cambridge: Cambridge University Press, 1994); J. Elsner (ed.), *Art and Text in Roman Culture* (Cambridge Studies in New Art History and Criticism; Cambridge: Cambridge University Press, 1996); N. K. Rutter and B. A. Sparkes, *Word and Image in Ancient Greece* (Edinburgh: Edinburgh University Press, 2000); J. P. Small, *The Parallel Worlds of Classical Art and Text* (Cambridge: Cambridge University Press, 2003); E. James, *Art and Text in Byzantine Culture* (Cambridge: Cambridge University Press, 2007); Z. Newby and R. Leader-

artifact. The fragments of a miniature codex may serve as the instance of the use of a manuscript as an artifact:[3] *P.Ant.* I 13,[4] a parchment folio from the fourth century (7.2 × 8.7 cm) with text from the *Acta Pauli et Theclae*, here from the *Acts of Thecla*, is described by its editor, Colin H. Roberts, as a '*de luxe* codex' which manifests extraordinary features as far as its material ('which is thin and translucent to an unusual degree') and script ('in its regularity and delicacy reminiscent of the great biblical codices') are concerned. The 'exceptional quality' of the manuscript raises several questions: why had someone in the fourth century any interest in producing or possessing such an extravagant miniature book? Why did someone want to have a lavishly produced copy of the *Acts of Thecla*? Did someone regard that copy as being more than a book with text alone, as being something very precious and exceptional?[5]

The interaction between material, script and actual text of a manuscript are worthy of being discussed in more detail elsewhere. In this study the even more complex interrelation between iconographical and textual elements on the one and material and design on the other hand will take centre stage. What appears rather theoretical and artificial becomes self-evident with the help of the following test case: the fragments of a Byzantine armband with rests of Greek Psalm 90, figurative or pictorial representations and symbols.

2. The Socio-cultural Context: Objects with Greek (Septuagint) Psalm 90

2.1 Purpose and background of objects with Greek (Septuagint) Psalm 90

The armband belongs to a large group of objects with Greek (Septuagint) Psalm 90 that can be subdivided into several categories. In order to identify and understand the purpose and background of the armband, its context will be briefly sketched.

Newby (eds), *Art and Inscriptions in the Ancient World* (Cambridge: Cambridge University Press, 2007). Further, see, with a focus on private settings, J. Elsner, *Roman Eyes: Visuality and Subjectivity in Art and Text* (Princeton: Princeton University Press, 2007).

   3 Cf. A. M. Hansen et al. (eds), *The Book as Artifact: Text and Border* (Variants, 4; Amsterdam and New York: Rudopi, 2005), although the contributions are mainly dedicated to more modern times and approaches.

   4 Edited by C. H. Roberts, *The Antinoopolis Papyri. Part I* (Graeco-Roman Memoirs, 28; London: Egypt Exploration Society, 1950), pp. 26–28 and plate I.

   5 See, for instance, P.Oxy. I 6 (= *Cambridge Univ. Libr. Add. MS* 4028), another parchment fragment of a miniature codex (6.7 × 7.3 cm) from the fifth century, also with extracts from the *Acts of Thecla*: although material and script are of considerable quality, this copy does not bear comparison with the *de luxe* copy discussed above. Cf. B. P. Grenfell and A. S. Hunt (eds), *The Oxyrhynchus Papyri. Part I* (Graeco-Roman Memoirs, 1; London: Egypt Exploration Society, 1898), pp. 9–10.

Recently, two new papyri with verses from Septuagint-Psalm 90 ($=$ Psalm 91 according to its number in the Masoretic text) were published, both of them – P.Duk.inv. 778[6] and P.Duk.inv. 448[7] – from the papyrus collection of the Duke University and both of them considered as amulets. This verifies (a) that we must reckon with more objects with verses of this psalm coming to light in the future and (b) that in principle, it is quite common to find a biblical psalm serving a magical, here an apotropaic, purpose, above all Psalm 90. It has repeatedly been pointed out that this psalm was outstandingly popular with early Christians,[8] a fact that originates from (a) the specific function it had in Judaism as a 'song against demons' and for believers under pressure (see, for instance, Talmud Yerushalmi yShab 6.2.8b; yEr 10.11.26c)[9] and (b) the peculiar content of the psalm in both its Hebrew and Greek versions.[10] Thus, this psalm was predestined to serve an apotropaic purpose, and by applying it in such a circumstance people hoped to gain divine protection against all kinds of evil powers from the very early state of the transmission of Psalm 90 [91].[11]

Being curious and at the same time fascinated by the various and varied objects preserving words and/or verses of Greek Psalm 90, I dedicated some effort to the accumulation of data on all accessible objects that might provide any evidence of the apotropaic use of the Greek version of this psalm.[12] While I reflected on the method of producing a collective edition of the relevant material, I came across several difficulties, for

---

6   Cf. C. A. La'da and A. Papathomas, 'A Greek Papyrus Amulet from the Duke Collection with Biblical Excerpts', *BASP* 41 (2004): 93–113.

7   Cf. A. Delattre, 'Un extrait du Psaume 90 en copte', *BASP* 43 (2006): 59–61.

8   See, for instance, L. Amundsen, 'Christian Papyri from the Oslo Collection', *SO* 24 (1945): 141–7; R. W. Daniel, 'A Christian Amulet on Papyrus', *VigChr* 37 (1983): 400–4; D. Jordan, ''Αλλο ἑνα παράδειγμα του Ψαλμοῦ 90.1', *Εὐλιμένη* 3 (2002): 201; La'da and Papathomas (see note 6), pp. 107–10.

9   See in detail B. Rebiger, 'Die magische Verwendung von Psalmen im Judentum', in E. Zenger (ed.), *Ritual and Poesie. Formen und Orte religiöser Dichtung im Alten Orient, im Judentum und im Christentum* (HBS, 36, Freiburg: Herder, 2003), pp. 265–81.

10   In due course I intend to address the relationship between the Hebrew of the Masoretic and the Qumran texts and the Greek of the Septuagint in more detail so that it becomes evident whether or not the Septuagint might even have amplified the magical tendencies in Psalm 90 [91].

11   See, for instance, an Aramaic magic bowl from Iraq (Jewish Historical Museum, Belgrade, no. 242/1) with Psalm 91.1[MT] (J. Naveh and S. Shaked, *Amulets and Magic Bowls: Aramaic Incantations of Late Antiquity* [Jerusalem: Magnes Press, 3rd edn, 1998], pp. 185–187 and pl. 27 [Bowl 11] and an amulet from the Cairo Genizah (T-S K 1.127) with a paraphrase of Ps. 91.10[MT] (Naveh and Shaked, *Amulets and Magic Bowls*, pp. 237–8 and pl. 39 [Geniza 7]).

12   See T. J. Kraus, 'Psalm 90 der Septuaginta in apotropäischer Funktion', in J. Frösén, T. Purola and E. Salmenkivi (eds), *Proceedings of the 24th International Congress of Papyrology, Helsinki, 1st-7th of August 2004. Vol. I* (Commentationes Humanarum

instance, (1) that certain objects that do not carry this psalm must also be regarded as they do add to the category and classification the specific Psalm-90-object under discussion belongs to and (2) that these categories and classes must be investigated on their own.

2.2. *The objects in general – a brief overview in categories*

All in all, I have data available of eighty-two objects at the moment, although the database is gradually growing. Twenty-two of them are *papyri* in the wider sense of its meaning[13] with two Coptic ones included.[14] Three other items belong to the so-called '*Bous'-tablets*, which themselves form a group of their own consisting of twelve tablets. These are linked with each other by certain elements and the key for understanding lies in the interaction between the Decan divinity Βωϛ, the Egyptian magical name Βαινχωωωχ (or Βαινχωωχ) and Psalm 90.[15] There are eleven *medallions, other kinds of pendants and icons* that, apart from other iconographical and textual elements, preserve words, phrases or verses of the popular psalm. Six items are *rings or ring bezels*, seven *door lintels* from different buildings (mostly from Syria). Seven others form a group of *miscellaneous epigraphic objects* with an inscription from a *pastophor-ion*[16] of a church in Petra, a long inscription on the door of a Christian tomb on the Crimean peninsula, two inscriptions at a cemetery (one in a burial chamber and another at a cemetery chapel), an inscription of a

---

Litterarum, 122.1; Helsinki: Societas Scientiarum Fennica, 2007), pp. 497–514, and, updated and enlarged, idem, 'Septuaginta-Psalm 90 in apotropäischer Verwendung: Vorüberlegungen für eine kritische Edition und (bisheriges) Datenmaterial', *BN* 125 (2005): 39–72.

13   For the discussion of the papyrological determination of objects as 'papyri', see T. J. Kraus, '"Pergament oder Papyrus?": Anmerkungen zur Signifikanz des Beschreibstoffes bei der Behandlung von Manuskripten', *NTS* 49 (2003): 425–32 and, enlarged, idem, '"Parchment or Papyrus?": Some Remarks about the Significance of Writing Material when Assessing Manuscripts', in idem, *Ad fontes. Original Manuscripts and their Significance for Studying Early Christianity – Selected Essays* (Texts and Editions for New Testament Study, 3; Leiden and Boston: Brill, 2007), pp. 13–25.

14   See notes 6 and 7. There are further Coptic papyri, for instance, a magical handbook with spells, prayers, the Abgar correspondence, the list of seven sleepers of Ephesos and forty martyrs of Sebasta, the beginning of the four Canonical Gospels, and Psalm 90. Cf. W. Pleyte and P. A. A. Boeser, *Manuscripts coptes du Musée d'Antiquités des Pays-Bas à Leide* (Leiden: Brill, 1897), pp. 441–79. How to deal with the growing number of published, categorized *and*, on the Internet, catalogued Coptic manuscripts in respect of an edition with objects with the Greek Psalm 90 will be a methodological issue.

15   For further details see T. J. Kraus, 'Βουϛ, Βαινχωωχ und Septuaginta-Psalm 90? Überlegungen zu den so genannten "Bous"-Amuletten und dem beliebtesten Bibeltext für apotropäische Zwecke', *ZAC* 11 (2008): 479–91.

16   A *pastophorion* is one of the two apartments at the sides of the *bema* or sanctuary, as it is still known in the modern Orthodox Church.

dwelling house in Salamis-Constantia on Cyprus, and two inscriptions on Sarcophagi, both from Midjeleyya in Upper Syria.

Of the total number of eighty-two objects with Septuagint-Psalm 90, twenty-five are still without mention here. These are part of a group of thirty-four *armbands* distinguished by specific features from other armbands (see below); and this is the category the fragmentary armband under discussion belongs to. That is why special attention is paid to the description and analysis of this item and identification and interaction of its textual, pictorial and symbolic elements.

3. A Closer Look at the Armbands with Focus on One Newly Edited in the British Museum

3.1. A descriptive overview

Recently I have edited the fragments of an armband of the British Museum in London (*BM* AF 255 + 289) with the initial verse of Septuagint-Psalm 90.[17] As already mentioned, this artifact belongs to a larger group of thirty-four armbands, probably from the middle of the sixth and the seventh century, which are listed and described in my study in order to contextualize the armband in London.[18] Although the individual items differ from each other in respect of artistic quality, details of the iconographic program employed and textual elements, the overall conception of the group can be defined as follows: 'Members of the group have a thin flat band showing from one ... to eight ... iconographic or inscriptional medallions, with those bearing four medallions...being the most common.'[19] With Gary Vikan's concise description, the most significant and conjunctive features of the armbands are given. The majority of these armbands were found in Egypt and in the region of Syria/Palestine,[20] so that either all of them derived from a common origin or these two geographical groups developed independently and parallel to

17 T. J. Kraus, 'Fragmente eines Amulett-Armbands im *British Museum* (London) mit Septuaginta-Psalm 90 und der Huldigung der Magier', *JAC* 48/49 (2005/2006): 114–27 and plates 2–3.

18 See, above all, Kraus, 'Fragmente eines Amulett-Armbands' (see n. 17), pp. 120–7.

19 G. Vikan, 'Two Byzantine amuletic armbands and the group to which they belong', *The Journal of the Walters Art Gallery* 49/50 (1991/1992): 34 (= idem, *Sacred Images and Sacred Power in Byzantium* [Variorum Collected Studies Series; Aldershot/Burlington: Ashgate Publishing, 2003], article X, p. 34).

20 La'da and Papathomas (see n. 6), p. 107 n. 16, exclude *SB* I 1577–1579 (see J. van Haelst, *Catalogue des papyrus littéraires juifs et chrétiens* [Université de Paris IV Paris-Sorbonne. Série «Papyrologie» 1; Paris: Publications de la Sorbonne, 1976], nos. 189–191) from their appendix of parallel attestation 'as they come from Syria'. For an adequate understanding of the type of armbands under discussion (above all their origin and their use), however, geographical limitations are inappropriate.

each other in two subgroups.[21] In my edition of the armband in the British Museum I propose a common origin of these armbands in Syria/Palestine.

Most of the armbands are made of silver or bronze, but there are also others for which copper, a coppery alloy or just plain iron were used. Depending on their diameter the armbands were worn around the forearm or upper arm. Most of the objects investigated are about 7.5 cm wide so that they could have been put on the forearm just above the wrist, maybe even in pairs or one left and one right. The smaller diameter of two other armbands indicates that their wearers' wrists and forearms must have been slimmer, so that they were possibly meant for children. The diameter of 4 cm of another armband even more obviously proves that it was designed for the slender arm of a child.

The distinctive elements on their bands and their medallions – above all the Rider Saint, 'the evil eye', some magical signs and symbols, and Septuagint-Psalm 90 – denote that the armbands were worn as protective amulets. Only nine of the thirty-four armbands are without any verse of Psalm 90 (mainly 90.1, but occasionally also longer passages); four carry only decorations. The conceptual program of the armbands depends on a pool of textual (e.g., the Εἷς θεός formula, the *trisagion*, and invocations) and iconographic elements (the Annunciation, the birth of Jesus, the homage of the μάγοι, the Holy Trinity, the baptism and crucifixion of Jesus, women at the tomb, the Rider Saint, the Ascension, 'the evil eye', and other less common pictorial scenes). In addition, there are elements that evidently indicate their Christian background, while others are clearly of non-Christian origin (e.g., depiction of Chnubis,[22] 'the evil eye', various magical signs and symbols, maybe also the stern symbol, the ἄφλαστον[23]). Only the investigation into the complete set of armbands forming this specific group allows one to draw methodologically appropriate conclusions and to apply these to the textual and iconographical concept behind these armbands and their function. For details on all the thirty-four items,

---

21   In my study (Kraus, 'Fragmente eines Amulett-Armbands' [see n. 17], p. 116) I favour the first alternative with a preference for Syria/Palestine as provenance. Nonetheless, some of the many diverse elements appear to derive from an Egyptian background, whereas others apparently indicate that the armbands were individually designed and their elements arranged according to the tastes dominant in a specific culture or region.

22   For more information about the lion-headed serpent divinity often used in amulets and on other magical papyri (mainly in *voces magicae*), see R. Kotansky, 'A Silver Phylactery for Pain', *The J. Paul Getty Museum Journal* 11 (1983): 172–3.

23   For the background of the ἄφλαστον cf. L. Casson, *Ships and Seamanship in the Ancient World* (Princeton: Princeton University Press, 1971), images nos. 114, 116, 119–21 etc.; G. Vikan, '"Guided by Land and Sea": Pilgrim Art and Pilgrim Travel in Early Byzantium', in E. Dassmann and K. Thraede (eds), *Tesserae. Festschrift für Josef Engemann* (Jahrbuch für Antike und Christentum, Ergänzungsband 18; Münster: Franz Joseph Dölger-Institut, 1991), p. 90 and pl. 11 f-g (= idem, *Sacred Images and Sacred Power in Byzantium* [see n. 19], article VIII, pp. 90–91).

I refer to the descriptions in my study.[24] Nevertheless, there are also pendants, medals and medallions, pilgrim phials (*ampullae*), gems etc. with similar textual and iconographic elements, which served the same apotropaic purpose as the armbands. Thus, people in those days really believed in such a protection against demonic powers.

3.2. *Focus on British Museum, AF 255 + 289*

Sir August Wollaston Franks, Kustos of the British Musuem, donated more than 3,300 rings to the British Museum in 1897, among them the two fragments AF 255 + 289. Unfortunately, the provenance of these is unknown as, sadly enough, can be said of so many archaeological findings from the end of the nineteenth century. O. M. Dalton catalogued the fragments as parts of rings and with a brief description,[25] but later on the two fragments could be joined together successfully so that it became quickly clear that half of an armband is to be talked about here. Although the bronze armband is heavily oxidized (thus the greenish corrosion of the copper material), the textual and iconographic elements preserved on the medallions and the remains of the band can easily be described and identified: one medallion, with the stylized 'evil eye' on its left and right on the band, reads ο κατοικον εν βοη, the beginning of Greek Psalm 90 written in three lines, thus originally as OKATO I IKONE I HBOH.[26] The other medallion depicts a scene very similar to that shown on the Michigan armbands with a smaller sitting figure on the lap and another figure on the other, the right side. All figures have a nimbus and in the middle between them is a round object at face level.

Of major help to find out more about text, elements and the figure constellation are three other armbands:

(1) An armband kept in a private collection in Munich (inv. 1743) with five medallions which, according to its editor, Gisela Zahlhaas, bear the Annunciation, Psalm 90.1 in three lines († ο κα I τοικο I ν εν), the Rider Saint (see the description of the next armband), and the women at the tomb; the fifth medallion is blank

---

24 Cf. Kraus, 'Fragmente eines Amulett-Armbands' (see n. 17), pp. 120–7.

25 See O. M. Dalton, *Catalogue of Early Christian Antiquities and Objects from the Christian East in the British Museum* (London: Printed by the Order of the Trustees [British Museum], 1901) nos. 157 and 191.

26 Septuagint-Psalm 90.1, according to Rahlfs' Goettingen edition, reads: ὁ κατοικῶν ἐν βοηθείᾳ τοῦ ὑψίστου ἐν σκέπῃ τοῦ θεοῦ τοῦ οὐρανου αὐλισθήσεται – 'He that dwelleth in the help of the Highest, shall sojourn under the shelter of the God of heaven.'

and was meant for closing the armband.[27] The narrow band presents 'the evil eye' in an almost identical way to the armband of the British Museum. Interesting is how some of the figures have crossed their arms, especially the women at the tomb, which almost gives the impression that the women are carrying something. Also the drapery of the clothes is very similar to the presentation of the figures on the armband in the British Museum. Furthermore, it might be debatable if the fourth medallion really shows the Annunciation. There are two figures with nimbus facing each other, one sitting on a chair (throne?) on the left and another on the right. In between them there is a cross at face level and below it seems to be a smaller figure with nimbus. Possibly, this scene is similar to the relevant medallion of the armband in the British Museum and should be treated analogously as the homage of the μάγοι (in front of Maria with the child Jesus).[28]

(2) Mich. 26131 + 26160 (= Bonner 322[29]) kept in the Kelsey Museum of Archaeology of the University of Michigan is made of bronze and was found in Aleppo in Syria. Its diameter of about 7.5 cm indicates that it was worn on the upper arm. The armband consists of a blank medallion in order to close it and three others with text and images on them: one medallion shows a rider on horseback with a spear and a person lying prostrate underneath the horse. Such a depiction was widespread and very popular with people in those days. It is the Rider Saint who fights against evil powers manifested by the lying person. It is not the place here to discuss this context further; however, the names Sisinnos, Solomon (and the magical signet ring he received from the Archangel Michael), and Lilith (as the manifestation of evil) indicated how complex an exact interpretation of the definite background of the Rider Saint might be.[30] Another medallion shows a sitting (female) figure with a smaller one on her lap on the left and a standing figure looking at the first two on the right side. Each of the three has a nimbus and in the middle between them there is a cross. The third medallion has + ο κα | τοικο | ν εν inscribed in three lines. The remnants of the band show stylized

27   Cf. L. Wamser (ed.), *Die Welt von Byzanz – Europas östliches Erbe. Glanz, Krisen und Fortleben einer tausendjährigen Kultur* (Schriftenreihe der archäologischen Staatssammlung, 4; München-Darmstadt: Wissenschaftliche Buchgesellschaft, 2004), p. 326 nos. 626–8.

28   See Kraus, 'Fragmente eines Amulett-Armbands' (see n. 17), p. 119.

29   C. Bonner, *Studies in Magical Amulets Chiefly Graeco-Egyptian* (Ann Arbor and London: University of Michigan Press, 1950), pp. 306–7 (no. 322).

30   For a concise discussion of the various ways in which the Rider Saint could be presented, see J. Engemann, 'Palästinische frühchristliche Pilgerampullen. Erstveröffentlichungen und Berichtigungen', *JAC* 45 (2002): 159–60.

blind eyes, the symbol for 'the evil eye', which can be found so
often on such objects. As usual a circle is inscribed around the text
and the pictorial elements.

(3)   The third armband of major interest, Mich. 26198 (= Bonner
321), is also from the Kelsey Museum of Archaeology.[31] It is made
out of bronze and from Syria, too, and consists of five medallions,
of which one is blank and was destined for closing the armband
(see the previous two armbands). The other four have the Rider
Saint, the same figure constellation as the other Michigan
armband (person with a smaller person on the lap opposed to
another person, nimbus, and in the middle here a stylized star), ο
κα Ι τοικο Ι ν εν βο Ι ηθια in four lines, and women left and right to
a standing figure, all of them, of course, with nimbus, usually
taken as the women at the tomb (but maybe this is the scene of the
raising of Lazarus). Again the band shows the typical form of
blind eyes, i.e., a stylized eye with diagonal lines through it, as a
representation of 'the evil eye' on the band, always close to the
medallions.

A comparison of the first medallion AF 255 with the relevant ones of
other armbands proves that it was a custom to arrange the text as it is
done rather clumsily on the armband in the British Museum. Even 'the
evil eye' as a means of protection against all kinds of evil[32] seems to go
stereotypically with this kind of arrangement. The second medallion with
the three figures also belongs to a typical and programmatic setting: the
drapery (cf. the other three armbands discussed above) reveals the sitting
person as a woman wearing a dress or, at least, a skirt-like gown. So, the
context together with the small figure on the lap suggests that we have
here Mary with the child Jesus sitting on a chair or throne (see the stylized
cross on the armband of the British Museum). In the middle there is the
star (carried out as a cross on Bonner 322; cf. the armband in the private
collection in Munich, inv. 1743; see above) and on the right there is a
figure that appears to be a woman at first glance. Campbell Bonner wrote
'worshipper, apparently female'.[33] This is based on a bosom-like shape at
breast height. However, the drapery and the fact that inscribing in crude
bronze a figure carrying a gift at breast-height may have been too difficult
for accuracy are reasons enough to search for a logical explanation of the
scene: here we have the somewhat awkward picture of a μάγος presenting

---

31   Bonner, *Studies in Magical Amulets* (see n. 29), pp. 306–7 (no. 321).

32   See, for instance, O. Jahn, *Über den Aberglauben des bösen Blicks bei den Alten*
(Berichte über die Verhandlungen der sächsischen Gesellschaft der Wissenschaften.
Philologisch-historische Klasse, 7; Leipzig: S. Hirzel, 1855), pp. 28–110; J. Engemann, 'Zur
Verbreitung magischer Übelabwehr in der nichtchristlichen und christlichen Spätantike',
JbAC 18 (1975): 22–48; Bonner, *Studies in Magical Amulets* (see n. 29), nos. 298–301.

33   Bonner, *Studies in Magical Amulets* (see n. 29), p. 306 (no. 322).

his gift (cf. Mt. 2.1-12). Of course, it was also difficult and probably regarded as redundant to present more than one μάγος. Perhaps it was regarded as sufficient to illustrate just one μάγος that accounts for the other missing ones, no matter how many the inscriber primarily had in mind. One may even wonder whether the artist may have trusted in the Gospel tradition or in some apocryphal text as far as the μάγοι tradition and the number of the μάγοι is concerned. Besides, the star (or cross) between the two adult figures that are looking at each other heavily supports this interpretation (cf. the other three armbands mentioned above). Consequently, this scene is that of the homage of the μάγοι, a scene obviously popular with people who wore such armbands.

Moreover, it seems likely that the armband originally consisted of five medallions if the estimated diameter had been similar to that of the two Michigan and the Munich armbands, i.e., 7.5 cm. The length of the band between the two medallions, however, suggests that the armband in the British Museum might have been more similar to Mich. 26198, so that it originally had four medallions with textual and iconographical elements and one blank medallion needed to close the armband. Nonetheless, it cannot be ruled out that the armband originally comprised only three medallions (with an additional fourth to close the band). But what then about the third missing medallion and the text, image or sign/symbol it might have carried? Of course, any reflection in this respect remains speculative. However, the program of textual and iconographical elements and the similarity with other armbands from this category motivate the idea that one of the missing medallions or the missing one might have carried the Rider Saint who is often inscribed on many different objects in late antiquity and in the Byzantine epoch. Be that as it may, other combinations with the homage of the μάγοι and Greek Psalm 90 are possible, too. Unfortunately, there is no other medallion preserved here in the case of the armband in the British Museum with another incident from the programmatic 'Life of Jesus circle'. Thus, theories about the likelihood of this or that element for the missing medallion(s) remain pure speculation.

All in all, the sequence Septuagint-Psalm 90 and the homage of the μάγοι appears to have been quite popular if not even part of a fixed set of a text-picture program. The armbands in the British Museum, in Munich and the two in the Kelsey Museum of Archaeology at the University of Michigan preserve this sequence. Another armband kept in Berlin[34] also bears witness to this set of text and specific scene. Besides, all five armbands carry the blind eyes ('the evil eye') on their bands and, with the

---

34   Cf. O. Wulff, *Altchristliche Bildwerke und mittelalterliche byzantinische und italienische Bildwerke, Teil I: Altchristliche Bildwerke* (Berlin: Akademische Verlagsgesellschaft, 1909), no. 1109 and pl. LV.

exception of AF 255 + 289, four of them present the Rider Saint on one of their medallions.[35] Although the pool of textual, iconographic and symbolic elements allowed a multitude of individually designed armbands, this program seems to be one of the many possible for designing armbands that served an apotropaic purpose in Byzantine days.

4. Scripture as Artifact – Artifact as Scripture?

Although some of the armbands forming this specific category of objects are rather filigree and represent a piece of art and decoration, most of the others are carried out in a clumsy way. Not too much effort was used to inscribe textual and iconographical elements, especially as far as the four bronze armbands are concerned that have been discussed in more detail above. The armbands, as can be seen by the Rider Saint, 'the evil eye', and the Greek Psalm 90, to mention only the most prominent features, served a specific purpose: to protect their wearers from evil powers that seemed to be omnipresent threats to the people in those days. Aggressive magic (for example, represented by 'the evil eye') made it necessary to apply counter measures, i.e., to ban the devastating effect of 'the evil eye' by a crossed-out depiction of blind eyes that embody 'the evil eye'. In addition, it is obvious that Greek Psalm 90 was perfectly destined to protect a person from all kinds of evil: it summoned the protection of the wearer of an amulet, here of an armband, and that protection came from the 'Highest', from God. The armbands themselves are determined by a kind of 'Life of Jesus chronology' that is manifested in an iconographical program. Therefore, by highlighting only a few scenes from the life of Jesus, the whole Gospel chronology is summoned. Occasional invocations and underlining quotations from the Gospels prove that the overall conception was to bring biblical texts in the form of illustrative scenes together with magical elements, to combine popular images with the 'Life of Jesus chronology', and to provide a network of texts, images and symbols in order to protect the wearers of the amulet. However, it can be doubted that the people who manufactured the armbands and those who wore them cared about such distinctions at all. Probably, all they did was just to think of a most effective way to gain protection. Thus, the artifact 'armband' was worn as a sort of effective expression of protection, maybe in some cases also as a sort of decoration, but always visible to others and always determined by its specific purpose and the manifest belief of its wearer in its necessity and efficacy.

---

35 The armband in Berlin (Wulff 1109; see n. 34), however, is quite different from the other four: it is made of silver and its design is more filigree as its band consists of rhombi-shaped elements and four small medallions in addition to the three ordinary sized ones, not to mention some additional pictorial elements.

PUBLIC AND PRIVATE – SECOND- AND THIRD-CENTURY GOSPEL MANUSCRIPTS[*]

Scott D. Charlesworth

1. *Introduction*

Early gospel MSS were used in two general settings – publicly in corporate worship, and privately by individuals. It will be shown that the majority of *second-century* gospel manuscripts (MSS) can be designated 'public', in the sense that they were intentionally produced to be read aloud by lectors in Christian meetings. Rightly dividing the continuous lines of letters in ancient texts (*scriptio continua*) in order to break through to the underlying meaning was not easy.[1] In a public setting where immediacy was called for, punctuation, lectional aids and various kinds of sense breaks in the text could greatly assist the task of the lector (ἀναγνώστης). This seems to be why such 'reader's aids' are found in most second-century gospel MSS. In contrast, sense breaks, punctuation and lectional aids are not present in many *third-century* gospel MSS. This may be because in private settings where MSS were read by individuals or where 'private' readings for family or friends were conducted, there was more leisurely interaction with the text and the need for reader's aids was less

---

[*] This chapter, which first appeared as 'Public and private – second- and third-century gospel manuscripts', *Buried History* 42 (2006): 25–36, has undergone substantial revision.

[1] On the private use of Christian books see H. Y. Gamble, *Books and Readers in the Early Church: A History of Early Christian Texts* (New Haven: Yale University Press, 1995), pp. 231–7, and on the difficulties of reading *scriptio continua* see ibid., pp. 203–4, 228–30; cf. R. Cribiore, *Writing, Teachers and Students in Graeco-Roman Egypt* (ASP, 36; Atlanta: Scholars Press, 1996), pp. 148–9; and eadem, *Gymnastics of the Mind: Greek Education in Hellenistic and Roman Egypt* (Princeton: Princeton University Press, 2001), pp. 190, 203. B. M. Metzger and B. D. Ehrman (*The Text of the New Testament: Its Transmission, Corruption, and Restoration* [New York: Oxford University Press, 4th edn, 2005], pp. 22–3) are more optimistic in arguing that because texts were read aloud syllable by syllable, *scriptio continua* presented no 'exceptional difficulties'. However, even if differentiation of words was not normally affected by ambiguity, the problem of where clauses began and ended would remain.

pressing. But a more likely explanation is to be found in the different kinds of settings in which gospel MSS were copied/produced.

It will be argued that a correlation can often be found between intended use and the kind of setting in which a MS was copied/produced. Again in general terms, early gospel MSS intended for public use were produced in controlled settings, while MSS intended for private use were copied in casual settings where quality controls over copying/production were lacking (which would go some way towards explaining an absence of reader's aids). That is to say, it is often possible to make a distinction between 'controlled' production for public use and 'uncontrolled' production for private use when it comes to early gospel MSS. However, it is important to recognize that the categories of 'public/controlled' and 'private/uncontrolled' should not be seen as inflexible classifications to be imposed on the evidence. A MS could potentially be used in both public and private settings, or an individual might make or obtain a copy of a 'public' MS for 'private' use or vice versa. Nonetheless, the documentary evidence clearly sustains the notion that early gospel MSS were produced and used in broad 'public/controlled' and 'private/uncontrolled' settings.

2. Scribal Method

2.1. *Text division and lectional aids*

One of the features of Christian MSS in comparison with Ptolemaic and Roman literary texts is the frequent use of sense breaks or text division. The enlargement of the first letter of the first word in a text, new section or clause, the practice of 'leaving spaces between words or more often groups of words', and *ekthesis* or projection into the margin of the first and sometimes second letter of a line following a break in sense or meaning, were all scribal practices borrowed from documentary texts.[2] Spaces were not used in Ptolemaic and Roman literary papyri, and *ekthesis* is generally limited to commentaries and lists of the Roman period.[3] Not of documentary origin are the punctuation and lectional aids (apostrophe, trema or diaeresis marking an initial ϊ or ϋ; rough breathings also marked by ¨ or ʽ) found in early Christian papyri.[4] These also occur in literary papyri, but less commonly or at least not in the same proportions as in

---

2   C. H. Roberts, *Manuscript, Society and Belief in Early Christian Egypt* (Schweich Lectures, 1977; London: Oxford University Press, 1979), pp. 14–18. Enlargement of initial letters also accentuates lines in some school texts written by teachers: see Cribiore, *Writing*, p. 99.

3   See Roberts, *Manuscript*, pp. 16–18, for examples. Cf. E. G. Turner, rev. P. J. Parsons, *Greek Manuscripts of the Ancient World* (BICS.SP, 46; London: Institute of Classical Studies, 2nd edn, 1987), p. 8.

4   Roberts, *Manuscript*, p. 21 and n. 4. The use of accents is random and rare.

some Christian texts.[5] It should also be noted that punctuation, in the form of the medial or high point (·), dicolon (:), diastole (,), and dash (–), can be seen as both lectional aid and sense/text division marker.[6]

Early Christian scribes also seem to have been influenced by Jewish practices.[7] In the Qumran scrolls the Hebrew text was divided into sections by spaces in general accordance with a system called *parashiyyot*, which was later used in the Masoretic Text (MT).[8] A vacant line end corresponds to a major subdivision ('open section' in MT) and a space in the middle of a line to a minor subdivision ('closed section' in MT) within the paragraph.[9] Space division into smaller sense (verse) units occurs in only a few Hebrew biblical MSS because these sense breaks were part of the oral tradition of Torah reading in the synagogues (perhaps dating from the second century BC).[10] But verse divisions are marked in the early Aramaic and Greek translations where they were supplemented according to the syntax and conventions of the translation language itself.[11] On the Greek side, the use of spaces for verse division is attested in a number of Jewish Septuagint (LXX) MSS dated to the first century BC.[12]

The *paragraphos* (a horizontal stroke written below the line at the left margin) was used to mark the change of speaker in Greek dramatic texts, to separate metrical elements in lyric, and was also employed in documents to separate the main text from the *subscriptio* (although rarely elsewhere).[13] According to Johnson, in Greek literary texts the *paragraphos* served as an aid for reading aloud.[14] But again, the degree of Jewish influence on text division in Christian MSS should not be

---

5   The following details are taken from Roberts, *Manuscript*, pp. 21–2.

6   For discussion of the various punctuation and lectional signs see Turner, *Greek Manuscripts*, pp. 8–12; and L. Threatte, *The Grammar of Attic Inscriptions*, vol. I: *Phonology* (Berlin: de Gruyter, 1980), pp. 73–98. For a dated survey of the use of text division markers and punctuation in Jn 13.31–16.33 in NT MSS up to the fourth century see P. Gächter, 'Zur Textabteilung von Evangelienhandschriften', *Bib* 15 (1934): 301–20.

7   For a discussion of the influence on the early codex of Near Eastern scribal habits generally see J. Ashton, 'The persistence, diffusion and interchangeability of scribal habits in the ancient Near East before the codex' (unpubl. PhD diss., University of Sydney, 1999), pp. 166–86.

8   E. Tov, *Textual Criticism of the Hebrew Bible* (Minneapolis: Fortress, 2nd edn, 1992), pp. 210–11; cf. 51–4.

9   E. Tov, *Scribal Practices and Approaches Reflected in the Texts Found in the Judean Desert* (STDJ, 54; Leiden: Brill, 2004), pp. 143–9.

10   Ibid., pp. 135–40, 159–62.

11   Ibid.

12   Ibid., pp. 299–315, esp. 304–5, 311. The point is also used in two texts (p. 311) and enlarged letters in two others (Roberts, *Manuscript*, p. 18 and n. 3).

13   Turner, *Greek Manuscripts*, pp. 8–9.

14   W. A. Johnson, 'The function of the paragraphus in Greek literary prose texts', *ZPE* 100 (1994): 65–8.

underestimated.[15] Although its ultimate derivation may be Greek, the *paragraphos* marks divisions in four early Jewish LXX MSS,[16] and is also found in other Greek and Aramaic texts and in biblical and non-biblical texts written according to Qumran scribal practice.[17] *Paragraphoi* mark text divisions in the Christian MSS P.Beatty 10 (Daniel and Esther), P. Bodmer 24 (Psalms), Pap. W (Freer Minor Prophets), and occasionally in tandem with vacant line ends in P.Beatty 6 (Numbers and Deuteronomy).[18] So it is unlikely that Jewish scribal conventions used in the production of LXX MSS were wholly ignored by Christian scribes.[19]

Should a lack or paucity of text division, punctuation and lectional aids be attributed to the scribe or his exemplar?[20] Turner reached the general conclusion that 'if punctuation was present in the exemplar it was the first scribe's duty to copy it'.[21] In his important work on the literary roll Johnson found reason to agree with this assessment: 'Substantial portions of details like adscript and punctuation seem to be part of what was traditionally copied, part of the paradosis.'[22] 'The scribe attempted to copy the "original" punctuation, that is, the sort of bare-bones punctuation existing before reader intervention', but also incorporated 'corrections or additions as he saw fit'.[23] Lectional aids may also have been part

15 Though used in only a small number of early LXX MSS, *ekthesis* is also attested: 8HevXIIgr, P.Oxy. 54.4443, P.Scheide + P.Beatty 9 (Tov, *Scribal Practices*, p. 161).

16 4QLXXLev[a], P.Fouad inv. 266b, 4QPapLXXLev[b], 8HevXIIgr: ibid., p. 304.

17 Tov, *Textual Criticism*, p. 216; cf. pp. 108–11.

18 Tov, *Scribal Practices*, pp. 305–6.

19 R. A. Kraft, 'The "textual Mechanics" of early Jewish LXX/OG papyri and fragments', in S. McKendrick and O. A. O'Sullivan (eds), *The Bible as Book: The Transmission of the Greek Text* (London: The British Library, 2003), pp. 51–72, shows that Roberts erred in rejecting Jewish influences, but goes too far in the other direction.

20 Cf. the small amount of evidence for female scribes prior to the fourth century in K. Haines-Eitzen, *Guardians of Letters: Literacy, Power, and the Transmitters of Early Christian Literature* (New York: Oxford University Press, 2000), pp. 41–52. See also R. S. Bagnall and R. Cribiore, *Women's Letters from Ancient Egypt, 300 BC – AD 800* (Ann Arbor: University of Michigan Press, 2006). The letters all come from the upper social and economic strata of Egyptian society, from women who were more likely to use an amanuensis. 'Only occasionally can we be confident that a letter is written in a woman's own hand' (p. 7).

21 Turner, *Greek Manuscripts*, p. 10.

22 W. A. Johnson, *Bookrolls and Scribes in Oxyrhynchus* (Toronto: University of Toronto Press, 2004), p. 8; cf. pp. 15–37, esp. 35.

23 Ibid., pp. 58–9. Cf. 'As a rule, scribes copied the divisions between section units from their *Vorlagen*, but they sometimes deviated from them, and it is difficult to determine under which conditions they did so... Beyond this description, scribes must have felt free to change the section divisions of their *Vorlage* and to add new ones in accord with their understanding of the context' (Tov, *Scribal Practices*, p. 150 [cf. p. 144]; regarding section divisions in Hebrew MSS).

of the paradosis, and were copied 'when they appeared to be part of the original copy'.[24]

As regards scribal tendencies in the production of literary rolls, the evidence demonstrates the 'dominance, indeed near uniformity, of professionalism'.[25] But when copying a gospel exemplar, Christian scribes were not copying a literary text into a roll, but something like a 'paraliterary' text into a codex.[26] Nevertheless, a professional scribe trained in copying texts of various kinds and working in a Christian copying centre, should have understood that his task involved copying the text division, punctuation and lectional aids in his exemplar. Moreover, if the client supplied an exemplar which lacked reader's aids, they could be inserted at sense breaks or from an in-house master copy (see below). Therefore, paucity or irregularity of text division, punctuation and lectional aids will be taken to be an indication that a MS was produced for private rather than public use, especially when coupled with a documentary or scholarly rather than a literary or semi-literary hand. (We can visualize broad but non-exclusive categories of second- and third-century hands ranging from literary and semi-literary through informal to documentary and scholarly.[27]) Furthermore, rather than just being illustrative of the intent of the scribe, the lack of such features will often be traceable to an uncontrolled production setting.

2.2. Early gospels: representative and conventional

It was previously assumed that New Testament (NT) MSS of Egyptian provenance originated there and were examples of local text-types.[28] But Hellenistic and Roman period papyri testify to a constant flow of written material from Alexandria to the Mediterranean world and vice versa in the early centuries of our era. The Hellenistic and Roman state postal services were used solely for official and military purposes. Yet despite

24 Johnson, *Bookrolls*, p. 36. Later readers often added 'breathings, accents and adscripts, just as they added punctuation', so 'in the case of lectional aids it seems the scribe copied from his model the essentials, but remained attentive to the need to reproduce a clean, unencumbered text' (p. 36).

25 Ibid., p. 160.

26 The similarities to Graeco-Roman commentaries have been alluded to above. On commentaries see E. G. Turner, *Greek Papyri: An Introduction* (Oxford: Oxford University Press, 1968; rev. edn. 1980), pp. 112–24.

27 On the 'rapid, informal hand' of scholars see Roberts (*Manuscript*, pp. 15, 25, 66); Turner (*Greek Papyri*, pp. 92–4); idem, 'Scribes and scholars of Oxyrhynchus', in H. Gerstinger (ed.), *Akten des VIII. Internationalen Kongresses für Papyrologie, Wien 1955* (MPER n.s. 5; Vienna: R. M. Rahrer, 1956), pp. 141–6.

28 See, for example, K. W. Clark, *The Gentile Bias and Other Essays* (Leiden: Brill, 1980), p. 127: 'All the manuscripts so far discovered, including the most sensational of recent discoveries, may enable us to recover no more than the early text in Egypt.'

some difficulties – delivery times might increase dramatically if a letter carrier were unreliable or a boat unavailable – private senders were able to find carriers and letters regularly moved with relative ease,[29] making their way to Egypt from such places as Ravenna, Macedonia, Asia Minor, Seleucia, Ostia, Rome and Constantinople.[30]

By the same means, gospel MSS could have found their way to Egypt from elsewhere.[31] For instance, P[52] demonstrates that the Gospel of John, though apparently written in western Asia Minor (Irenaeus, *Haer.* 3.1.1), was probably circulating in Egypt in the first half of the second century.[32] Thus, although the early gospel papyri were all found in Egypt, they may well be representative of the gospel text from around the Mediterranean world.[33] To some extent the 'coherence of the early Church must have depended' on the efficient movement of communications and literature.[34] When the remarkable Christian preference for the codex as against the roll

29 That is, until the Diocletianic persecution at the end of the third and beginning of the fourth century. See S. R. Llewelyn, *New Documents Illustrating Early Christianity* (vols 6–7; Sydney: Macquarie University, Ancient History Documentary Research Centre, 1997–98; vols 8–9; Grand Rapids, MI: Eerdmans, 1997–2002), VII,1–57; idem, 'Sending letters in the ancient world', *TynBul* 46 (1995): 337–56; E. J. Epp, 'New Testament papyrus manuscripts and letter carrying in Greco-Roman times', in B. A. Pearson et al. (eds), *The Future of Early Christianity: Essays in Honor of Helmut Koester* (Minneapolis: Fortress, 1991), pp. 35–56, esp. 43–51. See also A. Harnack, 'Excursus. Travelling: the exchange of letters and literature', in idem, *The Expansion of Christianity in the First Three Centuries*, trans. J. Moffatt (2 vols.; London: Williams and Norgate, 1904), I, 462–72.

30 Turner, *Greek Papyri*, pp. 50–1, 96.

31 On the movement of written communications and MSS between early Christian groups see also Gamble, *Books and Readers*, pp. 108–32; M. B. Thompson, 'The holy internet: communication between churches in the first Christian generation', in R. J. Bauckham (ed.), *The Gospels for All Christians: Rethinking the Gospel Audiences* (Grand Rapids, MI: Eerdmans, 1998), pp. 49–70; L. Alexander, 'Ancient book production and circulation of the gospels', in ibid., pp. 71–105.

32 Roberts urged caution but cited an impressive array of papyrological authorities who supported his dating. See C. H. Roberts, *An Unpublished Fragment of the Fourth Gospel in the John Rylands Library* (Manchester: Manchester University Press, 1935), with 2 pll.; repr. with corrections in idem, 'An unpublished fragment of the fourth gospel in the John Rylands Library', *BJRL* 20 (1936): 44–55 and 2 pll.; and with critical notes and bibliography in idem, *P.Ryl.* 3 (1938): 1–3. It remains to be seen whether the criticisms of B. Nongbri, 'The use and abuse of P[52]: papyrological pitfalls in the dating of the fourth gospel', *HTR* 98 (2005): 23–48, will find any support.

33 Cf. Epp, 'Letter carrying', p. 56; idem, 'The papyrus manuscripts of the New Testament', in B. D. Ehrman and M. W. Holmes (eds), *The Text of the New Testament in Contemporary Research: Essays on the status quaestionis. A Volume in Honor of Bruce M. Metzger* (SD, 46; Grand Rapids, MI: Eerdmans, 1995), pp. 3–21 (9). Chance preservation also applies in the case of Christian MSS that escaped deliberate destruction. This adds weight to the possibility that the gospel papyri are representative.

34 C. H. Roberts, 'Books in the Graeco-Roman world and the New Testament', in P. R. Ackroyd et al. (eds), *The Cambridge History of the Bible* (3 vols; Cambridge: Cambridge University Press, 1963–70), I, 48–66 (64).

(particularly for writings regarded as sacred text[35]) and the ubiquitous use of the *nomina sacra* convention[36] are added to the equation, there is a strong case for there having been 'a degree of organization, of conscious planning, and uniformity of practice' in the early church.[37]

This is verified by codicological features common to early gospel MSS and summarized in Table 1 below. The MSS are listed according to date and by Turner Group in order of increasing page size. The following details are provided in the columns for each MS:

1   NT papyrus number;
2   size (W × H cm);[38]
3   lines per column;
4   Turner grouping (related to codex size);[39]
5   gospels held (M = Mt., m = Mk, L = Lk., etc.);
6   description of the hand (see below);
7   types of text division and/or punctuation;
8   intended use/type of production. The intended use can be either public or private, and the type of production controlled (= c) or uncontrolled (= u).

Johnson's three categories of hands parallel those used here: (1) 'formal, semi-formal, or pretentious'; (2) 'informal and unexceptional'; (3)

---

35   See the recent statistical analysis of L. W. Hurtado, *The Earliest Christian Artifacts: Manuscripts and Christian Origins* (Grand Rapids, MI: Eerdmans, 2006), pp. 43–61, esp. 57–60. See also C. H. Roberts and T. C. Skeat, *The Birth of the Codex* (London: Oxford University Press, 1985), and Gamble, *Books and Readers*.

36   Of around 300 Christian MSS earlier than 300 the number without *nomina sacra* 'can be counted on the fingers of our two hands': L. W. Hurtado, 'P[52] (P.Rylands Gk. 457) and the *nomina sacra*: method and probability', *TynBul* 54 (2003): 1–14 (5). See idem, *Earliest Christian Artifacts*, pp. 95–134, for an informative discussion of the *nomina sacra*.

37   Roberts, *Manuscript*, p. 41.

38   In the majority of cases, codex size and line count figures are based on my own calculations (working from scaled images). Turner's rule of thumb, that 2:3 is generally the proportion of upper to lower margins, was followed (see E. G. Turner, *The Typology of the Early Codex* [Philadelphia: University of Pennsylvania Press, 1977], p. 25). Thus, a 1 cm upper margin should have a 1.5 cm lower margin (total 2.5 cm), and a 1.6 cm upper margin should have a 2.4 cm lower margin (total 4 cm). So in the absence of physical evidence, 2.5 cm (the hypothetical lower limit) and 4 cm (the hypothetical upper limit) are added to estimates of column height, while side margins are assumed to be 1.5 cm wide (total 3 cm). Generally, my figures approximate closely to those found in K. Aland, *Repertorium der griechischen christlichen Papyri*, vol. I: *Biblische Papyri: Altes Testament, Neues Testament, Varia, Apokryphen* (PTS, 18; Berlin and New York: de Gruyter, 1976); J. van Haelst, *Catalogue des papyrus littéraires juifs et chrétiens* (Série «Papyrologie» 1; Paris: Publications de la Sorbonne, 1976); E. G. Turner, *The Typology of the Early Codex* (Philadelphia: University of Pennsylvania, 1977); and the various papyrological editions.

39   For details see Turner, *Typology*, pp. 13–34.

'substandard or cursive'.[40] The following abbreviations are used in describing the hands:

    bk   = literary/bookhand;
    doc. = documentary/cursive hand (with arrows indicating whether it is closer to a bk← or →doc. hand);
    inf.   = informal hand (which is in between [↔] the other two hands).

The following abbreviations for types of text division and punctuation are also used:

    pg.   = *paragraphos*;
    vac. = vacant line ends;
    ek.   = *ekthesis*;
    en.   = enlarged first letter of verse or chapter;
    sp.   = space;
    ·   = medial/high point;
    :   = dicolon;
    '   = apostrophe or line filler;
    >   = diple line filler; and
    ⁄   = acute-like text division marker or miscellaneous stroke.

Table 1: Gospel MSS arranged by date and Turner grouping

MS	Size (W × H)	Lines/col.	TG		Gosp.	Hand	Text Div./Punct.	Use/Prod.
Second century								
P^{103}	10 × 13–14.5	19/20	10	M		semi-literary, bk←	·	public/c
P^{77}	11 × 13.5–15	21	10	M		semi-literary, bk←	· pg. vac. ek.?	public/c
P^{90}	12.5 × 15–16.5	22/24	9.1	J		semi-literary, bk←	ek. en. sp.?	public/c
P^{104}	13 × 17–18.5	c. 30	9.1	M		formal round	sp.?	public?/c?
P^{64+67}	13.5 × 17–18.5	36/39	9.1	M		bibl. majuscule	· : ek.	public/c
P^{52}	18 × 22.5	18	5^Ab	J		semi-literary, bk←	sp.?	private?/u?
Second/third century								
P^{4}	13.5 × 17	36	9.1	L		bibl. majuscule	· : ek. pg.	public/c[41]
P^{66}	14.2 × 16.2	14/25	9	J		decorated round	· : ' > - , vac. ek. sp.	public/c
Third century								
P^{53}	10.8 × 16.5–18	24/25	9.1	M		near doc./cursive	sp.?	private?/u?
P^{108}	14.5 × 18.6	23/24	9.1	J		semi-literary, bk←	?	public?/c?
P^{101}	12 × 24.5–26	32/33	8	M		inf., bk↔doc.	nil	?/?
P^{75}	13 × 26	38/45	8	LJ		elegant majuscule	· : > sp. ek. pg.	public/c
P^{69}	12–14 × 30.5–32	45	8.1	L		inf., bk↔doc.	?	private/u
P^{95}	12 × 20–21.5	35/36	8.2	J		bibl. majuscule	nil	public?/c?
P^{107}	12 × 22.5–24	33/34	8.2	J		semi-cursive, doc.	?	private?/u?

40 Johnson, *Bookrolls*, p. 102; cf. 161. The vast majority of literary rolls in his samples fall into the first and second categories.

41 There are a number of problems with the effort of T. C. Skeat, 'The oldest manuscript of the four gospels?' *NTS* 43 (1997): 1–34 (repr. in J. K. Elliott [ed.], *The Collected Biblical Writings of T.C. Skeat* [NovTSup, 113; Leiden: Brill, 2004], pp. 158–92) to show that P^{64+67} and P^4 come from the same four-gospel, single-quire codex. See my article 'T. C. Skeat, P^{64+67} and P^4, and the problem of fibre orientation in codicological reconstruction', *NTS* 53 (2007): 582–604.

MS	Size (W× H)	Lines/col.	TG	Gosp.	Hand	Text Div./Punct.	Use/Prod.
P[106]	12 × 24	35/36	8.2	J	non-literary, →doc.	nil	private/u
P[70]	13 × 23–24.5	26	8.2	M	semi-literary, bk←	sp.	public?/c?
P[109]	13 × 23.5–25	25/26	8.2	J	non-literary, unprof.	nil	private?/u?
P[5]	13 × 24–25.5	27	8.2	J	semi-literary, →doc.	sp.	public/c
P[1]	13 × 24–25.5	37/38	8.2	M	inf., bk↔doc.	·	private/u
P[28]	14 × 22.5–24	25/26	8.2	J	→doc./cursive	nil	private/u
P[39]	14.5 × 26	25	8.2	J	bibl. majuscule	sp.	public/c
P[111]	15.5 × 22.5–24	22	7	L	semi-doc.	nil	private/u
P[45]	20 × 25	39/40	4	M-J	elegant majuscule	· ´	private/u
P[22]	roll *c.* 30 H	47/48	-	J	→doc./cursive	nil	private/u
Third/fourth century							
P[102]	12 × 26.5–27	34/35	8	M	semi-literary, bk←	·	public/c
P[37]	16 × 25.5–27	33	7	M	doc./cursive	sp.? ´	private/u
0171[42]	11–12 × 15	24	X^{15-12}	ML	careful majuscule	´ sp.? vac.? ek.	private/u
[0162	14.6 × 16.2	19	$X^{15-12sq}$	J	literary majuscule	· sp.	public/c[43]]
[P[7]	15 × 22	18	7.1	L[44]]			
[P[62]	P.Oslo. inv. 1661, University Library, Oslo; Mt. 11.25-30[45]]						
[P[80]	P.Barc. inv. 83, Fundación San Lucas Evangelista, Barcelona; Jn 3.34[46]]						

Analysis of the table suggests a number of preliminary conclusions. (1) If we focus for a moment on the first ten papyri, the small size of second-century and second/third-century gospels is immediately noticeable (P[52] is the exception). This appears to support the proposition that portability (and hence transportability) played a significant part in

42   0171 is a parchment codex designated NT Parch. 51 by Turner. Many of the examples in this category are early, but there is little correspondence with papyrus formats (Turner, *Typology*, pp. 28–9, 31–2).

43   0162 (P.Oxy 6.847) is probably to be dated to the fourth century: cf. III/IV, K. Aland et al. (eds), *Kurzgefasste Liste der griechischen Handschriften des Neuen Testaments* (Berlin: de Gruyter, 2nd edn, 1994), p. 33; IV, B. P. Grenfell and A. S. Hunt (*P.Oxy.* 6 [1908]: 4–5), van Haelst (*Catalogue*, no. 436), Turner (*Typology*, p. 159).

44   Petrov 553, Kiev, Ukrainian National Library, F. 301 (KDA), preserving Lk. 4.1-2: see Aland, *Liste*, p. 3 (III/IV?). For an edition based on that of C. R. Gregory (*ed. pr.*) see K. Aland, 'Neue neutestamentliche Papyri', *NTS* 3 (1957): 261–5. Gregory dated the MS IV-VI, but it was never photographed and has been lost, so the dating cannot be checked or the original format (roll or codex) determined. Cf. Aland, *Repertorium*, p. 225; van Haelst, *Catalogue*, nos 1224, 1225.

45   P[62] is probably outside our period. It is dated early IV, L. Amundsen ('Christian papyri from the Oslo collection', *SO* 24 [1945]: 121–40); IV, K. Aland and B. Aland (*The Text of the New Testament*, trans. E. F. Rhodes [Grand Rapids, MI: Eerdmans, 2nd edn, 1989], p. 100), van Haelst, *Catalogue*, no. 359; ?IV, Turner, *Typology*, p. 148.

46   P[80] is probably later than III/IV since other MSS containing *hermeneiai* of John are fifth-century or later: see D. C. Parker, 'Manuscripts of John's gospel with *hermeneiai*', in J. W. Childers and D. C. Parker (eds), *Transmission and Reception: New Testament Text-Critical and Exegetical Studies* (Text and Studies, 3.4; Piscataway, NJ: Georgias Press, 2006), pp. 48–68 (51). Cf. III, Aland, *Liste*, p. 14; late III, R. Roca-Puig, 'Papiro del evangelio de San Juan con "Hermenia"', in *Atti dell'XI Congresso Internazionale di Papyrologia, Milano, 2–8 Septembre 1965* (Milan: Instituto Lombardo di Science e Lettere, 1966), pp. 225–36; early IV, van Haelst, *Catalogue*, no. 441; and V–VI, Turner, *Typology*, p. 150.

Christian preference for the codex. Even in the third century the increased height of gospel codices should not have inhibited portability.

(2) If the Turner Group 10 is considered a sub-group of Group 9,[47] there is remarkable uniformity in the sizes of gospel codices in each century. Based on the extant evidence, we may infer that Christians favoured a codex size for gospels approximating the Group 9.1 format (W11.5–14 × H at least 3 cm higher than W) in the second century, and the 8.2 Group format (W12–14 × H not quite twice W) in the third century.[48] This is verified by the size of other early Christian codices as given by Turner. Like some third-century gospel codices, P^{46} (P.Beatty 2 + P.Mich. inv. 6238; III) which contains the Pauline letters, P.Mich. inv. 917 (*Hermas*; III), and P.Oxy. 4.656 (Genesis; II/III), are in Turner's Group 8. So too P.Beatty 9–10 (Ezekiel, Daniel, Esther; III) is in Turner's Group 8.1, and P.Bodmer 24 (Psalms; III/IV) in Group 8.2.[49]

(3) Conventional Christian approaches to MS production – uniformity in size, hands in the semi-literary to (formative) biblical majuscule[50] range, and the use of text division to facilitate easy public reading – support the idea that most of the first dozen or so codices listed in the table were produced in controlled settings, i.e., in small copy centres (rather than 'scriptoria'[51]) comprised of two or more scribes.[52] Where these factors are present *as a group* (as in P^{77}, P^{90}, P^{64+67}, P^4, P^{66} and P^{75}), controlled production is certainly taking place. It is reasonable to suggest that such copy centres existed in the second century in Christian centres such as Antioch, Alexandria, Caesarea, Jerusalem and Rome.[53]

47   'Group 10 is only a special case in a slightly smaller format of Group 9' (Turner, *Typology*, p. 25).

48   These figures correct an inadvertent error in the *Buried History* version of this chapter.

49   See Turner, *Typology*, pp. 20–1. P.Beatty 6 (Numbers, Deuteronomy; III) is an exception (Turner's Group 3 Abberants).

50   Turner (*Greek Manuscripts*, p. 25) gives biblical majuscule (which had developed by the fourth century) as one example of three types of formal, round, bilinear (i.e., written between two notional lines) hands: 'each letter (ι only excepted) occupies the space of a square (ε θ ο ς being broad circles) and only φ and ψ reach above and below the two lines' while 'υ regularly and ρ often reach below the line'. For a succinct but more detailed description see G. Cavallo and H. Maehler, *Greek Bookhands of the Early Byzantine Period A.D. 300–800* (University of London Institute of Classical Studies Bulletin Supplement, 47; London: Institute of Classical Studies, 1987), p. v.

51   See A. Mugridge, 'What is a scriptorium?' in J. Frösén et al. (eds), *Proceedings of the* 24th *International Congress of Papyrology, Helsinki, 1–7 August, 2004* (Commentationes Humanarum Litterarum, 122.2; Helsinki: Societas Scientiarum Fennica, 2007), pp. 781–92, who shows that the word 'scriptorium' or a Greek equivalent was not used in the early period.

52   Gamble, *Books and Readers*, pp. 120–1.

53   See G. Zuntz, 'The text of the epistles', in his *Opuscula selecta: Classica, Hellenistica, Christiana* (Manchester: Manchester University Press, 1972), pp. 252–68, esp. 266–8; idem, *The Text of the Epistles: A Disquisition upon the Corpus Paulinum* (Schweich Lectures, 1946;

(4) Although certainty is difficult, the aberrant sizes of P^{52} and P^{45} suggest production in private/uncontrolled settings. The remaining third-century gospel codices also seem to fall into the same category. Paradoxically, standard sizes were still preferred, suggesting that in most cases fashion/convention was strong enough to dictate size even as the number of private copies of the gospels increased. This in turn supports the argument that conventional textual practices already existed among Christians at an early time, at least as far as the East is concerned.[54]

3. Scribal Milieu

Examination of all early gospel codices is impossible within the scope of this chapter, so I have chosen to discuss just three MSS. Two of these can be viewed as unambiguous examples of 'public' (P^{75}) and 'private' (P^{37}) MSS. At first glance the third MS might be thought to be 'public' as well, but despite its obvious quality 'public' indicators as a group are not present in P^{45}. It will illustrate very well the sometimes ambiguous nature of the evidence to be considered when deciding on the production setting and use of gospel MSS.

In what follows sense breaks in two of the three papyri discussed are compared to chapter, verse breaks and verse subdivisions in Nestle-Aland (NA^{27}).[55] This has the appearance of working backwards from later to earlier evidence. But according to its editors, the text divisions in NA^{26} correspond to the divisions found in ancient MSS, presumably B and ℵ in particular.[56] It is not unreasonable to assume that the text divisions in these later codices took over and further developed sense breaks in earlier MSS like P^{75}, so comparison with NA^{27} should be enlightening. It should also be noted that the occasional use of the adjective 'liturgical' as a

---

Oxford: Oxford University Press, 1953), pp. 271–5; Roberts, *Manuscript*, p. 24; Gamble, *Books and Readers*, p. 121. 'There is, however, no direct evidence for a library in Alexandria, and its existence in the second and third centuries can only be inferred' (Gamble, *Books and Readers*, p. 161).

54   Cf. E. J. Epp, 'The significance of the papyri for determining the nature of the New Testament text in the second century: a dynamic view of textual transmission', in W. L. Petersen (ed.), *Gospel Traditions in the Second Century: Origins, Recensions, Text, and Transmission* (Christianity and Judaism in Antiquity, 3; Notre Dame: University of Notre Dame Press, 1989), pp. 71–103 (91).

55   B. Aland and K. Aland et al. (eds), *Novum Testamentum Graece* (Stuttgart: Deutsche Bibelgesellschaft, 27th edn, 2001).

56   According to K. Aland et al. (eds), *Novum Testamentum Graece* (Stuttgart: Deutsche Bibelgesellschaft, 26th edn, 1979), 44*, its text divisions correspond to the divisions found in ancient manuscripts, and with rare exceptions NA^{27} reproduces the system of punctuation and paragraphing used in its predecessor (46*).

synonym for 'public' implies nothing other than the reading aloud of gospels in early Christian meetings/worship gatherings.[57]

3.1. *A 'public'/liturgical MS: P^{75} (P.Bodmer 14–15)*[58]

Turner argues that some Christian MSS were written with larger characters to make public reading easier. Comparable codices of Greek prose literature contain significantly more letters per line than both P^{66} and P^{75}. Such MSS, he says, are 'the work of practiced scribes writing an ordinary type of hand, but writing it larger than usual'.[59] Thus, the spacious script of P^{66} appears to be stretched horizontally.[60] Furthermore, no traces of any *kolleseis*/joins between sheets are visible in the Bodmer photographs of the MS, suggesting that the final physical form or appearance of the codex was an important consideration.[61] So in P^{66} we appear to have a codex designed to take a central place in public worship.

Although they are not as pronounced, the same features can be seen in the third-century P^{75} which preserves in good condition significant parts of Luke and John.[62] The page measures 13 × 26 cm, so the open codex had a square shape.[63] According to Turner, a Group 8 book of these

---

57 According to Justin, the gospels were read in the context of worship for 'as long as time permits' (*1 Apol.* 67).

58 P.Bodmer 14–15 is now housed in the Biblioteca Apostolica Vaticana, Rome. For editions see V. Martin and R. Kasser, *Papyrus Bodmer XIV: Evangile de Luc chap. 3–24* (Cologny-Genève: Bibliotheca Bodmeriana, 1961); V. Martin and R. Kasser, *Papyrus Bodmer XV: Evangile de Jean chap. 1–15* (Cologny-Genève: Bibliotheca Bodmeriana, 1961); and for identification of fragments see K. Aland, 'Neue neutestamentliche Papyri III', *NTS* 20 (1974): 376–81; M.-L. Lakmann, 'Papyrus Bodmer XIV–XV (P^{75}): neue Fragmente', *MH* 64 (2007): 22–41 and pll. I–X.

59 *Typology*, pp. 85–6.

60 Turner, *Greek Manuscripts*, p. 108, no. 63. The scribe would not have been worried about running out of space in a codex made up of multiple quires to which another quire could easily be attached (Turner, *Typology*, p. 73).

61 Turner (*Typology*, pp. 49–50) is making the point that when the sheets used to make P^{66} and P^{75} were cut from rolls, the makers tried to keep the sheets join-free. On methods of cutting sheets from a roll minus the joins see *Typology*, p. 52. Although he had not personally inspected this manuscript, from the photographs Turner's conclusions appear sound. However, it can be 'particularly difficult' to detect joins in photographs because the photographer is focused on producing 'maximum contrast between the writing and its background': idem, *The Terms Recto and Verso: The Anatomy of the Papyrus Roll* (Papyrologica Bruxellensia, 16; Actes de XVe Congrès International de Papyrologie, Première Partie; Bruxelles: Fondation Égyptologique Reine Élisabeth, 1978), p. 15.

62 The MS is dated 175–225, Martin and Kasser, *Luc*, pp. 13–14; II-III, Aland, *Liste*, p. 14; early III, B. M. Metzger, *Manuscripts of the Greek Bible: An Introduction to Greek Palaeography* (New York: Oxford University Press, 1981), p. 68; 225–75, Turner, *Typology*, p. 95 (cf. *Bib.* 49 [1968]: 110; and *Greek Papyri*, p. 174 n. 37).

63 Martin and Kasser, *Luc*, p. 9.

dimensions was intentionally manufactured (B = $\frac{1}{2}$ H).[64] Aland describes the script as a beautiful, upright majuscule, Martin and Kasser as elegant and careful.[65] Some letters, such as o and ω, are much smaller than average. There are 38–45 lines to the page (only 3 pages have under 40 lines and the average is 42),[66] and 25–36 letters to the line.[67] Because he had underestimated the number of sheets required, as he proceeded the scribe's writing became progressively smaller in an effort to fit everything in. Martin and Kasser note that the number of lines is considerably greater in the second half of the codex.[68] Turner comments on the same phenomenon, but still regards P[75] as another example of a Christian MS written in a larger script for reading aloud.[69] The margins are quite generous and the occasional *kollesis* can be seen on the photographs, but the relative paucity of such joins may indicate that like P[66] this codex was intended to play a visible part in public worship.

Punctuation takes the form of high, medial and low points, but if any rationale governs the different heights it is difficult to discern.[70] The trema over ι and υ is used frequently but not systematically, and rough breathings are often used over pronouns to differentiate them from homonyms (e.g., ἐῖς, ἐν, ἐξ).[71] Individual Semitic names are marked with an apostrophe or point,[72] and the former is also used after ουκ and between double consonants,[73] probably 'in the interests of clarity of pronunciation' in public reading.[74]

The point followed by one or more vacant spaces and one-letter *ekthesis* on the following line is the usual method of chapter and paragraph division.[75] However, the dicolon and *paragraphos* are used very occasionally in lieu of or with other markers. In comparison to NA[27], about two-thirds of chapter breaks and one-third of paragraph breaks are marked in the non-fragmentary pages of the MS. More noteworthy is the consistently high rate of verse division corresponding to NA[27]. The

---

64   *Typology*, p. 23.

65   Aland, *Repertorium*, p. 310; Martin and Kasser, *Luc*, p. 13.

66   Martin and Kasser, *Luc*, p. 10.

67   Van Haelst, *Catalogue*, no. 406.

68   Near the start of the codex one page corresponds to about 30 lines of the 1961 edition of Nestle, while the second half increases to 41 lines of Nestle: Martin and Kasser, *Luc*, p. 10.

69   *Typology*, pp. 74, 86.

70   Cf. Martin and Kasser, *Luc*, p. 16, who think that high and low points correspond to non-final (our commas and colons) and final stops respectively (see also Turner, *Greek Manuscripts*, p. 11). This system may at times apply.

71   Martin and Kasser, *Luc*, p. 17. There are no soft breathings.

72   Ibid.

73   Metzger, *Manuscripts*, p. 68.

74   B. M. Metzger, 'The Bodmer Papyrus of Luke and John', *ExpTim* 73 (1962): 201–3 (201).

75   See the plates in Martin and Kasser, *Luc* and *Jean*.

rounded percentages of marked as against unmarked verse breaks per
chapter are as follows: (**Luke** 10) 82 : 18; (11) 93 : 7; (12) 98 : 2; (13) 94 : 6;
(14) 94 : 6; (15) 72 : 28; (16) 71 : 29; (22) 72 : 28; (23) 82 : 18; (**John** 1) 70 :
30; (2) 72 : 28; (3) 75 : 25; (4) 81 : 19; (5) 64 : 36; (8) 86.5 : 13.5; (9) 77.5 :
22.5; (10) 86 : 14.[76] On average the verse breaks in P^{75} agree with those in
NA^{27} about 80 percent of the time.[77] We are more than justified,
therefore, in seeing the text divisions in P^{75} as ancestors of those found in
B and ℵ.

3.2. A 'private'/non-liturgical MS: P^{37} (P.Mich. 3.137)[78]

P^{37} consists of two abutting fragments which make up a single codex leaf.
It measures 13.5 × 22.4 cm and preserves Mt. 26.19-37 (↓) and 26.37-52
(→). There were originally 33 lines per page and, based on the extant text,
the column measured about 13 × 23 cm and the page 16 × 25.5–27 cm
(Turner's Group 7).[79] If we were to imagine a range of hands starting at
the literary end with the formative biblical majuscule of P^4, at the opposite
extreme we would find P^{37} with its documentary hand.[80] The hand is a
very informal cursive, and according to Sanders 'every letter seems to
present most of its conceivable forms'. He concluded that the writer 'was
an educated man, but not a practised scribe' and finds parallel hands in
documentary papyri.[81]

There is only one rough breathing (↓8), but the trema is used
regularly over initial ι (and once medially at ↓11, εσθίοντων). A
correction at ↓12 where εκαλασεν was written, then the whole word
except for the augment crudely crossed out and κλασεν written by the
same hand[82] above the crossed-out letters, gives an impression of haste
as though the whole document was written quickly. A long omission
(Χαῖρε ῥαββί, καὶ κατεφίλησεν αὐτόν. ὁ δὲ ᾽Ιησοῦς) in vv. 49–50
probably results from a scribal leap from ειπεν to ειπεν.[83] There are also

---

76 The actual figures in the extant text are: (Luke 10) 28, 6; (11) 50, 4; (12) 58, 1; (13) 33,
2; (14) 33, 2; (15) 23, 9; (16) 22, 9; (22) 23, 9; (23) 45, 10; (John 1) 35, 15; (2) 18, 7; (3) 27, 9; (4)
43, 10; (5) 14, 8; (8) 32, 5; (9) 31, 9; (10) 12, 2.

77 The averaged agreement in Luke and John is 84.2 and 76.4 percent respectively.

78 For editions see H. A. Sanders, 'An early papyrus fragment of the Gospel of Matthew
of the Michigan Collection', *HTR* 19 (1926): 215–26; idem, *P.Mich.* 3 (1936): 9–14 and pl. 1.

79 Cf. 15 × 25 cm: *ed. pr.* (p. 215), van Haelst (*Catalogue*, no. 378), Aland (*Repertorium*,
p. 259); 12+ × 25 cm: Turner, *Typology*, p. 147.

80 Cf. Turner, *Greek Papyri*, pp. 88–96.

81 *Ed. pr.*, pp. 216–17.

82 Sanders, *P.Mich.* 3 (1936): 12 n. 26.

83 See ibid, *P.Mich.* 3 (1936): 13 nn. 49–50.

11 singular readings, including three additions,[84] and a number of spelling variants.[85]

The writer used no punctuation, but at times seems to have left spaces between words or letters that coincide with NA[27] verse breaks (vv. 21, 23, 27, 30, 31, 42, 44, 46, 50, 51), or that appear to introduce speech (↓25, →5) or function like commas (→12, 20). However, other verse breaks are not so marked (vv. 22, 24, 25, 26, 29, 32, 33, 36, 38, 40, 41, 43, 45, 49); and two vacant spaces in the text appear not to serve any function (↓6, 8). So while some vacant spaces appear to function as punctuation, that may often be more by accident than design, the chance result of a rapidly written hand.

Sanders thought a second hand had added the short raised strokes (´) where spaces had been left at the end of phrases.[86] Certainly, a space and stroke sometimes occur together where the text corresponds to a paragraph (v. 31) or verse break (vv. 23, 27, 30, 42, 46, 51) in NA[27], but strokes are not present in a number of places where spaces have been left (↓6, 8, 25; →12), and both 'markers' are also lacking in two places where they might have been expected (vv. 38, 45). Moreover, although strokes frequently correspond to paragraph and verse breaks (vv. 22, 23, 27, 29, 32, 33, 36, 40, 41, 42, 43, 44, 46, 49, 51) or verse subdivisions (vv. 22, 25, 26, 27, 39², 40, 41, 42, 44², 45, 50) in NA[27], just as often there is no verse subdivision correspondence (vv. 21², 22², 24, 25, 26², 27², 31, 32, 33, 36, 39, 40², 45³, 46, 47²), or apparent sense divisions lack a clear rationale (vv. 24², 42², 43).[87]

It is the last category that calls into question the idea that the strokes may have assisted with reading in public.[88] However, if the MS were altered by a second hand to help with public reading, it must have been a privately produced MS that was modified subsequently. The first hand is undoubtedly documentary and by no means bilinear, and for both reasons far from suitable for public reading. The second hand has made corrections above the line in three places.[89] But there is no correction of the long scribal leap by the second hand, another factor that would seem

---

84   ταυτα is added before τη νυκτι ταυτη, v. 31; και before ο ι͞η͞ς, v. 34; δε before ωδε, v. 38. Besides the large omission in vv. 49–50, ελθητε in v. 41 lacks the prefix εις, and των omitted from v. 51.

85   εγρηγορειτε : γρηγορειτε, vv. 38, 41; εγρηγορησαι : γρηγορησαι, v. 40; ισχυσαν : ισχυσατε, v. 40. Cf. P. M. Head, 'Observations on early papyri of the synoptic gospels, especially on the "scribal habits"', *Bib* 71 (1990): 240–7 (244).

86   Ibid., p. 10.

87   A superscript number indicates more than one occurrence in the verse.

88   This is the view of the *ed. pr.*, p. 217.

89   At ↓9 (ν is written above the ν in εγενηθη, v. 24), ↓16 ([εκ]χυνομενον is corrected to εκχυννομενον by writing ν above and between υν, v. 28), ↓17 (του is added above the line to be read after τουτου, v. 29): see Sanders, *P.Mich.* 3 (1936): 12 nn. 24, 28, 29.

to rule out use of the modified papyrus in a worship setting.[90] The second hand has attempted to insert, or perhaps to clarify or supplement, text division in the MS, but a number of the strokes appear to be study aids that mark something of interest in the text. So the modified MS was probably for 'private' use as well.

3.3 P^{45} (P.Beatty 1[91] and P.Vindob. G. 31974[92]): 'public' or 'private'?

P^{45} is comprised of 30 fragmentary leaves of a codex dated *c.* 250 which preserve parts of the four Gospels and Acts.[93] Not one complete page survives; the top of the single column is preserved in most cases, but its base is missing on every page. In Luke and John one side of the column survives, but in Matthew and Mark both sides of the column are damaged.[94] Each page measured 20 × 25 cm (Turner's Group 4).[95] Judging from leaves 25–30, the upper margin was around 3.2 cm and the lower probably larger; the inner margin where it is twice preserved is 1.9 cm, and Kenyon estimates that the outer margin was about 2.5 cm.[96] This means the written area was about 15.5 × 19.5 cm. On reconstructed figures there were 39/40 lines per page and 50 characters per line.[97] Because Mark and Acts were next to each other in the lump of papyrus that arrived in England, Kenyon thought that the Gospels may have been in the Western order.[98] Skeat agrees with this on the basis of the acute-like strokes added by a second hand that appear in Mark and Acts but not

---

90   However, several difficult to decipher letters which are not noted or discussed by Sanders have been written above ειπεν on →25.

91   F. G. Kenyon, *The Chester Beatty Biblical Papyri: Descriptions and Texts of Twelve Manuscripts on Papyrus in the Greek Bible*, Fasc. 2: *The Gospels and Acts, Text* (London: Emery Walker, 1933), *The Gospels and Acts, Plates* (London: Emery Walker, 1934). For recent editions of fragments see T. C. Skeat and B. C. McGing, 'Notes on the Chester Beatty biblical papyrus I (Gospels and Acts)', *Hermathena* 150 (1991): 21–5 and pll.; and W. J. Elliott and D. C. Parker (eds), *The New Testament in Greek*, vol. 4.1: *The Gospel according to St. John: The Papyri* (International Greek New Testament Project; NTTS, 20; Leiden: Brill, 1995): pp. 52–67.

92   H. Gerstinger, 'Ein Fragment des Chester-Beatty Evangelienkodex in der Papyrussammlung der Nationalbibliothek in Wien', *Aeg* 13 (1933): 67–73; G. Zuntz, 'Reconstruction of the leaf of the Chester Beatty papyrus of the Gospels and Acts (Mt. XXV, 41–XXVI, 39)', *CE* 52 (1951): 191–211 and pll.

93   It is dated III[1-2], Kenyon (*Text*, p. x) citing Bell and Schubart; III, R. Seider (*Paläographie der griechischen Papyri* [3 vols; Stuttgart: Hiersemann, 1967–90], II, p. 118), and Turner (*Typology*, p. 148); and III[3-4] by Hunt, cited by Kenyon (*Text*, p. x).

94   Kenyon, *Text*, pp. v–vi.

95   Van Haelst, *Catalogue*, no. 371.

96   Kenyon, *Text*, p. vi.

97   Aland, *Repertorium*, p. 270; van Haelst, *Catalogue*, no. 371.

98   Kenyon, *Text*, p. viii.

elsewhere. These would be easier to account for if Mark and Acts were adjacent.[99]

Skeat calculates the codex would have contained 56 sheets or 224 pages (Mt. 49, Jn 38, Lk. 48, Mk 32, Acts 55).[100] The scribe managed to fit the Gospels and Acts into a codex of this size only by using a small script and a larger page and written area.[101] Kenyon describes the script as 'small and very clear', approximately square (in height and width), 'very correct, and though without calligraphic pretensions...the work of a competent scribe'. Although 'characteristic of good Roman hands', it has a marked slope to the right.[102] Zuntz agrees that the scribe's hand is 'on the whole amazingly even, and his practice with regard to orthography [and] punctuation...astonishingly consistent'.[103]

As for the editorial activity in the MS, Colwell concludes it is indicative of an uncontrolled tradition. The scribe freely improves the reading of his exemplar and is not constrained by any need to reproduce it verbatim.[104] Generally, there seems to be a desire to remove unnecessary words while producing a smoother text.[105] Details are often omitted in the interests of conciseness, clarity and style, especially when they have been mentioned previously or can be understood from the context.[106] Clarification also motivates the scribe of P^{75}, but most of the time is overcome by the desire to make an exact copy.[107] In contrast, the copying in P^{66} is careless, but numerous corrections against a second exemplar are indicative of

99   T. C. Skeat, 'A codicological analysis of the Chester Beatty papyrus of the Gospels and Acts (P45)', *Hermathena* 155 (1993): 27–43 (31–2), repr. in Elliott, *The Collected Biblical Writings of T. C. Skeat*, pp. 141–57. Kenyon had previously noted that a later hand had added the 'heavy dots or strokes above the line' (*Text*, p. ix).

100   Skeat, 'Codicological analysis', pp. 27–43.

101   Roberts and Skeat, *The Birth of the Codex*, p. 66.

102   Kenyon, *Text*, pp. viii–ix; cf. Zuntz, 'Reconstruction', p. 193.

103   What follows is based on Zuntz, 'Reconstruction', pp. 192–3. J. R. Royse, *Scribal Habits in Early Greek New Testament Papyri* (Leiden: Brill, 2008), pp. 114, 119–20, finds only 8 orthographic errors in 227 singular readings.

104   E. C. Colwell, 'Method in evaluating scribal habits: a study of P^{45}, P^{66}, P^{75}', in his *Studies in Methodology in Textual Criticism of the New Testament* (NTTS, 9; Leiden: Brill, 1969), pp. 106–24 (117–18).

105   218 of 227 (96 percent) of readings produced by the scribe 'read more or less smoothly': Royse, *Scribal Habits*, p. 123.

106   Colwell, 'Method in evaluating scribal habits', p. 119.

107   'In P^{75} the text that is produced can be explained in all its variants as the result of a single force, namely the disciplined scribe who writes with the intention of being careful and accurate' (ibid., p. 117). Royse (*Scribal Habits*, pp. 625, 630–1) identifies 116 corrections (with only 5 by other hands), the vast majority of which correct 'scribal blunders' to the reading in B, which suggests that 'there was little if any attempt to revise the text by a second exemplar'.

conscientious efforts to produce a good final copy.[108] This suggests that the scribe of P[45] rather than the exemplar is responsible for the contents of the MS.

Ekthesis, vacant line ends, spaces, and the *paragraphos* were not used. A rough breathing sometimes appears with the article and relative pronouns, *iota* adscript consistently occurs after η and ω (but not α), and the trema is used regularly over initial ι and υ (sometimes appearing as a small line over υ).[109] Text division in the form of a medial point is employed inconsistently by the first hand, but more often heavier strokes (′), blobs, or dots, are added by a second hand. The latter, which do not occur in Matthew, Luke and John, are often thick, intrusive and rough, and in marked contrast to the elegant hand. The only strokes that approach the size of this text marker in Mark are the downward strokes on α and δ, but they are not as thick. There is no doubt that the markers were produced by a different reed, and probably by a different hand at some later time.[110] If the markers were made during production, they would have spoiled the efforts of the first copyist to produce an attractive MS. Thus, contemporaneity is virtually ruled out.

It appears that several *Vorlagen* were used. This is suggested by the sparse use of points in Mark, their excessive use in John (10.10-16 in particular), and their absence in Acts. Mark was certainly copied from a different exemplar, one that contained early readings that flowed into the later Byzantine tradition,[111] and this almost certainly accounts for its paucity of points. The same was probably the case with Acts and perhaps John. Thus, the scribe seems to have reproduced points as he found them in the various exemplars, and did not add them to P[45] when copying Acts. As for other markers of text division, it is highly unlikely that all of the exemplars lacked *ekthesis*, vacant line ends and/or spaces, and the *paragraphos*. Therefore, the copyist seems to have ignored these when he encountered them, perhaps because the exemplars were all different in this regard, and this kind of variation would be more visible than inconsistent use of the point. This explanation is feasible because the same kinds of minor scribal changes to the text are found in Mark as in the other Gospels. We can conclude then that although he copies points, the copyist

108   G. D. Fee, 'The corrections of Papyrus Bodmer II and early textual transmission', *NovT* 7 (1964/65): 247–57.

109   Kenyon, *Text*, p. ix, notes that when 'two letters occur together, as in υιος, three dots are placed above them'. On the scribe's very consistent use of the *iota* adscript see Zuntz, 'Reconstruction', p. 192 n. 5.

110   Kenyon, *Text*, p. ix; Skeat, 'Codicological analysis', pp. 31–2.

111   B. Aland, 'The significance of the Chester Beatty papyri in early church history', in C. Horton (ed.), *The Earliest Gospels: The Origins and Transmission of the Earliest Christian Gospels. The Contribution of the Chester Beatty Gospel Codex P[45]* (JSNTSup, 30; London: T. & T. Clark, 2004), pp. 108–21 (113).

of P^{45} rather than his exemplars has determined the layout and character of the MS. This conclusion is supported by the absence of chapter and paragraph text division markers, the unfashionable page size, the small script and compressed layout, and the small number of corrections.[112] All of these factors point to uncontrolled production and mark P^{45} as an individualistic early witness.

In the few small fragments of Matthew that are preserved, medial points have been inserted quite regularly[113] to mark verse breaks or verse subdivisions. Apparently, because this was the case the second hand did not add any raised strokes. (There is, however, no guarantee that the same situation pertained in the rest of Matthew.) In contrast, in Mark the second hand added strokes to indicate verse breaks or subdivisions which had not been marked in the exemplar.[114] Sometimes these were entered where medial points had previously been (inconsistently) placed. In Luke and John points were used with some consistency in the exemplars, and for this reason strokes were not entered by the second hand.[115] But again, there is no way of knowing if this was the case throughout both of these books. In Acts, where the point was not used at all, raised strokes are reintroduced by the second hand. From the end of 6.9 the strokes become small, dark oval blobs and then dots which Kenyon records as high points in his edition.[116] The scribe apparently decided to decrease the size of the division marker.[117] There is little doubt, however, that the same second hand is again at work because, although the strokes are generally shorter and thinner from this point (than in Mark), small raised ovals or blobs also occur along with the occasional longer stroke (of Mark) from fol. 27^r onwards.[118]

The low importance placed on signalling text division in P^{45} is more

---

112   Royse finds only 14 corrections in P^{45}, two of which are by a second hand (Mt. 25.42; Acts 7.12): see *Scribal Habits*, p. 114.

113   Although several verse breaks are not marked in fol. 2^v of the Beatty fragments and on the → of P.Vindob. G. 31974, there is consistency elsewhere. But it should be noted that many verse breaks in Matthew coincide with lacunae in the papyrus.

114   I proceed here in the order of the gospels in the *ed. pr.*, rather than in the Western order.

115   If the gospels were in the Western order (Matthew, John, Luke, Mark), the use of medial points must have been quite inconsistent in John and Luke before grinding to a halt early in Mark.

116   See fol. 19^v (Acts 6.7–7.2). Note also that throughout the transcription Kenyon records medial points as high points.

117   This was anticipated at the ends of Mk 9.26 and 12.27 where a blob of ink was written instead of a stroke. Short raised strokes are missing in fol. 23^v, but they resume in the next folio (24^v) where a thinner pen begins to be used.

118   Where blobs are again inaccurately marked as high points in Kenyon's edition.

indicative of a MS made for 'private' rather than 'public' use.[119] Indeed, the very sparse text division in Mark and the complete absence of text division in Acts, as far as the work of the first copyist is concerned, would seem to be decisive in this regard. It might be said with some justification that Acts may not have been read in public worship and, given its very poor preservation in comparison with other gospel papyri, the same may often have been true of Mark as well. But the later addition of strokes, besides underlining the importance of reading aids if MSS were to be read publicly, would seem to indicate the opposite in both cases. So P^{45} does not seem to have been prepared with any lector in mind. Still, the regular use of points in Matthew, Luke and John mean that an intended public use cannot be ruled out entirely, although it is unlikely since the copyist is merely reproducing his exemplars. Nonetheless, the small hand and compressed layout, combined with the 'free' scribal approach and lack of correction against the exemplars or another MS,[120] as well as the odd size of the codex (when pressure to conform to third-century fashion or expectations in terms of size must have been significant[121]), denote production in an uncontrolled setting.

4. *Elaborating on Public and Private Production Settings*

Ancient literary works were distributed as individuals borrowed and copied texts owned by their friends.[122] Gamble conceives of this taking place among small groups of Christians. Among the members of a congregation competent to make copies, he lists the 'few educated members', 'slaves trained for scribal tasks or professional scribes experienced especially in documentary work', and proposes that 'even small-business-persons accustomed to dealing with records would have

---

119   Cf. G. N. Stanton, *Jesus and Gospel* (Cambridge: Cambridge University Press, 2004), pp. 198, 73 n. 38, citing a private communication from T. C. Skeat. In contrast, Hurtado (*Earliest Christian Artifacts*, pp. 174–7) favours public use. He suggests that the MS was intended 'for the edification of an ecclesiastical readership' (idem, 'P^{45} and the textual history of the Gospel of Mark', in Horton, *Earliest Gospels*, pp. 132–48 [146–7]). This is a possibility since an educated reader (or readership) familiar with the content would be better able to make sense of an inconsistently divided text.

120   As P^{66} and P^{75} demonstrate, such a mindset would be alien in a controlled production setting.

121   In Table 1 above other third-century gospel MSS designated private nevertheless conform to third-century fashion or expectations concerning the size of gospel codices.

122   R. L. Starr, 'The circulation of literary texts in the Roman world', *CLQ* 37 (1987): 213–23 (213), envisions texts circulating 'in a series of widening concentric circles determined primarily by friendship'. Cf. the discussions of Gamble, *Books and Readers*, pp. 83–93, esp. p. 88; and Johnson, *Bookrolls*, pp. 158–9.

been able to write a clear, practical hand'.[123] While this scenario is very plausible, he assumes that copies would be produced for the corporate use of the group as a whole rather than for the private or personal use of individuals. But this is by no means assured. Christians were able to obtain and own personal texts ranging from ornate miniature codices to simple amulets used for apotropaic purposes.[124]

In contrast, Horsley argues that initially Christian groups commissioned copies of their texts from 'established scriptoria', and that it was only as demand increased that they set up their own 'scriptoria which produced serviceable, "in-house" copies with growing proficiency'. By the fourth century these had become 'highly professional scriptoria which set great store not only by accuracy but also by aesthetic appeal'.[125] While Christian copying was probably a factor from the very beginning,[126] there were undoubtedly times when Christians had recourse to outside copying centres. That is, Christians probably obtained copies of gospel MSS in much the same way as one obtained copies of literary works in the ancient world. Copies might be commissioned from outside scribes, or be made by the borrower or Christians known to him with the ability to transcribe MSS.

There are also grounds for placing Horsley's second phase, that of 'growing proficiency' in the in-house production of MSS, at an earlier time than he seems to have entertained. It was certainly well advanced by *c.* 175, as Table 1 shows. MSS produced in early Christian copy centres had a number of identifiable features that when present as a group point to controlled production for public or liturgical use. These include semi-literary or literary hands, lectional aids in the form of punctuation and text division to facilitate public reading, and the use of the codex in sizes conventional in the second and third centuries. The converse is also true. Codices with informal or documentary hands and lacking features conducive to public reading, even though they may come in conventional sizes, were very probably copies made without controls for private use. For our purposes, therefore, 'private' denotes all gospel MSS produced outside Christian copying centres.

---

123   Gamble, *Books and Readers*, p. 78.

124   For miniature codices see Turner, *Typology*, p. 22. For a list of apotropaic texts see 'Papyri from the Rise of Christianity in Egypt: Conspectus of Texts', §§ X–XII, produced by the Ancient History Documentary Research Centre (AHDRC), Macquarie University (at http://www.anchist.mq.edu.au/doccentre/PCEhomepage.htm, accessed 6 Sept. 2008).

125   G. H. R. Horsley, 'Classical manuscripts in Australia and New Zealand, and the early history of the codex', *Antichthon* 27 (1993): 60–85 (74–5).

126   The very early and almost universal practice of contracting *nomina sacra* is a strong argument in favour of Christian scribes and copyists: Gamble, *Books and Readers*, p. 78.

As seen in Paul's use of literary assistants,[127] there is no reason to think that 'private' copying, or indeed access to the materials and tools needed for writing,[128] was limited to scribes.[129] When students at school progressed from the first two levels of letters and alphabet to syllabaries, lists of words and writing exercises, papyrus and its requisite tools were needed.[130] Though expensive for ordinary villagers or farmers, papyrus was quite affordable in higher social contexts.[131] School papyri from villages and towns as against *metropoleis* come from the social level represented by 'landowners, soldiers, businessmen and so on'.[132] A limited number of individuals went to school, and most did not stay 'long enough to develop firm habits of writing'.[133] But three years was long enough to learn to read and write slowly, and a range of abilities should be envisaged even at this stage of literacy.[134] Some pupils in the larger cities and also in the larger villages reached 'rather high levels' of instruction.[135]

127 Among Paul's personal retinue were Silas who co-authored a couple of letters (1 Thess. 1.1; 2 Thess. 2.1), and Timothy, the son of a Greek father and Jewish mother from Lystra in Asia Minor (Acts 16.1-3), who shared in the authorship of a number of letters (2 Cor. 1.1; Phil. 1.1; Col. 1.1; 1 Thess. 1.1; 2 Thess 2.1; Phlm. 1). Other persons who could supply literacy to the Pauline mission were Apollos, an Alexandrian rhetorician (ἀνὴρ λόγιος, Acts 18.24), Sosthenes, who co-authored a letter (1 Cor. 1.1; perhaps an *archisynagogos*, Acts 18.17), Tertius, one amanuensis of a number (Rom. 16.22), and Luke, the physician who went on to write a Gospel and the book of Acts (Col. 4.14; 2 Tim. 4.11; Phlm. 24): see E. A. Judge, 'The early Christians as a scholastic community', *JRH* 1 (1960/61): 4–15, 125–37 (131–4); repr. in idem, *The First Christians in the Roman Empire: Augustan and New Testament Essays* (ed. J. Harrison and E. Mathieson; Tübingen: Mohr Siebeck, 2008), pp. 526–52.
128 For a discussion of writing tools see Turner, *Greek Manuscripts*, pp. 6–7.
129 Cf. Cribiore, *Writing*, pp. 3–11.
130 Ibid., pp. 69–72; Turner, *Greek Papyri*, p. 89 and n. 44.
131 T. C. Skeat, 'Was papyrus regarded as "cheap" or "expensive" in the ancient world?' *Aeg* 75 (1995): 75–93, concludes that a roll of *c.* 11 m would cost about 2 dr, so a single sheet suitable for writing a letter 'would cost one-fifth of an obol – surely not an excessive expense' (p. 90).
132 T. Morgan, *Literate Education in the Hellenistic and Roman Worlds* (Cambridge: Cambridge University Press, 1998), p. 46. In Graeco-Roman Egypt 'the elite were concentrated in the cities': P. van Minnen, 'Boorish or bookish? Literature in Egyptian villages in the Fayum in the Graeco-Roman period', *JJP* 28 (1998): 99–184 (100).
133 H. C. Youtie, 'βραδέως γράφων: between literacy and illiteracy', *GRBS* 12 (1971): 239–61 (252).
134 Cf. ibid., pp. 239–61; Cribiore, *Writing*, pp. 104, 151–2. Slow writers ranged from the illiterate feigning ability to write to those who could write with difficulty in poor hands a short subscription under a text written on their behalf. On possible alternative routes to literacy other than schooling see N. Horsfall, 'Statistics or states of mind', in M. Beard et al., *Literacy in the Roman World* (JRA Supplementary Series, 3; Ann Arbor: University of Michigan Press, 1991), pp. 59–76.
135 Cribiore, *Writing*, p. 20; cf. pp. 132–5. At a slight remove from the slow writer were those who could write 'an epistle in quivering but somewhat empowering characters' (eadem, *Gymnastics*, p. 159), and then those who could more easily write at length, and so on.

Although most literate people came from the middle and upper strata of society,[136] private writers of modest income certainly existed. Apollonios and his brother Ptolemaios, who lived in the Memphite Serapeum in the mid-second century BC, were able to copy Greek literature with different levels of ability.[137] Apollonios, the younger and more proficient writer with an education extending 'somewhat beyond the primary level', was capable of writing letters to officials. He joined the army and eventually became assistant to the chief of police on the necropolis.[138] In a similar vein, Apion, a new recruit to the Roman army in the second century AD, wrote to his father at Philadelphia in large, round capable letters that resemble a teacher's hand. The indications are that he had 'at least some grammatical' or secondary education.[139]

In the early third century a certain 'Antonius Dioskoros, son of Horigenes from Alexandria', was considered suitable for minor public office in his home town of Arsinoe. Like the other applicants he was 'an urban shopkeeper or craftsman of moderate means', but he was also a Christian. His *duo nomina* 'after the Roman fashion, with a Roman *gentilicium* and Greek *cognomen*', and the Alexandrian connection suggest a social position somewhat above the other candidates.[140] Generally speaking, administrative officials had duties requiring literacy, and Antonius Dioskoros should not be seen as one of only a small number of Christians in such roles.[141] Perhaps he was among those who attended a church conference held at Arsinoe in the third century.[142] At the conference the bishop of Alexandria called together the presbyters and teachers of the surrounding villages to examine a book containing the millenarian teachings of a former local bishop. Clearly, non-Christian

---

136   See E. A. Judge and S. R. Pickering, 'Papyrus documentation of church and community in Egypt to the mid-fourth century', *JAC* 20 (1977): 69–70. Cf. Turner, *Greek Papyri*, pp. 82–8; and W. Clarysse, 'Literary papyri in documentary "archives"', in E. Van 't Dack et al. (eds), *Egypt and the Hellenistic World, Proceedings of the International Colloquium, Leuven, 24–26 May 1982* (StHell, 27; Leuven: Peeters, 1983), pp. 43–61.

137   See D. J. Thompson, 'Ptolemaios and the "lighthouse": Greek culture in the Memphite Serapeum', *PCPhS* n.s. 33 (1987): 105–21.

138   Cribiore, *Gymnastics*, pp. 188–9. On writing of letters see pp. 215–19.

139   Ibid., pp. 245–6 (BGU 2.423).

140   P. van Minnen, 'The roots of Egyptian Christianity', *APF* 40 (1994): 71–85, esp. 75–7.

141   See P.Col. 8.230 (early III? Karanis), the deacons Anchophis and Sansneus are nominated as *sitologoi*; P.Oxy. 10.1254 (260, Oxyrhchus), Petrus is appointed to an expensive public office; and P.Cair.Isid. 114 (304, Karanis), Johannes, a former gymnasiarch. For other Christian papyri and letters see M. Naldini, *Il Cristianesimo in Egitto: lettere private nei papiri dei secoli II-IV* (*Biblioteca Patristica*; Firenze: Nardini Editore, rev. edn 1998); Judge and Pickering 'Papyrus documentation'; and 'Conspectus', AHDRC, Macquarie University.

142   See Eusebius, *HE* 7.24.

'Egyptian priests were not the only ones assiduously reading and interpreting' and *copying* religious texts in the villages of the Fayum.[143] By this time, levels of Greek literacy had probably increased along with Hellenization in areas such as Egypt where literacy had formerly been confined to specific 'social and geographic milieus'.[144] At a very general level, this may have contributed to the increase in 'private' gospel MSS, apparently produced in uncontrolled settings, in the third century.

In practice, however, gospel MSS and particularly small fragments can sometimes be difficult to categorize (see the number of designations qualified by question marks in column 8 of Table 1). Often the uncertainty is because the fragment does not provide enough evidence to allow us to be decisive either way. But in other cases, certainty is hindered by mixed signals. This should come as no surprise given the range of variables that might come into play. For example, did the exemplar have public or private characteristics, or both? Was the copying done in a controlled or uncontrolled setting for public or private use? What changes might have been made to an exemplar during production to bring about a desired outcome in terms of enhanced readability? And the question that naturally follows on from these: to what extent do these variables undermine the validity of 'public' and 'private' as categories? A hypothetical comparison of copying in controlled and uncontrolled settings, though inevitably somewhat speculative, may help to provide an answer.

Christian copying centres in major cities would probably have maintained master copies of *public* gospel MSS. Copying MSS was, after all, their *raison d'être*. This may explain the greater consistency in the transmission of 'public' features (text division, punctuation and lectional aids) which seems to have characterized controlled production. When working from a gospel exemplar provided by a client rather than an in-house master copy, trained scribes working in Christian copying centres would understand their task involved copying text division, punctuation and lectional aids where they were original to the exemplar. If they were lacking in the exemplar provided, they could be inserted at sense breaks or by reference to a master copy.[145] This can be taken a step further. If such copying centres were attached to larger churches, the 'master' copies were probably MSS read in the church. As P[37] and P[45] demonstrate, later readers of MSS (not to mention lectors and/or clergy who regularly read or

---

143   Van Minnen, 'Boorish or bookish?' p. 184. He argues that Christians must have comprised at least 25 percent of the population of Egypt in the early fourth century ('Roots', p. 73). R. S. Bagnall, *Egypt in Late Antiquity* (Princeton: Princeton University Press, 1993), p. 281, estimates that Christians were in the majority by the death of Constantine in 337.

144   W. V. Harris, 'Literacy and epigraphy, I', *ZPE* 52 (1983): 87–111 (97).

145   See Johnson, *Bookrolls*, pp. 58–9; and Tov, *Scribal Practices*, p. 150 (cited above in n. 23).

consulted MSS) marked the text to assist comprehension and public reading. Over time the added sense breaks, whether they were marked in the same way or otherwise, might have found their way into copies made from the 'master'. Indeed, this was probably an important stimulus to the development of the systematic use of punctuation and lectional aids. Moreover, as just mentioned, there is reason to believe that this process was well advanced in Christian copying centres in the second half of the second century.

In private/uncontrolled settings copies would be made from whatever MS could be obtained. 'Cross-fertilization' was probably always a factor, but the evidence suggests that the exemplars used often had 'private' characteristics. Over time this would naturally change as private readers marked sense breaks, 'public' features in exemplars increased, and Christian copying centres assumed the entire burden of producing copies of the new scriptures. The varying levels of ability of private or casual copyists should also be considered.[146] Untrained copyists would not attach the same importance to reproducing reader's aids as trained scribes, and would be more likely to overlook or reproduce them only some of the time. Educated Christians and Christian public officials or business people used to dealing with records might fall into this category. Commissioned non-Christian scribes or Christian scribes working in secular settings would be more likely to reproduce the reader's aids in the exemplar. The needs of the 'customer' – i.e., intended private/non-liturgical use – was probably another factor that affected 'the presence or absence of lectional signs'.[147] This could also apply when copies were made by trained scribes among the slaves or freedmen of Christians. That is, if MSS were being produced in uncontrolled settings for private/non-liturgical use, the reproduction of reader's aids would be a lower priority. But because trained copyists could still be involved, it is not possible to equate strictly the public/controlled and private/uncontrolled categories with professional/trained scribes and untrained copyists, respectively.

As noted at the beginning of this chapter, there are other complicating factors. An individual might make or obtain a copy of a 'public' MS for 'private' use, or a MS could potentially be used in both public and private settings. In some areas churches might have had no option but to use gospel MSS lacking 'public' characteristics in public worship. In such cases lectors would need to have become very familiar with the contents of the text. But the evidence shows that this level of familiarity must have been the exception rather than the rule. The use and consolidation of text division, punctuation and lectional aids in second- to fourth-century public MSS, the later addition of text division markers to P[37] and P[45], and

---

146 Of course, this was also a factor in controlled production settings.
147 Johnson, *Bookrolls*, p. 17.

ɪes may also have existed at Smyrna and Oxyrhynchus[153]
ɪ end of the second century. 'If so, that is all the more reason to
ɪ scriptoria in Alexandria and other Christian centers at an earlier
ɪ4 Much early Christian literature was written with a wide
ɪership in mind, e.g., the Apocalypse and the catholic and pseud-
ɪymous epistles,[155] and more significantly the gospel MSS themselves
strongly suggest that this was the case.

5. *Conclusion*

As the authoritativeness of the four Gospels increased in the third century,
it was to be expected that uncontrolled copying of gospel MSS for private
use would increase. It seems as the number of churches and the demand
for gospel MSS grew, so did the number of gospels produced in private
settings. It is also likely that individuals could more easily make or
commission copies for personal use as the number of gospels in circulation
increased. Third-century codices are still quite narrow physically (i.e., they
remain within a range of about 10–14 cm), but heights increase
significantly.[156] Nevertheless, MSS produced for private use in casual
settings usually conform to third-century 'standards'. This should come as
no surprise. The dictates of third-century convention were obviously of
some importance. Indeed, the conventional features of the MSS themselves
provide evidence that cannot be ignored for the existence of communication and consensus between early Christian groups.

However, as P[45] has demonstrated, there are sometimes a number of
complicated factors to be weighed against each other when deciding
whether a particular MS is 'public' or 'private'. Although there was clearly
variation in the use of lectional aids and text division markers,[157]

153 Roberts, *Manuscript*, p. 24.
154 Gamble, *Books and Readers*, p. 122. On the problems with using the word
'scriptorium' with reference to the first few centuries see n. 51.
155 Gamble, *Books and Readers*, pp. 104–7.
156 Of the codices listed in Turner's Group 8 (in which breadth is about half height) and
its two sub-classes, 30 of 38 are dated III or IV (Turner, *Typology*, pp. 20–1).
157 In comparing text division in P[66] and P[75] Martin and Kasser (*Luc*, p. 15) note
agreement and disagreement and conclude that the practice was still in its developmental
phase. By the time of the great fourth- and fifth-century codices, the primary markers of text
division (*ekthesis* and vacant line ends) are virtually settled, but there are still individual
differences. My own examination of quality facsimiles found that Sinaiticus has *ekthesis*,
vacant line ends, the occasional medial point or dicolon, but not the *paragraphos*. Likewise,
Vaticanus contains *ekthesis*, vacant line ends, and a very occasional high point, but also
vacant spaces in the text, the *paragraphos*, and dicola at the end of Matthew, Mark and John,
but not Luke. While Alexandrinus has *ekthesis*, vacant line ends, vacant spaces in the text
and medial points, but not the *paragraphos*.

conventional textual and codicological features when considered *as a group* are important indicators of the setting in and purpose for which gospel MSS were produced. Such features provide an additional way of weighing the reliability of textual witnesses. The same controls were not in place when gospel MSS were copied privately in casual settings.

The influence of convention on the production of the four Gospels in the second and third centuries can be seen in preference for the codex in certain sizes, the ubiquitous presence of the *nomina sacra* convention, and the use of text division, punctuation and lectional aids.[158] When third-century gospel MSS lack reading aids and text division, it is likely that private/uncontrolled copying and/or production for non-liturgical use are responsible. Uncontrolled copying is also discernible in documentary and informal hands, an absence of collation, correction, or similar quality control, and in scribal approaches that take significant liberties with the text. Thus, even an impressive MS like P[45] can be designated 'private'.

---

158 The second-century evidence itself vitiates any perceived circularity in the argument.

O

A JOHANNINE READING OF OXYRHYNCHUS PAPYRUS 840

Pamela Shellberg

A small piece of parchment catalogued as P.Oxy. 840 contains the account of an exchange between Jesus and a chief priest in the temple in which the two debate what kind of bathing is required to be clean. The contrast between moral and ritual purity led earliest interpreters to judge the fragment an apocryphal elaboration of the Synoptic Gospels. However, research developments in the past few decades across a number of related fields have brought its Johannine features into sharper relief. Characteristics recognized as hallmarks of the Fourth Gospel appear in the fragment's dominant water motif and Jesus' critique of ritual practices: the text on the fragment bears the distinctively Johannine phrase, 'living water'; there is an allusion to foot washing; the episode takes place near an immersion pool at the temple, a setting matched only in the Fourth Gospel's report of the invalid near the Sheep Gate.[1]

Recent archaeological evidence confirms the accuracy and detail of the fragment's description of a stepped immersion pool. Studies of purity in Second Temple Judaism suggest that the author of the parchment text was actually quite familiar with the ritual of body immersion required for entrance into the temple and aware of debates about what constituted valid water for purification purposes. This research makes it plausible to locate the author of the text closer to the pre-70 CE time period and revives the question of the episode's historical veracity. Scholarly reconstructions of the Johannine community at its earliest stages have identified a Samaritan influence, the language and theology of which may account for some otherwise difficult features in the parchment text. An intertextual analysis of the fourth evangelist's exegesis illuminates a hermeneutic interest in immersion pools clearly shared by the fragment's author.[2] The

---

1 The invalid at the Sheep's Gate pool is in Jn 5.1-18; the phrase 'living water' is in 4.10, 4.11, and 7.38. All biblical references are taken from the NRSV.

2 Raymond E. Brown, *The Gospel According to John 13–21* (AB, 29; Garden City, NY: Doubleday, 1970); idem, *The Community of the Beloved Disciple: The Life, Loves, and Hates of an Individual Church in New Testament Times* (New York: Paulist, 1979); Craig R.

fragment has still more to yield and so this essay contributes to the recently revived conversation about P.Oxy. 840 by extending further attention to its Johannine aspects.

The History of P.Oxy. 840[3]

When Bernard P. Grenfell and Arthur S. Hunt published the 1905 discovery of P.Oxy. 840, they relied on the highly esteemed Emil Schürer for its interpretation. Schürer determined that the author of the parchment text could not possibly have been well acquainted with the temple or its attendant ritual practices. On the basis of Schürer's expertise, the fragment was dated to the late second century, characterized as an apocryphal elaboration of Mt. 15.1-20 and Mk 7.1-23, and then, after a flurry of initial attention, largely disregarded.[4] Joachim Jeremias studied the fragment again in 1947.[5] On the weight of archaeological findings, exegetical comparisons to the Synoptic Gospels, and his reading of the Mishnah and Talmud, Jeremias demonstrated that many of Grenfell and Hunt's conclusions about P.Oxy. 840 could no longer be sustained. Yet, even after its inclusion in the 1958 publication of Jeremias's *Unknown Sayings of Jesus*, P.Oxy. 840 received no substantive attention again until after the year 2000; François Bovon argued that the fragment was a polemical work reflecting early Christian baptismal controversies and, after analyzing the fragment's paleography, Michael J. Kruger proffered an answer to the question of whether the vellum leaf had been part of an amulet or of a miniature codex.[6] However, neither scholar took up the

---

Koester, *Symbolism in the Fourth Gospel: Meaning, Mystery, Community* (Minneapolis: Fortress, 1995); Carol B. Selkin, 'Exegesis and Identity: The Hermeneutics of *miqwā'ôt* in the Greco-Roman Period' (PhD diss., Duke University, 1993).

3   Jack Finegan (*Hidden Records of the Life of Jesus* [Philadelphia: Pilgrim, 1969], p. 226) notes that although this fragment was found and subsequently catalogued as a papyrus along with the other papyri found at Oxyrhynchus, it is actually a parchment fragment. This distinction could suggest a place of origin other than Egypt. Since it has been speculated the fragment was originally part of an amulet worn around the neck, that it somehow traveled *to* Egypt most likely explains its presence there.

4   B. P. Grenfell and A. S. Hunt, *The Oxyrhynchus Papyrus, Part V* (London: Egypt Exploration Fund, 1908), p. 4.

5   J. Jeremias, 'Der Zusammenstoss Jesu mit dem pharisäischen Oberpriester auf dem Tempelplatz. Zu Pap. Ox. V, 840', in *Coniectanea Neotestamentica XI in honorem Antonii Fridrichsen* (Lund: C. W. K. Gleerup, 1947), pp. 97–108.

6   J. Jeremias, *Unknown Sayings of Jesus* (London: SPCK, 1908), pp. 36–49; F. Bovon, 'Fragment Oxyrynchus 840: Fragment of a Lost Gospel, Witness of an Early Controversy Over Purity', *JBL* 119 (2000): 705–28; M. J. Kruger, 'P. Oxy. 840: Amulet or Miniature Codex?' *JTS* 53 (2002): 81–94. David Tripp also argued that P.Oxy. 840 reflected early Christian baptismal controversies in 'Meanings of the Foot-washing: John 13 and Papyrus

issue of the historicity of the fragment's text against the background of Judaism.

Kruger then extended his research beyond codicology and paleography to include the first comprehensive analysis of the fragment. In his 2005 monograph, *The Gospel of the Savior*, Kruger deals fully with issues of historicity, language, provenance, and theology. Comparing P.Oxy. 840 to the canonical gospels, he accentuates similarities between the text of the fragment and two Fourth Gospel texts in particular: the festival of Booths (John 7) and Jesus washing the disciples' feet (John 13.1-20).[7] He describes the composition as a conflation of elements from the canonical gospels like other second-century apocryphal works; the style of this fragment imitates the canonical gospels' presentation of Jesus but at the same time also accurately and correctly reflects first-century Jewish ritual purity practices.[8]

Synopsis of Text and Translation

Jesus enters the temple court with his disciples and encounters the priest, a certain Levi, who challenges Jesus' presence there because Jesus has not bathed nor have his disciples washed their feet. There is an exchange between them about what is required in order to be ritually clean. Jesus asks Levi about his own state of cleanliness, to which Levi responds with a very detailed description of his immersion in the Pool of David and subsequent clothing in clean and white garments. Jesus charges Levi with having bathed in unclean water and having washed in the secular manner of harlots and pipe-girls. He rejects Levi's charge that he and his disciples have not been bathed themselves because, in fact, they have been dipped in the water of life.

[21]And the Savior immediately stood still with his disciples and responded to him, 'Are you, then, being here in the temple, clean?'

And he said to him, 'I am clean

[25]for I washed in the pool of David and having descended by a staircase by another I ascended, and white garments I put on and clean, and then I came in and looked upon these holy

---

Oxyrhchus 840', *ExpTim* 103 (1992): 237–39. On the question of amulet or codex, see also Thomas J. Kraus, 'P. Oxy. V 840 – Amulett oder Miniaturkodex? Grundsätzliche und ergänzende Anmerkungen zu zwei Termini', *ZAC* 8 (2005): 485–97.

7 M. J. Kruger, *Gospel of the Savior: An Analysis of P.Oxy. 840 and its Place in the Gospel Traditions of Early Christianity* (Leiden: Brill, 2005), 176–82.

8 Ibid., pp. 203–205. Kruger dates the fragment to the early- to middle-second century and offers the tentative conclusion that P.Oxy. 840 was written by a Nazarene group with two purposes in mind: first, to defend against the criticisms of rabbinic Jews by claiming that they, the Nazarenes, had been made clean in Jesus Christ; second, to refute the Ebionites who had splintered off over the question of Jewish self-identity and the role of the laws of ritual purity in the construction of that identity (pp. 203–5).

³⁰things.' The Savior answering him
said, 'Woe, you blind ones, not seeing!
You bathed in these poured out
waters in which dogs and pigs have been
lying
night and day, and washing
³⁵the outside skin you have wiped yourself
off which also
the prostitutes and the pipe girls
pour perfume and wash and wipe off
and beautify the face for the desires
of men. But inside they are filled

⁴⁰with scorpions and
all manner of evil. But I and
my disciples, whom you say have not
washed, we have been dipped in
living waters having come from . . [.]
⁴⁵but woe to you [. . .]

Archaeological Evidence for miqwa'ôt

Among the evidence advanced by Schürer that the author of this passage was unfamiliar with the temple or temple practices was the supposedly 'fanciful' description of the stepped pool. Grenfell and Hunt concluded that the two stairways leading into and out of the pool of David seemed to be a detail 'invented for the sake of rhetorical effect'.[9] Recent archaeological evidence proves, however, that stepped pools used for the purpose of purification were not an invention of the author's imagination.[10] In fact, this description is consistent with descriptions of immersion pools, first identified as *miqweh* or, in the plural, *miqwa'ôt*, on an archaeological dig in the mid-1960s when two such water installations were discovered at Masada. Since then, more than 100 stepped pools in Israel have been identified as *miqwa'ôt* from the Second Temple period, including several in close proximity to the Temple Mount.[11] Approximately 60 have been found in the Upper City of Jerusalem, noteworthy and relevant as will be shown below for being the residence of the priestly aristocracy.

9   Grenfell and Hunt, *Oxyrhynchus Papyrus*, p. 3.
10   E. P. Sanders, *Jewish Law from Jesus to the Mishnah* (Philadephia: Trinity Press International, 1990), p. 39. In contrast to disputes over the purity practice of handwashing, Sanders judges that a dispute over the construction of immersion pools would necessarily show an extensive knowledge of Judaism.
11   Selkin, 'Exegesis', pp. 78–79. See also Ronny Reich, 'The Synagogue and the *miqveh* in Eretz-Israel in the Second-Temple, Mishnaic, and Talmudic Periods', in *Ancient Synagogues: Historical Analysis an Archaeological Discovery* (ed. D. Urman and P. V. M. Flesher; Leiden: Brill, 1995), p. 296. For a discussion of the cautions in archaeological interpretation, see Benjamin G. Wright, 'Jewish Ritual Baths – Interpreting the Digs and the Texts: Some Issues in the Social History of Second Temple Judaism', in *The Archaeology of Israel: Constructing the Past, Interpreting the Present* (JSOTSup, 237; ed. N. A. Silberman and D. B. Small; Sheffield: Sheffield Academic press, 1997), pp. 193–96. There is a range of interpretation given to the presence of *miqwā'ôt*. Reich and Sanders accept that almost all of

Interestingly, no early *miqwa'ôt* have been located outside Palestine, providing clues about the possible location of the author of P.Oxy. 840.[12]

A number of *miqwa'ôt* from the Second Temple Period contain partitions – either constructed or hewn into the bedrock – extending from the entranceway and down the middle of the steps.[13] In other *miqwa'ôt* there are instead two sets of steps probably serving to separate the impure on their way into the pool from the purified on their way out.[14] The archaeological data thus corroborate the description given in the passage of the Pharisee's immersion in a stepped pool.

Literary Evidence for the Practice of Ritual Immersion

The water in the *miqweh* also had to be 'living water' (according to Lev. 11.36; 15.13) which meant naturally flowing or moving, not drawn, water.[15] While there is evidence for sectarian debate over non-scriptural details about the storage of pure water and the blending of pure and impure water, there was considerable agreement about the basic nature of living vs. drawn water. Similarly, despite the diversities of Second Temple Judaism there was remarkable unanimity that it was living water in which the ritually impure must wash by full body immersion.[16] This distinction is made plain in the parchment text when Jesus contrasts the water in which Levi has bathed, χεομένοις ὕδασι, or 'poured out water', with the water in which Jesus and his disciples have bathed, ὕδασι ζωῆς, or 'waters of life'.[17]

---

the pools are *miqwā'ôt* while Wright, concerned about the dearth of textual evidence concerning ritual bathing from the Second Temple period, considers some to have had industrial or other uses.

12   Selkin, 'Exegesis', p. 94. The single reference to immersion in the Diaspora is found in Justin's *Dialogue with Trypho* (46.2), where Justin accuses the Jews of digging pits or cisterns which purify only the body; in Sanders, *Jewish Law*, p. 360, n. 11 and Wright, 'Jewish Ritual Baths', p. 206.

13   Selkin, 'Exegesis', pp. 88–89.

14   Sanders, 'Jewish Law', pp. 217–18.

15   Marianne Sawicki (*Crossing Galilee: Architectures of Contact in the Occupied Land of Jesus* [Harrisburg: Trinity Press International, 2000], p. 23) describes the water suitable for the purifications prescribed in Jewish law as 'running water or, more exactly, water whose natural downward valence from the heavens has not been interrupted by human hands... But cistern water cannot be used, because it has been lifted, and thus is perceived to have acquired a contrary valence.'

16   Wright, 'Ritual Baths', p. 213.

17   This reconstruction of lines 43–44 is given by both Grenfell and Hunt, *Oxyrhynchus Papyrus*, pp. 7–10, and Finegan, *Hidden Records*, pp. 229–30. Grenfell and Hunt reconstruct the text ἐν ὕδασι ζω[ῆς αἰωίνου τοῖ]ς ἐλθοῦσιν ἀπό..., 'into the waters of eternal life', but acknowledge in their notes that it could be ζῷσι, 'with another word in place of αἰωνίου'. Finegan's reconstruction is ἐν ὕδασι ζω[ῆς...τοῖ]ς ἐλθοῦσιν ἀπό..., 'in the waters of life'. It

In Second Temple Jewish writings, there is very little evidence from which to construct a detailed picture of the practice of ritual immersion.[18] The bulk of the information comes from Philo and Josephus writing from Diaspora communities where, curiously, no *miqwa'ôt* have been uncovered. However, it is clear from this literature that Jews did in fact bathe their bodies to remove various states of impurity that would prevent access to the temple.

Of some interest at this point is a discussion attributed to the Houses of Shammai and Hillel.[19] The debate is over rules, attributed to the Shammaites, opposing two practices: immersing in drawn water, and bathing after immersion by having clean, drawn water poured over the bather.[20] The existence of these rules suggests that not everyone accepted the pharisaic definition of valid water, and that it is the aristocrats of the Upper City of Jerusalem against whom, in particular, this decree might be directed. It is important to keep in mind at this point that the water in a *miqweh*, while ritually pure, would not be considered clean by any standards of hygiene. In fact, the water in the single-pool *miqweh* often and regularly was somewhat fetid and stagnant. Those who could afford to do so probably bathed again after their ritual immersion in hygienically clean water. Evidence has shown that houses in the Upper City of Jerusalem had both *miqwa'ôt* and bathtubs.

The Samaritan Influence

In the Fourth Gospel, the evangelist departs from what is known of Jesus' ministry in the Synoptic Gospels with a story of travels through Samaria where Jesus wins a whole Samaritan village over to the belief that he is the Savior of the world (4.42).

In his reconstruction of the historical development of the Johannine community, Raymond E. Brown posits an original group into which a

---

seems to me that the better reconstruction is ζῶσιν, a dative plural to stand with the ἐν ὕδασι. I suspect the theology of 'eternal life' was congenial to Grenfell and Hunt and that Finegan chose to omit their speculation on the missing word in his translation. However, in omitting the αἰωίνου he omits the reason for the genitive ζωῆς. I would translate it literally as something like 'into life waters'. Kruger reconstructs εν υδασι ζω[σιν εκ του ουρανο] υ ελτηουσιν, *Gospel of the Savior*, p. 68.

18 Wright, 'Ritual Baths', pp. 205–10. Reading Philo, Josephus, 2 Maccabees, and Judith, Wright concludes that, in contrast to the substantial attention given to immersions in the rabbinic literature, there is little information about what constituted valid water for the immersions or where they were performed.

19 Sanders, 'Jewish Law', p. 224, following Neusner, dates the debate as late pharisaic rather than early rabbinic.

20 Ibid., p. 226.

second group of Christians was converted.[21] He reads the episode of Jesus' interaction with the Samaritan woman at the well and the generally positive portrayal of Samaritans as evidence of their entrance into the community. The charge against Jesus by Jews, 'Are we not right in saying that you are a Samaritan and have a demon?' (8.48) indicates that the Johannine community was regarded by Jews as having Samaritan elements.[22] Brown further posits that this second group 'consisted of Jews of peculiar anti-Temple views who converted Samaritans and picked up some elements of Samaritan thought, including a Christology that was not centered on a Davidic Messiah'.[23]

Brown's theories are relevant for the study of P.Oxy. 840 for at least two reasons. First, the theory of Samaritan influence is linked to the story of the woman at the well, the episode which contains a reference to ὕδωρ ζῶν, 'living water' (4.10, 11). This is a phrase and concept unique to the Fourth Gospel, and a verbal link to the parchment fragment. Second, the only reference to Jesus as 'Savior' in the whole of the gospel is here in this passage.[24] Scholars who date P.Oxy. 840 to the second century or later have done so, in part, on the basis of identification of Jesus as Savior as an indication of gnostic influence.[25] If Brown's reconstruction is accepted as a premise, then the term 'Savior' may appear on the parchment as a marker of the influence of Samaritan Christology.[26] By itself the occurrence of σωτήρ is not enough to identify a Samaritan influence. But, in combination with the anti-temple practice polemic presented by this text and its satirical rejection of things Davidic, a stronger case can be made for it. If the author of P.Oxy. 840 is associated in some way with the Johannine community, or is in contact with its emerging theology and Christology, then the identification of Jesus as Savior is not anomalous, and a second-century dating or gnostic influences are not necessary to explain it.

21   Brown, *Community*, pp. 36–54.
22   Ibid., p. 37.
23   Ibid., p. 38.
24   Jn 4.42: 'They said to the woman, "It is no longer because of what you said that we believe, for we have heard for ourselves, and we know that this is truly the Savior of the world."' There are only two occurrences of σωτήρ in the Synoptics, both in Luke: 'my spirit rejoices in God my Savior', (1.46), and 'for to you is born this day in the city of David, a Savior, who is Christ the Lord' (2.11).
25   Finegan, *Hidden Records*, p. 230. Finegan characterizes the usage as 'more like the usage in gnostic texts than in the canonical gospels'.
26   The idea that the history of a Johannine community can actually be reconstructed has and will continue to be debated and explored. Brown's theories have been challenged, but not abandoned, and still shape historical-critical studies of the Fourth Gospel. For a general discussion of the *status quaestiones*, see Robert Kysar, 'The Whence and Whither of the Johannine Community', in *Life in Abundance: Studies of John's Gospel in Tribute to Raymond E. Brown* (ed. John R. Donahue; Collegeville, MN: Liturgical, 2005).

Jesus as miqweh *of Israel*

Carol Selkin focuses on the hermeneutics of the *miqwa'ôt* and argues, in part and through an exegesis of Jn 5.1-18, that the author of the Fourth Gospel was delivering a first-century commentary on the word *miqweh*.[27] Her study of the story of the invalid healed by Jesus at the pool by the Sheep Gate is an intertextual one, and the word *miqweh* is explored in its juxtaposition with 'the fount of living water' in Jer. 17.13.

> O LORD, the hope of Israel,
> all who forsake thee shall be put to shame;
> those who turn away from thee shall be written in the earth,
> for they have forsaken the LORD, the fountain of living water.
> Heal me, O LORD, and I shall be healed;
> save me, and I shall be saved.[28]

Selkin notes that the word *miqweh* never appears in the Hebrew Bible in its technical sense of a ritual bathing pool, although it appears occasionally as a 'gathering of water'. Her analysis centers on its alternative meaning, 'hope', and she argues that Jeremiah's juxtaposition of the 'hope of Israel' with 'fountain of living water' leads to an interpretation in the Johannine community consistent with its interest in a kind of replacement theology: Jesus, represented as fulfilling or abolishing Jewish cultic institutions, becomes the *miqweh* of Israel. By appropriating the text from Jeremiah in the story of the invalid at the Sheep Gate pool to attack the laws against healing and carrying on the Sabbath, and probably also legal issues around the use of *miqwa'ôt*, the gospel argues for its own non-halakhic hermeneutic in understanding the scriptures.[29]

Selkin's work establishes a link between Jesus, the *miqwa'ôt*, and the concept of living water in the Fourth Gospel. These same links are suggested in P.Oxy. 840.

A Johannine Reading of P.Oxy. 840

A Certain Pharisee

Jesus brings the disciples into the place of purification, but it seems that he himself moves on to walk about in the Temple Court. He is addressed by 'a certain Pharisee, a chief priest, Levi by name'. This is a curious amalgam of titles and roles, historically all distinct, but narratively one. While the chief priests were usually Sadducees, there were instances of high priests who were Pharisees, making the combination of Pharisee and

---

27   Selkin, 'Exegesis', p. 182.
28   This is Selkin's translation of Jer. 17.13 ('Exegesis', p. 180).
29   Selkin, 'Exegesis', p. 216.

chief priest here a legitimate one.[30] The name given to this Pharisee, Levi, may echo the *Testaments of the Twelve Patriarchs*, where the patriarch Levi recalls specific instructions given to him regarding ritual bathing: 'And before entering into the holy place, bathe; and when thou offerest the sacrifices wash; and again, when thou finishest the sacrifice, wash'.[31] It may also simply refer to the Levites, or to Levitical practices. Josephus reported that Levites were allowed white robes in 65 CE; this would cohere with the reference by the Pharisee to the 'clean and white' clothes he put on after immersing in the pool.[32]

Jesus' opponents are much more likely to be generalized in the Fourth Gospel without the sectarian distinctions characteristic of the Synoptics. The evangelist refers to 'the chief priests and Pharisees' but makes no mention of other groups known to have been present in Jesus' time, such as the Sadducees, Herodians, zealots, or scribes. The gospel was written after 70 CE, a time when many of the religious distinctions of Jesus' day no longer had any meaning. The destruction of the temple had simplified Judaism and such that only the chief priests and Pharisees remain in John – the chief priests because their role in the Sanhedrin and the trials of Jesus was too essential a part of the story to be omitted; the Pharisees because they are the sect that survived the temple's destruction in 70 CE.[33] The text of P.Oxy. 840 may reflect a similar process of simplification.

However, the amalgamation of Pharisee, Sadducee, and Levite into one person may also suggest an author who was perhaps more closely related to the pre-70 CE time period and was quite intentionally rendering the religious distinctions meaningless, critiquing all forms of priestly/temple leadership as a single unity because, on the matter of purity regulations, Jesus (and the group he represents) stood outside of all the in-house debates.

The Pool of David

When Jesus asks Levi if he is clean, the Pharisee describes his own immersion in 'the pool of David'. According to Jeremias, and undisputed since, the Pool of David in Jerusalem is nowhere else attested. However, many scholars would agree that the fact that it has not been located does not prove that it never existed. Similarly, the pools known as Bethzatha

---

30   Grenfell and Hunt, *Oxyrhynchus Papyrus*, p. 8; Kruger, *Gospel of the Savior*, pp. 98–100.

31   *T. Levi* 9.

32   Josephus, *Ant.* 20.216-18, quoted in Sanders, *Jewish Law*, p. 37.

33   Brown, *Gospel*, p. lxxii. He observes, 'the disappearance of these groups is the work of simplification and the change of historical perspective'.

and attested only in John 5 have also not been uncovered.[34]

However, uncertainty about whether the pool existed does not translate into a certainty that it did. It is entirely possible that the pool, or at least its designation as the 'Pool of David', is the author's construction revealing the previously posited Samaritan influence. Since the whole of Samaritan theology was directed against the claims of the Davidic dynasty and of Jerusalem, the Davidic city, the fragment's author may be satirizing the *miqweh*, which here is the site of the anti-temple polemic, as the Pool of David.[35]

Jesus describes Levi's immersion in particular terms and, with the phrase νιψάμενος τὸ ἐκτὸς δέρμα ἐσμήξω, claims that Levi has washed his outer skin and wiped himself off just as the harlots do when they anoint themselves, then wash and wipe themselves off. This sequence is very similar to that described and prescribed for the Roman bath.[36] Jesus' characterization of Levi's bath more closely describes what happens in a Greco-Roman bath, not a *miqweh*.[37] The sensuousness of the mention of the pipe-girls is also in keeping with Roman bathing customs – a detail alluding to secular style bathing. The presence of the harlots is consistent with the sexual and moral corruption associated with baths and which drew the greatest public censure.[38]

The descriptions of the *miqweh* and the Roman-style bath indicate that the author of P.Oxy. 840 was well acquainted with the water installations in Palestine and their relevance for temple rituals, and with pre-rabbinic debates about acceptable bathing practices. Through Jesus a critique appears to be leveled at those who are observing a practice in the wrong sequence. While Levi may have washed in the Pool of David and thereby considers himself ritually clean, he may have then also bathed in a secular bath that makes him no more pure than dogs and swine. This bath is not a bath of living water, but of waters that have been 'poured out' and

---

34   Selkin, 'Exegesis', pp. 175–79. Selkin encourages cautious and restrained judgments when interpreting texts that reference particular sites: 'Lack of knowledge about the site makes it impossible to know with certainty whether the gospel might have been satirizing a particular institution or practice, since if we can't be sure of the location, we surely can't be definite about how the site functioned within the variegated Judaism of the time.'

35   Brown, *Community*, p. 44.

36   Fikret Yegül, *Baths and Bathing in Classical Antiquity* (New York: The Architectural History Foundation, 1992), p. 34. Roman bathing began in the *sudatoria*, a kind of sauna or hothouse, and, after a time of working up a good sweat, the bather would move to the *caldarium* where hot water would be sprinkled on the body. It was customary to end this hot bath by rubbing the body with specially prepared cosmetics and perfumed oils. A slightly curved metal blade called a strigle was then used to scrape down sweat and excess oils from the body. After a plunge in the cold pool of the *fridigarium*, the body was wiped off with cloths or sponges.

37   Sawicki, personal correspondence, September 2003.

38   Yegül, *Baths and Bathing*, p. 40.

therefore also drawn. The secular bath would make a person clean, that is hygienic, but not pure according to Levitical standards. Jesus therefore accuses Levi of being like the harlots and pipe-girls who, in the secular bathhouse, also wash and beautify just the outer skin. At this point in the text, the argument seems to follow the logic of the pharisaic debate: because Levi did not follow his secular style bath with immersion in the *miqweh*, he remains as the harlots and pipe-girls – with scorpions and all manner of unrighteousness within. The striking similarity to debates about internal and external purity found in Mk 7.1-8, Mt. 15.1-9, and Mt. 23.27-28 is what led Jeremias to speak of P.Oxy. 840 as 'an unknown gospel of Synoptic type'.[39]

But if the text represents the debate about a proper bathing-immersion sequence, then one must ask what the significance is in having Jesus challenge Levi over what is, in fact, an in-house debate. Perhaps Jesus, or the author through Jesus, criticizes the ways or means by which water is transferred into the *miqweh*. It is possible that Jesus represents a position outside the debate that would strictly define living water in terms of natural water – rivers, creeks, and springs, for example – and therefore would disallow any artificial structure.

However, similarities with the Fourth Gospel caution against reading this as a purity debate. It is more likely that, through Jesus, the author is critiquing the entire intra-Jewish conversation about living and drawn water – and the use of immersion pools at all.[40] Regardless of whether Levi has immersed in a secular bath or in a *miqweh*, he is still charged with bathing in a manner and in water that is different than the manner and water in which Jesus and his disciples have been immersed.

Washing and Ritual Bathing

In one of the last lines on the parchment Jesus says, 'But I and my disciples whom you say have not washed, have been dipped/ βεβάμμεθα in living water.' The perfect middle/passive form of the verb βάπτω, 'to dip', has been reconstructed here at a lacuna, only μμεθα showing on the fragment.[41] In Second Temple Jewish literature, seven words are found for washing and bathing but with no one word consistently designating the performance of ritual bathing. Of those seven, three are present in

39 J. Jeremias, 'Oxyrhynchus Papyrus 840', in Wilhelm Schneemelcher (ed.) *New Testament Apocrypha, Vol. 1: Gospels and Related Writings* (trans. R. McL. Wilson; Louisville: Westminster John Knox, 1991), p. 94.

40 In a discussion of the extensive disagreements about purity within Judaism, Sanders observes that menstrual impurity and the water used in immersion pools fell into the category of the most serious purity issues, especially among pietist groups (*Jewish Law*, p. 41).

41 Grenfell and Hunt, *Oxyrhynchus Papyrus*, p. 10; Finegan, *Hidden Records*, p. 229; Kruger, *Gospel of the Savior*, p. 91.

various forms in P.Oxy. 840: βαπτίζω, ἐκνίπτω, and λούω.[42] These three words primarily denote washing/bathing/sprinkling actions taken by a human subject. The possibility that the reconstruction is inaccurate notwithstanding, it is interesting that the word on the lips of Jesus, βάπτω, is outside of this group and is distinct from the other bathing words used in the text. It draws attention to a different kind of process or practice – one distinct from traditional rites and also one not initiated by the individual human agent.

Like the author of the Fourth Gospel, the author of P.Oxy. 840 seems to know a great deal about Judaism and is concerned to critique purity rituals involving water. The reference to 'living water' links the fragment thematically to the gospel, and Jesus' critique of the Pharisee's immersion practice (and perhaps the debates about the immersion rites) coheres with the evangelist's concern to demonstrate how the cultic institutions of Judaism had lost their significance for those who believed in Jesus.[43]

Levi reproaches Jesus for not having bathed but also because the disciples' feet have not been washed. Both the foot-washing and the bathing were required of the priests prior to their service in the temple, and there is evidence to suggest that in the time of Second Temple Judaism the requirements were extended to the common people as well.[44] Laymen entering the 'Inner Court', the Court of the Israelites, could do so only after Levitical purification that required both bathing/immersion and washing their feet (Lev. 14.9; 15.13; Num. 19.19).[45]

Different words are used in P.Oxy. 840 to distinguish the two kinds of washing activity. Jesus has not bathed/λούω, a word that refers, as a rule, to a washing of the whole body. It is the word that has attracted the sense of full body immersion. In middle forms (as here in line 14, λουσαμένῳ) it refers to religious washings; it is defined, with specific reference to P.Oxy. 840, as 'the act of purification necessary before entering the temple'.[46] This is the same term the Pharisee uses when he reviews the purity requirements for entering the temple (line 19) and when he speaks of his own bathing (line 24). It is also the word used when Jesus charges him with ritually bathing in impure water. In these three cases, the middle form is used. The word is also seen in its present active indicative form in

42 Wright, 'Jewish Ritual Baths', pp. 206–7. The four other words are ἀπολούω, προσαποπλύω, λουτρόν, and ῥαντός.

43 Brown, *Community*, pp. 48–49.

44 Robert L. Webb, *John the Baptizer and Prophet: A Socio-Historical Study* (JSNTSup, 62; Sheffield: Sheffield Academic Press, 1991), p. 110.

45 Jeremias, *Unknown Sayings*, p. 41; Adolph Büchler, 'The New "Fragment of an Uncanonical Gospel"', *JQR* 20 (1907–08): 334–36.

46 Frederick W. Danker (ed.), *A Greek-English Lexicon of the New Testament and Other Early Christian Literature* (Chicago: University of Chicago Press, 3rd edn, 2000), p. 603.

line 37; the harlots and the pipe-girls 'wash, λούουσιν, and wipe clean [their skin]'. A distinction is made here from religious washings.

A different kind of washing, νίπτω, is introduced later in the text, in Jesus' description of how Levi has washed and wiped himself clean. The plain sense of νίπτω is that of ordinary, or non-ritual, washing, and is generally used for the washing of a body part, not the entire body. Finally, the word used in Levi's complaint that the disciples' feet have not been washed is βαπτίζω. This word also means 'wash', but specifically in reference to ritual washings.[47]

Levi probably makes the observation that Jesus and his disciples are not bathed or washed on the basis of a dusty or dirty appearance and, in the case of Jesus, the absence of clean garments. He likely assumes they cannot be ritually clean because the water of immersion or foot washing would have given them a more externally clean appearance. There may be nothing more here than the initiation of the conflict that serves as a catalyst for the rest of the episode: Jesus and his disciples fail to observe the cultic regulations and the Pharisee's reproach leads to Jesus' critique of bathing practices and water purity. This is certainly suggested by the ritual connotations of λούω and βαπτίζω. However, read against the background of the foot-washing episode of John 13, several points are worth noting. It is curious that Levi did not have the same expectations of the whole group – Jesus and the disciples together; either all should have bathed or all at least should have washed their feet. The text, however, suggests that Levi accuses Jesus alone of not bathing, while the charge that the disciples' feet have not been washed is something separate.

The fourth evangelist uses νίπτω for Jesus' action in washing the disciples' feet in chapter 13. This is important because it was not the evangelist's intention to portray Jesus as instituting a new or replacement ritual. Rather, the act of washing feet is significant because of its symbolic expression of Jesus' death.[48] In that death, all are made 'clean', rendering superfluous the need for any other kind of washing: Jesus said to [Simon Peter], 'He who has bathed/λελουμένος does not need to wash/νίψασθαι, but he is clean all over' (13.10a).[49] Signified by the 'washing' is what it accomplishes, a spiritual cleansing as complete as a full physical bathing and, since offered in Jesus' death, one that cannot and will not be repeated.[50]

If the author of this parchment text was familiar with the foot-washing tradition or acquainted with Johannine soteriology, the detail of the

---

47   BAGD, 164.

48   Brown, *Commentary*, pp. 565–68; James D. G. Dunn, 'The Washing of Disciples' Feet in John 12.1-20', *ZNW* 61 (1970): 249–51.

49   Georg Richter, 'The Washing of Feet in the Gospel of John', *TD* 14 (1966): 200–03.

50   Dunn, 'Washing', pp. 249–50.

disciples' unwashed feet would be consistent with a belief that as a result of the salvific death of Jesus, there was no longer a need for physical washings. That Jesus' feet are not mentioned coheres with the gospel tradition of Jesus having washed the feet of the others.[51]

Jesus accuses the Pharisee of being blind, of not seeing that the water he has bathed in is 'poured out' water, not 'living water', and therefore impure.[52] Jesus' accusation is delivered in the plural, οὐαὶ τυφλοὶ μὴ ὁρῶντες, suggesting perhaps that all of them – Pharisee, Sadducee, and Levite – are blind, but then addresses Levi in the singular when he talks about his bathing practice. Jesus contrasts the Pharisee's bathing (in impure water) and washing (like the harlots and the pipe-girls) with a different kind of experience, 'having been dipped'/βεβάμμεθα in the 'life waters'.

Finegan reconstructs a lacuna in line 44 so that βάπτω is repeated but he renders it both times 'immersed': 'But I and my disciples, of whom you say we have not immersed ourselves, we have been immersed, βεβα [μμένους βεβά]μμεθα. . .'.[53] This reconstruction and translation loses the distinction the author is making between the Pharisee's expectation of how Jesus should have bathed and the newly introduced 'dipping'.

I am more inclined to follow Grenfell and Hunt who reconstruct the lacuna as βεβα[πτίσθαι βεβά]μμεθα and translate, 'But I and my disciples, who you say have not bathed, have been dipped in the waters. . .' because the distinction between ritual bathing and the new 'dipping' is preserved.[54] However, I would preserve the reference to the initial occurrence of βαπτίζω in line 16, the accusation that the disciples' feet are not washed,

51   At the risk of pushing the comparisons too far, I could not help but note that Jesus tells Simon Peter that if Peter will not allow Jesus to wash his feet, he will have no inheritance or share/μέρος with Jesus. Traditionally it is Levi and his tribe who are given no share of the promised land upon entering (Num. 18.20; Deut. 12.12; 14.27).

52   Jeremias, like Grenfell and Hunt, describes P.Oxy. 840 as presenting a synoptic gospel-like contrast between inward and outward purity, made plain in the contrast between the external bathing prescribed by Jewish law and the immersion of Jesus and his disciples in living water. While I would like to make a case for the closer Johannine comparison, the 'Woe, you blind ones' phrase in this particular context could hardly be more Matthean. In the 'woes to the scribes and Pharisees' of Mt. 23.13-32, Matthew calls the scribes and Pharisees 'blind guides' (23.16, 24), 'blind fools' (23.17), 'blind men' (23.19), and one 'a blind Pharisee' (23.26). These epithets punctuate many examples of what Jesus perceives to be the Pharisees' hypocrisy, several of which have to do with the same point made here in the parchment fragment, that they are worried about outer cleansing and appearances of purity when inside they are full of extortion and rapacity, hypocrisy and iniquity.

53   Finegan, *Hidden Records*, p. 230.

54   Kruger reconstructs line 44 as do Grenfell and Hunt, βεβαπτισθαι βεβαμμεθα, but translates the line, 'But I and my disciples, who you say have not bathed, have been bathed in living waters' (*Gospel of the Savior*, p. 68). Like Finegan's translation, the rendering βεβαμμεθα as 'bathed' misses the point the author is making by introducing βάπτω, 'dipped'.

by translating, 'But I and my disciples, who you say have not **washed**, we have been **dipped**...'. A Johannine reader would remember that in the gospel account, Jesus does not wash his disciples' feet in a ritualistic way – as suggested by the use of νίπτω. By recalling the reference to the ritual washing of feet by the Pharisee's use of βαπτίζω in line 16 and contrasting it with 'dipping', the ritual sense of βαπτίζω is subverted. The disciples' feet were not washed/βαπτίζω because they had already been washed/νίπτω; νίπτω in John 13 symbolized the salvific death which is expressed here in 'dipping'.

All that being said, the 'dipping'/βάπτω is really something of a puzzle. It is difficult to be sure how the author understood the meaning of this word. It may be that there was intentional effort made to not associate this 'dipping' with Christian baptism. To the degree that the intensive form, βαπτίζω, carries such strong connotations of purity and did so with respect to Jewish ritual practice, a Johannine author would not likely use a word that would suggest Christian baptism was connected with purity. Such a connection is not found in the Johannine writings.[55]

But that is to argue for why a certain word is not used, not why one is chosen. The word βάπτω has only four other NT occurrences. One is in Lk. 16.24 where the rich man in Hades asks Abraham to have Lazarus 'dip' his finger into water and cool his tongue. The second and third are in Jn 13.26, an extension of the foot-washing episode, where Jesus identifies his betrayer as the one to whom he will give a morsel that he has 'dipped'. The final occurrence is in the ambiguous text of Rev. 19.13, 'He is clad in a robe dipped in blood, and the name by which he is called is The Word of God'.

The Samaritan converts to the Johannine community expected not a messiah, but a *taheb*, one whom, among other roles, was a 'revealer'.[56] The idea of revelation is very prominent in the Johannine writings, as here the dipped morsel reveals Judas as Jesus' betrayer.[57] In P.Oxy. 840, perhaps, it is Jesus, similarly dipped in the divine 'life waters', who is revealed as the Savior.

---

55   Richter, 'Washing', p. 201.
56   Brown, *Community*, p. 44.
57   Koester, *Symbolism*, p. 163. With reference to another example of the water motif in the Fourth Gospel, Koester suggests that revelation replaces purification: 'The transformation of the water at Cana indicates that purification would now be accomplished through revelation... Through that revelation God "cleanses" by transforming sin into faith, and in so doing replaces the system of Jewish ritual purification.'

Conclusions

P.Oxy. 840 can be read as a non-canonical expression of the replacement theology so prominent in the Fourth Gospel. Selkin offered an intertextual and canonical argument for Jesus as the *miqveh* of Israel; this little parchment fragment may bear noncanonical witness to the same. Brown, in talking about the theme of replacement in the Fourth Gospel, said, 'This replacement is a sign of who Jesus is, namely, the one sent by the Father who is now the only way to the Father. All previous religious institutions, customs and feasts lose meaning in his presence'.[58] The message of the parchment text seems to be the same, specifically, that the institution of washing feet and immersion before entering the temple has lost meaning in the presence of Jesus, whose having been 'dipped in the living water' reveals God's salvation and makes all people clean.

58   Raymond E. Brown, *The Gospel According to John 1–12* (AB, 29; Garden City, NY: Doubleday, 1966), p. 104.

HOW LONG AND OLD IS THE CODEX OF WHICH P.OXY. 1353 IS A LEAF?

Don Barker

Introduction

P.Oxy. 1353 is held at the United Theological Seminary, Dayton, USA.[1] P.Oxy. 1353 consists of four fragments of a leaf from a parchment codex containing 1 Pet. 5.5-13 and written with iron gall ink (see Figure 1). The leaf has been damaged by acid from the ink and it appears also to have some water damage. Although P.Oxy. 1353 has been edited by Grenfell and Hunt another look at the manuscript is warranted because of the misreading of the page number on the verso and a late dating of the manuscript, most probably due to the unfounded notion of the lateness of the refined 'biblical uncial' hand.[2]

The Dimensions of P.Oxy. 1353

The dimensions of the original page were c.13.5 (H) × c.10.1 cm (B). The top margin, c.11 mm, bottom margin, c.23.5 mm, left margin c.13 mm and right margin c.11 mm. P.Oxy. 1353 is a leaf from what would have been a small deluxe parchment edition. Of the sixty-four New Testament codices from the second to the early fourth century, according to most scholars, approximately 7.8 percent are written on parchment. As can be seen from Table 1, New Testament texts from II–early IV, written on parchment,

---

1   I am greatly indebted to the Faculty of the United Theological Seminary, Dayton and especially to Professor Larry Welborn for the invitation to study and to conserve their papyri. I wish also to give thanks to Tim Blinkley whose helpfulness was very much appreciated.

2   Bernard Grenfell and Arthur Hunt, *The Oxyrhynchus Papyri* 11 (Oxford: Oxford University Press, 1915), pp. 5, 6. Like so many early papyrologists, it seems that Grenfell and Hunt presumed that the 'biblical uncial' hand was a late development, but as we argue elsewhere, this view has no real evidence to support it and there are good reasons to suggest that the style is quite early in its appearance.

Fig. 1. P.Oxy. 1353 (recto)

tend to be deluxe editions. For images of these manuscripts see Figures 9–13.[3]

Table 1 Books of the New Testament II–early IV on parchment in codex form

Sigla	Date	Prov.	NT	Size (cm)	Book Style
P.Berl. inv.11765	II/III	unknown	**Acts 5**	[11.5 × 12]	Semi-deluxe Ed.
P.Ant. 1.12	III?	Antinoopolis	**2 John 1**	9 × 10	Deluxe Ed.
P.Berl. inv. 11863 + PSI 1.2 + 2.124	III/IV	Hermopolis	**Matt. 10, Luke 22**	[12 × 15]	Deluxe Ed.
P.Oxy. 6.847	III/IV	Oxyrhynchus	**John 2**	14.6 × 6.2	Deluxe Ed.
Oslo, Schøyen Coll.	III/IV	Old Cairo	**Rom. 4, 5**		Deluxe Ed.

3 By deluxe editions it is meant that the letters are written in careful block lettering and bilinearity is observed by the scribe.

The Text of P.Oxy. 1353

The Alands classify the text of P.Oxy. 1353 as belonging to category three: which they describe as a manuscript of distinctive character with an independent text. Lines 6,7 of the recto of P.Oxy. 1353 (1 Pet. 5.7) has the textual variant ἐπιρίψατε, agreeing with Augustinus. This agreement with Augustinus and along with the parchment codex material may indicate that the codex might have had its origins outside of Egypt.

The Dating of P.Oxy. 1353

Although giving no reasons, Grenfell and Hunt (ed.pr.) dated P.Oxy. 1353 to the fourth century, presumably on the basis of the style of the hand. The script is a carefully executed large (3 mm) round block lettering, written slowly with decorative serifs on most letters and contrasting thick and thin strokes (Grenfell and Hunt's 'biblical uncial'). The hand of P. Oxy. 1353 is also marked by the obliques of alpha, delta and lambda often meeting at the top and continuing upward in a vertical. The diagonals of the upsilon are quite widespread, and the mu is formed in four movements. Bilinearity is maintained except for psi, upsilon, and iota.

To narrowly date this type of hand is problematic as there are very few dateable examples by which we may judge what period the manuscript could fall. The dateable biblical uncials are as follows:

Fig. 2. P.Oxy. 1.20. = P.Lond. Lit.7, Homer, *Iliad* II

The hand has a firm second-century date. The recto contains Homer's *Iliad* written in a large calligraphic uncial. On the verso are some accounts in a cursive hand of the late second/early third century. According to Roberts this could possibly date the hand on the recto to the mid-second century.[4]

P.Ryl. 1.16 is a fragment of an unknown Comedy. Latter part of II? This literary text has on the verso a letter (P.Ryl. 2.236) dated AD 255/256. Hunt (ed.pr.)

Fig. 3. P.Ryl. 1.16

4   Colin Roberts, *Greek Literary Hands, 350 BC–AD 400* (Oxford: Clarendon Press, 1955), p. 16.

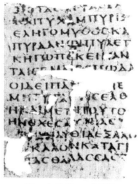

Fig. 4. P.Oxy. 4.661,
Callimachus, Iambi

says of 16 that it therefore could not be later than 215.[5]

On the verso of P.Oxy. 4.661 is a cursive hand which, according to Grenfell and Hunt, is not later than the third century and which quite likely falls within the second. The hand of the verso could therefore be dated to the second century. According to Roberts this is one of the earliest datable examples of the biblical uncial style.[6]

The Dating of the Biblical Uncial Hand

Cavallo, *Richerche sulla Maiuscola Biblica* (1967), bases the dating of the 'biblical uncial' hands on the assumption that there is a diachronic development in the hand so that the characteristics associated with it become more marked in time. Cavallo argues from this evolutionary thesis that the biblical uncial style took its classic shape in the middle to late second century AD.[7] On this basis he dates 1353 to the late fourth century. Peter Parsons of Oxford notes that following Cavallo's thesis, P.Oxy. 1353 should be assigned to the later fourth century because of the script's monumental stance and the very heavy contrast between the thick and thin strokes, however he rightly notes that, 'the objection to this assumption is that the objectively datable examples are too few to prove that the more developed examples of the script are always later than the less developed ones, it may just be that the more and the less developed are the work of the more and the less artistic scribes working in the same period'.[8] Parsons is correct in this observation and this of course makes a narrow dating of P. Oxy. 1353 problematic. From Table 2 it can be observed that there are enough similarities to suggest that P.Oxy. 1353 could be contemporary with P.Oxy. 661, which has been dated to the late II. In view of this it may be safer to suggest, until further evidence is forthcoming, to give a rather broad date for P.Oxy. 1353 from early III to the mid-IV.

The page number on the top right corner of the verso has been added by a different hand (see Figure 5). Grenfell and Hunt read the first letter of the page number written in a different hand on the flesh top left side of the

5   Roberts, *Greek Literary Hands*, p. 22.
6   Roberts, *Greek Literary Hands*, p. 12.
7   G. Cavallo, *Richerche sulla Maiuscola Biblica* (Firenze: Le Monnier, 1967), pp. 13–44.
8   Peter Parsons, email message to the author, 3 June 2007.

Table 2 Comparison of letter formation between 1353 and 661 (mid – late II)

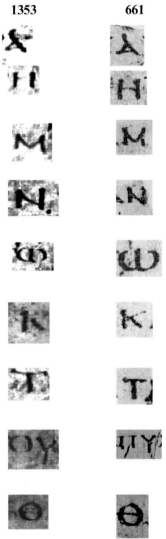

leaf as being a sigma, that is, the number 200. The second letter they read as a possible kappa and the third letter as theta, which gives the page number as 229 (ΣΚΘ).[9] However, on closer inspection, the sigma that

---

9   Grenfell and Hunt, *Oxyrhynchus Papyri*, p. 5.

Fig. 5. The length, dimensions and contents of P.Oxy. 1353

Grenfell and Hunt read is unmistakably an omega (the number 800), with a supralinear line to signify that it is a number. The second letter, given its position and what remains, could either be a kappa, as Grenfell and Hunt suggested, or an iota. Therefore the page number is either 829 (ΩΚΘ) or 819 (ΩΙΘ).

What were the possible contents of this large and bulky codex? There are some examples in the period III–IV of codices which include combinations of Christian literature as well as 1 Peter. They are as follows: the Crosby-Schøyen, Dishna, codex dated III containing 1 Peter (Coptic), with Melito of Sardis, 2 Macc., Jonah and a homily; P. Bodmer 8, dated III/IV, Panopolis?/Dishna? containing 1 Peter and 2 Peter. The page number of P.Oxy. 1353, however, gives evidence of a much larger codex. Could it have contained a collection of New Testament epistles? The average number of characters on the page of P.Oxy. 1353 is c. 250. The total number of characters (NA^{26} text) from Romans to 1 Peter is c. 194,500 which makes about 778 pages of 250 characters. This number includes the usual *nomina sacra*. If we then allow for sense spaces and spacing between epistles the end result is that Romans to 1 Peter could be included in the pages before the P.Oxy. 1353 fragment. Of course this is not evidence that they did. There well may indeed have been other combinations which included the *Shepherd of Hermas* as well as other books that made it into the canon. The type of combinations would depend very much on when and where the codex was produced.

Conclusion

If we can locate the production of P.Oxy. 1353 in the third century or possibly even earlier it joins at least two to three other highly calligraphic second/third-century New Testament manuscripts, P.Oxy. 1780 (Figure 9) P.Med. inv. 69.24 and P.Ant. 1.12. P.Oxy. 1780 is a leaf from a papyrus codex, the original page measuring c. 26 × 18 cm. The hand is a highly calligraphic, 'biblical majuscule'. Grenfell and Hunt assigned a fourth-century date to 1780. Turner, however, dates the hand to the late third,[10] Roberts and Skeat to the first half of the third century.[11] Whilst not

10   E. G. Turner, *The Typology of the Early Codex* (Philadelphia: University of Pennsylvania Press, 1977), p. 147.

11   K. Aland, *Studien zur Überlieferung des Neuen Testaments und seines Textes* (Berlin: de Gruyter, 1967), p. 105 n. 4.

1780 = P39 in Oxy. Vol. XV

excluding a third-century dating a late second-century date may also be entertained. The hand of P.Oxy. 1780 may be compared to P.Oxy. 4708, which is a less formal but a comparable hand (epsilon has a longer middle horizontal stroke and is formed with a straight vertical stroke; mu has a rounded saddle but deep overhang on the delta; omega rises to full height in its centre; and omicron is full size; see Table 3). D. Obbink assigns 4708 to the late second century comparing the hand to Roberts *GLH*, 20b, edict of a prefect, AD 206 and BGU V 1210.[12] See also P.Oxy. 4302 and P.Oxy. 661 (later II). Most likely the codex contained only the Gospel of John.[13] P.Med. inv. 69.24 is very similar in style to P.Oxy. 1780 and is therefore possibly dated to the same period. P.Ant. 1.12 is a parchment fragment of a codex that contained 1 John. The dating of P.Ant. 1.12 by scholars varies. Cavallo gave no basis for his dating of P.Ant. 1.12 to IV/V whilst Aland listed P.Ant. 1.12 as V/IV, again without giving a reason. Comfort, on the basis that it is a precursor to the formal Coptic Uncial, dated P.Ant. 1.12 to the III/IV. Roberts, the ed.pr., compared the hand to P.Lond. Lit. 192, P.Oxy. 656 and P.Beatty 10 and dated the hand to III. He also argued that the size of the codex, 8.8 × 9.9 cm is a common format in early codices, and that the peculiar forms of the *nomina sacra* found in the text strengthen the case for an early date. We should most probably therefore locate its production somewhere in the III.

After surveying the writing styles in the early Christian papyri, K. Haines-Eitzen states that:

> there are no second and third century Christian papyri that exhibit the highly calligraphic features of the best literary hands...whose strict bilinearity, regularity and formality suggest a highly trained scribe specializing in the art of copying books.[14]

She further argues that the scribes who produced Christian books in the second and third centuries were trained in a general way to be multifunctional, that is, their style of writing betrays a documentary influence yet they write in such a way to achieve legibility.[15] This may be the case for the majority of the early Christian manuscripts but there are exceptions. As we have noted above, P.Oxy. 1780, P.Med. inv. 69.24 and P.Ant. 1.12 show a high degree of skill and expertise. The calligraphic nature of these Christian manuscripts along with P.Oxy. 1353 is evidence of early Christian manuscripts being produced by highly trained scribes. Perhaps a wealthy Christian financed these deluxe editions for his or her

12 Nicholas Gonis and Dirk Obbink, *The Oxyrhynchus Papyri*, 69 (Oxford: Oxford University Press, 2005), p. 18.
13 Aland, *Studien zur Überlieferung*, p. 105.
14 Kim Haines-Eitzen, *Guardians of Letters* (Oxford: Oxford University Press, 2000), p. 67.
15 Haines-Eitzen, *Guardians of Letters*, pp. 63–75.

own personal use or for a church, or it may be that a number of members of a church contributed financially to their production for use in their meetings. Whatever may have been the financial support for such deluxe copies and their subsequent use, they must be taken into account in our understanding of early Christian book production and the socio-economic makeup of the early Christian churches.[16]

Fig. 6. P.Oxy. 1780

Fig. 7. P.Oxy. 62 4302

16   When considering how representative the published New Testament Oxyrhynchus papyri are, we need to keep in mind that if Christian books belonging to churches were burnt in times of persecution perhaps they were the more highly calligraphic editions. As far as I am aware no Christian papyrus fragments found at Oxyrhynchus show signs of being burnt, but have most probably ended up in the rubbish mounds as discards, because they have worn out. Furthermore, of the 900 boxes of papyri taken by Grenfell and Hunt from the Oxyrhynchus site only 151 (16.8 percent) have been processed and of the approximate fifty thousand papyri found in Oxyrhynchus approximately 1 percent have been edited and published.

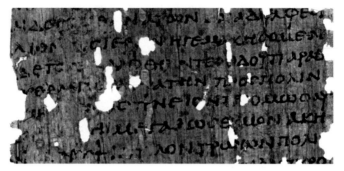

Fig. 8. P.Oxy. 69 4708

Table 3 Comparison between letter formation of P.Oxy. 4708 and P.Oxy. 1780

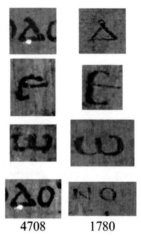

4708   1780

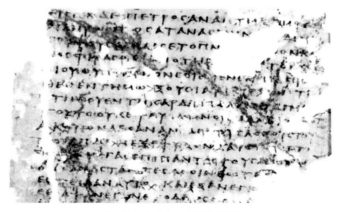

Fig. 9. P.Berl. inv. 11765 II/III

Fig. 10. P.Ant. 1.2 III/IV

Fig. 11. P.Oxy. 847

Fig. 12. PSI 1.2

Fig. 13. Oslo, Schøyen Coll, MS 113; 0220

Letter Carriers in the Ancient Jewish Epistolary Material

Peter M. Head

1. *Introduction*

The aim of this paper is to investigate the extant ancient Jewish epistolary documents and literature in order to ascertain what we can learn about the delivery of these letters and the role of the letter carriers in the communication between sender and receiver.[1] In comparison with the wealth and breadth of epistolary material preserved among papyrological documents from Greco-Roman Egypt, and the huge numbers of letters associated with elite literary figures, such as Cicero, relatively few letters reflecting Jewish authorship and milieu are extant from the period 200 BC–AD 200. Philip Alexander collected around 90 examples comprising 28 manuscript letters from the Judean desert, 16 letters quoted in 1–3 Maccabees, 37 letters cited in Josephus, 8 letters preserved within the rabbinic traditions, and an assortment of letters either contained within or expressed as pseudepigraphical material.[2] These comprise diverse types of letter and very diverse settings, but may be treated here together in terms of any information contained within them (or their traditions) about delivery and carrying.[3]

---

1 An earlier form of this paper was presented to the Seminar in Hebrew, Jewish and Early Christian Studies in the Faculty of Divinity in Cambridge (29 May 2006). Thanks are due to the Chairman, Professor William Horbury, and the members of the seminar for their encouragement.

2 P. S. Alexander, 'Epistolary Literature', in *Jewish Writings of the Second Temple Period: Apocrypha, Pseudepigrapha, Qumran Sectarian Writings, Philo, Josephus* (CRINT, 2.1; Assen: Van Gorcum; Philadelphia: Fortress, 1984), pp. 579–82. Cf. also H.-J. Klauck (with D. P. Bailey), *Ancient Letters and the New Testament: A Guide to Context and Exegesis* (Waco, TX: Baylor University Press, 2006), pp. 229–97.

3 This paper forms one part of a more extensive research project investigating the background to and role of letter carriers in early Christianity.

2. Manuscript Letters

Although some epistolary material from earlier periods survives (especially from Tel Arad, Lachish, Elephantine),[4] the manuscript material from our period is all from the Dead Sea area: Murabbaat, Nahal Hever, Nahal Seelim, Nahal Mishmar, and Masada; in Hebrew, Aramaic and Greek.[5] These letters are unique among the material to be surveyed in this paper since unlike the other material (in which letters are incorporated into other texts or are themselves literary compositions), 'they alone exist in their physically original form'.[6] In fact, of course, very few of them remain 'in their physically original form'. Most are quite damaged and fragmentary. Among those that are preserved many are quite brief.

a) The Letters from the so-called 'Cave of the Letters' in the northern cliffs of Nahal Hever belong to the period of the Bar Kokhba revolt (132–135).[7] There are fifteen letters, ten in Aramaic, three in Hebrew and two in Greek, mostly addressed from Bar Kokhba (or one of his aides) to Yehonathan (sometimes rendered Jonathan) and/or Mesabala (his officers in Ein Gedi), often apparently concerning the movement of personnel, but with little information about the means of delivery. Many are damaged and fragmentary. At least two of the Aramaic letters appear to have been

---

4   For this more ancient material see D. Pardee, *Handbook of Ancient Hebrew Letters: A Study Edition* (SBLSBS, 15; Chico, CA: Scholars, 1982); B. Porten and A. Yardeni, *Textbook of Aramaic Documents from Ancient Egypt*, Vol. I: *Letters* (Winona Lake, IN: Eisenbrauns, 1986); B. Porten (with J. J. Farber, C. J. Martin, G. Vittmann, Leslie S. B. MacCoull, Sarah Clackson, and contributions by Simon Hopkins and Ranon Katzoff), *The Elephantine Papyri in English: Three Millennia of Cross-Cultural Continuity and Change* (Leiden: Brill, 1996); J. M. Lindenberger, *Ancient Aramaic and Hebrew Letters. Second Edition* (SBLWAW, 14; ed. K. H. Richards; Atlanta, GA: SBL, 2003) [contains text and translation of 79 letters].

5   In addition to literature cited below cf. B. Lifshitz, 'The Greek Documents from Nahal Seelim and Nahal Mishmar', *IEJ* 11 (1961): 60–61; B. Lifshitz, 'Papyrus grecs du désert de Juda', *Aeg* 42 (1962): 240–58.

6   Alexander, 'Epistolary Literature', p. 589. For a discussion of the physical form of these letters see B. Porten, 'Aramaic Papyri and Parchments: A New Look', *BA* 42 (1979): 74–104.

7   These have been published together in Yigael Yadin, Jonas C. Greenfield, Ada Yardeni and Baruch A. Levine, *The Documents from the Bar Kokhba Period in the Cave of Letters 3: Hebrew, Aramaic, and Nabatean-Aramaic Papyri* (Judean Desert Studies, 3; Jerusalem: Israel Exploration Society; Institute of Archaeology, Hebrew University; Shrine of the Book, Israel Museum, 2002). I have followed their referencing system and translation. For earlier discussions see Y. Yadin, 'Expedition D', *IEJ* 11 (1961): 36–52; 12 (1962): 227–57; Y. Yadin, *The Finds from the Bar Kokhba Period in the Cave of Letters* (Judean Desert Studies; Jerusalem: Israel Exploration Society, 1963); N. Lewis (ed.), *The Documents from the Bar Kokhba Period in the Cave of Letters* (Judean Desert Studies; Jerusalem: Israel Exploration Society); J. A. Fitzmyer and D. J. Harrington, *A Manual of Palestinian Aramaic Texts (Second Century B.C. – Second Century A.D.)* (Rome: PBI, 1994) [henceforth H&F].

dictated to a scribe.[8] The letters were probably delivered by personal courier, but there are few specific indications of this.[9] Two examples certainly seem to support this, and provide two examples of named couriers.

> P. Yadin 53 (= 5/6Hev 53 = H&F 55): 'A letter of Shim'on, son of Kosibah: Peace! To Yehonathan, so[n of] Ba'yah: (Be advised) that whatever Elisha tells you, do for him, and try to do well with him [in eve]ry task. Fare you well!'

This letter (P. Yadin 53) serves as something like a letter of introduction for Elisha to Yehonathan. It authorizes Elisha as the carrier of additional (possibly secret) information or perhaps orders and instructions. Although not specified, it was normal for this type of letter to be carried by the person named within it. Yadin wrote: 'The substance of Bar Kokhba's order was apparently secret, but Elisha was authorized to transmit it by word of mouth to Yehonatan, who was instructed to assist Elisha in its execution.'[10]

> P. Yadin 52: 'Soumaios to Yonathes son of Beianos and to Masabala greetings. Since I have sent you Agrippa, hurry to send me wands and citrons, as much as you will be able to, for the camp of the Jews, and do not do otherwise. It (the letter) was written in Greek because of our inability (to write?) in Hebrew letters. Release him (Agrippa) more quickly on account of the festival, and do not do otherwise. (Second hand) Soumais, Farewell.'

This letter in Greek (P. Yadin 52) also names and specifies the letter carrier – Agrippa – using an expression that is common in Greek letters: ἐπιδὴ ἔπεμσα πρὸς ὑμᾶς …[11] Agrippa's role is to take the letter and return quickly with the 'wands and citrons' (note the urgency:

---

8   P. Yadin 54 (= 5/6Hev 54 = H&F 53) includes final signature: 'Shemu'el [Samuel], son of 'Ammi' in a different hand (so Yadin, *IEJ* 11 [1961]: 42). P. Yadin 50 (= 5/6Hev 50 = H&F 56) includes an explicit note about the scribe: 'Simeon, son of Judah, wrote it'. P. Yadin 52 (Greek Letter from Soumaios to Yonathes and Masabala) also includes a final signature in a different hand from the main text.

9   P. Yadin 49 (= 5/6Hev 49): nothing explicit on courier; P. Yadin 50 (= 5/6Hev 50 = H&F 56): note about scribe; courier implied but no mention; P. Yadin 51 (= 5/6Hev 51): very fragmentary, no courier; P. Yadin 54 (= 5/6Hev 54 = H&F 53): nothing on courier; P. Yadin 55 (= 5/6Hev 55 = H&F 59): P. Yadin 56 (= 5/6Hev 56 = H&F 58): fragmentary, interchange of personnel (?); P. Yadin 57 (= 5/6Hev 57 = H&F 60): movement of personnel – and donkeys: courier implied but not mentioned; P. Yadin 58 (= 5/6Hev 58 = H&F 57): fragmentary, no courier.

10   Yadin, *IEJ* 11 (1961): 43; cf. H&F: 'this is a letter from Bar Chochba to Jonathan that the latter should carry out an order to be transmitted orally by a certain Elisha' (p. 215).

11   So also Cotton in Yadin, *Documents*, p. 361.

σπουδάσατε πέμσε μοι ... lines 5–6; αὐτὸν ἀπόλυσαι τάχιον διὰ τὴν ἑορτὴν ... lines 15–16).[12]

b) There are seven documents identified as letters (in Hebrew) from the period of the second revolt found among the 173 documents found at the Wadi Murabba'at.[13] But little or nothing can be discerned about the delivery of these letters. P. Mur. 42 – 'from the village managers of Beth-Mashko, from Yeshua and Elazar, to Yeshua son of Galgula, camp commander' – deals with the ownership of a cow (the cow had been taken from Yaaqov son of Yehuda, a resident in Beth-Mashko, by Yehosef son of Ariston – the letter makes clear that the cow belongs to Yehosef, although it doesn't disclose any other aspect of this 'transaction'). The text is clearly dictated to a scribe in the presence of various witnesses who also sign the letter, but no information is given about the delivery of the letter.[14] P. Mur. 43 – 'from Shimon ben Kosiba to Yeshua ben Ga[l]gula and the men of your company' – threatens imprisonment to any who allow harm to come to some Galileans. The text is clearly dictated to a scribe, but no information is given about delivery. P. Mur. 44 – 'from Shimon to Yeshua son of Galgula' – deals with instructions for the transfer of a shipment of wheat. Un-named persons will deliver and then pick up the wheat, but no letter carrier is named or indicated.[15]

c) A letter to Shimon ben Kosibah (in Hebrew) (XHev/Se 30) from Nahal Hever, although damaged, is of interest:

---

12   Cf. Josephus, *Ant.* 13.372: 'it was a custom among the Jews that at the festival of Tabernacles everyone holds wands made of palm branches and citrons'. Background: Lev. 23.40 (cf. Josephus, *Ant.* 3.245). See also P. Yadin 57 for a similar request in the same collection.

13   P. Benoit, J. T. Milik and R. de Vaux, *Les Grottes de Murabba'at (Texte)* (DJD, 2; Oxford: Clarendon Press, 1960) [Milik, pp. 155–68]; cf. Pardee, *Handbook*, pp. 114–39.

14   The letter concludes with a list of six names and a brief description of their role. Milik took the final name, 'Yaaqov son of Yehosef', and description, *m'yd*, as 'sans doute' the signature of the scribe: *Les Grottes de Murabba'at*, p. 158 (Pardee disagrees on the ground of the difference in handwriting from the main text – *Handbook*, p. 126).

15   Of the other 'letters' P. Mur. 45, 46, 47, 48 are too incomplete to warrant treatment here (49–52 even more so: although they were labeled 'Lettres (?)' by Milik only odd words and letters are extant). 4Q342 and 4Q343 ('alleged Qumran texts') are also provisionally identified as letters by their editors, but the extant texts are also exceedingly fragmentary and little content is discernible. H. M. Cotton and A. Yardeni, *Aramaic, Hebrew, and Greek Documentary Texts from Nahal Hever and Other Sites, with an Appendix Containing Alleged Qumran Texts (The Seiyâl Collection II)* (DJD, 27; Oxford: Clarendon Press, 1997), pp. 285–88. Perhaps here we could also note MasOstr (H&F 36): '[Menah]em, son of Ma'azi, greetings! That you ... [you] are to pay the sum, five zuzim (in) number ...' – fragmentary, insufficient details, no courier. For publication see J. Aviram, G. Foerster and E. Netzer (eds), *Masada I: The Yigael Yadin Excavations, 1963–1965, Final Reports*; Y. Yadin and J. Naveh, *Aramaic and Hebrew Ostraca and Jar Inscriptions*; Y. Meshorer, *The Coins of Masada* (The Masada Reports; Jerusalem: Hebrew University of Jerusalem; Jerusalem: Israel Exploration Society, 1989), no. 554 (pp. 49–50).

To Shim'on son of Kosibah, the prince of Israel, from Shim'on son of
Mtnym/h; ... Greetings. Let it be known to you that ... [*several lines
missing*] ... that brothers (?) were ... and we have not been among them
(?). Greet[ings.] Shim'on son of *Mtnh*.
The verso adds: *'El... to Shim'on*

In this text, the signature is in a different hand from the main body of the
letter, indicating that the letter was dictated to a scribe. The editors
suggest that the first word on the verso might be *'Eli'ezer*, a different name
from the sender who might 'perhaps' have been 'the carrier of the letter'.[16]
Although clearly possible, there is no positive evidence for it, and
analogies in Greco-Roman letters are against it, since the letter carrier is
not customarily named on the outside of the letter; rather, the message is
normally a message to the letter carrier (such as 'deliver this letter to
Shimon').

d) There are relatively few identifiably Jewish letters among the breadth
of documentary material, almost entirely in Greek, among the papyri.[17]
Only two letters within our time-frame (i.e. 200 BC–AD 200) are catalogued
in the *Corpus Papyrorum Judaicarum*.[18] Of subsequently published
papyrological material concerning Judaism,[19] only one is a letter,

16   H. M. Cotton and A. Yardeni, *Aramaic, Hebrew, and Greek Documentary Texts from
Nahal Hever and Other Sites, with an Appendix Containing Alleged Qumran Texts (The Seiyâl
Collection II)* (DJD, 27; Oxford: Clarendon Press, 1997), p. 103 [Yardeni] (plate XX).

17   There is practically no evidence for Jews in the papyri for the two centuries following
the suppression of the Jewish revolt in 115–117. The lack of evidence in this period is
commonly attributed to the decimation of the Jewish population and the intentional public
invisibility of the surviving Jewish communities. See D. Frankfurter, 'Lest Egypt's City be
Deserted: Religion and Ideology in the Egyptian Response to the Jewish Revolt (116–117 C.
E.)', *JJS* 43 (1992): 203–20 [203]; R.S. Bagnall, *Egypt in Late Antiquity* (Princeton: Princeton
University Press, 1993), pp. 276–78; G. M. Horsley, 'Divine Providence in a Letter of Judas',
New Docs. 3 (1983): 141–48 (esp. 142); E. J. Epp, 'The Jews and the Jewish Community in
Oxyrhynchus: Socio-Religious Context for New Testament Papyri' in *New Testament
Manuscripts: Their Texts and Their World* (eds T. J. Kraus and T. Nicklas; TENT 2; Leiden:
Brill, 2006), pp. 13–52 (esp. 15–16). On the difficulty in defining criteria for identifying
documents as 'Jewish' see G. Bohak, 'Good Jews, Bad Jews, and Non-Jews in Greek Papyri
and Inscriptions', in *Akten des 21. Internationalen Papyrologenkongresses, Berlin, 13.-
19.8.1995* (ABF Beiheft 3; ed. B. Kramer et al.; Stuttgart and Leipzig: B. G. Teubner, 1997),
pp. 105–12; and Epp, 'The Jews in Oxyrhynchus', pp. 16–32.

18   V. A. Tcherikover and A. Fuks (eds), *Corpus Papyrorum Judaicarum* (3 vols;
Cambridge: Magnes Press, Hebrew University, 1957–64). For letters outside our time-frame
see *CPJ* 4 (P. Edg. 84, 257 BC); *CPJ* 5 (P. Edg. 13, 257 BC); *CPJ* 12 (P.Cair.Zen. 59509, III
BC); *CPJ* 128 (P. Enteux. 23, 218 BC); *CPJ* 469 (P. Princ. 73, III AD). *CPJ* 13 (P.Cair.Zen.
59377, III BC), noted by Alexander, 'Epistolary Literature', p. 579 n. 1 is not actually a letter.

19   Cf. I. F. Fikhman, 'Les Juifs d'Égypte à l'époque Byzantine d'après les papyrus
publiés depuis la parution du "Corpus Papyrorum Judaicarum" III', *Scripta Classica
Israelica* 15 (1996): 223–29; I. F. Fikhman, 'L'état des travaux au "Corpus Papyrorum
Judaicarum" IV', *Akten des 21. Internationalen Papyrologenkongresses, Berlin, 13.-19.8.1995*

P.Oxy. 3314, known as the letter of Judas, but it is fourth-century and not definitively Jewish.[20] Neither of the two catalogued letters contain any absolutely explicit indications of being written by a Jew, and only one contains information about the delivery of the letter. The first, P.IFAO 104 (*CPJ* 141), is a letter from Herakles to Ptolemaios (first half of first century BC); it contains a reference to Jews in the content of the letter: 'you know that they loathe the Jews', which makes it possible that the author is identifying with 'Jews',[21] although other possibilities also exist. There is no address, no information about delivery, and no letter carrier mentioned. The second of these two letters is P. Bad. 35 (*CPJ* 424), a letter from Johanna to Epagathos (15 Dec. 87 AD). This is a private letter, 'in a most illiterate Greek', and was identified as Jewish only by the name of the sender.[22] The letter contains no information about the letter carrier. There is an address on the outside of the letter: εἰ]ς Πτολεμαιείδα τὴν Ἑρμε[ίου]. | [δὸς κω]μοφύλακι ὥστε Ἐπαγ[άθῳ φέρειν]. ET: 'To Ptolemais Hermeiou. Give to the village-guard for delivery to Epagathos.' This suggests that the letter did not have a definite carrier, but was rather entrusted to more than one carrier for its delivery.

3. *Letters Preserved within Rabbinic Traditions*

Relatively few letters from our period are preserved within the rabbinic traditions.[23] Correspondence by letter did occur between Babylonian and Palestinian rabbis – the 'letter from the West' could be decisive in disputes about *halachah*.[24] No information about delivery is preserved, although

---

(ABF Beiheft 3; ed. B. Kramer et al.; Stuttgart and Leipzig: Teubner, 1997), pp. 290–96. P. Oxy. 2745 (an Onomasticon of Hebrew Names, third or fourth cent.); P.Oxy. 3203 (a lease from AD 400); P.Oxy. 3805 (accounts from AD 566 or later); CPR VII 2 (a list of names, first cent. AD).

20   For discussion (including defence of Judas as a Jewish name) see Epp, 'The Jews in Oxyrhynchus', pp. 38–43; Horsley, 'Divine Providence', pp. 141–48. Incidentally the text offers no clues about the delivery of the letter, and no reference to anyone who may have carried it.

21   So *CPJ* I.256.

22   See *CPJ* II.210, 211.

23   Alexander: eight texts; Sperling includes ten examples (some fragments), although several are not specifically letters (e.g. *M. Maaser Sheni* 5.8, 'Fragments', 196–97; *BT Pesahim* 3b, 'Fragments', 203–04).

24   For the generally decisive 'letter from the West' see *BT Sanhedrin* 19a ('We can produce a letter from the West that the halachah does not rest with R. Judah'); *BT Baba Bathra* 41b (R. Kahana: 'I can bring you a letter from the West to show that the halachah does not follow R. Simeon'); *BT Shebuoth* 48b ('I can bring a letter from the West that the law is not in accordance with R. Eleazar').

for many of these it seems likely that a personal courier would have been despatched.[25]

There is a letter from the Jews of Jerusalem to the Jews of Alexandria requesting the return of Judah b. Tabbai (to become patriarch of Jerusalem, or 'Nasi'): 'From Jerusalem the Great to Alexandria the Small. How long shall my betrothed remain with you while I remain grieving over him?' (*PT Hagigah* 77d; cf. also *PT Sanhedrin* 23c; *BT Sanhedrin* 107b; *BT Sotah 47a*). The historicity and details of this letter are unclear; no information is provided about the delivery of this/these letters.

Rabban Gamaliel wrote and despatched three letters (in Aramaic): 'to our brothers of Upper and Lower Egypt', 'to our brothers of the Upper and Lower South', and 'to our brothers belonging to the Babylonian diaspora': dealing with tithing and the intercalation of thirty days (*T. Sanhedrin* 2.6; *PT Sanhedrin* 18d; *PT Maaser Sheni* 56c; *BT Sanhedrin* 11a–b).[26] The date and identification is disputed, but the location 'on the steps of the temple mount' and the reference to sacrificial animals suggests that Gamaliel the Elder (grand/son of Hillel = Acts 5.34; 22.3) is in view.[27] The composition involves dictation to a scribe named Yohanan; no information is provided about the delivery of these encyclicals.

Two letters (in Hebrew) were sent jointly by Rabban Shimon ben Gamaliel and Yohanan ben Zakkai (*Midrash Tannaim* Deut. 26.23): 'from Simeon b. Gamaliel and from Yohanan b. Zakkai to our brothers in the Upper and Lower South, to Shahlil and to the seven southern toparchies', 'from Simeon b. Gamaliel and from Yohanan b. Zakkai to our brothers in the Upper and Lower Galilee and to Simonia and the Obed Bet Hillel ...': dealing with the removal of the tithed sacred produce so that the owner can recite the Confession.[28] Both letters close with a note 'we have not begun to write to you, but our fathers used to write to your fathers'.[29] The

25 For other references to letters from Palestinian sources see *BT Niddah* 68a (Rabin); *BT Baba Mezia* 114a (Rabin); *BT Ketuboth* 49b (Rabin); *BT Hullin* 95b (R. Johanan).

26 Texts, ET and discussion in S. D. Sperling, 'Fragments of Tannaitic Letters Preserved in Rabbinic Literature', in D. Pardee, *Handbook of Ancient Hebrew Letters* (SBLSBS, 15; Chico, CA: Scholars, 1982), pp. 183–211 (191–96); cf. also J. Neusner, *The Rabbinic Traditions about the Pharisees before 70* (3 vols; Leiden: Brill, 1971), pp. 356–8, 360, 361, 368 (ET and discussion), 372–3 (synopsis arrangement of the different texts).

27 So Sperling, 'Fragments', p. 195; Alexander is skeptical about the attribution ('Epistolary Literature', p. 581. n. 14); Neusner suggests that the first two letters (to North and South, dealing with tithing) may be genuine, and that the third (addressed to Babylonia and Medea [where few or no Pharisees are known], dealing with calendrical issues [that would have been determined by Temple authorities]) is likely not authentic (*The Rabbinic Traditions about the Pharisees before 70*, vol. I, pp. 356–8).

28 Cf. Deut. 14.22-29; 26.13; *M. Maaser Sheni* 5.6; Sperling, 'Fragments', p. 189.

29 Neusner argues that the setting and details are sufficiently different from the earlier letters from Gamaliel as to suggest the authenticity of these letters (*The Rabbinic Traditions about the Pharisees before 70*, vol. I, pp. 378–9).

composition involves both authors and dictation to a temple-scribe (named Yohanan); but no information is provided about the delivery of these encyclicals.

The opening portion of a letter from Judah the Patriarch (late II, early III) to the Emperor Antoninus exists in two versions: 'from Judah the Patriarch to our Lord King Antoninus', 'From Judah your slave to our Lord King Antoninus' (*Genesis Rabbah* 75.5).[30] The opening is dictated to Rabbi Afas, but no content is given and no information is recorded about delivery.

4. *Letters Cited in the Maccabean Literature (1 and 2 Maccabees)*

Letters of various types play an important role in the narratives of 1 and 2 Maccabees (less so in 3 Maccabees).[31] There are twelve letters referred to in 1 Maccabees, only two of which are actually (according to the narrative setting) composed by Jewish authors (5.10-13; 12.6-23), although the other letters are important as well as exhibiting expectations and assumptions about letter delivery.

The first letter in 1 Maccabees is in 5.10-13 which quotes from a portion of a letter (γράμματα) from Israelites in Gilead to Judas and his brothers. The quoted portion is clearly only a part of the letter consisting of the main body of the letter, and lacks any opening (perhaps partly paraphrased in v. 9f) or closing features. There is no note about delivery, although there is an interesting comment following the letter: 'while the letter (αἱ ἐπιστολαί) was still being read, behold, other messengers (ἄγγελοι ἕτεροι), with their garments rent, came from Galilee and made a similar report'. The combined effect of these messages galvanized Judas into action and men were sent both to Galilee and to Gilead.

In 1 Macc. 10.18-20 a letter (ἐπιστολάς) from Alexander (I Epiphanes) to Jonathan appointing him as high priest is quoted. This letter includes the opening address and a brief main body. No courier is mentioned.

1 Macc. 10.25-45 includes a letter from Demetrius to 'the Jews' offering various privileges in return for their allegiance. This is quite a long letter which includes the opening address, although it ends abruptly with no closing greetings (and there is no mention of delivery methods or any courier). Verses 46f note that Jonathan and the people did not believe these words in view of Demetrius' previous record.

1 Macc. 10.52-54 includes a letter from Alexander to Ptolemy, king of

30   Sperling, 'Fragments', pp. 197–201.
31   There are two letters referred to in 3 Maccabees, both of which are open public letters from King Ptolemy [IV Philopator] to his whole kingdom. The letter of 3.12-29 orders the arrest of Jews throughout the kingdom; the letter of 7.1-9 overturns the first letter. There are no details about delivery.

Egypt.[32] This letter is sent through ambassadors (πρέσβεις), and is aimed at cementing their alliance through marrying Ptolemy's daughter.[33] Ptolemy accepted and replied positively and arranged a personal meeting (10.55-56).

1 Macc. 11.30-37 records a letter (ἐπιστολάς, v. 29) from Demetrius to Jonathan incorporating a copy of a previous letter from Demetrius to Lasthenes. This letter reiterates some of the promises made in 10.25-45 (later said to be broken, v. 53). There are no delivery details. In 1 Macc. 11.57 there is a brief note/letter from Antiochus (IV Epiphanes) confirming Jonathan as high priest. 1 Macc. 13.36-40 quotes from a letter (ἐπιστολήν) from Demetrius to Simon proclaiming peace between them. 1 Macc. 15.2-9 includes a letter (ἐπιστολάς) from Antiochus (VII Sidetes) to Simon, essentially offering a continuation of the provisions made previously. In none of these cases is there any information about delivery.

In 1 Macc. 12.6-23 there is a letter (τὸ ἀντίγραφον τῶν ἐπιστολῶν) from Jonathan to the Spartans (6–18, with appended copy of previous letter from Arius, king of Spartans to Onias the high priest, 19–23). This letter, designed to confirm an alliance with the Spartans, includes explicit named letter carriers. Their role is ambassadorial, and in fact the process has already been narrated in 12.1-4 before the letter is quoted:

> We therefore have chosen Numenius the son of Antiochus and Antipater the son of Jason, and have sent them to Rome to renew our former friendship and alliance with them. We have commanded them to go also to you and greet you and deliver to you this letter from us concerning the renewal of our brotherhood. (12.16-17)

In 1 Macc. 14.20-23 we have a letter (τὸ ἀντίγραφον τῶν ἐπιστολῶν) from the Spartans to Simon and the Jewish people on hearing news of Jonathan's death (said to have been written on bronze tablets in order to renew their alliance, v. 18). This includes explicit reference to the previous envoys: Numenius and Antipater:

> The envoys (οἱ πρεσβευταί) who were sent to our people have told us about your glory and honour, and we rejoiced at their coming. And what they said we have recorded in our public decrees, as follows, 'Numenius the son of Antiochus and Antipater the son of Jason, envoys of the Jews (πρεσβευταὶ Ἰουδαίων), have come to us to renew their friendship with us. It has pleased our people to receive these men with

---

32   This is not listed by Alexander but is clearly a written letter (introduced with similar expression to other letters: ἀπέστειλεν ... κατὰ τοὺς λόγους τούτους, cf. 10.17; Ptolemy's reply promises to do what Alexander had written, 10.56)

33   Regarded by Goldstein as the composition of the author (J. A. Goldstein, *I Maccabees* [Anchor Bible, 41; Garden City, NY: Doubleday, 1976], p. 416).

honour and to put a copy of their words in the public archives, so that
the people of the Spartans may have a record of them.' (21–23)

Here we have confirmation that on the occasion of their ambassadorial
visit to the Spartans, Numenius and Antipater had supplemented the
written correspondence with further explanations. Immediately following
this we read: 'after this Simon sent Numenius to Rome with a large gold
shield weighing a thousand minas, to confirm the alliance with the
Romans' (14.24).

1 Macc. 15.16-21 reports that Numenius arrives back from Rome
bearing a letter from Lucius, consul to the Romans, to King Ptolemy,
noting the role of 'the envoys of the Jews' (οἱ πρεσβευταὶ τῶν Ιουδαίων),
accepting the gold shield and offering protection to the Jews.

> The role of Numenius as envoy carrying official letters demonstrates the
> way in which Jonathan (and his staff) 'were ready and able to use for
> their own benefit the established methods of the Hellenistic world'.
> (Goldstein, 447)

There are seven letters referred to in *2 Maccabees*, which opens with two
important letters, the only ones which are actually composed by Jewish
authors, although a later letter (11.17-21) reveals more about Jewish letter
carriers.

2 Macc. 1.1-10 begins 'The Jewish brethren in Jerusalem and those in
the land of Judea, to their Jewish brethren in Egypt'. The letter refers to a
previous letter and now urges that the Egyptian community 'keep the feast
of booths in the month of Chislev' (in 124 BC). This letter contains no
reference to delivery, although the form is similar to other letters from
Jerusalem regulating the calendar with respect to the observation of
festivals.[34]

2 Macc. 1.10–2.18 contains a long letter from 'those in Jerusalem and
those in Judea and the senate and Judas, to Aristobulus, who is of the
family of the anointed priests, teacher of Ptolemy the king, and to the
Jews in Egypt', which explains and justifies the new eight-day festival of
Hanukkah (commemorating the restoration/rededication of the temple
which will be narrated in 10.1-8). No details are given about the delivery
of this letter, which may not reflect a historical letter situation.[35]

2 Macc. 9.19-27 records a letter of Antiochus (IV Epiphanes) 'to his
worthy Jewish citizens', calling for their support of his son (Antiochus V
Eupator). 2 Macc. 11.17-21 records a letter from Lysias (one of Antiochus
V's chief officials, cf. 10.11; 11.1) following Maccabeus' defeat of Lysias

---

34   Cf. 2 Chron. 30.1-9; Est. 9.20-32; cf. the Elephantine Passover Letter (*TAD* A4.1, 419/
18 BC) [point of origin not specified]; Tos. Sanh. 2.5f (discussed); *TB Sanhedrin* 11a–b.

35   Cf. J. A. Goldstein, *2 Maccabees* (Anchor Bible, 41A; Garden City, NY: Doubleday,
1983), pp. 157–67, 540–45 (anti-Oniad propaganda).

and referring to their peace terms which had previously been 'delivered to Lysias in writing' from Maccabeus (11.15):[36]

> Lysias to the people of the Jews, greeting. John and Absalom, who were sent by you, have delivered your signed communication and have asked about the matters indicated therein. I have informed the king of everything that needed to be brought before him, and he has agreed to what was possible. If you will maintain your good will toward the government, I will endeavour for the future to help promote your welfare. And concerning these matters and their details, I have ordered these men and my representatives to confer with you ('to discuss the details with you' AB). Farewell. (164 BC)

This letter reveals that John and Absalom had acted as couriers of the letter setting out the terms of peace from Maccabeus to Lysias.[37] As Lysias notes, they not only delivered the letter but also pressed personally the point of the letter.[38] They are also sent back (with representatives of Lysias) to confer further about these matters.

2 Macc. 11.23-26 contains the letter from Antiochus V to Lysias, allowing the Jews to 'live according to the customs of their ancestors' (with no details about delivery). This is followed immediately by 2 Macc. 11.27-33 which contains the letter from Antiochus V 'to the senate of the Jews and to the other Jews' granting a pledge of friendship and permission 'for the Jews to enjoy their own food and laws'. Antiochus refers to Menelaus as having informed him of Jewish wishes 'to return home and look after your own affairs' (v. 29). The same person is named in the closing sentence of the letter: 'I have also sent Menelaus to encourage you' (πέπομφα δὲ καὶ τὸν Μενέλαον παρακαλέσοντα ὑμᾶς, v. 32). 2 Macc. 11.34-38 contains a letter from two Roman envoys supporting these arrangements.

First and Second Maccabees reflect knowledge of the way in which royal emissaries could supplement and reinforce the epistolary correspondence which they carried. There are several clear indications of the important role of these ambassadorial letter carriers in personally advocating the causes contained within the written letter and mediating its reception.

---

36   See Goldstein, *2 Maccabees*, p. 408 for defence of the authenticity of the letter.

37   'John' was a very common name so it is not possible simply to identify this 'John' with the brother of Judas Maccabeus (cf. 1 Macc. 2.2; 9.35-38), who in any case is not mentioned in 2 Maccabees.

38   Goldstein acknowledges that this is the narrative perspective: 'Jason followed his probably erroneous assumption, that John and Absalom represented Judas, and deduced, from "submitted" in vs. 17, that Judas submitted peace terms in writing for Lysias to consider' (*2 Maccabees*, p. 408).

5. *Letters Cited in Josephus' Works*

Josephus cites a large number of letters throughout the *Antiquities*, beginning with correspondence that bears some relation to biblical events (Josephus often introducing specifically epistolary vocabulary and forms). This includes correspondence between Solomon and King Eiromos of the Tyrians (*Ant.* 8.50-52 [Solomon to Eiromos]; 8.53-54 [Eiromos to Solomon][39]); Cyrus' letter to the Satraps in Syria (11.12-17; cf. 1 Esdr. 6.27; Ezra 6.6); the letter from the people of Syria, Phoenicia, Ammon, Moab and Samaria to Cambyses (Cyrus' son = Artaxerxes; 11.22-25 = 1 Esdr. 2.16-24; Ezra 4.7-16); together with a reply from Cambyses to Samaritans (11.26-28; cf. 1 Esdr. 2.25; Ezra 6.17). There is a letter from Darius to Sisines and Sarabazanes (11.104; cf. 1 Esdr. 6.34; Ezra 6.12).

In *Antiquities* 11.118-119 (cf. 1 Esdr. 6.27-31; Ezra 6.6-10) Josephus records a letter from Darius to the Samaritans, referring to an embassy from the Jews (11.16) which had complained about their treatment. The letter of Darius refers to these envoys (πρεσβευταί) by name as Zorobabelos, Ananias and Mardochaios,[40] who clearly accompanied this letter:

> It is my will, therefore, that when you have read this letter, you shall furnish them [i.e. the envoys] out of the royal treasury, from the tribute of Samaria, everything which they may need for the sacrifices as the priests request, in order that they may not leave off their daily sacrifices or their prayers to God on behalf of me and the Persians. (11.119).

Josephus also includes a letter from Darius' son Xerxes (= biblical Artaxerxes), authorizing Ezra to lead the Jewish return to Jerusalem (11.123-130; cf. 1 Esdr. 8.9-24; Ezra 7.11-24).

The royal mounted couriers play an important part in the biblical book of Esther, enabling the decree of Ahasuerus, which allowed Jews to gather and defend their lives to be carried to the 127 provinces: 'letters were sent by mounted couriers riding on swift horses that were used in the king's service, bred from the royal stud...so the couriers, mounted on their swift horses that were used in the king's service, rode out in haste, urged by the king's command' (Est. 7.10, 14 RSV). Josephus' retelling of the story includes a text of the letter dependent on the Greek Additions to Esther (*Ant.* 11.273-283; Greek Esther Addition E; or 16.1-24), followed by several references to those who carried the letters; in one of these the

---

39   Said by Josephus to be preserved in the Tyrian archives (*Ant.* 8.55; *Apion* 1.106-111); they paraphrase information from 1 Kings 5 (cf. Eusebius, *Praep. Ev.* 9.33f for reference to Eupolemus, second cent. BC, as source).

40   Cf. *Ant.* 11.16 which refers to Zorobabelos and four other leaders as the envoys: καὶ πρεσβεύουσι Ζοροβάβηλος καὶ ἄλλοι τῶν ἀρχόντων τέσσαρες. Cf. Ezra 2.2; Neh. 7.2 for Hananiah and Mordecai as leaders with Zerubbabel.

bearers of the king's letter 'announce' (Loeb), or perhaps 'explain' (δηλόω) the main point of the letter: that on the thirteenth day of the month they will destroy their enemies (οἱ κομίσαντες τὰ τοῦ βασιλέως γράμματα ἐδήλουν ...).

Josephus also cites various letters from the Letter of Aristeas, Demetrius to Ptolemy, 12.36-39 (*Ep. Arist.* 28–32); Ptolemy to Eleazar, 12.45-50 (*Ep. Arist.* 35–40) and Eleazar to Ptolemy, 12.51-56 (*Ep. Arist.* 41–46). The letter from Ptolemy to Eleazar, announcing the decision to have the Law translated and requesting six men from each tribe in order to undertake the translation, includes reference to two men, presumably the letter carriers, who are able to discuss the matters further, and who are also bringing gifts. The men are recommended as 'greatly honoured', which further strengthens their role in carrying forward the discussion about such matters:[41]

ἀπέσταλκα δέ σοι περὶ τούτων διαλεξομένους Ἀνδρέαν τὸν ἀρχισωματοφύλακα καὶ Ἀρισταῖον ἐμοὶ τιμιωτάτους ...[42]

Other letters include Antiochus (III) to Ptolemy (12.138-144); Antiochus to Zeuxis (governor of Lydia) (12.148-152), neither of which include any discussion of delivery. In *Ant.* 12.226-227, Josephus includes a copy of the letter from Areios, king of Sparta, to Onias the high priest, which was already discussed above as included in 1 Macc. 12.20-23. Josephus adds both an introductory note that an embassy accompanied the letter (Ἄρειος πρεσβείαν τε ἔπεμψε καὶ ἐπισταλός), and includes a note within the letter stating that 'Demoteles, the courier, is bringing this letter to you' (Δημοτέλης ὁ φέρων τὰ γράμματα διαπέμπει τὰς ἐπιστολάς).[43]

A number of further official letters are quoted by Josephus which refer to the accompaniment of envoys who accompany (and reinforce the letter): Samaritans to Antiochus (IV) Epiphanes (12.258-261[44]); the reply from Antiochus to Nicanor (12.262-263) explicitly mentions the role of

---

41 The ET in *OTP* misses this in describing the men as 'held in high esteem *by you*', which is in no way justified by the slightly different formulation in *Aristeas* (τιμωμένους παρ᾽ ἡμῖν) [cited from H. B. Swete, *An Introduction to the Old Testament in Greek* (Cambridge: Cambridge University Press, 1990), p. 559 who refers to no variants at this point].

42 'I have sent Andreas, the commander of the bodyguard, and Aristaeus – men whom I hold in the greatest honour – to discuss these matters with you, and by their hands I have also sent dedicatory offerings as first-fruits for the temple, and one hundred talents of silver for sacrifices and other purposes' (*Ant.* 12.50).

43 The letter of Areios refers to a document about the common ancestry of Jews and Lacedaemonians [or Spartans], which is probably what is meant by the plural here (?). Demoteles is referred to again in connection with the acceptable reception of this letter in 13.167.

44 *Ant.*, 12.258: πέμψαντες ουν πρὸς τὸν Ἀντίοχον πρέσβεις καὶ ἐπιστολὴν ἐδήλουν τὰ ὑπογεγραμμένα.

these envoys: 'the men sent by them have represented to us ...' Other letters can simply be noted (not including any details about delivery):

> 13.45: From Alexander to Jonathan (= 1 Macc. 10.18-20)
> 13.48-57: From Demetrius to Jonathan (= 1 Macc. 10.25-45)
> 13.65-68: Onias to Ptolemy and Cleopatra
> 13.70-71: Ptolemy and Cleopatra to Onias (reply)
> 13.126-128: Demetrius to Jonathan (= 1 Macc. 11.30-37)

In *Antiquities* 13.166-170 Josephus includes a copy of the letter from Jonathan and the Jews to Sparta (= 1 Macc. 12.6-18), which we have discussed at some length already (as concerned the named letter carriers mentioned in 1 Macc. 12). Josephus' version adds the small but significant detail concerning Numenius and Antipater that they are leaders among the Jews and 'are held in honour by us': τῶν ἀπὸ τῆς γερουσίας ὄντων παρ' ἡμῖν ἐν τιμῇ.

Other letters in Josephus include: Dolabella (governor of Asia) to Ephesus (14.225-227; cf. also 230; 233: additional short letters/decrees); Laodicea to Gaius Rabirius (14.241-243), which refers to an envoy from Hyrcanus carrying the letter to which this one is the reply; Publius Servilius Galba to Miletus (14.244-246).

During the trial of Antipater, for plotting against Herod (*Antiquities* 17),[45] Herod's men intercepted a letter from Antiphilus (then in Egypt) to Antipater which referred to a letter from Acme that Antiphilus was sending on to Antipater (17.134). This includes an interesting detail about letter-carrying:

> The king then looked for the other letter as well but it was not visible, and the slave of Antiphilus, who had brought the letter just read, denied that he had received any other. The king was therefore at a loss what to do but one of his friends noticed that there was a patch sown on the slave's inner tunic – he was wearing two of these – and guessed that a letter was hidden with this fold. And this was in fact the case. (pp. 135–136)[46]

Couriers are also mentioned (as being delayed) in the correspondence from Gaius to Petronius (18.304; cf. earlier letters mentioned in 301): 'Petronius did not receive it [Gaius' letter] while Gaius was alive since the voyage of those who brought the message was so delayed that before it arrived Petronius had received a letter with news of the death of Gaius' (18.305). Four named letter bearers are also mentioned within Claudius'

---

45   This same context refers to a letter from Herod to Caesar which was accompanied by men 'to inform him by word of mouth about the villainy of Antipater' (17.133).

46   Further letters (involved in a complex conspiracy of forged letters) are cited: Acme to Antipater (17.137); Acme to Herod (17.139). The whole complex intrigue is recounted at length in *War* I.602–661.

letter to the rulers and people of Jerusalem (*Ant.* 20.10-14): 'the bearers of this letter are Cornelius son of Ceron, Tryphon son of Theudion, Dorotheus son of Nathanael, and John son of John', but no specific role is specified.

Some more letters are mentioned or quoted in Josephus' *Life*. In one episode (*Life* 48–51) Philip ben Jacimus, having escaped from the besieged royal palace in Jerusalem, sent letters to Agrippa, and had one of his freedmen convey the letter to Varus, Agrippa's viceroy, who fearing that he would be out of a job, killed the letter carrier. Philip had been expecting the courier to return (with news), and so 'dispatched a second with further letters and to bring him word what had happened to cause the delay of his first courier' (*Life* 51). These events illustrate the importance of the carrier to the sender, since it was anticipated that the courier would return with news about the reception of the letter. Obviously in this case 'letter carriers live dangerously'.[47]

In another interesting passage Josephus tells a story in which the letter carrier has a crucial, albeit unusual role, not in aiding the communication, but in some ways subverting the point of the letter by telling more of the situation than would have otherwise been known (*Life* 216–228). Josephus' Jewish opponents attempt to entrap him and write him a letter to invite him to a meeting, as long as he brings only a few companions (*Life* 217–218, for the letter). This letter was carried by 'an insolent young fellow' who delivered the letter with an account of the senders and a request for a speedy reply (*Life* 220–221).[48] Josephus managed to gain the courier's confidence sufficiently to invite him to share a drink, and as a result he 'indulged so freely with the wine that he became intoxicated and unable to keep his secrets any longer to himself' (*Life* 225). The courier divulged the plot and Josephus escaped, sending a reply with a group of Galileans who were instructed to greet the embassy but not to speak further (he places a trusted soldier with each one to ensure 'that no conversation took place between my emissaries and the other party', *Life* 228).[49] This episode illustrates that it was a widely held assumption that letter couriers were party to additional information.

In general we might note that Josephus is very familiar with the form and function of letters (of course he does say at one point that he had received 62 letters from Agrippa II, praising his history of the Jewish War, *Life* 364–366). He understands the conventions associated with royal and official correspondence and their accompanying embassies; but he also

---

47   Klauck, *Ancient Letters*, p. 257.

48   This request comports with one of the emphases of the letter itself: 'we request you to come to us with all speed' (*Life* 218).

49   Josephus later sets guards over the routes whereby this group would send letters: to intercept any couriers and forward on the letters (*Life* 240–241; cf. 245).

understands that couriers could have a significant role in less official correspondence. Letter carriers can reinforce the message of the letter in person, or carry conversation further, or bring news back of how the letter was received. Careless couriers can sometimes subvert the message of a letter.

6. *Letters in Philo's Works*

By and large Philo is relatively unconcerned with matters epistolographical.[50] In his reasonably capacious works he uses the noun ἐπιστολή only twelve times, and eleven of these are within *The Embassy to Gaius*. Similarly he uses the verb ἐπιστέλλω only nine times, eight of which occur within the same work, *The Embassy to Gaius*.[51] He does not, however, quote many letters, preferring, as we shall see, to summarize the content of the communication.

Embassy 199–203 refers to a letter from Capito (collector of the imperial revenues in Judea) to Gaius, with summary and some quotation (but incomplete); no details about delivery. *Embassy* 207 refers to a letter from Gaius to Petronius (Roman legate in Syria), with summary and description of tone but no quotation and no details about delivery. *Embassy* 248–254 refers to a letter, or indeed letters from Petronius to Gaius, with a summary (of the reasons for delay in the erection of the statue). Of these letters it is said that Petronius appointed active men 'who were accustomed to make a rapid journey' to convey them (254), although no more is said of these men after their delivery to Gaius who reacts angrily to Petronius' excuses, although he sends a calm reply which concealed his anger (*Embassy* 259–260).[52] *Embassy* 276–332 quotes a long letter from Agrippa I to Gaius (which itself contains references to other

---

50   There is very little secondary literature on the subject of Philo's view of communication by letter-writing. Neither of the two major Philonic bibliographies provided even a single discussion of letters in Philo: Roberto Radice and David T. Runia, *Philo of Alexandria: An Annotated Bibliography, 1937–1986* (Supplements to Vigiliae Christianae, 8; Leiden: Brill, 1988); David T. Runia, *Philo of Alexandria: An Annotated Bibliography 1986–1996* (Supplements to Vigiliae Christianae, 57; Leiden: Brill, 2001). Letters in the other sense – γράμμα and γράμματα – are referred to fairly frequently in Philo (*The Philo Index*, p. 78 [see next note] lists 55 occurrences), and also appear in discussions of Philo's letter–spirit contrast, but do not concern us here.

51   Cf. P. Borgen et al. (eds), *The Philo Index: A Complete Greek Word Index to the Writings of Philo of Alexandria* (Grand Rapids, MI: Eerdmans, 2000), p. 144: ἐπιστολή: *Prob.* 96; *Legat.* 199, 207 (2 ×), 254 (2 ×), 259, 291, 301, 303, 314, 315; ἐπιστέλλω: *Mos.* 1.83; *Legat.* 209, 248, 261, 276, 305, 311, 313, 314.

52   An interesting note is that on receipt of Petronius' letter Gaius is said to have read it, become angry, and then made marks on every page (*Embassy* 254). This would seem to correspond to an initial reading of the letter and then a reading with annotations or marks for reference (more like studying the letter).

letters in 291, 301, 303, and 305; and a complete transcription of another letter, 314–316), urging toleration for Jewish scruples in view of the favourable attitudes of Augustus and Tiberius to the Jews.[53] Agrippa's letter is written, sealed and sent, but no details about delivery are given. Gaius' reception is described rather fully (331–333) in terms of receiving the letter, reading it and considering each suggestion, before acquiescing to withdraw the plan for the erection of his statue. Letters are written and dispatched to Petronius (*Embassy* 333–334) advising him of this.

We thus learn nothing about letter carriers named within letters; we hear once of official and experienced Roman couriers taking mail from Syria to Rome, and we might presume that they (or their official colleagues) also made the return journey, but no role is given to them in these communications. The letters are clearly important; indeed Agrippa's letter is depicted as powerfully fulfilling his aim and halting (at least at that point) the emperor's plan.

7. Conclusion

Given the variety of material considered it is important to note that any generalizations will be a little dangerous. It is clear that the letter carriers do sometimes have an important role in the communication process (esp. when named, where it is generally assumed that they will have a larger role). An important place is given to specifically ambassadorial language in connection with the role of envoys/embassies in the delivery of official and royal letters. This can be both real/historical and redactionally introduced (e.g. in Maccabean literature and Josephus). From the notes of the Bar Kokhba revolt through to the royal letters of Jewish kings we do find letter carriers involved in reinforcing and supplementing the message of the written letter and thus facilitating the communication process envisaged by the author and sender of the letter.

---

53 It is interesting that Agrippa is depicted as having access to earlier relevant official letters during the composition of this one.

'I WAS INTENDING TO VISIT YOU, BUT …'
CLAUSES EXPLAINING DELAYED VISITS AND THEIR IMPORTANCE IN PAPYRUS LETTERS AND IN PAUL

Peter Arzt-Grabner

The Genre of Paul's Letters

The distinction between letter and epistle by A. Deissmann is classical. According to him, a letter is 'something non-literary, a means of communication between persons who are separated from each other. Confidential and personal in its nature, it is intended only for the person or persons to whom it is addressed, and not at all for the public or any kind of publicity.'[1] Contrary, an epistle has to be seen as

> an artistic literary form, a species of literature… It has nothing in common with the letter except its form; apart from that one might venture the paradox that the epistle is the opposite of a real letter. The contents of an epistle are intended for publicity – they aim at interesting 'the public'. If the letter is a secret, the epistle is cried in the market; everyone may read it, and is expected to read it: the more readers it obtains, the better its purpose will be fulfilled… Most letters are, partly at least, unintelligible unless we know the addressees and the situation of the sender. Most epistles are intelligible even without our knowing the supposed addressee and the author… The epistle differs from a letter…as art differs from nature. The letter is a piece of life, the epistle is a product of literary art.[2]

---

1 Adolf Deissmann, *Light from the Ancient East: The New Testament Illustrated by Recently Discovered Texts of the Graeco-Roman World* (trans. Lionel R. M. Strachan; London: Hodder and Stoughton, rev. edn, 1927), p. 228.

2 Deissmann, *Light*, pp. 229–30.

These definitions are still more or less valid and practical to distinguish a private, personal, or family letter[3] from an epistle as a solely literary genre. But a true problem of modern classification[4] is caused by the fact that in Graeco-Roman antiquity not only personal, administrative, or business letters were written in the form of a letter but also several other types of documents (e.g., receipts, different types of deeds, petitions) that we today would not classify as such.[5] More or less everything that functioned as a written piece of communication in antiquity could be, and

---

3 On the type and the different parts of a personal letter see Heikki Koskenniemi, *Studien zur Idee und Phraseologie des griechischen Briefes bis 400 n.Chr.* (Helsinki: Suomalainen Tiedeakatemia, 1956); John L. White, *Light from Ancient Letters* (Philadelphia: Fortress Press, 1986), pp. 187–220; idem, 'Epistolary Formulas and Cliches in Greek Papyrus Letters', in *SBL 1978 Seminar Papers*, vol. 2, pp. 289–319; idem, 'The Greek Documentary Letter Tradition Third Century B.C.E. to Third Century C.E.', *Semeia* 22 (1981), pp. 89–106; John L. White and Keith A. Kensinger, 'Categories of Greek Papyrus Letters', in *SBL 1976 Seminar Papers*, pp. 79–91; Rodolfo Buzón, 'Die Briefe der Ptolemäerzeit: Ihre Struktur und ihre Formeln' (diss., Heidelberg, 1984); Abraham J. Malherbe, *Ancient Epistolary Theorists* (Atlanta: Scholars Press, 1988); Stanley K. Stowers, *Letter Writing in Greco-Roman Antiquity* (Philadelphia: Westminster Press, 1986); Hans-Josef Klauck, *Ancient Letters and the New Testament: A Guide to Context and Exegesis* (Waco: Baylor University Press, 2006), pp. 9–42, 67–77 (with bibliography pp. xxi–xxiii); Hermann Probst, *Paulus und der Brief* (Tübingen: Mohr, 1991), pp. 56–60; Christopher Kumitz, *Der Brief als Medium der* αγαπε*: Eine Untersuchung zur rhetorischen und epistolographischen Gestalt des Philemonbriefes* (Frankfurt a.M.: Peter Lang, 2004), pp. 36–39. On the form of New Testament letters (in comparison with papyrus letters) see especially Deissmann, *Light*; Peter Arzt-Grabner, *Philemon* (Göttingen: Vandenhoeck & Ruprecht, 2003) (with bibliography); Peter Arzt-Grabner et al., *1. Korinther* (Göttingen: Vandenhoeck & Ruprecht, 2006); William G. Doty, 'The Classification of Epistolary Literature', *CBQ* 31 (1969): 183–99; idem, *Letters in Primitive Christianity* (Philadelphia: Fortress Press, 1973); John L. White, 'New Testament Epistolary Literature in the Framework of Ancient Epistolography', in *ANRW* II.25.2, ed. Wolfgang Haase, pp. 1730–56 (Berlin and New York: Walter de Gruyter, 1984); Stanley K. Stowers, 'Social Typification and the Classification of Ancient Letters', in *The Social World of Formative Christianity and Judaism: Essays in Tribute to Howard Clark Kee* (ed. Jacob Neusner et al.; Philadelphia: Fortress Press, 1988), pp. 78–90; Klauck, *Ancient Letters*, pp. 299–435; E. Randolph Richards, *Paul and First-Century Letter Writing: Secretaries, Composition and Collection* (Downers Grove, IL: InterVarsity Press, 2004); Catherine Salles, 'L'épistolographie hellénistique', in *Paul de Tarse: Congrès de l'ACFEB (Strasbourg, 1995)* (ed. Jacques Schlosser; Paris: Éditions du Cerf, 1996), pp. 79–97.

4 On this problem, and on a critical review of Deissmann's work cf. especially Doty, 'Classification'; Greg H. R. Horsley, 'The Fiction of "Jewish Greek"', in idem, *New Documents Illustrating Early Christianity*, vol. 5, *Linguistic Essays* (Sydney: Macquarie University, 1989), pp. 5–40.

5 Also the so-called cheirographon as the most widely attested documentary type of private law, obviously, has its stylistic origins in those of the private letter, and developed its own distinct style not earlier than during II BCE (cf. Hans Julius Wolff, *Das Recht der griechischen Papyri Ägyptens in der Zeit der Ptolemäer und des Prinzipats*, vol. 2, *Organisation und Kontrolle des privaten Rechtsverkehrs* [Munich: C. H. Beck, 1978], pp. 109–10).

also was, styled in the form of a letter.[6] Moreover, a clear distinction between letter and epistle does not work for documents that show typical characteristics of private letters and of literary epistles as well.[7] This is, e.g., true for letters that, on the one hand, contain very personal parts and passages that are not clearly understandable for a reader who is different from the primary recipient, and neither familiar with her or his historical situation nor with that of the sender, and, on the other hand, also contain parts that go beyond a specific personal and historical situation and express timeless and commonly understandable ideas that could address almost everyone anytime. This is true for Paul's letters as well as for many personal letters of other authors or philosophers of Graeco-Roman antiquity. It is important to realize that these letters preserved their personal identity even after reaching a broader public, published and sold in a bookstore later on, although they underwent a process of transmission and redaction.[8] Not only in this respect, the personal letters preserved on papyrus and the so-called literary letters preserved in ancient and medieval manuscripts can be compared to one another to reach a better understanding of New Testament letters.[9] Even the length of a Pauline letter, or its sophisticated style must not be seen anymore as features reserved for literary epistles, but are also attested by private letters on

---

6   Doty, 'Classification', pp. 196–97, distinguishes between three groups of 'more private letters' and five groups of 'less private letters', the latter groups again dividing in several sub-groups; the eight main groups distinguished by Doty are: *more private letters*: 1. writer to individual person, 2. writer to discrete group, 3. writers to addressees; *less private letters*: 4. official (administrative military or non-military, administrative Christian, commercial, foreign affairs, legal documents), 5. public ('open' letters, school exercises), 6. 'non-real' (pseudonymous, imaginary, letters from heaven or the gods, epistolary novel), 7. discursive (magical, scientific, religious, literary-critical, historical, knowledge-in-general, paraenetic, didactic), 8. other special types (amorous, erotic, poetic, inserted [stylized to fit content], consolation, dedication, introduction, congratulation). On the problem of classification see also Stowers, 'Social Typification'; White and Kensinger, 'Categories'; for additional bibliography see Klauck, *Ancient Letters*, p. 67.

7   Cf. Klauck, *Ancient Letters*, pp. 70–71.

8   On the redaction of Paul's letters see especially David Trobisch, *Paul's Letter Collection: Tracing the Origins* (Bolivar: Quiet Waters Publication, 2001); idem, *The First Edition of the New Testament* (Oxford: Oxford University Press, 2000); on several scribal features see also Larry W. Hurtado, *The Earliest Christian Artifacts: Manuscripts and Christian Origins* (Grand Rapids: Eerdmans, 2006), pp. 95–189.

9   Cf. Klauck, *Ancient Letters*, p. 103. An overview of Greek and Latin literary letters is presented by Klauck, *Ancient Letters*, pp. 103–48. On the criteria for comparing both see especially Arzt-Grabner, *Philemon*, pp. 44–56; idem, 'The International Project "Papyrological Commentaries on the New Testament" (Papyrologische Kommentare zum Neuen Testament): Methods, Aims, and Limits', in *Proceedings of the 24th International Congress of Papyrology, Helsinki, 1–7 August, 2004*, vol. 1 (ed. Jaakko Frösén; Helsinki: Societas Scientiarum Fennica, 2007), pp. 53–57.

papyrus (cf. P.Ammon I 3 [348 CE?]; abbreviations of papyri, ostraca, and tablets according to Oates et al., *Checklist*).[10]

This article addresses a particular type of passage that is not found outside personal letters. To inform the recipient of a letter about one's desire to visit her or him, and to explain the reasons for a delayed visit is typical for a private correspondence, as one of its main goals is to stay in touch even when being apart. On the contrary, it would not make any sense for an author of a literary epistle to talk about plans to visit his audience, as epistles are pieces of literature with their authors' only intention to be read by a public audience. In this sense, when Paul several times expresses his intention to visit a Christian community, or explains why he had to delay a planned visit, this clearly attests to the character of his letters as real, personal letters, not literary epistles.

Delayed Visits Mentioned by Paul in his Letters

As with many senders of private papyrus letters, Paul emphasizes several times that he intended to visit his addressees earlier but for some reason could not or did not do so: In 1 Thessalonians, Paul expresses his eagerness and desire to see the faces of his sisters and brothers, and that he wanted to visit them more than once but was hindered by Satan (2.17-18; cf. 3.6). Concerning the community at Philippi, Paul is convinced he will be able to come shortly (2.24; cf. also 1.27).

Paul's Corinthian correspondence in particular contains several passages dealing with the apostle's plans to visit the Christian Corinthians. In 1 Cor., Paul more than once assures them to visit the community soon, although some of them – in their arrogancy – might not trust him (4.18-19; cf. 4.21; 16.2-7). In 2 Cor. 1.15-16, Paul writes about his former plans to visit Corinth, then go for a mission to Macedonia, and come back to Corinth before leaving for Judaea. And he tries to explain why he altered his plans, and (most probably) returned to Ephesus after a severe conflict arose during his second visit. His return to Corinth *after* his travels through Macedonia is overdue, yet it seems to be too early for him to visit the community right now, and risk another disappointing meeting (cf. 2.1-

---

10   John F. Oates et al., *Checklist of Editions of Greek, Latin, Demotic and Coptic Papyri, Ostraca and Tablets* (Oakville and Oxford: Oxbow, 5th edn, 2001); online version: http://scriptorium.lib.duke.edu/papyrus/texts/clist.html (accessed December 2007). – P.Ammon I 3 deals throughout with family affairs, and was at least (the letter is not completely preserved) as long as Gal.; some examples for private letters written in a sophisticated or even poetic style are, besides P.Ammon I 3: *BGU* IV 1141 (with *BGPA* III, 17; XI, 25; Bror Olsson, *Papyrusbriefe aus der frühesten Römerzeit* [Uppsala: Almquist & Wiksell, 1925], no. 9; 14–13 BCE); P.Sarap. 85; 89 (both 90–133 CE); P.Oxy. XLII 3057 (I–II CE).

3).[11] From Macedonia he writes 2 Corinthians instead, explaining his intention to spare the members of the Christian community (1.23), and to come for a third visit after sending Titus and two other brothers with the letter that is aimed at preparing his visit, and in particular the collection for the communities in Judaea (cf. especially 12.14, 20–21; 13.1-2).

Finally, in Romans, Paul's only letter which is addressed to a community that he has not visited before, Paul emphasizes that for many years it has often been his purpose to visit the Christians in the empire's center (cf. 1.10, 13; 15.22-23).

Delayed Visits in Papyrus Letters and their Impact on Paul's Clauses

As it is one of the primary purposes of a letter to function as an alternative to a personal visit, letter writers not only attempt to remember their relatives and friends, to pray for them almost all the time, and use every opportunity to send them a letter, but they also emphasize that they would prefer to visit them in person. According to the actual situation, those letter writers explain more or less extensively why it was, and still is, impossible for them to visit. To study and explain those passages in papyrus letters, their different forms and functions, is the basis for comparing them with the relevant passages in Paul's letters which will lead to a better understanding of the epistolary functions of these passages.[12]

Examples for reporting a delayed visit, and sometimes also explaining the reasons for the delay are manifold. It always seems to be a good excuse to blame it on an illness or just too much work. Official duties seem to be the reason for a certain Demetrios who sent a letter to Zenon that was – as confirmed by Zenon on the back of the papyrus sheet – received on 2 January, 252 BCE. The final lines of this letter (P.Lond. VII 1979, 17–19) read: ἐβουλόμην | μὲν οὖν καὶ αὐτὸς ἀναπλεῦσαι πρός σε, ἀλλ᾽ οὐκ ἐκπεποίηκέ μοι. γράφει γὰρ Ἀντιλέων | πρός σε ἐπιστολὴν ὑπὲρ μοῦ ('I myself am anxious to sail up to meet you, but I did not have time to do so. For Antileon is writing the letter to you on my behalf'). It seems that Demetrios had been urgently called away from Alexandria where he had his office, and not only lacked time to visit Zenon in Philadelphia but even

---

11   According to my interpretation, 2 Cor. 2.3-4 deals with 2 Cor., and not with the letter mentioned in 7.8-12 (see Peter Arzt-Grabner and Ruth E. Kritzer, *2. Korinther* [Göttingen: Vandenhoeck & Ruprecht, forthcoming]).

12   This is also part of a long-term research project at the Department of Biblical Studies and Ecclesiastical History at the University of Salzburg, Austria. The current project is sponsored by the Austrian Science Fund (FWF) and focused on commenting on 1 and 2 Thess. from a papyrological perspective (see http://www.uni-salzburg.at/bwkg/pknt).

had to commission a business associate, Antileon, to write the present letter on his behalf.[13]

P.Fay. 123 is a letter addressed to Sabinus, the son of Gemellus, sent by a brother named Harpocration around 100 CE.[14] A molestation kept him from going to Sabinus, and to prove that he really intended to go there he confirms that he already sent another letter the day before in relation to this. Right at the beginning of his letter, Harpocration now writes – 1. 3–9: καὶ ἐκ|θές σοι ἔγραψα διὰ | Μάρδωνος τοῦ σοῦ γ|νῶναί σε θέλων ὅ|τι διὰ τὸ ἐπηρεᾶσθαι | οὐκ ἠδυνήθην κατελ|θεῖν ('I also wrote to you yesterday by your servant Mardon, desiring you to know that owing to having been molested I was unable to come down').[15]

A certain Herakleides, all of a sudden, became ill, and, therefore, was not able to visit Helene. So, in P.Freib. IV 56 (I–II CE), he requests her to arrange for the harvest of a crop of reeds, something that *he* was supposed to do as they are running a business together. It seems that they are the lessors or sellers of one or several vineyards whose duty it was to provide a sufficient quantity of reeds and cord to be used by the lessee or buyer to maintain the vineyard. Herakleides writes – 1. 2–9 with *BGPA* IX, 90: ἐπεὶ τῇ η ἀπὸ <νό>σου ἐνω|θρευσάμην καὶ οὐκ ἰσ|χύω{ι} κατελθεῖν, | εὖ ποιήσεις προνοήσα|σα κοπῆναι τὸ καλαμί|διον προχρήσασα τοὺς | μισθοὺς μέχρι οὗ κατέλ|θω{ι} ('since on the 8th day I got so worn out because of a disease and do not have the strength to come down, you will do well to arrange for the reeds to be cut, advancing the wages until I come down').[16]

According to P.Oxy. XLVI 3313 (II CE), Apollonios and Sarapias are a married couple living in Oxyrhynchus in the second century CE and running a florists. The necessary recovery from some disease as well as the forthcoming periodic review of the financial and judicial affairs of each nome by the Roman governor keeps them from visiting a certain Dionysia, and especially from attending her son's wedding. They write that Dionysia filled them with joy by announcing the good news of the wedding of her son, and that they would have come immediately to serve him on a day so greatly longed for, 'but', as they add in 1. 6–8 'because of the conventus and because we are recovering from illness we could not come' (ἀλλὰ διὰ τὸν | δι[αλο]γισμὸν καὶ ὅτι ἀναλαμβάνομεν ἀπὸ

---

13 Cf. Th.C. Skeat in P.Lond. VII, p. 74.

14 = C.Pap.Jud. II 431; Sel.Pap. I 110; Olsson, *Papyrusbriefe*, no. 65; White, *Light*, no. 99.

15 Similar examples are P.Mich. VIII 479,15–17 (= White, *Light* no. 111; early II CE); P.Oxy. X 1345 (late II or III CE); P.Flor. II 156,2–10 with *BGPA* I, 150 (249–268 CE); III 365,6–9; P.Oxy. XLII 3082, 8–11 (both III CE); *PSI* VIII 971,3–14 (III–IV CE).

16 Similar P.Lips. I 108,4–6 (II–III CE).

νωθρείας | οὐκ ἠδυνήθημεν ἐλθεῖν).[17] They continue to explain what arrangements they have made to supply flowers for the wedding. Dionysia, naturally, had ordered a large quantity of roses and narcissi. Now, Apollonius and Sarapias send 1,000 roses and 4,000 narcissi, and they apparently refuse payment, saying that they love the kids as if they were their own.

The examples presented so far display very clearly some of the important aspects of the topic: a letter is somehow a less valuable alternative to a personal visit, but on the other hand it is a very good medium in which to act according to the importance of the things that have to be done. Practically, the letter has the function of resolving issues that require immediate action without delay.

In some cases, after a visit was delayed or just impossible, letter writers try to figure out whether a visit is still necessary or not. E.g., the sender of P.Cair.Zen. IV 59593 (mid. III BCE) tells Zenon that he tried to meet him, as requested by Zenon, but somehow it did not work. And he adds in l. 9: εἰ οὖν τι ἀναγκαῖόν ἐστιν, γράψομ (l. γράψον) μοι ὅπως παρα[γένωμαι] ('if there is something urgent, just write to me, so that I come'; cf. also l. 14).

During the second century CE, a certain Sarapammon writes to a sister Thaesis at the end of his letter – P.Oxy. XII 1488,20–25 with *BGPA* III, 138: ἔμελ|λον γὰρ ἀνελθεῖν, καὶ | ὑπερθέμην ἔστ' ἂν | μάθω πότερον ἐρά|ισας ἢ οὐ, καὶ εἰ χρεία | ἐστὶ τοῦ με ἀνελθεῖν ('for I intended to come up, but have put it off until I learn whether you have recovered or not, and whether there is need for me to come').[18]

The more a letter writer is able to convince the addressee that she or he had a good reason to delay or even put off some intended or already arranged visit, the more the addressee is supposed to and ready to accept the letter as a valid substitute for it. The sender of the letter confirms and insists that it was truly impossible for her or him to come, and expects the addressee to believe it and to accept the letter as a sufficient excuse. In P. Oxy. XIV 1773 (III CE)[19] a certain Eutychis recounts her difficulties in

17 The Greek term διαλογισμός is equivalent to the Latin *conventus*; cf. J. R. Rea in P. Oxy. XLVI, pp. 102–03: 'This refers to the periodic review of the financial and judicial affairs of each nome by the Roman governor … Presumably Apollonios expected to be called to appear in court.' On the *conventus* see also Naphtali Lewis, 'The Prefect's Conventus: Proceedings and Procedures', *Bulletin of the American Society of Papyrologists* 18 (1981): 119–28.

18 See also P.Mil.Vogl. I 24,10–12 with *BGPA* VI, 84 (7 December, 117 CE); *SB* XXIV 16268,3–6 (II CE); P.Oxy. XIV 1678,3–13 (= Giuseppe Ghedini, *Lettere cristiane dai papiri greci del III e IV secolo* [Milano: Vita e Pensiero, 1923], no. 7; Mario Naldini, *Il Cristianesimo in Egitto: Lettere private nei papiri dei secoli II–IV* [Fiesole: Nardini, 1998; nuova edizione ampliata e aggiornata], no. 9; III CE).

19 = Ghedini, *Lettere*, no. 8; Naldini, *Cristianesimo*, no. 10.

traveling to Oxyrhynchus from an unknown point in the Thebaid. She tells her mother – ll. 5–16: γεινόσκιν (l. γινώσκειν) σε θέ|λω ὅτι ἀπὸ τριακάδος τοῦ Τῦ|βι ἦλθον εἰς τὸ Τυράννιν καὶ | οὐκ εὗρον πῶς ἔλθω πρὸς ὑμᾶς, | [τ]ῶν καμηλιτῶν μὴ θελησάν|[τ]ων ἐλθεῖν εἰς Ὀξυρυγχείτην. | [ο]ὐ μόνον, ἀλλὰ καὶ εἰς Ἀντινόου | [ἀ]νῆλθα χάριν πλύου (l. πλοίου) καὶ οὐ|κ εὗρον. νῦν οὖν ἐσκεψάμην | τοὺς γόμους μου ἀρῖν (l. ἀρεῖν) εἰς Ἀν|τινόου καὶ μῖνε (l. μεῖναι) ἐκεῖ ἄχρι οὗ πλῦ|ον (l. πλοῖον) εὕρω καὶ καταπλεύσω ('I want you to know that I came to the Tyrannion on the 30th of Tybi, and I could not find any way to come to you, because the camel drivers refused to go to the Oxyrhynchite. Not only that, but I went up to Antinooupolis for a boat and did not find any. So now I am considering bringing my cargo to Antinoou and staying there until I find a boat and sail down').

The content of P.Oxy. XLII 3065 (III CE)[20] is tantalizing. Unheard-of atrocities are the reason why Arius is not yet able to get out of the city of Alexandria and visit his parents. He writes in ll. 4–9: ἤδη πολλὰς ἐπιστο|λὰς ὑμῖν ἔγραψα δηλῶν ὅτι μ[έλλ]ω πλ{ε}εῖν καὶ σωθῆ|ναι τῆς πόλεω[ς] τάχα δὲ ...... περὶ τῶν ἐνθάδε | γενομ[έ]ν[ω]ν. τοιαῦ[τ]α γέγονεν οἷα οὐδέποτε ἐκ τοῦ | αἰῶν[ο]ς γέγονεν. νῦν ἀνθρωποφαγεία ἐστὶν καὶ οὐ πόλε|μος ('I have already written you many letters saying that I'm about to sail and get clear of the city. Perhaps...about what's happened here. Things have happened, the like of which hasn't happened through all the ages. Now it's cannibalism, not war.') In the third century CE, battles rather frequently took place in and around Alexandria – the massacre under Caracalla (215), the contest between Macrinus and Elagabalus, the rising of Macrianus and Quietus, the Palmyrene wars, the revolt of Domitius Domitianus – or the incidental wars and pogroms. But, as the editor of the letter, Peter Parsons, wrote: 'I see no way of choosing among these.'[21] In lines 16–17, the writer of our letter again confirms: ἐγὼ γὰρ ἤθελον [π]ρὸς σὲ{ν} ἐλθεῖν, ἡ δὲ τῆς | πόλεως ανθρω...ια οὐκ ἀφῆκέν με ('I wanted to come to you, but the cannibalism[?][22] of the city did not allow me').

If the cause of a delayed or failed visit is explained very extensively, this can be estimated as a sign either of a deep personal relationship, or an uncertainty on the side of the sender whether she or he can explain sufficiently the cause for not visiting. P.Mich. III 203, e.g., is a letter written between 114 and 116 CE by the soldier Satornilos who is on active duty, perhaps as a member of the auxiliary cohorts at Pselkis. The letter is

---

20 Giuseppe Tibiletti, *Le lettere private nei papiri greci del III e IV secolo d. C. Tra paganesimo e cristianesimo* (Milano: Vita e Pensiero, 1979), no. 10.

21 P. J. Parsons in P.Oxy. XLII, pp. 156–57.

22 Cf. P. J. Parsons in P.Oxy. XLII, p. 158: 'Probably ἀνθρωποφαγία again, though the space is a little short. The traces are no more than scattered spots of ink.'

sent back home to his mother Aphrodus in Karanis. Satornilos leaves no doubt that he is extremely eager to see his mother again. He writes that if he does not make the journey soon, he will not see her for another eighteen months because he will then leave Pselkis for a tour of duty in a frontier garrison. He has a plan for getting himself to Karanis, but it requires most careful preparation and execution. The right moment is not yet at hand, and, as he says in lines 19–20, πάντα εἰς τὴν στρατειὰν (l. στρατιὰν) | [μετ' εὐ]καιρείας [γ]είνεται ('everything in the army runs with a favourable chance'). So, his plan is – according to Herbert C. Youtie's interpretation of this letter – to be sent on a mission to Alexandria with military correspondence to the prefect of Egypt. But, 'at the very time that Satornilos is writing this letter to his mother, the rumor is circulating in the camp that the prefect is indeed on the road. If Satornilos were to set out now, he might encounter the prefect before reaching his destination, and that would be most unfortunate for him because the prefect would of course relieve him of the correspondence, which he was after all taking north for delivery to the prefect. There would be no reason for him to continue his journey, and the prefect would order him to return to his unit at Pselkis. The whole affair would for him be abortive, he would not see his mother, and the expense to which he had been put would have been of no avail'[23] (cf. ll. 7–21). Large parts of the letter are an extensive description of Satornilos' desire and of his efforts to visit his mother that go far beyond a neutral explanation of the whole situation.

P.Mich. XV 751 (= *New Docs.* II, pp. 63–64) is a much shorter example. By the end of the second century CE this letter was sent by Sempronius to his mother Satornila, filled with concerns about her welfare and about some unknown family matters.[24] He blames his mother for having not written to him, neither through a certain Celer nor through one Sempronius. Those two guys, however, had put forward an excuse: the letter writer was on the road (ll. 5–8), who later on writes – ll. 26–30: ἐβουλόμην πᾶν ποιῆσε (l. ποιῆσαι) | κὲ ἐλθῖ[ν] πρὸς ὑμᾶς πρῶτον μὲν προσκυνῆσε (l. προσκυνῆσαι) σου τὸ ἀγαθὸν | καὶ φ[ι]λότεκνον ἦθος, δεύτερον κὲ περὶ τούτων. οὐ νῦν | δὲ [.]ν εὗρον ἀφορμ[ήν], ἀλλὰ πρὸς ἀποδημίαν ὧν ἔγραψά | σοι περὶ αὐτῶν τούτων ('I would have done everything to come to you, in the first place to make obeisance to your good and child-loving character and in the second place also because of these matters. Now I did not find an opportunity; but I rather wrote to you about these matters because I am travelling').

The examples are very well comparable with the Pauline passages, but 2

23   Herbert C. Youtie, 'P.Mich. III 203', *Zeitschrift für Papyrologie und Epigraphik* 20 (1976): 288–92, here: 288–89.

24   On the small family archive of Sempronius see especially A. Papathomas in P.Heid. VII, pp. 117–18.

Cor. 1.23 is different as Paul admits: 'It was to spare you that I refrained from coming to Corinth.' This specific function is restricted to the letter, and could not be fulfilled through a personal visit. At least one example from the papyri shares this particular aspect with 2 Cor.: P.Oxy.Hels. 48 (II–III CE) was written by a certain Ammon, and addressed to his business partner Dionysios. We may assume that they were both dyers. Ammon insists that he had never ceased to inquire about his addressee's health whereas Dionysios had never remembered him when writing to his sister (ll. 3–7). And Ammon continues – ll. 7–11: ἕτοιμος οὖν ἤμην | ἐλθεῖν πρὸς σὲ ἡνίκα ἤμην ἐν | Βουβάστῳ, ἀλλ᾽ ἐπεί, ὡς πρόειπον, | περὶ ἐμοῦ οὐδὲν ἐπέστειλας, διὰ | τοῦτο ἐπέσχον ('so I was ready to visit you when I was in Boubastus, but since you, as I have already said, did not send any message concerning me, I refrained from coming'). But this defiant attitude is not final, as Ammon continues (ll. 1–15): 'Provided you know that we could find a letter of credit at your place in order to pay the money there, I am willing to come to you to purchase the wool.' Obviously, it is not just for business reasons that he is ready to visit again. Near the letter closing, we find a whole list of salutations before Ammon adds a very unique form of final greeting in ll. 25–27: ἐρρῶσθαί σε εὐχόμεθα πανοι-| κησία διὰ βίου πολλὰ πράσ|σοντα ('we pray that you and all yours may enjoy good health and much prosperity all your lives').[25]

Messengers as Representatives of Letter Senders

Paul usually emphasized his messengers as special co-workers or trustworthy people, an aspect which hints at the function of the letter itself: the letter frequently represents a substitute for the personal presence of the sender. Now and then, to compensate for the impossibility of visiting the addressee, a messenger functions as a representative for the sender of the letter. In particular, the three messengers who are sent to Corinth by Paul to deliver 2 Cor. are entrusted to act as the apostle's representatives, in order to prepare the collection for the communities in Judaea (cf. especially 2 Cor. 9.3-5). Detailed papyrological examples are not very numerous, perhaps because it was not necessary to describe the messenger as a representative explicitly, as he could give a verbal explanation by himself, as it was required, probably, to understand the exact meaning of ostracon *SB* XIV 11580 (second half II CE): Θέσιδι Διτύμη (1. Διδύμη) χαίρειν. | ἐτεμάκην (1. ἡτοιμάκειν) αἱματὴν (1. ἐμαυτὴν) ἐρθῖν (1. ἐλθεῖν). | Ἀπολλῶς ἀδὼς (1. αὐτὸς) ἤρηγέ (1. εἴρηκέ) μοι | ἐρθὼν (1. ἐλθὼν) μεθ᾽ ὑγ <ι> είας ἔρθου (1. ἔλθου) | εἰς {ζ} οἶκόν σου ὡς δέκης (1.

---

25   Other examples of delayed visits are *PSI* VIII 974, Verso 28–29 (late I/early II CE); P. Rain.Cent. 70,8–12 (II–III CE); P.Stras. IV 233,4–5.7–8 (2nd half III CE); P.Lond. II 479 (p. 255),5–8 (III CE?).

τέκης). | ἤαν (l. ἐὰν) θέλης, γράψον | ἐπὶ μαὶ (l. μὲ) καὶ ἐρχο{ν}|μαι. ὁ τίτων (l. δίδων) σοι | τὸ ὄστρακον δοῦ|το (l. τοῦτο) αὐτός μοι | ἤρηγαι (l. εἴρηκε) μεῖ|νον ἐκεῖ|{ν}. The interpretation of the text is difficult. Most probably, Didyme wished to travel to her mother in order to give birth to a child at her mother's home. Her husband Apollos had already left on business, and therefore could not stay with his wife. For some reason, Didyme did not dare to ask her mother in a simple and straightforward way if she would be allowed to come over to her house. She refers to the recommendations of her husband, instead, and to those of the letter carrier who, of course, also had the opportunity to speak to Thesis in person, and to explain Didyme's desire in detail. I suggest the following translation: 'To Thesis, Didyme, greetings. I had prepared myself for coming. Apollos himself told me as he was leaving, "If you are well go to your home to give birth." If you want, write to me, and I will come. The bearer of this ostracon told me, "Remain there."'[26]

A further example was written during the time of Paul: a certain Zosimos writes at the beginning of his letter to Sarapion – *BGU* III 830, 3–7 with *BGPA* I, 70 (= Olsson, *Papyrusbriefe*, no. 71; I CE): δ[ιε]πεμψάμην σ[οι τὸ]ν ἐμὸν | ἄνθρωπον, ὅπ[ως] καλῶς | ποιήσις συμβαλὼν χάρ[ακα] | περὶ τοῦ ἐ[λαιῶν]ος ἰδίου | αὐτοῦ τοῦ ἐνθάδε ('I am sending you my man so that you do well to put a fence around your own olive grove there'). As we can read in the following lines, Zosimos had been informed by the tenant of the olive grove that he was reminded by the tax collectors to build the fence. Therefore, Zosimos promised to care for it, and he now sends his messenger as his representative.[27]

The two best examples originate from the second or third century CE: A certain Horion writes to Heron – P.Lips. I 108,3–9 (II or III CE): ἐπεὶ ὁ υἱός μου Διονύσιος ὢν παρ' ἐμοὶ | ἔγραψέ σοι, ὡς ἐμοῦ μέλλοντος ἐλθεῖν | πρός σε καὶ οὐκ ἠδυνήθην διὰ τὸ ἐμὲ | μετρείως ἔχοντα, ἔπεμψα δέ σοι | τὸν ἀδελφὸν αὐτοῦ Δίδυμον ποιοῦν|τά μου τὸν τόπον ὡς ἐμοῦ ὄντος παρά | σοι ('because my son Dionysios who is with me writes to tell you that I had the intention of coming to you but could not because I am quite poor, I am sending you his brother Didymos, so that he takes my place as if I were with you'). A representative function could not be expressed more clearly although the sender does not even mention which concrete task Didymos shall perform instead of him.

P.Flor. II 156 (249–268 CE) belongs to the so-called Archive of

---

26   A different interpretation was presented by the first editor of this ostracon (cf. John C. Shelton, 'Four Private Letters on Ostraca', *Zeitschrift für Papyrologie und Epigraphik* 21 [1976]: 261–64, and plate V, here: 261–62), and by Roger S. Bagnall and Raffaella Cribiore, *Women's Letters from Ancient Egypt, 300 BC–AD 800, with contributions by Evie Ahtaridis* (Ann Arbor: University of Michigan Press, 2006), p. 284.

27   For another, albeit indirect example, of a messenger acting as a representative in the same letter see ll. 12–13.

Heroninos; the letter was sent by Alypios to his 'lord' Heroninos whom he informs that he wanted to come to check the vineyards, and the harvest work, but because certain necessities pressed him to go to town, he sends Philippus 'so that he checks everything, and informs me' (ll. 9–10: ἵνα πάντα ἐπί[δῃ καὶ] | μεταδῶ μοι).

Conclusions

The clauses and passages that explain a delayed or put-off visit are not mere phrases explaining simply that the letter writer could not visit his addressee (or, in other words: these clauses are not just philophronetic), but in a direct combination with such clauses, the letter writer informs the addressee, more or less clearly, about the original and primary intention of the letter. Sometimes, a letter merely functions to ease the writer's personal desire for the addressee, or to confirm the ongoing good relationship between the two of them. Concerning Paul, this is especially true for 1 Thessalonians, and – at least in part – Philippians.

Sometimes, it is the writer's intention to express via a letter exactly what she or he had wished to express on the occasion of a visit (cf. Rom., 1 Cor., and Phil). But there are also examples where a writer obviously explains something different, and deals with information, queries or expectations in a way that is different from what she or he would have done when visiting the addressee in person (cf. especially 2 Cor., but also 1 Cor.). In any case, the relevant clause explains a lot about, and hints directly at, the main intention of the letter, be it the confirmation of a good relationship, or the sorrow about a difficult one, or a strategy to improve, and fight for it.

ADVICE TO THE BRIDE:
MORAL EXHORTATION FOR YOUNG WIVES IN TWO ANCIENT LETTER
COLLECTIONS[*]

Annette Bourland Huizenga

In the New Testament letter to Titus, the pseudonymous author 'Paul' sketches a scenario for the moral training of younger women within a Christian community in the late first or early second century:

> But you [Titus] speak what is fitting for the healthy teaching ... older women likewise to be in a reverent demeanor, not slanderers nor enslaved to much wine, good teachers, so that they might bring the young women to their senses, to be loving of husbands, loving of children, moderate [σώφρον], pure, house-workers, good, being subordinate to their own husbands, so that the word of God might not be defamed. (Titus 2.1, 3–5)[1]

This 'healthy teaching' for women's moral behavior is echoed in the two other New Testament letters by this author, 1 and 2 Timothy, so that throughout the Pastorals' letter collection, the author sporadically, but consistently, offers *paraenesis* about proper activities for women in the domestic household and in the 'household of God' (οἴκῳ θεου, 1 Tim. 3.15).

When the instructions in the Pastorals that concern women are considered together, they raise questions about the practice of moral-philosophical training for women in the Roman world. How do the teachings of the Pastorals correspond to a typical ἄσκησις ('exercise') for women as delineated by other authors? How does the literature

* My work on these letters has been generously funded by an American Dissertation Fellowship from the AAUW Educational Foundation.

1 Σὺ δὲ λάλει ἃ πρέπει τῇ ὑγιαινούσῃ διδασκαλίᾳ.... . πρεσβύτιδας ὡσαύτως ἐν καταστήματι ἱεροπρεπεῖς, μὴ διαβόλους μὴ οἴνῳ πολλῷ δεδουλωμένας, καλοδιδασκάλους, ἵνα σωφρονίζωσιν τὰς νέας φιλάνδρους εἶναι, φιλοτέκνους σώφρονας ἁγνὰς οἰκουργούς ἀγαθάς ὑποτασσομένας τοῖς ἰδίοις ἀνδράσιν, ἵνα μὴ ὁ λόγος τοῦ θεοῦ βλασφημῆται. It is serendipitous that parts of these verses appear in the very early papyrus fragment P32, dated ca. 200 CE, and held by the Rylands Library of the University of Manchester.

characterize the complementary roles of *teachers and learners*? What *instructional methods* are used? What *topics* were considered appropriate for women to 'study'? One final question leads to the investigation of this essay: what *educational texts* were available for women and how might an audience read such texts?[2]

Scholars have already located numerous ancient parallels to the Pastorals' instructions regarding women's moral behavior and social roles,[3] but among these, one set of texts stands out: the letters and discourses attributed to women from the Pythagorean philosophical communities. Under the names of five women (Melissa, Myia, Theano, Periktione, and Phintys) there are twelve extant texts – nine letters and three discourses.[4] Here I concentrate on five letters supposedly authored by Melissa, Myia, and Theano.

Many extant sources speak to the production of texts, in particular, philosophical letters, as a means of and resource for moral-philosophical instruction. Such letters are almost always ascribed to male authors (who take the role of teacher), and likewise addressed to male recipients (in the position of learners): for example, the letter collection of Seneca to Lucilius, the letters attributed to Apollonius of Tyana, and the Cynic and Platonic epistles (a few of which do feature female recipients). While evidence about women's moral-philosophical education in antiquity is somewhat sparse, the letters attributed to Pythagorean women present remarkable information about the process of virtue-training for women.

For many centuries, up to and including today, the Pythagorean

2   The hermeneutical framework of my research uses the terminology and concepts of more modern learning theory in order to analyze the various components of the Pastorals' teachings for and about women.

3   Often cited are: Plato, *Republic* 451C–461E; and *Laws* 6.780E–781D, 7.804E–806C, 8.838A–839B; Xenophon, *Oeconomicus* 7; Musonius Rufus, *Or.* III, *That Women Too Should Study Philosophy*, and *Or.* IV, *Should Daughters Receive the Same Education as Sons*; Plutarch, *Advice to the Bride and Groom*; Philo, *De Vita* 32–33, 68–69. A comprehensive listing of parallel texts and inscriptions is found in Ceslas Spicq, *Les Épîtres Pastorales*, vol. I (Paris: Gabalda, 4th edn, 1969), 'Excursus I: La Femme Chrétienne et Ses Vertus', pp. 385–425. For references to Jewish, inscriptional, and later Christian texts, see Martin Dibelius and Hans Conzelmann, *The Pastoral Epistles* (trans. P. Bottolph and A. Yarbro; Hermeneia; Philadelphia: Fortress, 1972), esp. pp. 45–49, 73–76, 139–41; as well as Jerome D. Quinn, *The Letter to Titus* (AB 35; New York: Doubleday, 1990), esp. pp. 118–22, 134–38. On philosophical texts that treat women's household roles, see David L. Balch, *Let Wives Be Submissive: The Domestic Code in I Peter* (SBLMS, 26; Atlanta: Scholars Press, 1981).

4   These are: (a) three treatises in Stobaeus, *Anthologium*: Periktione, *On the Harmony of a Woman* (in two fragments); Periktione, *On Wisdom*; Phintys, *On the Sophrosyne of a Woman* (in two fragments); (b) five letters known from Renaissance manuscripts: *Melissa to Kleareta*, *Myia to Phyllis*, *Theano to Euboule*, *Theano to Nikostrate*, *Theano to Kallisto*; and, (c) four letters in one manuscript (Vat. Gr. 578 [sixteenth cent.]): *Theano to Eurydike*, *Theano to Timaionides*, *Theano to Eukleides*, *Theano to Rhodope*.

women's letters have been copied and studied as a collection mainly due to their inherent 'female-ness': they feature female authorial pseudonyms, pseudonymous female recipients, and feminine topics.[5] The impetus for composing such letters seems to have come from the remembrance that women joined with men as members of the original Pythagorean communities. Thus, these pseudonymous letters draw upon the prestige of Theano, the wife of Pythagoras himself, along with that of Myia, his daughter, and upon the positive connotations adhering to the name Melissa (who is otherwise unknown as an individual woman or as a Pythagorean).[6] Additionally, the letters *Melissa to Kleareta* and *Myia to Phyllis* are identified as Pythagorean because they are found in the Doricized Greek that characterizes many other pseudo-Pythagorean texts.

In these five letters, the author-teachers instruct the recipient-learners on how women (as distinct from men) can attain virtue, especially in their important roles as wife, mother, and mistress of a household.[7] When the Pythagorean women's letters are read as a group, this commonality of feminine topics is quite pronounced, as can be seen from their supposed epistolary occasions:

(1) *Melissa to Kleareta*: a chaste (σώφρον) woman advises a new bride on how to conduct herself as a wife.

(2) *Myia to Phyllis*: Pythagoras' daughter Myia advises a new mother about the hiring of a wet-nurse and the care of a newborn.

(3) *Theano to Euboule*: Pythagoras' renowned wife Theano censures a mother who is spoiling her young children.

(4) *Theano to Nikostrate*: Theano censures a wife who is reacting angrily to her husband's affair with an *hetaira*.

(5) *Theano to Kallisto*: Theano advises another new bride on how to manage her household slaves.

The dating of these letters is now generally accepted as not before the first century BCE, and more probably later – according to Alfons Städele, in the

---

5   Interest in the Pythagorean women's texts has grown since the advent of women's studies in the 1970s. English translations of the letters and treatises are found in Mary Ellen Waithe (ed.), *A History of Women Philosophers, Volume I: Ancient Women Philosophers, 600 B.C.–500 A.D.* (Boston: Martin Nijhoff, 1987), omitting *Melissa to Kleareta*; Prudence Allen, *The Concept of Woman, Vol. I: The Aristotelian Revolution, 750 B.C.–A.D. 1250* (Grand Rapids, MI: Eerdmans, 2nd edn, 1997); and I. M. Plant (ed.), *Women Writers of Ancient Greece and Rome: An Anthology* (Norman, OK: University of Oklahoma Press, 2004).

6   Neither are the named female addressees otherwise known from Pythagorean lore and literature.

7   Together the letters address all three roles prescribed for women in their households: as wives, mothers, and household-managers. This triad corresponds to the male roles in the three pairs of relationships defined by Aristotle as essential to well-ordered households: husband–wife, father–child, master–slave (*Pol.* I 1253b.1–14), and conveyed in other philosophical writings, as well as in the New Testament (see again, Balch, *Let Wives*).

second century CE.[8] Thus, the Pythagorean women's letters are in close temporal proximity to the Pastoral Letters, and in fact share a common gendered worldview.[9]

This essay focuses on these five letters as textual artifacts, because the papyrological remains show how the letters might have been composed and read as instructional resources for the moral training of young women. However, it is not simply the *composition* of individual letters, but their subsequent *positioning* within larger epistolary collections that is a notable piece of evidence. My thesis is that because the Pythagorean women's letters are framed *in the format of a collection*, the composite arrangement enhances their instructional effectiveness in these ways: (1) the letter collection as a whole *enlists* and, at the same time, *expands the authority* of the respected Pythagorean philosophical tradition, relying especially on that movement's notoriety for including women; and (2) more than for the study of a single letter, the format of letters-in-collections promotes a *reading strategy* that allows for the re-reading of any part of a letter and for subsequent cross-referencing of the individual letters with one another. This means that the collection was organized to be read *as a whole* in order to comprehend the full range of ideas being expressed.

I begin by explaining the papyrological and later manuscript evidence for the collecting of the five Pythagorean letters, and then describe how the collection might be read as an instructional resource. The conclusion compares my findings about this Pythagorean *corpus* with the New Testament epistolary collection known as the Pastoral Letters.

Papyrus Hauniensis II.13 – Two Pythagorean Women's Letters

The earliest textual evidence for the Pythagorean women's letters is a copy of the letter *Melissa to Kleareta* and part of the letter *Theano to Euboule* found in one papyrus document, Papyrus Hauniensis II.13, dated to the

---

8 Alfons Städele, *Die Briefe des Pythagoras und der Pythagoreer* (Beiträge zur Klassischen Philologie, 115; Meisenheim am Glan: Verlag Anton Hain, 1980), pp. 256, 269, 287, 293, 308, 325, and 332.

9 I do not argue that the Pastorals are dependent upon these texts, nor even that the Christian author had knowledge of the Pythagorean texts. Instead, it is more likely the case that, as Hans-Josef Klauck states: 'In the daily life of the newly converted Christians, codes that they had brought with them and that were presupposed as something taken for granted continued in force, thanks to their inherent plausibility', *The Religious Context of Early Christianity: A Guide to Graeco-Roman Religions* (trans. Brian McNeil; Minneapolis: Fortress, 2003), pp. 427–28.

third century CE.[10] The Pythagorean writings appear on the *verso* of the papyrus, while the *recto* records an unpublished official document. The upper right hand corner on the *verso* is missing, and the letter of Melissa has been written on what remains available, indicating that this was a piece of recycled papyrus. There is no *kollesis*, and the editor speculates that this document was originally a scroll. Analysis of the writing gives 'the general impression ... of a literary hand'.[11] My translation of this letter follows:

> Melissa to Kleareta. Greetings.
>
> It appears to me that you possess most good attributes on your own. For your earnest wishing to hear about a wife's decorous behavior gives a good hope that you are going to reach maturity in accordance with virtue. Therefore, the moderate [σώφρον] and married woman must belong to her lawful husband, being adorned with silence, in clothing that is white and clean, plain but not very expensive, simple but not elaborate or excessive; for she ought to reject the [± 8], and clothing shot through with purple and gold, since this sort is useful to the courtesans [ἑταίραι] for their hunting of more men. But the adornment that belongs to the woman who is well pleasing to her very own [husband] is her way of life, and not her robe. For the married and moderate [σώφρον] woman is to appear fair of form to her own husband, but not to the neighbor: on the one hand, having a modest blush on her face is better than rouge and white paint, and, on the other, goodness and the height of decorum and moderation [σωφροσύνη] instead of gold and emerald. For the woman who strives for moderation [σωφροσύνη] ought not [strive] for the extravagance of clothing and of the body, but for the management and salvation of her household. And she should please her own moderate [σώφρον] husband by accomplishing his wishes, for the wishes of her husband ought to be engraved for the decorous woman, according to which she must live. And she must consider that, along with herself, her orderly behavior has been offered as her best and greatest dowry. For she must trust in the beauty and wealth of her soul rather than in that of her possessions and looks; for time, jealousy, sickness, and fortune take away from possessions and bodies, but the decorum of the soul is at hand until death for the women who have acquired it.

After a forked *paragraphus*, a letter by Theano begins; the break is also indicated with an 'enlarged *theta*' in the author's name.[12]

10   Edition of P.Haun. II.13 by Adam Bülow-Jacobsen (ed. and trans.), *Papyri Graecae Hauniensis*, vol. II: *Letters and Mummy Labels from Roman Egypt* (Bonn: Habelt, 1981), pp. 1–10.
11   Bülow-Jacobsen, *Papyri*, p. 2.
12   Bülow-Jacobsen, *Papyri*, p. 8.

Theano to Euboule. Greetings.

I hear you are raising [your children delicately]. But the domain of [a good   ± 9] mother is not [care for the pleasure] of her children, but [guidance toward the moderate (σώφρον)]. Therefore, watch out, lest [*the remaining letters are illegible and the papyrus breaks off*][13]

With the addition of these last few lines, the papyrus text provides the earliest evidence of the collecting of the Pythagorean women's letters.

Melissa to Kleareta and *Theano to Euboule* have not been found in any other papyrus documents, but they have been transmitted in some twenty Renaissance codices. In the twenty-two manuscripts containing *Melissa to Kleareta*, this letter is written in a Doricized Greek. A word-for-word comparison of the texts shows that in P.Haun. II.13, those Doricisms are consistently represented by Koiné forms of the same words.[14] The text also shows that Koiné words have been substituted for some of the more unusual Doric forms.[15] It seems more likely that the Doricized text of the later manuscripts is yet prior to this papyrus version in Koiné, since one can more easily conceive of a scribe changing the less familiar Doric into a more understandable Koiné, rather than the other way around. This means that the Doric version offers the more difficult reading. Furthermore, each addition or change to Koiné in the papyrus can be explained as a *lectio facilior*, in Bülow-Jacobsen's phrasing, that would assist an audience unfamiliar with Doric in the reading of the letter.[16]

Another noteworthy difference is that the papyrus text is about 10 percent longer than the later manuscripts (roughly 240 vs. 212 words), since in P.Haun. II.13, there are nine *additions* to the Doric text,[17] while there are a few less significant and shorter *omissions*.[18] Therefore, in the case of almost all of the textual differences, the Doric version found in the Renaissance manuscripts is the shorter reading. These text-critical

13   The portions of *Theano to Euboule* in brackets have been reconstructed by Bülow-Jacobsen based on Städele's edition.

14   I count more than seventy small differences in this category; see also Bülow-Jacobsen, *Papyri*, p. 3.

15   For example, τελειοῦσθαι ('to become perfect') takes the place of the rare πολιοῦσθαι ('to grow gray') in line 8.

16   Bülow-Jacobsen, *Papyri*, p. 10. In his analysis of P.Haun. II.13, E. A. Judge states: 'In the case of Melissa we are apparently dealing with the modernisation of the text by an editor, which must surely imply that it would be more effectively communicated in the *koine*' 'A Woman's Behaviour', *New Docs* 6 (1992): 23.

17   For example, in line 13, P.Haun. II.13 adds to the description of modest clothing that it ought to be 'simple but not very expensive', and in line 30, the papyrus clarifies that the husband too ought to be moderate (*sophron*).

18   There are four omissions: ἦμεν ('to be', a Doric infinitive, line 11); καί ('and', line 12); δὲ αὐτάν ('but she', line 30); along with dropping the unusual word γλιχομέναν ('be enthusiastic', line 28).

principles serve to establish P.Haun. II.13 as a copy of a Koiné version of an originally Doricized text. The letter *Theano to Euboule* does not exist in a Doric dialect, and, unfortunately due to the fragmentary nature of the papyrus, comparisons with the later manuscripts yield little in the way of similarities or differences in the text.

Pythagorean Women's Letters in Collection

After a gap of about nine centuries, the textual history of the Pythagorean women's letters resumes with the Renaissance codex manuscripts, appearing first in *Harleianus* 5610, variously dated from 1200 CE to the early fourteenth century CE.[19] All five letters next appear in twenty-two fifteenth- and sixteenth-century manuscripts,[20] often being found with other letters from male Pythagoreans.[21] Further examination of the manuscripts evinces a two-letter collection (always in the order *Melissa to Kleareta* and *Myia to Phyllis*, *MM*) and a three-letter collection (always in the order *Theano to Euboule*, *Theano to Nikostrate*, and *Theano to Kallisto*, *TH3*). The collection *TH3* usually follows the paired letters of *MM* (Composite A), but occasionally precedes them (Composite B), as shown in Chart A. The shifting placement of *TH3* can be explained by the theory that these letters form another small collection on their own, which is supported by the fact that *TH3* appears in six manuscripts that do not contain *MM* at all.[22]

Chart A

Order of Letters-in-Collections	Number of MSS.
Composite A: $MM \rightarrow TH3$	17
Composite B: $TH3 \rightarrow MM$	3
$TH3 \rightarrow XX \rightarrow MM$[23]	2
$TH3$	6

19   For a complete textual history, brief commentary, and linguistic parallels, see Städele, *Die Briefe*.

20   One of these manuscripts, *Ms. Chicago* 103 (olim Ry. 9, 15th cent.), is held by the Newberry Library, Chicago. Here each text begins with the author's name and an initial letter in red ink.

21   This is true of *Ms. Chicago* 103, which includes letters by: Alciphron, Melissa, Myia, Theano (three letters), Hippocrates, Heraclitus, Diogenes, Crates, and Aeschines.

22   These are: (1) *Mutinensis Gr.* 54 (15th cent.); (2) *Leidensis Vossianus Gr.* Q 51 (15th cent.); (3) *Laurentianus Gr.* 55.2 (15th cent.); (4) *Vindobonensis phil. Gr.* 59 (15th cent.); (5) *Ambrosianus* 348 (1462); and (6) *Parisinus Gr.* 3054 (15th cent.). See Städele, for a list of the manuscripts, and diagrams of their relationships (*Die Briefe*, pp. 65 and 136).

23   Here *XX* represents texts from another author inserted between the women's sub-collections. According to Städele, in *Vaticanus Gr.* 1467, it is texts by Musonius, in this arrangement: *TH3* 126^r – 131^r; Musonius; *MM* 135^v – 137^v. In *Harleianus* 5635 (15th cent.), the order is: *TH3* 109^r–113^v; the letters of Apollonius of Tyana; then *MM* 127^r –128^v.

To summarize, in the manuscript tradition the five letters most often form a composite collection, built out of two sub-collections.

A neatly-ordered text history of the letter collection from the extant papyrus to the codices is complicated because the letter *Myia to Phyllis*, which is later so tightly paired with *Melissa to Kleareta*, is not present at all in P.Haun. II.13. Since *Melissa to Kleareta* starts at the very top of the sheet, Bülow-Jacobsen rightly concludes there was no other text preceding it. Then, although there is no formal closing to the letter, the opening of *Theano to Euboule* is made clear by the forked *paragraphus* and the larger theta, so that it is probable that whoever copied this papyrus did not know of the later persistent connection between the letters of Melissa and Myia. What remains in P.Haun. II.13 is the smallest collection possible, of two letters, by women affiliated with Pythagoreanism.[24]

While the absence of *Myia to Phyllis* in P.Haun. II.13 is problematic, the earliest sequence of the two letters persists in the later manuscripts after a fashion. That is, the most common order of Pythagorean women's letters in the codices – Composite A, which begins with *Melissa to Kleareta* followed by the letters of Theano – is supported by the papyrus evidence. Also, the later fixed order of Theano's three-letter sub-collection, with *Theano to Euboule* in first position, is somewhat confirmed by the fact that this is the letter that appears right after *Melissa to Kleareta* in P. Haun. II.13. Thus, all extant copies of *Melissa to Kleareta* are transmitted along with at least one letter of Theano,[25] suggesting a perduring impulse to collect the Pythagorean women's letters. However, between the copying of P.Haun. II.13 in the third century CE, and the earliest humanist manuscript from the twelfth century or so, we have no records of or attestations to these letters, so further determinations about the collecting and copying processes cannot be made.

Authority of Letters in a Collection

The evidence of P.Haun. II.13 shows that, although both letters it contains probably circulated separately at some early point, within a century or so of their composition, these texts appear as a collection of at least two letters. In the later codices, the collection has grown to include

---

24 Bülow-Jacobsen considers what might have come after the few lines of *Theano to Euboule*, where the bottom of the papyrus has broken off. Calculating that *Theano to Euboule* would take about 67 lines in this format, and assuming a roll with several columns, he speculates that the other two letters from Theano might have followed (*Papyri*, p. 1). If that were true it would have been helpful to my argument, but a final determination is impossible.

25 On the other hand, the collection *TH3* evidently existed independently of Melissa's letter, as shown in the later manuscripts.

five letters.[26] As these letters became aggregated to each other, they acquired a certain weightiness: *literally*, by adding to the number of pages of Pythagorean women's writings, but more importantly, *figuratively*, by accumulating an authoritative influence. This enhanced influence would operate in a circular fashion, with individual letters adding their authority to and, at the same time, acquiring more authority from the other letters in the collection. Their authority surfaces first from the prestigious reputations of the pseudonyms of both authors and recipients,[27] so that when the letters are positioned in a collection, the honor of each name extends to the others in the collection. In this way, the collection as a whole creates a picture of virtuous female Pythagoreans communicating with one another. Although we only hear one side of an epistolary dialogue in these texts, the letters' form and contents imply companionable relationships between senders and addressees, with each sender claiming some special knowledge of the addressee's individual circumstances. In addition, in the Renaissance codices, we have the congenial situation of the famed Theano authoring three letters, while her own daughter Myia has written another.

The women's letters are often transmitted with other letters ascribed to male Pythagoreans, including: *Pythagoras to Hieron*, *Lysis to Hipparchos*, and the letters of Apollonius of Tyana. Yet in no extant manuscript do all these Pythagorean letters from women and men follow sequentially, and an examination of these manuscripts reveals no stable ordering that might suggest an overall 'Pythagorean collection'.[28] The regularity of the ordering of the Neopythagorean women's letters in both their composite and sub-collections is all the more conspicuous by comparison. Still, that other Pythagorean letters are often found nearby the women's letters

---

26   Not much mention can be made here of the four other letters attributed to Theano extant in the singular Vatican manuscript. Yet their existence further demonstrates how such letter collections could enlarge, as another pseudonymous author or scribe sought to acquire the cachet of Theano's authority for his later set of compositions.

27   The three authorial pseudonyms have attracted only positive connotations, with the names 'Melissa' ('honey-bee'), 'Myia' ('housefly'), and 'Theano' lauded in many other texts for their *sophrosyne* and proper feminine behavior. The recipients' names are value-laden as well: Kleareta ('called virtuous'); Phyllis ('leafy plant'); Euboule ('good counsel' or 'well-counseled'); Nikostrate ('victorious woman-warrior'); and Kallisto ('best' or 'noblest').

28   For example, it would be a nice touch if the letters of Theano followed that of her husband, *Pythagoras to Hieron*. Rudolf Hercher's edition of the Pythagorean letters does not reflect the manuscript tradition in the ordering of the letters, *Epistolographi Graeci: Recensuit, recognovit, adnotatione critica et indicibus instruxit Rudolphus Hercher* (Paris: Didot, 1873), pp. 601–08. Similarly, Holger Thesleff has gathered a variety of Pythagorean texts from many sources and simply placed them in English alphabetical order by pseudonymous author, a situation that never occurs in the manuscripts; *The Pythagorean Texts of the Hellenistic Period* (Acta Academiae Aboensis, Ser. A, Humaniora 30/1; Åbo, Finland: Åbo Akademi, 1965).

indicates that their supposed common origin was recognized, and sets the stage for extending their authoritative Pythagorean aura from one author and/or letter to another.

Reading Strategies for Letters-in-Collections

The fact that the Pythagorean women's letters survive materially as a *corpus*, rather than as individual letters, means that it has been possible to read and study them as a group. Thus, a letter-in-a-collection could be read not just alone, but with reference to the others, although perhaps a first reading would be conducted *seriatim*. Quintilian advocates such a strategy especially when reading a speech: '[we] must read through the whole work from cover to cover and then read it afresh ... .'[29] His advice is based on the assumption that there is a logic to the organization of any particular text, and that logic can be grasped by the reader. Similarly, with the study of letter collections, the order of the letters must be examined to determine if there is any perceivable significance to the organization. As Patricia Rosenmeyer argues with respect to the fictional letter collections of Aelian, Alciphron, and others, '... the collecting of individual letters into an anthology seems to us to presume some sort of organizing principle, whether by chronology, by addressee, or by subject matter.'[30] Rosenmeyer offers two ideas about reading the letters-in-a-collection one after the other. First, '... if we read sequentially, the meaning of each text is determined by that of the one that precedes it ....'[31] Second, she suggests that the opening letter in a collection was placed there by the author or editor to be read as programmatic for the rest of the collection.[32]

Applying Rosenmeyer's proposals to the Pythagorean women's letters, we find that the most common ordering in both P.Haun. II.13 and the codices with Composite A places *Melissa to Kleareta* first in each collection.[33] This letter might be thought of as 'programmatic' in that the occasion of the letter seems to be 'advice to a young bride', which is then followed by 'advice on mothering' found in either the letter *Theano to Euboule* (in the case of P.Haun. II.13) or *Myia to Phyllis* (in the codices).

---

29   *Inst.* 10.1.20; LCL, trans. H. E. Butler.

30   Patricia Rosenmeyer, *Ancient Epistolary Fictions: The Letter in Greek Literature* (Cambridge: Cambridge University Press, 2001), p. 215.

31   Ibid.

32   Ibid, p. 264.

33   On the other hand, the ordering principle for Composite B, where *Theano to Euboule* appears as the first letter of the five, may have something to do with Theano's prominence as a Pythagorean.

Greco-Roman social convention would certainly dictate this sequence of events: a (free) woman ought to be married *before* she has children, so that the children will be the legitimate children of her lawful husband, therefore a woman needs to know how to be a *sophron* wife before she learns how to be a *sophron* mother. The chronology of a woman's life-stages is then further indicated in the order of the letters in Composite A, with the insertion of *Myia to Phyllis* (to a mother of a newborn) before *Theano to Euboule* (to a mother of somewhat older children). Still, it is difficult to discern the ordering principle for the last two letters in the sequence, *Theano to Nikostrate* and *Theano to Kallisto*.

However, written texts offer the opportunity for second, third, and even further re-readings, again as noted by Quintilian:

> Reading ... does not hurry past us with the speed of oral delivery; we can re-read a passage again and again if we are in doubt about it or wish to fix it in the memory. We must return to what we have read and reconsider it with care, while, just as we do not swallow our food till we have chewed it and reduced it almost to a state of liquefaction to assist the process of digestion, so what we read must not be committed to the memory for subsequent imitation while it is still in a crude state, but must be softened and, if I may use the phrase, reduced to a pulp by frequent re-perusal.[34]

Furthermore, such 'frequent re-perusals' advocated by Quintilian would encourage moving forward or backward within a collection to check out a reference or a common motif in another letter, or, in the case of the Pythagorean letters, to find advice that might be especially relevant to a particular female reader's life circumstances. Such cross-referencing would be assisted by the relative compactness of the Pythagorean women's collection.[35]

Rosenmeyer describes such a 're-perusing' reading strategy in her analysis of the order of the letters in Aelian's collection *Letters of Farmers*. She states, 'The first two letters propel the reader forward; [while] the last letter functions as an explanation for the letters that precede it, tying the collection together as a whole.'[36] In that last letter, one of the farmers remarks that δικαιοσύνη (justice) and σωφροσύνη (moderation) are the most valuable crops to be harvested. Therefore, according to Rosenmeyer, 'With that assessment by an internal character, we turn back to the collection to (re)read it sophistically, to hunt for "wisdom" lurking in the

---

34 *Inst.* 10.1.20; LCL.

35 A total of about 225 lines, in Thesleff's edition, or about nine and a half pages, for example, in the fifteenth-century codex *Ms. Chicago* 103.

36 Rosenmeyer, *Ancient Epistolary Fictions*, p. 312.

lines.'[37] Studying letters-in-collections in this fashion is an approach akin to more modern methods of literary analysis.

Considering the manuscript tradition of the Pythagorean women's letters from this standpoint, *Theano to Kallisto* stands in the last position in Composite A as well as in *TH3*. In this letter, 'Theano' opens with a somewhat humorous assertion:

> To you younger women [νεωτέραις], authority has indeed been given by custom to rule over the household slaves once you have been married, but the teaching [ἡ διδασκαλία] ought to come from the older women [πρεσβυτέρων] because they are forever giving advice [παραινούντων] about household management. For it is good first to learn the things you do not know, and to consider the counsel of the older women the most suitable; for a young soul must be brought up in these teachings from girlhood.[38]

The assertion of an obligatory teaching–learning relationship between older and younger women leads a reader to the realization that all of the previous letters (i.e., in Composite A, or, at the least, in the sub-collection *TH3*) construct a similar instructional situation carried out by means of the letters. To go back and re-read all the letters from this perspective, we might justifiably conclude that each one contains *paraenesis* from a more mature married woman to a younger newly-wed woman. This conclusion is supported by the statement of Melissa to Kleareta: 'For your earnest wishing to hear about a wife's decorous behavior gives a good hope that you are going *to grow old* [πολιοῦσθαι] in accordance with virtue.'[39] Indeed, since both the first letter in the Composite A collection (*Melissa to Kleareta*) and the last (*Theano to Kallisto*) depict the epistolary relationship as an older sender writing to a younger recipient, the two letters function as an *inclusio* for that collection as a whole.

Comparisons with the Pastoral Letters

This analysis of the collection(s) of the Pythagorean women's letters highlights some correlations to the composition and reading of the

---

37 Ibid., p. 314.

38 Ταῖς νεωτέραις ὑμῖν ἡ μὲν ἐξουσία παρὰ τοῦ νόμου δέδοται τῶν οἰκετῶν ἄρχειν ἅμα τῷ γήμασθαι, ἡ δὲ διδασκαλία παρὰ τῶν πρεσβυτέρων ἀπαντᾶν ὀφείλει περὶ τῆς οἰκονομίας ἀεὶ παραινούντων. καλῶς γὰρ ἔχει πρότερον μανθάνειν ἃ μὴ γιγνώσκετε καὶ τὴν συμβουλὴν οἰκειοτάτην τῶν πρεσβυτέρων ἡγεῖσθαι, lines 2–7, my translation from Städele's edition.

39 τὸ γὰρ ἐσπουδασμένως ἐθέλεν τὺ ἀκοῦσαι περὶ γυναικὸς εὐκοσμίας καλὰν ἐλπίδα διδοῖ ὅτι μέλλεις πολιοῦσθαι κατ' ἀρετάν, lines 2–5 in Städele's edition. The unusual πολιοῦσθαι (lit.: 'to grow gray') has been changed to τελειοῦσθαι ('to reach maturity') in P.Haun. II.13; either infinitive suggests that Kleareta is not at present an older woman.

Pastoral letters within their own sub-collection and as component parts of the Pauline *corpus*.

Text History

The pseudonymous authors of the Pythagorean women's letters seem not to have possessed any actual letters by those women, but it was widely known that women were members of Pythagorean communities, and many female names arise in various biographical traditions. The author of the Pastorals was in a different position, having an ample familiarity with both Pauline biographical details as well as various Pauline letters. As pseudepigrapha, his letters are designed to develop and even correct the overall Pauline tradition for his own later audience, and he almost certainly had some of Paul's letters at hand.[40] In fact, he most probably possessed (or knew of) a *collection* of Pauline letters, and thus decided to write more than one letter himself, in an extended imitation of the existing collection.

Authorizing the Letters

As with the Pythagorean women's letters, the authority of the Pastorals registers first from the name and reputation of a famous author. However, here the addressees, Timothy and Titus, are also recognized personages from Paul's mission, so that the collection of three Pastoral letters gives a stronger impression of communication between Pauline associates, especially in the personal details 'Paul' notes about himself and Timothy, and in the more intimate 'testimonial' tone of 2 Timothy. The depiction of warm communication between these men validates the teachings passed on from the older Paul to his younger male subordinates, and from them to trustworthy male office-holders,[41] bringing the authoritative lineage of the Pauline school into the real author's own times.

When the Pastorals are read in their own sub-collection, and then

---

40   The author's studied use of several Pauline letters has been convincingly demonstrated by Annette Merz's study of the intertextuality of the Pastorals with other Paulines: *Die fiktive Selbstauslegung des Paulus: Intertextuelle Studien zur Intention und Rezeption der Pastoralbriefe* (Novum Testamentum et Orbis Antiquus/Studien zur Umwelt des Neuen Testaments, 52; Göttingen: Vandenhoeck & Ruprecht; Fribourg: Academic Press, 2004). The Pastorals' author probably also knew biographical (even legendary) information such as that found in the book of Acts and the *Acts of Paul and Thecla*.

41   I note briefly that in the Pastorals there are no women in this *teaching* chain-of-command who can serve as role models for other women, so the author sets up the older women of Titus 2.3 as suitable examples, the καλοδιδασκάλοι ('good teachers'), for younger women. In my view, these female teachers correspond to the author-teachers of the Pythagorean letters in their instruction of younger women.

attached to the larger Pauline corpus, the process of authorizing the texts works in the same way as it does for the Pythagorean women's letters: the Pastorals receive authority from and at the same time supplement the authority of the other Pauline letters. The eventual acceptance of the Pastorals as genuinely Pauline signaled the successful outcome of the author's use of a famous pseudonym: his letters have acquired the authority extended to the entire collection. Furthermore, for many centuries, the Pastorals have lent their own influence to the other Pauline letters, by expanding the collection in number, as well as by attempting to explain and correct Paul's teachings.

Re-reading

As with the Pythagorean women's letter collection, the Pastorals were composed for reading and re-reading, either within their own sub-collection, or in light of the whole Pauline *corpus*.[42] One could ask, as still happens today, 'What does Paul say about women?', and find many treatments of this topic in the entire letter collection attributed to him, some of them seeming ambiguous and even contradictory. The author of the Pastorals intended his instructions for and about women in the household of God to be the last, definitive Pauline teaching on the subject, and to a large extent, and for a long time, his purpose was achieved.

Except for the few partial verses of the letter to Titus in the very small fragment P32, the extant textual evidence for the Pastorals cannot be dated before the fourth century CE.[43] By the time of *Sinaiticus*, *Alexandrinus*, and later manuscripts, the Pastorals are found as a sub-collection, now called 'letters to individuals', positioned after Paul's so-called 'letters to churches.' They appear in the canonical order 1 Timothy–2 Timothy–Titus, followed by Philemon.[44] Considering the ordering of the Pastorals in light of Rosenmeyer's assertion that there is a logic to the arrangement of letters-in-a-collection, the present sequence seems to be based on the criterion of length, from longest to shortest.

However, if Jerome Quinn is correct in his conclusion that the original order of the Pastorals was Titus–1 Timothy–2 Timothy, as attested to by the Muratorian Fragment and Ambrosiaster,[45] then we have a different kind of reasoning at work. Looking just at the teachings about women, the pithy instructions in Titus 2.3-5 would then establish the general parameters of moral training for women in the author's assemblies, providing the lens through which to view the various teachings to and

---

42   Of course, the early Christian preference for the codex form may have assisted such a cross-referencing reading strategy.

43   There are attestations to the contents of the letters beginning in the second century.

44   All three letters are missing, along with Philemon, from the *Vaticanus* manuscript.

45   Quinn, *Letter to Titus*, pp. 19–20.

about women in the other two letters, but especially in 1 Timothy. Within the Pastorals' sub-collection, 'Paul's' command to Titus to establish the older women as virtuous teachers of the younger women is wholly consistent with the other instructions for women.[46] In any case, given the opportunity to re-read and cross-reference *all* the canonical Pauline letters, this same lens from Titus 2 could be focused on the instructions for women throughout the entire Pauline collection, and historically, of course, this is how the Pastorals' teachings on women have been studied. Therefore, both ancient and modern readers must examine both the Pythagorean and Pastoral letter collections, as a whole and through multiple re-readings, in order to comprehend the interlocking components each presumes and advises for the moral training of younger women.

Appendix: Transcription of Papyrus Hauniensis II.13, verso

Bülow-Jacobsen, Adam (ed. and trans.), *Papyri Graecae Haunienesis*. Vol. II: *Letters and Mummy Labels from Roman Egypt* (Bonn: Habelt, 1981).

- Provenance unknown; dated by the editor to the third century CE.
- 12 × 21.5 cm, with a broken-off corner around which the letter has been written.
- On the recto is a yet-unpublished official document.

Μέλισσα Κλεαρ[έτῃ]
χαίρειν. [α]ὐτομ[ατ-]
ως μοι φαίνη [πλεί-]
ονα τῶν καλῶ[ν ἔ-]
χειν· τὸ γὰρ ἐσ[πουδασμένως ἐθέλειν]
σε ἀκοῦσαι περ[ὶ γυναικὸς εὐκοσμίας]
καλὴν ἐλπ[ί]δα δ[ίδωσι ὅτι μέλλεις]
τελειοῦ[σ]θαι κατ' ἀ[ρετήν. χρὴ οὖν τὴν]
σώφρονα καὶ ἐλευ[θέραν τῷ κατὰ νόμον]
ἀν[δ]ρὶ προσῖναι ἧσ[... :κεκαλλωπισμέ-]
νην τῇ ἐσθῆτι λευ[κοείμονα καὶ κα-]
θάρειον, αφελῆ ἀλλ[ὰ μὴ πολυτελῆ,]
ἁπλὴν ἀλλὰ μη ποικίλην [καὶ περισσήν].
παραιτητέον γὰρ αὐτῇ τὰ [±8]
καὶ διαπόρφυρα ἢ χρυσόπα[στα τῶν ἐνδυ-]
μάτων. ταῖς γὰρ ἑταίραις τάδ[ε χρή-]
σ[ιμα] πρὸς τὴν τῶν πλειόν[ων θήραν,]
τῆς δὲ πρὸς ἕνα τὸν ἴδιον [εὐαρεστούσης]
γυναικὸς κόσμος ἐστιν ὁ τρό[πος καὶ οὐ-]

---

46 Some connection seems to be implied to the groups of older and younger widows in 1 Tim. 5.9-15.

χ ἡ στολή. εὔμορφον δὲ τὴν ἐλευ[θέραν]
καὶ σώφρονα ἰδέσθαι χρὴ τῷ ἑαυτῆ[ς ἀν-]
δρί, ἀλλ᾿ οὐ τῷ πλησίον. ἔχουσαν μὲν [ἐ-]
πὶ τῆς ὄψεως αἰδοῦς ἐρύθημα ἄμειν[ον]
φύκου καὶ ψιμιθίου, καλοκαγαθ[ί]αν δ[ὲ]
καὶ κοσμιότητα καὶ σωφροσύνην ἀ[ν-]
τὶ χρυσοῦ καὶ σμαράγδου. οὐ γὰρ ε[ἰ]ς τὴν [τ]ῆς
ἐσθῆτος καὶ τοῦ σ[ώ]ματος πολυτέλει[αν]
φιλοκαλεῖν δεῖ τὴ[ν] σώφρ[ον]α, ἀλλ᾿ [εἰς] οἰκ[ο]νο-
μίαν τε καὶ σωτηρίαν [τοῦ οἴ]κου, ἀρέσκειν
τε σωφρονοῦντι τῷ [ἑαυ]τῆς ἀνδρὶ ἐπι-
τελοῦσαν τὰς ἐκε[ίνου βο]υλήσεις· ἡ γὰρ
τοῦ ἀνδρὸς βούλησι[ς νόμ]ος ὀφείλει ἐν-
γραφῆναι κοσμίᾳ γ[υναικί, πρὸ]ς ὃν χρὴ
βιοῦν αὐτήν· νομίζει < ν > δὲ [πρ]οῖκα εἰσενη-
νοχέναι ἅμ᾿ α[ὑτ]ῇ καλλίστην καὶ μεγί-
στην τὴν εὐτα[ξί]αν. πιστεύειν δὲ χρὴ τῷ
τῆς ψυχῆς κάλλει τε καὶ πλούτῳ μᾶλλον
ἢ τῷ τῶν χρημάτων καὶ τῆς ὄψεως.
τὰ μὲν γὰρ χρήμα{σ}τα καὶ τὰ σώματα χρό-
νος, φθόνος, νόσος, τύχη παραιρεῖται·
ἡ δὲ τῆς ψυχῆς εὐκοσμία μέχρι θανά-
του πάρεστι ταῖς κεκτημέναις.

Θεανὼ Εὐβούλῃ χαίρειν. ἀκούω σε
[τὰ παιδία τρυφερῶ]ς τρέφειν· ἔστι δὲ
[ἀγαθῆς   ±9] μητρὸς οὐχ ἡ πρὸς
[ἡδονὴν ἐπιμέλεια τ]ῶν π[αίδ]ων, ἀλλ᾿ ἡ
[πρὸς τὸ σῶφρον ἀγωγή. βλέπε οὖ]ν μὴ
[   ] …

SCRIBAL TENDENCIES IN THE APOCALYPSE: STARTING THE CONVERSATION[1]

Juan Hernández Jr.

Introduction

In recent years, the role of theological controversies in creating textual variants has headlined text-critical discussions. While the Gospels and book of Acts have featured prominently in these conversations, the Apocalypse has been conspicuously absent. On occasion, textual critics will mention the work in passing; but for the most part, the Apocalypse has been little more than a silent partner.[2]

The fault, however, may not lie with textual critics. Unlike the Gospels and other NT writings, the Apocalypse's textual tradition resists untutored inquiries into its scribal tendencies. Not only is the Apocalypse the most poorly attested work in the NT, but also its earliest witnesses are extremely fragmentary.[3] To complicate matters further, the Apocalypse's principal text-types are arranged differently and accorded a different status than the rest of the manuscript tradition.[4] And, as if that

---

1 Originally presented as a paper in the New Testament Textual Criticism Section at the annual meeting of the SBL, Philadelphia, PA, 21 November 2005.

2 This is true even of Ehrman's important work, which includes only two references to John's Apocalypse. See Bart D. Ehrman, *The Orthodox Corruption of Scripture: The Effect of Early Christological Controversies on the Text of the New Testament* (Oxford: Oxford University Press, 1993), pp. 163, 272 n. 42.

3 Currently only 7 papyri (P^{18}, P^{24}, P^{43}, P^{47}, P^{85}, P^{98}, and P^{115}) and 11 majuscules (ℵ, A, C, P, 046, 051, 052, 0163, 0169, 0207, and 0229) preserve the work. Every pre-fourth-century manuscript contains only portions of the book of Revelation: P^{98} (2nd cent.) contains only 1.13-20; P^{47} (3rd. cent.) contains 9.10-11.3; 11.5-16.15; 16.17-17.2; P^{18} (3rd cent.) contains 1.4-7; and P^{115} (3rd/4th cent.) contains 2.1-3, 13-15, 27-29; 3.10-12; 5.8-9; 6.5-6; 8.3-8, 11-13; 9.1-5, 7-16, 18-21; 10.1-4, 8-11; 11.1-5, 8-15, 18-19; 12.1-5, 8-10, 12-17; 13.1-3, 6-16, 18; 14.1-3, 5-7, 10-11, 14-15, 18-20; 15.1, 4-7. The three manuscripts that are contemporary with the fourth century ℵ are also fragmentary: P^{24} contains only 5.5-8; 6.5-8; 0169 contains 3.19–4.3; and 0207 contains 9.2-15.

4 Josef Schmid, *Studien zur Geschichte des griechischen Apokalypse-Textes* (2 vols; Munich: Zink, 1956), II.146-50.

were not enough, the early controversies stirred by the Apocalypse appear to be unique to the work.[5] It is therefore quite understandable that our ongoing text-critical dialogue has been about less precarious works.

Nonetheless, the Apocalypse's manuscript tradition remains an area to be explored and raises the obvious question: Where do we begin? Here I suggest that the best place to begin is with the singular readings of Codex Sinaiticus – the earliest known manuscript to contain the entire work. By focusing on this majuscule's singular readings, we avoid committing ourselves to unexamined generalizations about the Apocalypse's textual relationships. Moreover, it is an approach well-suited to a manuscript rich in singular readings. Finally, it allows us to shelve any assumptions about scribal activity by examining precisely those readings that serve as irrefutable traces of corruption within the transcription process. Nevertheless, as I am not the first to examine this majuscule's singulars, I wish first to ground our discussion in the work of a few predecessors.

In 1882 Hort offered the following assessment:

> The singular readings [of ℵ] are very numerous, especially in the Apocalypse, and scarcely ever commend themselves on internal grounds. It can hardly be doubted that many of them are individualisms of the scribe himself, when his bold and rough manner of transcription is considered; but some doubtless are older.[6]

In this statement Hort brilliantly summarizes what any textual critic analyzing the Apocalypse is likely to find: a myriad of singular readings, most of which probably stem from the scribe himself rather than his *Vorlage*. What is omitted, and indeed precluded given Hort's own convictions, is that any of the singular readings stem from willful scribal tampering, least of all for theological ends. Moreover, as with most generalizations of this sort, many unanswered questions remain, such as: How many singular readings are there? What is it about the singulars that render them non-commendable? What about these so-called 'older' singular readings? How does one know they are older? Finally, can one say anything more about the scribe's transcription other than that it is

---

5 In addition to doubts over the work's authorship and apostolic status (Eusebius, *HE* 3.39.6; 7.25), concerns were raised early over its millennial teaching (Eusebius, *HE* 3.39.11-13), Jewish character (Eusebius, *HE* 7.24.1-5), depiction of angels (Epiphanius, *Pan.* 51.32.1, 7; 51.34.6-7), putative historical inaccuracies (Epiphanius, *Pan.* 48.33.1-4), and association with rogue prophetic movements (Epiphanius, *Pan.* 48.11.5-14.2). For a full discussion of these see Juan Hernández Jr., *Scribal Habits and Theological Influences in the Apocalypse: The Singular Readings of Sinaiticus, Alexandrinus, and Ephraemi* (WUNT, 2.218; Tübingen: Mohr-Siebeck, 2006), pp. 156–91.

6 B. F. Westcott and F. J. A. Hort, *The New Testament in the Original Greek: Introduction and Appendix* (2 vols; New York: Harper & Brothers, 1882), II.246-47.

'bold and rough'? As a result, Hort's summary raises far more questions than it answers.

Weiss's Study

To find answers to many of these puzzling questions we turn to Bernard Weiss's pioneering nineteenth-century monograph on the Greek text of the Apocalypse – a study dedicated entirely to the examination of variants in the Apocalypse's most important majuscules and written, in part, to compensate for Hort's silence on many individual textual problems.[7] To be sure, Weiss was not interested in scribal tendencies for their own sake; his primary concern was to use the internal evidence of readings to reconstruct the original.[8] Nonetheless, the bulk of Weiss's monograph is devoted to detailed discussions about how scribal proclivities impacted the Apocalypse's manuscript tradition. A good part of Weiss's study revolves around the role of singular readings within the majuscules, including Sinaiticus, dovetailing nicely with our present concern and rendering him an indispensable conversation partner. Weiss's work even trumps Schmid's monographic treatment in this regard, since Schmid only discussed those singular readings relevant to the question of textual relationships. Weiss, on the other hand, investigates the singular readings both individually and vis-à-vis each other, offering a specificity and comprehensiveness missing in Hort's generalization.

Recent Developments

Nonetheless, in many respects Weiss's work is sorely outdated and can only be consulted in conjunction with more recent studies. While his work was originally published in 1891, the following century witnessed a windfall of important papyrological discoveries,[9] theoretical and methodological refinements in the field, as well as the publication of landmark

---

7 Bernard Weiss, *Die Johannes-Apokalypse: Textkritische Untersuchungen und Textherstellung* (TU, 7.1; Leipzig: J. C. Hinrichs, 1891).

8 The structure of Weiss's study makes this clear, which concludes with a critically reconstructed text. See ibid., pp. 157–225.

9 These include the discovery of the Chester Beatty Papyri in 1930–31, which contained P^{47}. Subsequent analyses revealed that P^{47} was a close relative of ℵ. See Frederic G. Kenyon, *The Chester Beatty Biblical Papyri*, fasc. 3.1, *Pauline Epistles and Revelation Text* (London: Emery Walker, 1934), p. xii and Schmid, *Studien zur Geschichte des griechischen Apokalypse-Textes*, II,109–22.

studies on the Apocalypse.[10] These directly impact Weiss's data and inevitably alter his conclusions. For example, Weiss's original tally of 515 singular readings in Sinaiticus includes scores of singulars now found to have support within the Greek tradition. Moreover, Weiss's tally contains Greek singulars supported by the versions. Whether Weiss was aware of the inherent risks of using the versions to identify a particular Greek reading remains unclear. However, if we are attempting to isolate the scribal tendencies exhibited in a particular manuscript, prudence suggests that we begin by restricting our study to the Greek tradition alone.[11]

Finally, an important development to which Weiss was not privy is the text-critical sea change over how we assess scribal proclivities today. Ever since the landmark studies of Eldon Jay Epp[12] and Bart D. Ehrman,[13] it is no longer ill-advised to consider theological factors alongside more traditional ones when assessing transcriptional probabilities. Such an option naturally fell outside the purview of Weiss, who operated under Hort's dictum that there were 'no signs of deliberate falsification of the text for dogmatic purposes'.[14] We must, therefore, revisit many of Weiss's century-old conclusions in light of these newer considerations.

Methodological Considerations

To that end two basic questions govern this article. First: what are the singular readings of the Apocalypse in Codex Sinaiticus? Second: what do they tell us about scribal copying patterns in this manuscript? To answer these questions I follow the method originally articulated by E. C. Colwell in his programmatic 'Method in Evaluating Scribal Habits',[15] as well as its subsequent application and development in James R. Royse's 1981 dissertation, 'Scribal Habits in Early Greek New Testament Papyri'.[16] Royse's dissertation is critically important and serves as a model for our

---

10   Two of the most important works on the Greek text of the Apocalypse were published in the twentieth century: H. C. Hoskier, *Concerning the Text of the Apocalypse* (2 vols; London: Bernard Quaritch, 1929) and Schmid, *Studien zur Geschichte des griechischen Apokalypse-Textes*.

11   This measure is justified below.

12   Eldon Jay Epp, *The Theological Tendency of Codex Bezae Cantabrigiensis in Acts* (SNTSMS, 3; Cambridge: Cambridge University Press, 1966).

13   Ehrman, *The Orthodox Corruption of Scripture*.

14   Hort, *Introduction*, II,282.

15   E. C. Colwell, 'Method in Evaluating Scribal Habits: A Study of P^{45} P^{66} P^{75}', in *Studies in Methodology in Textual Criticism of the New Testament* (NTTS, 9; Grand Rapids, MI: Eerdmans, 1969), pp. 106–24.

16   James R. Royse, 'Scribal Habits in Early Greek New Testament Papyri' (ThD diss., Graduate Theological Union, 1981), now published as *Scribal Habits in Early Greek New Testament Papyri* (NTTS, 36; Leiden: Brill, 2007).

study insofar as it offers a comprehensive examination of the singular readings of P^{47} – a third-century papyrus containing Rev. 9.10–17.2 and judged by Schmid to belong to the same text-type as Codex Sinaiticus. With Colwell and Royse I consider singular readings to be 'created' readings. However, my study differs from theirs in that I exclude from consideration (at least for now) any Greek singulars supported by the ancient versions.[17] Practically speaking, what this means is that I count as singular those Greek readings that occur only in Codex Sinaiticus and that find no support in any witnesses – Greek or otherwise – listed in the apparatuses of Tischendorf,[18] von Soden,[19] Hoskier,[20] Schmid,[21] UBS[4], and NA[27].

Moreover, when I speak of scribal activity in Sinaiticus, I refer to the work of two scribes.[22] According to Milne and Skeat, Scribe A copied the first thirty-four and a half lines of the Apocalypse, while scribe D transcribed the rest. Not only were both scribes contemporary with the manuscript and therefore part of the original scriptorium, they were also responsible for corrections made at the time of the manuscript's production. In collations of Codex Sinaiticus, the corrections of these scribes are identified by the phrase *primâ manu*, which sets these corrections apart from those belonging to later correctors. This designation allows us to separate the singular readings that originated in the scriptorium from subsequent ones.

Finally, a word about the singular readings themselves: all of the singulars considered in this study are 'created' readings, insofar as they are obvious departures from the 'original'. This does not mean, however, that the two scribes of Sinaiticus created all of them. Some, no doubt, were already in the exemplar or exemplars of the scribes. What this does mean, however, is that the process of corruption includes Greek readings both created and inherited by the scribes of Sinaiticus. Either way, these readings reflect the scribal copying habits of this particular manuscript insofar as they survive nowhere else.

---

17   Here I follow Epp who suggests excluding singular readings with versional support when studying scribal habits. See Eldon Jay Epp, 'Toward the Clarification of the Term "Textual Variant"', in *Studies in the Theory and Method of New Testament Textual Criticism* (ed. Eldon Jay Epp and Gordon D. Fee; SD, 45; Grand Rapids, MI: Eerdmans, 1993), p. 60.

18   Constantine von Tischendorf, *Novum Testamentum Graece: ad antiquissimos testes denuo recensuit* (3 vols; Leipzig: Giesecke & Devrient, 1869–94).

19   H. F. von Soden, *Die Schriften des Neuen Testaments in ihrer ältesten erreichbaren Textgestalt hergestellt auf Grund ihrer Textgeschichte* (2 vols; Göttingen: Vandenhoeck & Ruprecht, 1913).

20   Hoskier, *Concerning the Text of the Apocalypse*.

21   Schmid, *Studien zur Geschichte des griechischen Apokalypse-Textes*.

22   H. J. M. Milne and T. C. Skeat, *Scribes and Correctors of the Codex Sinaiticus* (London: British Museum, 1938), pp. 18–21.

We can now begin with our basic tally. By my count there are 201 singular readings in the Apocalypse – a dramatic reduction of Weiss's original tally of 515. Of our 201 singular readings, forty-three (21.39 percent) are orthographic and nonsense singulars, leaving us with a total of 158 significant singulars. These readings take the form of additions, omissions, transpositions, various types of scribal harmonizing, and finally, potential theological singulars.

Significant Singulars: Additions

We begin with the additions. Of the 158 significant singulars, forty (25.32 percent) are additions. Twenty-six of these singulars consist of the addition of only one word, while the remaining fourteen add two or more words. The added words and phrases cut across a number of grammatical categories and stem from multiple factors. Twenty-seven of the additions appear to have been made by the scribes' careless assimilation to the immediate context. These singulars are 'careless' insofar as they do not improve the sense of the passage in any way; indeed, sometimes the created reading is awkward, though not nonsensical. Thirteen, however, not only render acceptable sense but also appear to stem from the scribes' deliberate attempt to harmonize a passage to its surrounding context. While I am unable at times to differentiate between changes that are deliberate and those that are careless, I consider 'deliberate' those scribal changes that result in significant grammatical, stylistic, and/or contextual improvements to the text. Virtually all of the additions – deliberate or otherwise – render good acceptable sense.[23]

When we consider how many words are added to the text, we find that our forty singular readings contribute an additional sixty-six words to the Greek text of the Apocalypse. What this means is that, on average, the scribes of Sinaiticus add 1.65 words per singular reading.[24]

Significant Singulars: Omissions

Turning our attention to the omissions, we find that forty-nine (31 percent) of our 158 singular readings are omissions. As with the additions, these scribal omissions cut across a cadre of grammatical categories and are produced by a variety of factors. Here, one-word omissions outnumber those of two or more words by a ratio of about one and a half to one (31.18). A critical difference, however, is discernible in the occasion for the omissions. Twenty of our forty-nine omissions are clear instances of

---

23 Hernández, *Scribal Habits and Theological Influences in the Apocalypse*, pp. 65–69.
24 Ibid., pp. 65–69.

haplography caused by either homoeoteleuton or homoeoarchton. Seventeen suggest no good explanation for the oversight other than pure negligence or arbitrariness on the part of the scribes. Only twelve of the omissions appear to have been made for the sake of grammar, style, emphasis, and/or contextual concerns. When we consider how many words are lost, we find that our forty-nine singular readings result in a loss of 116 words. That is to say, the scribes omitted an average of 2.37 words per singular reading.[25]

We can draw two preliminary conclusions from the data presented so far. First, the scribes of Sinaiticus clearly omitted with greater frequency than they added to the text of the Apocalypse (49.40). Second, their combined scribal activity resulted in a shorter text, since there is a net loss of fifty words (116–66 = 50). That is to say, the scribes not only omitted much more often than they added, they also omitted more of the text, in essence creating a shorter manuscript.[26]

Placing these results within the broader practice of textual criticism also means that the *lectio brevior potior* canon cannot be indiscriminately applied to the Apocalypse in Codex Sinaiticus.[27] The pioneering studies of Colwell and Royse on the papyri demonstrated that the general tendency during the earliest period of textual transmission was to omit. It is now clear, however, that the tendency to omit was also at work in a later period, at least in the case of the Apocalypse – a period, according to Hort, traditionally regarded as creating 'fuller texts'. Whether this is yet another one of the Apocalypse's idiosyncrasies or the result of applying a more rigorous method to a majuscule has yet to be determined. Nevertheless, we can confidently expand the claims of Colwell, Royse, Peter M. Head and even Michael W. Holmes (who considers the canon as relatively useless for the early papyri) and say that at least one majuscule during a later period of transmission exhibits a greater scribal tendency to omit than to add.[28]

---

25   Ibid., pp. 70–74.

26   Ibid., pp. 174–75.

27   The argument that the 'shorter' reading is preferable when choosing between two or more variants rests on the assumption that scribes tended to expand rather than shorten their texts. This argument, however, has undergone a vigorous reassessment over the past thirty years. See Eldon Jay Epp, 'Issues in New Testament Textual Criticism: Moving from the Nineteenth to the Twenty-First Century', in *Rethinking New Testament Textual Criticism* (ed. David Alan Black; Grand Rapids: Baker, 2002), pp. 26–30.

28   Colwell, 'Method in Evaluating Scribal Habits', pp. 106–24; Royse, *Scribal Habits*, pp. 616–20; and Peter M. Head, 'Observations on Early Papyri of the Synoptic Gospels, especially on the "Scribal Habits"', *Bib* 71 (1990): 240–47; 'The Habits of New Testament Copyists: Singular Readings in the Early Fragmentary Papyri of John', *Bib* 85 (2004): 399–408; and Michael W. Holmes, 'Reasoned Eclecticism in New Testament Textual Criticism', in

Transpositions

This scribal tendency to omit can also be seen in the manuscript's transpositions. Although these do not result in a net difference in the amount of words added or omitted from the text, they exhibit the scribal tendency to self-correct omissions. Codex Sinaiticus contains twelve transpositions, eight of which are clear instances of initial haplography – due to homoeoteleuton or homoeoarchton – followed by an immediate correction. In these particular instances the scribes became aware of their error before going too far. Three of the four remaining transpositions appear to be changes in word order for the sake of style or emphasis, while the last one is disputed.[29]

Harmonizing

We now come to the scribal tendency known as 'harmonizing'. Both Colwell and Royse found that it was an especially prevalent phenomenon in the early papyri, and Codex Sinaiticus is apparently no exception. There are a total of fifty-five instances of harmonizing among our singulars. Four of these are harmonizations to remote parallels. Four are instances of harmonizing to usage. Forty-seven, the overwhelming majority, are instances of harmonization to the immediate literary context.[30]

Singular Readings Reflecting a Heightened Christology

Finally, we grant some attention to those singulars that appear to reflect Christological concerns. It is important to note that Royse found *no* instances of such editorializing in P[47]. However, what these singular readings do is cast into bold relief the sudden appearance of Christological concerns in a majuscule dated to a century later and may reflect the increased dogmatic concerns of the fourth-century church. Here I do not propose a definite *Sitz im Leben* for these singulars as much as highlight how they improve the Apocalypse's unflattering or even 'unorthodox' portrayals of Jesus.

The Text of the New Testament in Contemporary Research: Essays on the Status Quaestionis (ed. Bart D. Ehrman and Michael W. Holmes; SD, 46; Grand Rapids, MI: Eerdmans, 1995), p. 343.

29   Hernández, *Scribal Habits and Theological Influences in the Apocalypse*, pp. 75–76.
30   Ibid., pp. 76–81.

Jesus Was Not Created

The first singular that offers the clearest example of a Christological change is found in 3.14. Here our scribes alter the universally attested title for Jesus as the 'beginning of the creation of God' (κτίσεως τοῦ θεοῦ) to the otherwise unattested 'beginning of the church of God' (ἐκκλησίας τοῦ θεοῦ) – a move that eliminates the possibility of placing Jesus within the created order. What makes this change so conspicuous is the fact that it occurs in a fourth-century manuscript – a manuscript produced during a period that was defined by its pitched theological battles over the precise nature of the Son. Moreover, it is remarkable how dangerously close the original language of the Apocalypse is to Arius's own musings about the Son. In the fragments of the *Thalia*, one of the few primary sources judged by Rowan Williams to contain direct quotations from Arius, the putative arch-heretic declares: 'The one without beginning (i.e. God) established the Son as the beginning of all creatures...'[31] This Arian formulation is nearly indistinguishable from the original text of the Apocalypse. The fact that our scribes eradicated such language from the manuscript appears to indicate that the Apocalypse's wording was perceived to be pregnant with heterodox possibilities. In response, our scribes harmonized this passage in the direction of the higher Christology of Colossians 1, where Jesus is the head of the church.[32]

Jesus Does Not Vomit

In 3.16, just a few lines down, we encounter one of the boldest textual changes to the portrait of Jesus in the Apocalypse. This verse contains Jesus' well-known threat to vomit the Laodiceans out of his mouth for their spiritual tepidity. Here our scribes engage in an unprecedented overhaul of the verse that removes any semblance of Jesus being capable of such a grotesque bodily function. Instead of vomiting the Laodiceans out of his mouth, the scribes record Jesus as saying that he was 'to stop their mouth(s)'. (παῦσαι ἐκ τοῦ στόματός σου). Again, the Christological controversies of the fourth-century church could prove illuminating here with their debates about how to understand properly passages that speak of the weakness of Jesus' bodily flesh. Passages that refer to Jesus eating, sleeping, being angry, or struggling at Gethsemane posed enough of a problem and were the subject of rigorous debate in the early church. What kind of scandal would a passage cause where Jesus threatens to vomit, especially since he is now exalted and has therefore abandoned bodily functions? Of course, this would also mean that our scribes misunderstood

31 Rowan Williams, *Arius: Heresy and Tradition* (Grand Rapids, MI: Eerdmans, rev. edn, 2001), p. 102.

32 For a full discussion see Hernández, *Scribal Habits and Theological Influences in the Apocalypse*, pp. 90, 172–78.

the metaphorical thrust of the passage. But given their 'bold and rough transcription', this should come as no surprise.[33]

The *Lamb Receives the Blessing, Honor, and Glory 'of the Almighty'*
In 5.13, we encounter an interesting change to the doxology offered to both the One who sits on the throne and to the Lamb. Here the majority of the Greek tradition reads: 'To the One who sits on the throne and to the Lamb be the blessing, honor, glory and power (καὶ τὸ κράτος).' Our scribes, however, rewrite καὶ τὸ κράτος as παντοκράτορος, so that the doxology now asserts that both God and the Lamb receive 'the blessing, honor, and glory of the Almighty...' What the singular reading does is to transform four individual qualities into *three* and unites all of them under the banner 'of the Almighty'. In other words, the singular reading appears to indicate that the qualities attributed to both the One who sits on the throne and to the Lamb proceed from the Almighty (παντοκράτορος), possibly without distinction.

It is difficult to exaggerate the significance of such a change. Turning again to Arius's own words in the *Thalia* fragments, we find that he differentiates between the degrees of glory ascribed to each member of the Godhead. Without equivocation Arius states: 'there exists a trinity in unequal glories, for their subsistences [*sic*] are not mixed with each other. In their glories, one is more glorious than another in infinite degree.'[34] In contrast, the language of our singular reading clearly precludes such distinctions within the Godhead. The fact that formulations like Arius's were circulating in the fourth century may have prompted our scribes to inoculate their text from similar Christological misapprehension.[35]

Conclusion

Other theological singulars that can only be mentioned in passing include readings that reflect an aversion to ascribing material corporeality to God (7.15; 10.1), as well as the denial that anyone can actually hear God's voice (21.3a).[36] Such singular readings are perfectly at home in a fourth-century context that spoke of God as ἀθάνατος, ἀόρατος, ἀψηλάφητος, and ἀχώρητος ('immortal', 'invisible', 'untouchable', and 'incomprehensible'). There are also singulars that resist the idea of direct angelic

---

33   Ibid., pp. 90–91, 178–80.
34   Williams, *Arius*, p. 102.
35   Hernández, *Scribal Habits and Theological Influences in the Apocalypse*, pp. 180–82.
36   Ibid., pp. 93–94, 183–85.

involvement in apocalyptic killing (9.15; 16.2; 16.3a), as well as singulars that heap greater condemnation upon the damned (20.13).[37]

What is fascinating about all these singulars in Revelation is that none of these passages appears to play any role as a proof text in early theological debates about the nature of Jesus or God. If it can be demonstrated that these Christological and broader theological concerns were beginning to surface in the fourth-century text of the Apocalypse, albeit sporadically, then we would be looking at a previously untapped primary source for understanding the influence of the early church and its concerns upon the manuscript tradition. Moreover, we would be compelled to explore the implications of the apologetic use of the Apocalypse in this regard. Could it be that the changes found here represent an early, although incomplete, attempt to make the Apocalypse theologically palatable for a wider audience, especially in light of fourth-century concerns about its usefulness for the church? Additionally, what does it mean that none of the controversies typically associated with the Apocalypse actually surfaces among our singular readings, such as concerns about its bizarre and esoteric symbolism, its grammatical solecisms, or its millenarianism? Should we even have expected those kinds of concerns to surface? To be sure, these are puzzling questions and cannot be answered with any certainty at this stage; but then again, this is only the opening conversation.

Appendix: The Singular Readings of Sinaiticus

Total Number of Singulars[38]
P^{47} = 76
א = 201

Insignificant Singulars

Orthography
P^{47} = 18
א = 19

Nonsense Readings
P^{47} = 5
א = 24

Significant Singulars

Additions
P^{47} = 6
א = 40

Omissions
P^{47} = 15
א = 49

37   Ibid., pp. 93–94, 185–91.
38   The figures for P^{47} are taken from James R. Royse, *Scribal Habits in the Early Greek New Testament Papyri* (NTTSD, 36; Leiden: Brill, 2007), pp. 359–98. The figures for א are taken from my *Scribal Habits and Theological Influences in the Apocalypse* (WUNT, 2.218; Tübingen: Mohr-Siebeck, 2006), pp. 49–95.

Transpositions
  P⁴⁷ = 2
  ℵ = 12

Significant Singulars: Harmonizations

Total Number of Harmonizations
  P⁴⁷ = 13
  ℵ = 55

Harmonization to Parallels
  P⁴⁷ = 0
  ℵ = 4

Harmonization to Context
  P⁴⁷ = 13
  ℵ = 47

Harmonization to Usage
  P⁴⁷ = 0
  ℵ = 4

Christ in the Apocalypse: Codex Sinaiticus

Jesus was not created
  Rev. 3.14

ἡ ἀρχὴ τῆς κτίσεως τοῦ θεοῦ ς ℵᶜ rell.
'The beginning of the creation of God.'

ἡ ἀρχὴ τῆς ἐκκλησίας τοῦ θεοῦ ℵ*
'The beginning of the church of God.'

  Arius:
'The one without beginning (i.e., God) established the Son as the beginning of all creatures.'[39]

Jesus does not vomit
  Rev. 3.16

μέλλω σε ἐμέσαι (ἐμιν ℵᶜ) ἐκ τοῦ στόματός μους rell.
'I am about to vomit you out of my mouth.'

παυσε (*sic.* παῦσαι) τοῦ στόματός σου ℵ*
'to stop your mouth'

The Lamb receives the blessing, honor and glory of the Almighty
  Rev. 5.13
  καὶ τὸ κράτος ς ℵᶜ rell
'...and the power'

παντοκράτορος ℵ*
'...of the almighty'

---

39 Rowan Williams, *Arius: Heresy and Tradition* (Grand Rapids, MI: Eerdmans, rev. edn, 2001), p. 102.

Arius: 'There exists a trinity in unequal glories... In their
                          glories, one is more glorious than another in
                          infinite degree.'[40]

40   Ibid.

'A THOUSAND BOOKS WILL BE SAVED': MANICHAEAN WRITINGS AND
RELIGIOUS PROPAGANDA IN THE ROMAN EMPIRE

Eduard Iricinschi

On 31 March 302, only three decades after Mani's death in the Sassanian
Empire, some thousand miles to the south-west, in the neighboring
Roman Empire, Julianus the Proconsul of Africa wrote a petition to
Emperor Diocletian, asking for punitive measures against the
Manichaean proselytizing missions in North Africa. Seizing the oppor-
tunity to describe the Manichaeans as a Persian fifth column whose
weapon of choice was 'a fantastic and lying imagination' – at the time, the
Roman Emperor was engaged in wars with his eastern neighbors, the
Sassanians – Diocletian ordered capital punishment for Manichaean
teachers, burning of their books, as well as death and confiscation of
worldly possessions for their followers.[1]

Modern scholarship takes the liberty of disagreeing with Emperor
Diocletian's vision of the Persian menace and places the sources of
Manichaean mission within the confines of the Roman Empire – in Syria,
to be more precise – rather than positing the direct import of their writings
from Persia to Egypt. By the end of the fourth century, however – within a

[1] 'As regards the Manichaeans, concerning whom your carefulness has reported to our
serenity, who, in opposition to the older creeds, set up new and unheard of sects, purposing in
their wickedness to cast out the doctrines vouchsafed to us by divine favor in older times, we
have heard that they have but recently advanced or sprung forth, like strange and monstrous
portents, from their native homes among the Persians – a nation hostile to us – and have
settled in this part of the world, where they are perpetrating many evil deeds, disturbing the
tranquility of the peoples and causing the gravest injuries to the civic communities; and there
is danger that in process of time, they will endeavor, as is their usual tactic, to infect the
innocent, orderly and tranquil Roman people, as well as the whole of our empire, with the
damnable customs and perverse laws of the Persians as with the poison of a malignant
serpent... We order that the authors and leaders of these sects be subjected to severe
punishment, and, together with their abominable writings, burnt in flames. We direct that
their followers, if they continue recalcitrant, shall suffer capital punishment, and their goods
be forfeited to the imperial treasury' (*Collatio Mosaicarum* xv 3, ed. and trans. Hyamson,
revised by Lieu, in Iain Gardner and Samuel N. C. Lieu (eds), *Manichaean Texts from the
Roman Empire* (Cambridge: Cambridge University Press, 2004), pp. 116–18).

hundred years of Mani's death – Manichaeism spread throughout the whole Roman Empire much faster and more effectively than had Christianity in its first two centuries. In 340, according to Athanasius' account, one could find St Anthony chastising neighboring Egyptian monks of Manichaean inclination.[2] Ten years later, in 350, one could see Didymus the Blind, the fourth-century Origenist writer and leader of the Catechetical School in Alexandria, unmasking the sophistic art of argumentation deployed by his Manichaean adversaries.[3] Next, one could discover Libanius, the famous Antiochean teacher of rhetoric, pleading in 364 with Priscianus, the governor of Palestina Prima, for religious toleration toward 'those who venerate the sun without performing blood sacrifices, and honor it as a god of the second grade and chastise their appetites'.[4] Palladius tells the story of a Christian holy man, Sarapion the Sidonite, who managed toward the end of the fourth century to convert a first-rank citizen of Sparta out of Manichaeism.[5] Finally, one could find out that the Manichaeans in Rome, around 370, like all good heretics, simply loved talking to women and proselytizing the weaker sex, apparently with a higher appetite for abstruse cosmologies.[6]

Although this paper will be concerned only with the spread of Manichaeism in the Roman Empire, one should keep in mind that successful proselytizing missions in Central Asia led to the hybridization of Manichaeism with Buddhism and Zoroastrianism, and insured its survival in Parthia and China well into the tenth century CE. What is the secret of this successful religious expansion across three continents and eight centuries? I have already alluded to its highly adaptive abilities across the religious cultures of late antiquity. Second, its universalistic message, together with Mani's presentation as the seal of the prophets, unveils the Manichaean ambition to supersede all existing religious forms. Finally, there is the strong association between Mani's prophetic status and his concern to couch his teachings in five or seven writings, together

---

2   *Vita Anthonii* 68, in Gardner and Lieu, *Manichaean Texts from the Roman Empire*, pp. 119–20.

3   Didymus Alexandrinus, *Expositio in Ecclesiastes* 9.9a, trans. by Lieu in ibid.

4   Libanius, *Ep. 1253*, by Lieu in ibid., pp. 125–26.

5   Palladius, *Historia Lausiaca* 37.8.

6   'Although this would fit all heretics, as they all inveigle themselves into houses and charm women with persuasive and crafty words, so that through them they might deceive the men in the fashion of the devil their father who defrauds Adam through Eve, it matches the Manichaeans above all others. None are so ruthless, so deceitful, so enticing as those whose practice is to cultivate one idea and declare another, say one thing in private and another in public.... They seek out women, who always want to hear something for sheer novelty, and persuade them through what they like to hear to do foul and illicit things. For the women are desirous to learn, though they do not possess the power of discrimination.' ('Ambrosiaster' in *ep. Ad Tim ii* 3.6-7.2, trans. S. Lieu in Gardner and Lieu, *Manichaean Texts from the Roman Empire*, p. 119).

with the prominent role granted by his disciples to the use of books as primary proselytizing tools.

The Cologne Mani Codex, a third-century tiny codex, written in Greek, on 'the Origin/Birth of his Body', includes a series of testimonies about Mani's life produced by his disciples. This almost biographical codex presents Mani's mission of religious propaganda as entrusted by his spiritual Twin, the 'splendid Syzygos'.

> You [Mani] have been sent out not only to this religion (*dogma*), but to every people, every school, every town and every place. For (by you) will (this) hope be explained and proclaimed to all (zones) and regions (of the world). In very great numbers will men (accept) your word. So, set out and go abroad; for I will be with you as helper and protector in every place, where you proclaim everything I have revealed to you.[7]

Scholars have dutifully identified the strong connection between the omnipresent reference to Mani's books and the rapid spread of Manichaeism from Syria into Egypt and Roman North-Africa in the fourth century, as a result of intense missionary efforts.[8] As for the Roman Empire, Manichaean missionaries entered Egypt in the late third century by land, via Palmyra, reaching Alexandria and Lycopolis, and by sea, across the Red Sea, and established contacts in the rich monastic environment of Egypt.[9] In East Asia, missionaries used the 'syncretistic' character of Mani's doctrine to connect to local religious features and convert the 'political leaders of the area'.[10]

---

7 *Cologne Mani Codex (CMC)*, 104–105, trans. S. Lieu in Gardner and Lieu, *Manichaean Texts from the Roman Empire*; see also Ron Cameron and Arthur Dewey (eds), *The Cologne Mani Codex (P. Colon. Inv. Nr. 4780) 'Concerning the Origin of His Body'* (SBL, Missoula, MT: Scholars Press, 1979); and Albert Henrichs, 'The Cologne Mani Codex Reconsidered', *Harvard Studies in Classical Philology* 83 (1979): 339–67.

8 Peter Brown, 'The Diffusion of Manichaeism in the Roman Empire', *The Journal of Roman Studies* 59/1,2 (1969): 92–103, esp. p. 98; Samuel Lieu, *Manichaeism in the Later Roman Empire and Medieval China* (Tübingen: J. C. B. Mohr, 1992), pp. 115–20; Richard Lim, *Public Disputation, Power, and Social Order in Late Antiquity* (Berkeley: University of California Press, 1995), pp. 70–108; and Gardner and Lieu, *Manichaean Texts from the Roman Empire*, pp. 1–45.

9 For the two-way missionary import of Manichaeism in Egypt, see Michel Tardieu, 'Les manichéens en Égypte', *Bulletin de la Société française d'Égyptologie* 94 (1982): 5–19; J. Vergote, 'L'expansion du Manichéisme en Égypte', in C. Laga, J. A. Munitiz and L. van Rompay (eds), *After Chalcedon: Studies in Theology and Church History* (Leuven: Orientalia Lovaniensia Analecta, 1985), pp. 471–78; and Serena Demaria, 'Die Griechischen Entlehnungen in den Koptischen Manichäischen Texten: Methoden und Ergebnisse', in A. Tongerloo and L. Cirillo (eds), *Il Manicheismo: Nuove prospettive della richerca* (Turnhout: Brepols, 2005), pp. 95–114.

10 Peter Bryder, 'The Zebra as Chameleon: Manichaean Missionary Technique', in H. Preissler and H. Seiwert (eds), *Gnosisforschung und Religionsgeschichte: Festschrift für Kurt Rudolph zum 65. Geburtstag* (Marburg: Diagonal Verlag, 1994), pp. 49–54.

That Syria occupied a central position for the importing of Manichaeism into Egypt becomes clear from the discovery of bilingual exercises 'written back and front on two wooden boards' at Kellis, in the Dakhleh oasis, the place of a fourth-century Manichaean mission. Apparently, the occupants of Kellis' House 3, where the bilingual exercises had been unearthed, were still prepared, later in the fourth century, to lend Syriac the mystique of a 'language of origins'. Third-century translation efforts rendered Syriac texts into Greek, as a lingua franca of the Roman Empire, whereas the fourth-century school exercises in an isolated southern oasis aimed at teaching Syriac to a rather Coptic-writing audience, bypassing Greek altogether.[11]

On the other hand, Richard Lim calls attention to the fluid aspects of Mani's *sancta ecclesia* and the problematic links between Mani's scriptures and his *ecclesia*. These writings could have been used for apotropaic reasons, as might have been the case with the miniature Cologne Mani Codex, or appropriated by groups already separated from Manichaeism. Lim identifies instead 'an overarching ideology of unity that served as the binding fiction for the growth of diverse local traditions from Roman Carthage to Ch'ang-an', created, no doubt, as the encounter between Manichaean missionary efforts and Catholic responses to them.[12]

What was the Role of the Books in Manichaean Revelation?

Modern students of Manichaeism do not miss a chance to call it 'the religion of the Book(s)', giving credit to its considerable literary developments, across three continents and several centuries, and placing it with full rights next to the other bookish religious enterprises, such as Buddhism, Judaism, and Christianity.[13] Manichaean books were not only

---

11   Majella Franzmann, 'The Syriac-Coptic Bilinguals from Ismant El-Kharab (Roman Kellis): Translation Process and Manichaean Missionary Practice', in Tongerloo and Cirillo, *Il Manicheismo*, pp. 115–22. See the Syriac/Coptic texts from Kellis in Iain Gardner, *Kellis Literary Texts*, vol. I (Oxbow Monograph, 69; Oxford: Oxbow Books, 1996), pp. 101–31; and see Brown, 'The Diffusion of Manichaeism in the Roman Empire', pp. 96–97, for Syria as the 'bridgehead of Manichaeism in the Roman Empire'.

12   Richard Lim, 'Unity and Diversity among Western Manichaeans: A Reconsideration of Mani's *sancta ecclesia*', *Revue des Études Augustiniennes* 35 (1989): 231–50, esp. 249. See, more recently, Richard Lim, 'The *Nomen Manichaeorum* and its Uses in Antiquity', in E. Iricinschi and H. M. Zellentin (eds), *Heresy and Identity in Late Antiquity* (Tübingen: Mohr Siebeck, 2008), pp. 143–67.

13   Friedrich Max Müller coined the term 'Buchreligion' in his 1873 *Introduction to the Science of Religion*; see Jürgen Tubach, 'Mani, der bibliophile Religionsstifter', in R. E. Emmerick, W. Sundermann and P. Zieme (eds), *Studia Manichaica: IV Internationaler Kongress zum Manichäismus, Berlin, 14–18. Juli 1997* (Berlin: Akademie Verlag, 2000),

overwhelmingly present in the Roman Empire, as instruments of bilingual religious propaganda; their illuminations, sizes, and titles made them also significantly more attractive than their Christian counterparts, as Robin Lane Fox reminds us: 'Like Protestants' texts in Europe just after the Reformation, Mani's books existed to be seen, not merely to be read.'[14]

To be sure, early Manichaean and heresiological sources do insist on establishing a close association between Mani's persona and his own books. For instance, *Acta Archelai*, a fourth-century 'transcription' by Hegemonius of a public disputation between Bishop Archelaus and Mani, presents a 'Manes' who displayed all the extravagant features of a happy wise man from the East.[15] His depiction of Mani is not far either from

---

pp. 622–38, esp. 623. See now Guy G. Stroumsa, *La fin du sacrifice: mutations religieuses de l'antiquité tardive* (Paris: Odile Jacob, 2005), pp. 63–101; and most recently, idem, 'The Scriptural Movement of Late Antiquity and Christian Monasticism', *Journal of Early Christian Studies* 16.1 (2008): 61–77, esp. 61–62.

14   Robin Lane Fox, 'Literacy and Power in Early Christianity', in A. K. Bowman and G. Woolf Greg (eds), *Literacy and Power in the Ancient World* (Cambridge: Cambridge University Press, 1994), pp. 126–48, esp. 131. Samuel Lieu notes that the fine quality of Manichaean codices, especially their beautiful binding, was 'mocked by Augustine, in c. Faust XIII, 6, and 18'; see idem, *Manichaeism in Mesopotamia and the Roman East* (Leiden: Brill, 1994), p. 64, n. 175. For Manichaean book-making see the following commentary by Keith Hopkins: 'In the magnificent 4th-c. Manichaean Psalm Book, each psalm was numbered, each page had a title with a psalm number and first line, and the book was finished with a 5-page, 2-column index, listing each of the 289 psalms. Religious knowledge, like tax knowledge, had to be ordered so that believers could find their place.' K. Hopkins, 'Conquest by Book', in A. Bowman et al., *Literacy in the Roman World* (Ann Arbor, MI: University of Michigan Press, 1991), pp. 133–58, esp. p. 140. If, as Hopkins argues, Coptic literacy increased as an answer to Roman administrative practices, this could have brought a higher interest in taxonomies. Hence, books had to be put in order, for a better, faster, proper use. For later Manichaean book painting in Central Asia (eighth to tenth century), see Zsuzsanna Gulácsi, *Manichaean Art in Berlin Collections: A Comprehensive Catalogue of Manichaean Artifacts Belonging to the Berlin State Museums of the Prussian Cultural Foundation, Museum of Indian Art, and the Berlin-Brandenburg Academy of Sciences, Deposited in the Berlin State Library of the Prussian Cultural Foundation* (Turnhout: Brepols, 2001), pp. 105–27; idem, *Mediaeval Manichaean Book Art: A Codicological Study of Iranian and Turkic Illuminated Book Fragments from 8th-11th Century East Central Asia* (Leiden: Brill, 2005).

15   Hegemonius, *Acta Archelai (The Acts of Archelaus)*, trans. Mark Vermes, introduction and commentary by Samuel N. C. Lieu (Turnhout: Brepols, 2001). See also Jason BeDuhn and Paul Mirecki (eds), *Frontiers of Faith: The Christian Encounter with Manichaeism in the Acts of Archelaus* (Leiden: Brill, 2007), esp. the two papers by J. Kevin Coyle, namely 'Hesitant and Ignorant: The Portrayal of Mani in the *Acts of Archelaus*' (pp. 23–32) and 'A Clash of Portraits: Contrasts between Archelaus and Mani in the *Acta Archelai*' (pp. 67–76).

Gerd Theissen's Cynic, wandering radicals of the earliest Jesus movement; but with a more daring style of clothing.[16]

> That very same day Manes arrived, bringing with him twenty-two elect young men and women... When he saw Manes, Marcellus was first astonished at the garments he was wearing. For he wore a kind of shoe which is generally known commonly as the '*trisolium*' [tripod sandals? E.I.], and a multi-colored cloak, of a somewhat ethereal appearance, while in his hand he held a very strong staff made of ebony-wood. He carried a Babylonian book under his left arm, and he had covered his legs with trousers of different colors, one of them scarlet, the other colored leek-green. His appearance was like that of an old Persian magician or warlord.[17]

Acta Archelai cannot be used as a source of information about the historical Mani, but it speaks volumes about early Christian perceptions of the role of books in Manichaean propaganda. As Eszter Spät showed recently, Mani's biography in *Acta Archelai* bears resemblance to the life of Simon Magus, the chief heretic figure.[18] For instance, the author of *Acta Archelai* traces Mani's heretical genealogy 'to the times of the apostles', more precisely to Scythianus, a rich merchant dealing between Egypt and Palestine, who adopted Pythagoras' dualism and rejected the scriptures. His disciple, Terebinthus, helped him write four books: *Evangelium*, the *Chapters* (our *Kephalaia*), the *Mysteries* and *Thesaurus*. Terebinthus traveled to Persia, changed his name to Buddha, married a widow and died. The widow bought a seven-year-old boy, Corbicius, and taught him how to read and write. It was this Corbicius who later changed his name to Manes.

It is not by mere coincidence that the above four titles could be found amongst Mani's original writings: *Acta Archelai* puts forth a caricature of Mani and his almost comic obsession with the books' virtues in spreading his religion. However, this apologetic misrepresentation cannot hide the strong link between Mani, his disciples, and their propagandistic use of the books.

> So when that boy [Corbicius/Manes] reached nearly sixty years of age, he had become learned in the doctrine that exists in those parts [Persia], ... yet he studied more diligently the things contained in those four

---

16   Gerd Theissen, 'The Wandering Radicals: Light Shed by the Sociology of Literature on the Early Transmission of Jesus Sayings', in David G. Horrell (ed.), *Social-Scientific Approaches to New Testament Interpretation* (Edinburgh: T & T Clark, 1999). Richard Lim points to the usefulness of Gerd Theissen's sociological model in interpreting the dynamics of Manichaean missions; see idem, 'Unity and Diversity among Western Manichaeans', p. 239.

17   Hegemonius, *Acta Archelai* 14.2-3, trans. Mark Vermes.

18   Eszter Spät, 'The "Teachers" of Mani in the *Acta Archelai* and Simon Magus', *Vigchr* 58.1 (2004): 1–23.

books. He also acquired three disciples whose names are as follows: Thomas, Addas, and Hermas. Then he took those books and copied them, not without inserting into them many other things of his own, that are like old wives' tales. So he had those three disciples who were fully aware of their wicked ways; moreover he attached his own name to the books, deleting the name of the former writer, as if he alone had written them all by himself. Next he decided to send his disciples with the things he had written in the books to the upper regions of the same province, and among the scattered cities and villages, in order to obtain some other people to follow him. Thomas decided to take the regions of Egypt, Addas those of Scythia, while only Hermas chose to remain with Manes.[19]

Failing to cure the Sassanian king's ill son, Mani winds up in prison, while outside it his disciples apparently faced strong Christian opposition to their proselytizing. According to Hegemonius, Mani's taste for book adulteration moved him from Scythianus' four writings to Christian literature. His prison notebooks must have been filled with glosses to scriptural places open to dualistic interpretation.

Now at last, while languishing in the prison, he [Manes] ordered that the books of the law of the Christians be obtained. For the men who had been sent by him had been treated in each city with great abhorrence by everybody, but especially by those who held the name of the Christians in respect. So they took a quantity of gold, and left for the areas where the books of the Christians were published, and pretending to be Christian initiates they requested that the books be made available for their purchase. To cut a long story short, they obtained all the books of our Scriptures, and delivered them to Manes residing in prison. This astute individual received the books and began to look in our writings for passages in support of his dualism – or rather not his but Scythianus', who had propounded this doctrine much earlier.... . So having put together these wicked interpretations, he [Manes] sent his disciples to preach these boldly fabricated and invented falsehoods and to announce the new and deceitful statements in every place.[20]

On the other hand, in the *Cologne Mani Codex* the revelation of Mani's prophetic persona is never separated from the act of writing down its content in apocalyptic books, just as his 'forefathers' did. Revelation came in waves, or in cycles, and was characterized in the *Mani Codex* by the willingness of the prophets themselves, or of their closest disciples, to write down its content.

For let him who is willing hear and attend how each one of the forefathers has made known his one revelation to his own elect, which

19 Hegemonius, *Acta Archelai* LXIV, 4–6; trans. M. Vermes.
20 Hegemonius, *Acta Archelai* LXV, 2–6; trans. M. Vermes.

> he chose and brought together in that generation in which he appeared, and has written about it and passed it on to posterity.... So, therefore, each of them, according to the period and course of his mission, spoke what he had witnessed and had written as a memorial, including about his rapture.[21]

Who are the authors of these apocalypses? The *Mani Codex* presents us with whole fragments from apocalypses written by Adam, Sethel, his son, Enosh, Shem, Enoch, or from Paul's second letter to the Corinthians (12.2-5) or to the Galatians (1.11-12). It concludes:

> In short, all the most blessed apostles, saviors, evangelists and prophets of truth – each of them observed, as the living hope was revealed to him for proclamation, and wrote and has handed it down and deposited for the reminding of the future sons of the (Holy) Spirit who would know the perception (of his) voice... For when each of them was seized, (everything he saw) and heard he wrote down and made known, and himself became a witness of his own revelation; while his disciples became the sealing of his sending.[22]

As David Frankfurter noticed, 'since Mani criticized Zoroaster, the Buddha, and Jesus for not writing down their *ipsissima verba*, Jewish apocalypses may have initially stood as the paradigms of properly recorded heavenly teachings'.[23] There are, however, no known parallels in the whole of ancient literature to the fragments preserved in the Mani Codex. Frankfurter argues that the alleged apocalyptic books invoked by Mani in the Cologne Codex – of Adam, Sethel, Enosh, Shem, and Enoch – embody the universalistic message of the antediluvian Hebrew patriarchs, similar to Mani's, and constitute the connecting lines between these 'prophets' and to the last one, Mani.

The first pages of the *Kephalaia*, a fourth-century Coptic text, originally written in Syriac, attributed to the first generation of Mani's disciples, present a Mani similarly preoccupied with turning his oral teaching into books. *Kephalaia*'s introductory section lists Mani's 'books of light': *The Great Gospel*, *The Treasury of Life*, *The Treatise* (Pragmateia), *The One of the Mysteries*, *The Writing about Parthians*, *The Epistles*, *The Psalms*, and *The Prayers*.[24] The same list appears on the *Psalms of the Bema* (CCXLI), from the *Psalm-Book*, another fourth-century Coptic text that compares

---

21   *CMC*, 47–48, trans. S. Lieu.
22   *CMC*, 62, 72.
23   David Frankfurter, 'Apocalypses Real and Alleged in the Mani Codex', *Numen* 44.1 (1997): 60–73, esp. 62.
24   *Kephalaia* 5.23-26. Edited text in H. J. Polotsky (ed.), *Kephalaia* (Manichäische Handschriften der Staatlichen Museen Berlin Bd. 1; Stuttgart: W. Kohlhammer, 1940); English translation in Iain Gardner, *The Kephalaia of the Teacher: The Edited Manichaean Texts in Translation with Commentary* (Leiden: E. J. Brill, 1995).

Mani to a 'great physician' in whose 'medicine chest' one could find his writings as healing tools and antidotes.

> He has the antidote that is good for every affection. There are two and twenty compounds in his antidote: His *Great Gospel*, the good tidings of all them that are of the Light. His water-pot is the *Thesaurus*, the Treasure of Life. In it there is hot water: there is some cold water also mixed with it. His soft sponge that wipes away bruises is the *Pragmateia*. His knife for cutting is the *Book of Mysteries*. His excellent swabs are the *Book of the Giants*. The *narthex* of every cure is the *Book of his Letters*.[25]

The *Kephalaia* also sets the educational frame for imparting the wisdom of these books in 'three great lessons'.[26] The author warns his readers, a few lines further, that since 'the cosmos did not allow Mani to write them down', these *kephalaia* represent a 'sub-canonical text',[27] conveying some of Mani's oral teachings.[28] His devotees wrote down the 'interpretations' (*hermeneia*), homilies and talks Mani had with his *archegoi*, elect, catechumen, and the free men and women. Similarly, Jesus and Buddha 'did not write their wisdom in the books', but left their disciples the task of immortalizing their master's voice.[29] This textual stratagem lends authority both to Mani's figure and to his disciples who would carry the *Kephalaia* westward, translating the original Syriac in Greek and Coptic. Moreover, the very act of further copying these translations carried ritual meaning, and it was later converted into a religious practice of its own: 'When you write down and are amazed by them ... enlighten greatly, and they shall give benefit and make free ... of the truth.'[30]

Another fourth-century Coptic Manichaean text, the *Homilies*, also names Mani's scriptures, adding several more to the *Kephalaia*'s list: *The Book of Giants*, his *Icon* and his *Revelations*.[31] It is not by accident that the Coptic translation includes Mani's apocalypses. Unlike *Kephalaia*'s quiet teaching setting, the *Homilies'* narrative genre highlights a far more authoritative role for its copyists and readers themselves, by way of a powerful prophecy about the resurrection of the textual body of the books. In particular, *The Sermon on the Great War* describes a future

---

25 C. R. C. Allberry, *A Manichaean Psalm-Book* (Stuttgart: W. Kohlhammer, 1938).

26 Or 'three great words': *pišamt nnač nceǧe* (*Kephalaia* 5.30).

27 According to Gardner's notes to his own translation (*Kephalaia*, p. 10).

28 *Kephalaia* 6.16.

29 *Kephalaia* 6.20-26; 7.23-26; 7.34–8.7.

30 *Kephalaia* 9.7-10 [translation by I. Gardner].

31 Coptic: *pǧōme nngigas ... tefhikon mnnefapokalypseis* (*Homilies* 25.4-5). Hans Jakob Polotsky, *Manichäische Homilien* (Stuttgart: W. Kohlhammer, 1934); see now Nils Arne Pedersen, *Manichaean Homilies: With a Number of Hitherto Unpublished Fragments* (Turnhout: Brepols, 2006).

textual community, whose survival depends mainly on its eschatological recovery of its books.

> Thousands of books will be sa[v]ed [*preserved*] by the believing [cat] echumen[s]. They will come into the hands of the righteous and the believers: [The] *[Go]spel* and the *Treasury of Life*; the *Pr[agma]teia* and the *Book of the Mysteries*; the *Bo[ok on] the Giants* and the *Epistles*; the *Psalms* a[nd the] *Prayers* of my lord; his *Image* and his rev [ela]tions; his parables and his mysteries. N[ot] one will be lost. How many will be lost, how many will be destroyed? Thousands were lost, and other thousands have come [into their] hands, [and] indeed [they have] found them in the end! They will kiss them and [say:] 'Oh, wisdom of the greatness! Oh, armor of the [Apost]le of Light! Where were you lost and [...]? From where are you coming? In which pl[ace] did they find you? [...] I rejoice that the books have come into their hands [...]' of his lord for they did not find it. You will find [them, reading] them publicly and proclaiming the n[ame ...] in them, the name of his lord and [...] him, and the name of all those who gave [...] and the name of the scribe who wrote it [and] also [the name] of he who put the punctuation marks in it.[32]

In the *Sermon on the Great War*, the postwar restoration of the books codifies the regeneration of the Manichaean community. In this Manichaean version of realized eschatology, what follows the 'great war' is a decidedly textual community, with a reader (anagnōstēs) occupying the center role. He or she – it's justified to say that here – will teach children to write, sing psalms and hymns, and read. In this version of Manichaean future, for instance, special attention will be given to the education of 'little girls'.

> How greatly will they love the reader (anagnōstēs), since thousands will come to visit him, male and female, masses and masses in every city! The churches and the catechumens' houses will be like schools... You will find them all, the great and the small, a large number of children of the catechumens, being given to righteousness in every city. You will find the little girls being taught to write and singing psalms and reading.[33]

Conclusion

The Homilies presents Mani's scriptures as virtual 'instruments of power' that have become even more effective with the 'birth of the codex' and its

---

32 Coptic: *an mpetafstize mmaph; Manichaean Homilies* (25.1-19); trans. Nils Arne Pedersen.

33 *Manichaean Homilies* 30.27–31.7, trans. Nils Pedersen.

wide use in Christian Egyptian circles.[34] The structures of everyday life in the Roman Empire were informed by textual culture, even when literacy rates dwindled to around 10 percent.[35] A missionary religion, such as Mani's, adapted its message not only to the social structures of early Christianity in Syria and Egypt, but also to the more subtle tones of the administrative and textual culture that permeated the Roman provinces.[36] According to Keith Hopkins, Coptic 'originated as a script of protest' against Greek speakers and Roman rule, embodying the 'anti-authoritarian ideologies' of Gnostic and Manichaean sub-elites.[37]

Werner Kelber discusses literacy in early Christianity from a similar theoretical position. He situates the many uses of scribality in Roman imperialism within the classic dichotomy of scribes with power versus scribes without power. Kelber regards 'the ancient media of orality and scribality as instruments of identity formation, control, and domination used both by elites and by marginalized groups'.[38] No matter how enticing the explanation of two sets of structures competing for domination and

34 Hopkins, 'Conquest by Book', p. 140; Colin H. Roberts and T. C. Skeat, *The Birth of the Codex* (London: Oxford University Press, 1983); C. H. Roberts, *Manuscript, Society, and Belief in Early Christian Egypt* (London: Oxford University Press, 1979). See also Harry Y. Gamble, *Books and Readers in the Early Church: A History of Early Christian Texts* (New Haven: Yale University Press, 1995) and Anthony Grafton and Megan Williams, *Christianity and the Transformation of the Book: Origen, Eusebius, and the Library of Caesarea* (Cambridge, MA: Belknap Press of Harvard University Press, 2006) for the use of codex in ancient Christianity.

35 For literacy in the ancient world, see William Harris, *Ancient Literacy* (Cambridge, MA: Harvard University Press, 1989), with the useful delimitations brought by the seminal works of Mary Beard, 'Writing and Religion: *Ancient Literacy* and the Function of the Written Word in Roman Religion', in M. Beard, A. Bowman et al., *Literacy in the Roman World* (Ann Arbor, MI: University of Michigan Press, 1991), pp. 35–58; Sebastian Brock, 'Greek and Syriac in Late Antique Syria', in Bowman and Greg, *Literacy and Power in the Ancient World*, pp. 149–60; Jonathan A. Draper (ed), *Orality, Literacy, and Colonialism in Antiquity* (Leiden: Brill, 2004); Fox, 'Literacy and Power in Early Christianity'; Martin D. Goodman, 'Texts, Scribes, and Power in Roman Judea', in Bowman and Greg, *Literacy and Power in the Ancient World*, pp. 99–108; and Werner Kelber, 'Roman Imperialism and Early Christian Scribality', in Draper, ed., *Orality, Literacy, and Colonialism in Antiquity*, pp. 135–53.

36 See especially Hopkins, 'Conquest by Book', for his discussion of Coptic literacy. 'The Roman empire was bound together by writing. Literacy was both a social symbol and an integrative by-product of Roman government, economy and culture. The whole experience of living in the Roman empire, of being ruled by Romans, was overdetermined by the existence of texts. I need hardly stress again that I am not arguing for near-universal literacy; only a minority of Roman men could read and write. But the mass of literates, the density of their communications, and the volumes of their stored knowledge, significantly affected the experience of living in the Roman empire. Literacy and writing were active ingredients in promoting cultural and ideological change.' (144)

37 Ibid., pp. 145–47.

38 Kelber, 'Roman Imperialism and Early Christian Scribality', pp. 135–37.

power through discourse may appear to the Foucauldian minded reader, it is bound, nevertheless, to lose some of the subtle nuances of the negotiation that took place between the two extremes. Preserving Hopkins's sociological terms, one could reasonably presume that the Manichaean sub-elite acquired its textual identity in Syria, becoming a 'religion of the Book' under Jewish influence, and had to adjust constantly this inherited textual identity in a complicated double negotiation, with Roman administrative structure and the formative Christian Church.[39]

---

39 Jürgen Tubach regards Mani's high respect for books as a 'legacy of Ancient Judaism', connecting it to the rabbinic conception according to which real piety comes with study of books ('Mani, der bibliophile Religionsstifter', p. 630).

THE DANISH HYMNBOOK – ARTIFACT AND TEXt

Kirsten Nielsen

Introduction

Brian Malley's book, *How the Bible Works*, has been an eye-opener to me. When I first read it, it became obvious that the Bible is not just a collection of texts to be interpreted; the Bible is also an artifact. When I read Malley's book, I had just begun writing a book about the reception and transformation of the Bible in modern Danish hymns.[1] But I had one problem. I had to admit in the introduction to my book that my analysis of the hymns was an exegetical analysis. Important issues such as the use of hymns in the liturgy and the fact that hymns are meant for singing were to be kept out of my book. I just did not know how to deal with issues like that. I still do not know much about it, but now I know more about what it is that needs clarifying. And that is why I decided to take the opportunity to discuss the Danish hymnbook as an example of 'Scripture as artifact'.

Normally, we do not talk about hymnbooks as scripture, but in Denmark the hymnbook is just as important to the congregation as the Bible and it may be even more important. Martin Luther called the Psalms in the Old Testament 'die kleine Biblia', 'the little Bible' and that is what the hymnbook is for many churchgoers in Denmark.

This article consists of three parts. In the first part, I will deal with the Danish hymnbook as artifact and I will try to draw some parallels between what Brian Malley says about the Bible as artifact and what I see as characteristic for the Danish hymnbook. Malley has done a lot of field work before publishing his work. I have not done that kind of research. What I present is first of all built on my own experiences and observations.

In the second part, I shall treat some phenomena that I am unable to combine with the hymnbook as artifact, if I use the word exactly the way

---

1 Kirsten Nielsen, *Der flammer en ild. Gudsbilleder i nyere danske salmer* (Frederiksberg: Aros Forlag, 2007).

Brian Malley does. Nevertheless, it would be wrong to label these phenomena 'text' if we understand text as meaning. I am thinking of the fact that hymns are supposed to be sung in the congregation. They are not only read and interpreted. They are a special kind of poetry that a Danish scholar has called 'Gentagelsens poesi',[2] 'poetry of repetition'. But the Danish word for repetition means more than just repeating. It also means to regain what otherwise might be lost. If we only repeat without interpreting the hymn, then we treat it as an artifact. But if we repeat it in order to keep the meaning of the hymn alive, then I would see the hymn not only as an artifact but also as a text whose meaning we try to regain.

In the third part, I shall present some of the results from my study of the use of the Bible as intertext for the Danish hymns. It will be very short but it is based on my own research.

In the conclusion, I shall argue that the authority of the Danish hymnbook is due both to its artifactual properties and to its use of the Bible as its dominant intertext.

I. *The Danish Hymnbook as Artifact*

Let us begin with a look at the Danish hymnbook. Until recently almost all hymnbooks found in the churches in Denmark had the same colour as the Bible. They were black. Nevertheless, on the day of their confirmation, most young girls got a nice little hymnbook with a white cover. An advertisement on the homepage of the Danish Bible Society presents a special hymnbook meant for young people at their confirmation.[3] They can choose between four colours for the cover: white or black, red or blue. The name of the hymnbook, 'Den Danske Salmebog', is in gold and the paper used for the sheets is extremely thin. The colours indicate that there are two possibilities for girls and two for boys: white or red for girls, black or blue for boys. The colour of the hymnbook corresponds with the gender of the young person and the colours white and black with the traditional dressing. The golden letters emphasize the importance of the book. The thin paper is traditional and signals the best quality. It is actually rather awkward to skip through a book with such thin sheets and it makes me suspect that this hymnbook is not meant for regular reading. It is first of all a kind of requisite that belongs to the dress code for confirmation.

The hymnbook is thus identified by its physical characteristics. It is a category designating a set of hymns bounded by conventions of the colour

2 Lotte Thyrring Andersen, *Gentagelsens poesi. Virkelighedsopfattelsen i Jørgen Gustava Brandts digtning* (København: Gads Forlag, 2003).
3 Cf. http://www.bibelselskabet.dk/boghandel/visProd.asp?id = 562 (accessed 29 January 2007).

of the cover.[4] Besides that, hymnbooks are personal belongings often received as a gift from a close relative and with the personal name printed in gold on the cover.

And let me continue with some more observations about the look of the hymnbook. If you open a modern Danish hymnbook, you will notice that it is authorized by the monarch. On one of the first pages it says that on the 29th July 2002 the Danish hymnbook was authorized by her Majesty, Margrethe the Second, to be used at the services in the Danish Church. The authorization by the queen thus marks an institutional boundary. The queen is mentioned on one of the first pages, but even before you come to the page with the name of the queen, you are faced with a page that shows drawings of the ten Danish cathedrals. Church authority comes first! I see this as another example of the fact that the hymnbook is identified by its physical characteristics.

A last example: In the past, most people died at home in their own bed. When the body had been washed and dressed, it was customary to place the hymnbook under the chin of the deceased and on the chest was placed a cross made by two straws, some steel and even some coins.[5] The reason seems to be to protect the deceased against evil. A more secular and pragmatic explanation says that the reason why old pictures so often show dead people with a hymnbook under the chin is not necessarily that people in those days were fond of singing hymns – but this small thick book was very suitable to keep the mouth shut, while the muscles get stiff![6] So much for what I would call the hymnbook as artifact.

II. *The Danish Hymnbook between Artifact and Text*

It is a characteristic of the hymnbook that it is authorized for use in the church. The church is a consecrated room. It has an altar where Bible and hymnbook are lying side by side. The service where the hymns are sung takes place on Sundays, a special day of the week, with a consecrated person leading the ceremony. And the same hymn may be sung at a specific moment in every service as part of the ritual.

The Danish ritual for the Holy Communion consists of prayers, citations from the Bible and the hymn, 'O Lamb of God'. This ritual use of the hymn may have as one of its consequences that the meaning of the hymn becomes less important than the mere fact that now we are singing

---

4 Cf. Brian Malley, *How the Bible Works: An Anthropological Study of Evangelical Biblicism* (Walnut Creek: Altamira Press, 2004), p. 145.

5 Cf. Troels Frederik Troels-Lund, *Dagligt Liv i Norden i det sekstende Aarhundrede. Illustreret Udgave, XIV Bog: Livsafslutning* (København, Kristiania: Gyldendalske Boghandel, Nordisk Forlag 1908[-1910]).

6 Cf. http:www.hanstedkirke.dk/traditioner.htm (accessed 29 January 2007).

the authorized hymn that signals Holy Communion.[7] But nothing prevents the churchgoers from trying to understand why Christ is called the Lamb of God. And if, for instance, the minister in his or her sermon has quoted Ps. 23, 'The Lord is my shepherd', the congregation may well begin to see a connection between the Old Testament and the image of Jesus as a good shepherd who even lays down his life for the sheep.

Brian Malley has observed that although older translations of the Bible may be preferred by some people even new translations of the Bible are regarded as Bible.[8] In Denmark we got a new Bible translation in 1992 and although the congregations worried a great deal about changes in well-known verses in the Bible, nobody argued that a new translation would not be a Bible. But when the bishops had to decide the wording of central biblical passages in the liturgy such as 'Our Father' and 'The Blessing', they kept the older translation but allowed the ministers to use the new translation. The repeated liturgical use of these words had made the very sound of the words so important that even a better translation should not be forced on ministers and congregations who wanted to use the older translation.

In particular the prayer Our Father is a problem, if it is changed. The congregation gets into problems if they do not use the same wording when praying *together*. In the authorized Bible from 1992 you will therefore find a version where only two words have been changed. The one is the verb in the prayer: 'Hallowed be thy name', where the Danish verb for 'to be' was a very old-fashioned one that was never used in Danish outside of this prayer. The second change was in the prayer: 'For thine is the kingdom, the power, and the glory for ever and ever.' Here the Danish word for 'for' was changed to a modern one. But the interesting thing is that the two 'new' words had the same number of syllables as the 'old' ones. This means that old and young members of the congregation can still say the prayer together and keep the same rhythm. It is vital for the prayer ritual that we can say the words together without being disturbed by new wording or a different rhythm in the text.

When new hymnbooks are published, the new hymnbook is not a translation of the old ones even though some of the words and images are difficult to understand for younger generations. The congregations do not want such changes. The churchgoers are used to singing the hymns and they may even have learned parts of them by heart. They want to be able to sing *together* without having to look at the wording all the time. They want to be absorbed in the collective singing, to be able to follow the tune and let the words come almost by themselves. Singing hymns is *not* the

---

7   Cf. Malley, *How the Bible Works*, pp. 82–83, who mentions the Buddhist tradition for learning by heart before even reflecting on the meaning.

8   Malley, *How the Bible Works*, pp. 37–41.

same as interpreting a text, although we sometimes manage to do both at the same time.

Singing hymns together was for many years part of a morning ritual in Danish schools. In the 1970s this ritual almost disappeared, but now it is back again in many schools. I do not know enough about the reason for this change, but it is my impression that it is first of all because hymns and songs are part of our tradition and therefore integral to the Danish identity. And one of the consequences of the fact that Denmark has more foreign inhabitants today than 40 years ago is that we are much more concerned about our Danish heritage and identity these days. Regular singing of hymns may for some participants end as a ritual where the feeling of fellowship is the only thing that matters. But for others or at other times, the hymns may give occasion for interpretation. And no matter what: singing together at the morning session at school becomes part of a ritual authorized by the state and thereby gives authority to the hymns.

Not only the hymnbook as such, but also individual hymns have authority in certain groups or families. Hymns are part of family traditions: there are hymns that have always been sung at weddings or funerals in 'my family'. And we sing them because our great-grandparents, our grandparents and our own parents did so. And I am sure that we use the same tune. Change of tune may spoil the whole idea of repetition. The tune may mean more for a family or a community than the words themselves.

I have now mentioned various issues that I find important if we want to know more about how the Danish hymnbook works, issues that show that the Danish hymnbook and the Bible in many regards work the same way.

III. *The Danish Hymnbook as Text*

My third part deals with the Danish hymnbook as text. As an exegete, I am first of all interested in the meaning of the hymns and how this meaning is expressed in the texts. In my book on the new Danish hymns I analyse the reuse of biblical images of God or, to put it differently, the Bible as intertext for the hymns. What I am going to present now is therefore some of the main results of my recent studies on Danish hymns.

By intertextuality I mean 'the function of older literature cited or in some way alluded to in later literature' as well as 'the interrelation between text and reader'.[9] It is obvious that a new hymn that begins with the words: 'My God, my God,/why have you forsaken me!' quotes Ps. 22

---

9 Cf. James A. Sanders, 'Intertextuality and Canon', in *One Way to Nineveh: Studies in Honor of George M. Landes* (ed. Stephen L. Cook and S. C. Winter; Atlanta: Scholars Press, 1999), pp. 316–33, 316–17.

in the Old Testament. And it is clear that the poet reuses not only the Old Testament psalm but also the New Testament as an intertext, when he in the first verse calls Jesus his brother and describes the day Jesus was crucified. The first verse of this new hymn sounds like this in my translation:

> My God, my God,
> why have you forsaken me!
> This was your last cry, my brother,
> the day when pain became too much,
> when you were brought down to your knees,
> firmly nailed to the tree of the cross:
> My God, my God,
> why have you forsaken me!

I could mention a lot of other examples of such quotations or allusions to biblical stories and expressions, but what I would like to argue in this article is something else, namely the reuse of biblical figures of speech in the new hymns. By this I mean the use of imagery when talking about God.

What is characteristic for imagery is that it acts in a specific context by an interaction between two different statements.[10] It is easily seen that metaphors act that way. The metaphor 'shepherd' in Ps. 23 creates an interaction between what is normally said about a shepherd and what is said about God. In modern Danish hymns, it is obvious that a lot of metaphors for God are taken from family life. God is described as a considerate parent who cares for his children. The word father may not be used directly, but the idea of God as a father lies behind the feelings and actions that are attributed to God. But even though the personal metaphors dominate in the hymns, it does not mean that God *is* a father or that Jesus *is* a brother. The words father or brother interact with what else can be said about God or Jesus.

The same kind of interaction is created by metonymies. When in Ps. 18 God is described as the agent behind natural phenomena like thunder and storm, the poet creates an interaction between the storm and God. The storm is *not* a metaphor for God, it is a real storm, a physical phenomenon, but through the interaction between storm and God we are told something about both God and the storm. There exists a metonymical relationship between God and the storm. In Danish hymns the sun (or light in general) plays a great role. The sun may be used as a metaphor for Christ, but the rise of the sun on Easter morning may just as

---

10 Cf. Kirsten Nielsen, *There is Hope for a Tree: The Tree as Metaphor in Isaiah* (Sheffield: JSOT Press, 1989), p. 65.

well be used as a metonymy. It is the rising Christ who is the agent behind the bright sunshine.

As a third kind of interaction I shall mention the parallelism. I understand the parallelism as a kind of extended metaphor. In his book on parallelisms, James Kugel defines parallelism like this: 'A and what is more B',[11] and I would like to argue that the main point is the interaction that is created between the two parallel lines. I have found that in some of the Danish hymns parallelism is used in a special way. First the poet describes natural phenomena like the great sea or the morning light and as a parallel to this description of nature he or she places a verse about God or Christ. The parallelism creates an interaction between the two verses. It is the well-known Danish nature, but God is the agent and nature bears witness to his creative powers.

I shall argue that exactly these three ways of speaking about God (metaphor, metonymy and parallelism) are taken from the Bible. The Bible itself stresses not only that God has revealed himself but also that God is different from what we know about human beings and about natural phenomena. The only way of speaking adequately about somebody/something like God is therefore to use a language that expresses both likeness and difference and thereby respects both the difference between God and human beings and the possibility of getting to know something about God.

The Bible is used as intertext for the Danish hymns. Reuse of biblical stories and expressions can be found again and again. But I find it important to stress that not only stories and themes but also the biblical way of talking of God by use of specific figures of speech is still normative for the way God is talked about in modern Danish hymns.

Conclusion: The Authority of the Danish Hymnbook

In many ways the Danish hymnbook works like the Bible. It is treated as an artifact. It is used in rituals. And it has a great deal of authority due not only to these characteristics but also to the fact that it has the Bible as its dominant intertext both when it comes to contents and when it comes to form.

---

11 Cf. James Kugel, *The Idea of Biblical Poetry: Parallelism and Its History* (New Haven and London: Yale University Press, 1981), p. 53.

Towards a Sociology of Bible Promise Box Use[1]

David J. Chalcraft

The classic sociological text, *The Protestant Ethic and the Spirit of Capitalism*, first published in 1904–5,[2] reveals the importance of understanding sociologically the role of biblical ideas and values in everyday life. Despite this classic example, sociology has been slow to pursue similar lines of enquiry. The following is one small attempt to begin to fill this large gap in sociological knowledge. I report on research undertaken into one biblical artifact, the Bible Promise Box, to understand changing attitudes and practices in the light of sociological theorizing about modernity.

What is a Promise Box?

A promise box is a box or other container in which individual biblical texts have been placed. There are two basic types. One type, which is probably the older of the two, is a cardboard box into which have been placed between 100 and 200 biblical texts, written or typed onto small slips of paper which have been rolled up into a tiny scroll. Often this type of Promise Box comes with a small pair of tweezers for the removal of the scroll.

---

1 I would like to dedicate this chapter to the memory of my maternal grandfather, Reginald Stanley Page, who died when my mother was still a young girl of nine in 1944, leaving a widow and five children. He was a respected and valued member of the Bexley Heath Corps and a Junior Band Leader. I have learnt lately that he was in the habit of placing a couple of scrolled Bible promises into his coat pocket as he left the house in case he needed to share 'the word' with someone during his travels in the course of the day.
I need to thank especially all the participants in the research for their sympathetic sharing of information and opinion. Many of them would recognize parts of their own story, even their own words, in my retelling, but I have attempted to conceal their identities.

2 English editions are mostly based on the revision to the text made by Weber in 1920, hence the 2nd edition. See Max Weber, *The Protestant Ethic and the Spirit of Capitalism*, new translation and introduction by Stephen Kalberg (Los Angeles: Roxbury, 1992).

The second type of Promise Box is a variation on the first type but where the scrolled texts have been replaced by small cards. These cards might carry a biblical text on both sides of the card, or one side of the card has a prayer or other thought considered appropriate to the biblical text. Given that cards instead of scrolls are used, there is more flexibility in presentation.

The biblical promises that are found in either type are selected from the huge number of available Bible verses (one count is 31,102 verses). There can be considerable variation between the biblical texts used, as well as there being texts that appear in almost all examples.

As the recent movie *Evan Almighty* amusingly demonstrates,[3] not all biblical texts lend themselves to be taken out of context, or turned into promises or demands. For Evan Baxter, the command in Genesis 6.14: 'Make thee an Ark of gopher wood' causes a fair degree of devastation of life, work and property. One is unlikely to find Genesis 6.14 chosen for a Promise Box. The potential randomness of selection is restricted a great deal by the appearance of well-worn, and tried and tested, favourites. Yet, people who drew promises were often challenged by them or reminded of what they saw as important truths.

The Research Process and Who was in the Research?

I anticipated that members of the Salvation Army may well be likely to have a tradition of Promise Box use. My intention was not to generate a large body of data through a carefully controlled random sample, but to explore in depth, from people who had used and/or continued to use a Promise Box, what they actually felt about doing so and the way that they did so.[4] A notice was placed in *The Salvationist*, describing my interest and the research project, and asking anyone with memories of Promise Boxes to get in touch. This called forth a number of telephone calls, private letters and emails. The sample, then, 'volunteered' itself.[5] I followed up the telephone calls with a questionnaire, and also, where people's letters suggested they might have more information and stories, followed up correspondents with a questionnaire.

Altogether there were 32 research participants. Of these 32, 26 completed the questionnaire. Of these 26, 6 also had a telephone conversation/interview with me. 18 people also sent letters or began an email correspondence with me. Of the 32 research participants, 25 percent

---

3 Tom Shadyac (dir.), *Evan Almighty* (Universal Pictures, 2007).

4 On various types of sampling see Colin Robson, *Real World Research* (Oxford: Blackwell, 2nd edn, 2002).

5 See Clive Seale and Paul Filmer, 'Doing Social Surveys', in C. Seale (ed.), *Researching Society and Culture* (London: Sage, 1998), pp. 125–45.

were male, 75 percent female. In terms of Christian denomination, 75 percent were Salvationists (24), 12.5 percent were Seventh Day Adventists, and 12.5 percent came from or 'belonged to' other denominations. The majority of respondents were from the UK but I was also contacted by people in the US, Canada and Australia. Of the 32 research participants, 73.9 percent were over 60, whilst 51.7 percent were between 70 and 79. The oldest participant was 92 (and still active in the local Salvation Army Band!). The research report draws on the data gathered from all these sources: telephone interviews, questionnaires, and autograph letters and emails.

Overall Trends in Promise Box Use across Time

In general, Promise Box use has declined among the Salvation Army and where its use continues it has moved from the public sphere of Army life to a more privatized and individualized setting. It was certainly the impression of informants that Promise Box use had dropped off considerably over the years. Respondents often expressed their regret that Promise Boxes no longer featured in public devotions nor during shared domestic times within the home. There was no doubt an element of general regret for 'the good old days' within these sentiments, and for some my research actually kindled nostalgic feelings. A respondent observed that 'promise boxes are not easy to purchase today', whilst another commented that 'it is a pity that they are not used so much today'; this sentiment was echoed by others who opined, 'They were used more in the past than they seem to be now, which is a pity'. For some the very research process seemed part of a needed revival: for example, someone said 'I was afraid it was a thing of the past and now it seems as if it is being revived. How wonderful!'

Within this general trend of decline and individualization, at least three historical trajectories can be traced. Firstly there were respondents who held fond memories of childhood where Promise Boxes had been used, and they now treasured those boxes that had been inherited as a form of family heirloom. However, they did not themselves make use of the Promise Box. A respondent shared, 'I inherited my parents' promise box – but must admit we stopped using it several years ago but keep it, I guess, for sentimental value'. In some cases, whilst the box itself had collapsed, the little scrolls had been kept in a safe place, and sometimes placed within another suitable receptacle.

A second pattern was found amongst respondents who, whilst having no childhood or teenage memories of Promise Boxes, had become Christians in adult life and had begun to use Promise Boxes. A respondent who falls within this category honestly stated that 'I only use my Promise

Box now and then, whenever I feel the need for a little scriptural uplifting. I do not have a set time and I do not have a ritual associated with it'. Whilst this comment evidences a general Protestant distaste for what might be seen as ritual, it is interesting that there was little routine in Promise Box use amongst those who had little tradition to draw upon.

A third pattern was when a respondent had experienced Promise Box use in various settings whilst growing up and had continued to use one during their lives up to and including the present day. As can be imagined, a life-long association with Promise Box use meant that some respondents were able to send me quite detailed accounts of their experiences and ideas. For example, Mrs K, recalling 1943, writes:

> After three years with four moves as a minister in various places my Promise Box was beginning to look bare and worst for wear. Why? Well, I had many women's meetings to lead, and every place I went I had one afternoon called The Promise Box, it was a bright hour, based on The Promises of God, and ending up with everyone having one of the Promises from my Box. So I went through many boxes.

In 1946, now serving at the rank of Captain, Mrs K was posted for Red Shield work to the Middle East to minister to members of the armed forces. She writes about this period as follows: 'I purchased a new Promise Box. I was in Benghazi, Tobruck, Cairo, and Port Said and I found that the Promise Box came in very handy, after counselling members of the forces, who asked for help, I asked them to take a promise.' In 1947, now back in the UK, she recalls working in North Allenton Prison. 'I found that a promise chosen by the men became a wonderful opening for conversation. Even the governor asked for one as he had heard about them.' Towards the close of her six-page letter, Mrs K goes on to say:

> I guess you are saying, 'Have you got one now?' Sure I have, standing in my bedroom on a shelf where I can easily get one out in the morning, but I've had it for 20 years now since my husband and I retired. But I have my eye on a new one... I shall still be using my Promise Box, as we are living in a Residential Quaker home and I shall one day put my Box in the dining room for the residents to take one if they wish. My husband and I lead the Christmas service in here, also a Good Friday service.

The above is an example of the public sharing of Promise Boxes. For many of the research participants, public sharing of biblical promises taken from a Promise Box form a sizeable part of their experience. The next few sections consider the various settings of Promise Box use.

Promise Box Use in Salvationist Public Meetings

A possible reason for the decline of the public use of Promise Boxes in Salvationist meetings depends on the type of meetings that were held in the past in which such a practice could operate, but which are seen to be now no longer viable. Promise Box use seems best suited to smaller gatherings. If each person is to select and then share their promise the group cannot be large. Also, the sharing of biblical texts, which can often be followed by an explanation of how that promise seems apposite to the person, requires a degree of trust and intimacy between the participants. A respondent informed me how the Promise Box mediated closer fellowship between a group of Salvationists who met regularly in each other's homes: 'Using the Promise Box brought any group into closer fellowship and helped us to understand each other's situations, so we prayed for each other.'

A respondent described a regular group meeting within a more domestic setting: 'Groups of soldiers used to come to my house for Bible Study, accordion band practice, fellowship meals etc. We always finished with a cup of tea, and we each chose a promise for the person on our left, or on our right whichever was agreed for the occasion. I would say that we each found comfort, and took new heart from the promises; and we could also learn from them.'

Another respondent spoke with regret about what she saw as changes within the Salvation Army itself and Corps life, and these changes presumably impacted on the popularity of Promise Boxes. She writes: 'Also in those far-off days certain people would issue invitation to Sunday Tea to young people, where the Promise Box would be produced and used. Sometimes a discussion would ensue. At an SA social gathering a box would be produced. I have not seen or heard of one being used in any of these capacities since not long after the war ended. When the men came back, life, Corps life, changed completely, and of course the SA is now vastly different from when I was young.'

Hence in circumstances where smaller meetings are no longer held, Promise Box use is less likely to take place. At the same time, however, even in smaller meetings it might no longer be acceptable to use Promise Boxes, which appear old fashioned and quaint. A general decline in sociability, even amongst members of the same religious community, means that the degrees of intimacy associated with sharing Bible promises is less likely to flourish, whilst increasing respect for privacy and individuality is evidenced.[6]

---

6 The nature of individuality and individualization in the rise of modernity and in contemporary modernity is discussed, respectively, by Emile Durkheim, *The Division of Labour* (Basingstoke: Macmillan, 1893), and by Ulrich Beck, *The Risk Society: Towards a New Modernity* (London: Sage, 1992).

The one meeting which still takes place in many Corps is the Home League meeting. This meeting was originally for women only, and even today can be attended solely by women although men can attend. During these meetings, if anyone has a birthday they are invited to take a promise. They may read the promise out loud or have it read to them. Then those gathered will sing 'Happy Birthday', with 'to Jesus be true' replacing the standard second line.

Mrs H, recalling mid-1940, wrote about Promise Box use in general that 'this idea is not so much used in public meetings these days. However I do recall that when a junior we had the promise box passed round then quoted the text we had received in public. These were very helpful to a great lot of people, as they were days in war time, and any comfort from such was good for those drastic days.'

A further memory from the same period also indicates how a Promise Box was used within a public setting, and seemed an appropriate action as each member stood on the threshold of the New Year. She recalls: 'One occasion has always stood out in my mind. It was the Watchnight service entering the year of 1947. In that year I was preparing myself for entering our International Training College in London for full time Officership in the Salvation Army. I was feeling a little apprehensive that the actual year was now upon me to enter in the August. All that Watchnight we had the promise box passed round, and I felt that my promise was extremely appropriate for my future, it was, "In all thy ways acknowledge Him and he will direct Thy paths." ... This was certainly a good thought to keep in mind in those formative days, and I can assure you that... [it has been]... a mainstay on many occasions since.'

A male respondent recorded: 'I am 77 and of an age when Promise Boxes were in use in Corps Fellowships, and especially "Cottage Meetings"; a phrase not used very often these days – when a few of us would meet for song, prayer and "The Word" at the house of an elderly or invalid member; those little paper-rolls and tweezers!'

The overall trend of decline of Promise Box use in public meetings can be seen from the above examples, and the manner in which such use created but also depended upon degrees of sociability and intimacy is underlined.

Use of Promise Boxes within the Family Home

One of the practices associated with Promise Boxes was the sharing of promises with guests at the home of a Salvationist, especially the sharing of promises after meals. One respondent explained: 'The Promise Box was often used after a meal with visitors (both Christian and non-Christian).

Each person took a promise and then each person read out their promise. Occasionally a visitor would ask to keep their promise.'

It transpired that many Salvationists remembered that the Sunday meal in the family home was also marked by the sharing of Bible promises from a Promise Box, normally at the meal's close. This formed a special time in the cycle of the family week, and was especially of interest to children. Children were invited to draw promises from the special box, to unravel the scroll, and to read out loud the promise that was intended just for them. Children could demonstrate their reading skills and be the focus of attention for a spell. When the promise needed further explication, one of the parents, normally the father, would provide some kind of explanation or application. A respondent from North America recalled that 'Occasionally a promise would speak to me but it was just a nice way of ending a special meal to draw our thoughts to God to thank Him for His provision for us in life.'

This respondent also helpfully described both the variety in practice and the manner in which a practice might be spread. She writes:

> At the end of the meal my mother would pass out the box around – everyone would draw a promise card and read both sides of it – no interpretation. In my parents' home that was it. Then I went to a Corps officer's house for dinner once and they had the tradition of having guests at the table sign their promise card and date it. Then any promise cards drawn with previous guests' names on them – after the reading of all the promise cards (both sides) then there would be a closing prayer during which each person whom had signed a card previously...would be remembered in prayer. I thought this was a lovely tradition to remember friends and acquaintances from times past in prayer and so I also adopted this tradition...

The Promise Box could also be used in the family home apart from family meals, and this was also seen as a special occasion and children were privileged to be able to take a promise. One respondent explained: 'We lived in a Church Hall. The Promise Box was kept over the fireplace in the small hall. The mission to the Jews had this Box and when my mother (Caretaker) did the cleaning she would let a curious child (namely myself) have a promise – a great treat for me.'

An elderly respondent recalled that 'My grandmother used it with us for family prayers. Each of us took our own promise, read it aloud, then replaced it'; and another mentioned that 'The promise box was an integral part of family life when I lived with my parents'. A ninety-two-year-old male respondent remembered:

> My mother and father had a promise box, there was six boys and my sister who was the youngest. We had family prayers on Sunday morning and we all got a promise from the Promise Box and we all had turns to

read our promise and say a few words of prayer. We lived in small house and it was a job getting us all out for Directory on Sunday morning.

Locating the Promise Box in the Private House

Promises Boxes are found in different locations within people's homes. Within sociology, the sociology of everyday life includes an interest in the cultural significance of social space and the material objects and social practices that appear to belong to different rooms and spaces within a house.[7] The place where a Promise Box is kept reflects in part the manner of its significance and use. Somewhat in parallel to the privatization and individualization of the Promise Box as its use moves out of public meetings, the Promise Box within people's homes is now most often found not in the public rooms, the 'front stages'[8] or in shared family space (e.g. living rooms/kitchens) but in the privacy of the bedroom. Nonetheless there are still a variety of places in which one might encounter a Promise Box in people's homes.

Informants told me that they kept their Promise Box(es) in the kitchen, in the living room, in the guest room, in their own bedroom, and in the dining room. Where the Promise Box was kept reflected the custom of usage in the house. People who regularly used the Promise Box located it where the routines of their daily lives were perhaps most predictable. Placement of the box also related to the attitude to witnessing to visitors and whether the owner minded 'giving away' promise texts. One respondent pointed out that hers was kept on the sideboard near the threshold of the house so that visitors on either arrival or departure could be offered one.

Other factors influencing this dimension include the design of the box itself. For example, a more ornamental type lends itself to being placed on the mantelpiece whereas a Bread of Life type suits the kitchen (the container for the promises is a loaf of bread and the cards are found inserted in the top of the loaf as if the bread were itself a toaster and the cards were the toast). Ceramic types, adorned with floral patterns, tend to appeal to the older generation, to women, and are often found on dressing tables. Teenage bedrooms might be the home for Promise Boxes reading 'Jesus Rules' in a contemporary graphic, or a child's bedroom might have a toy-like designed Promise Box, around the theme of Noah's Ark. Promise Boxes are available in more regular souvenir styles: for example,

---

7   See, for example, Tony Bennett, 'Home and Everyday Life', in T. Bennett and D. Watson (eds), *Understanding Everyday Life* (Oxford: Wiley-Blackwell, 1992).

8   A sociological dramaturgical distinction between front and back stages is developed by Erving Goffman, *The Presentation of Self in Everyday Life* (Hardmondsworth: Penguin, 1959).

in the shape of a lighthouse, and a visitor to Australia can purchase examples in the form of a kangaroo. It is most common today for Promise Boxes to be made by women engaged in home crafts, who can design and fill Promise Boxes depending on customer choice in a bespoke fashion.

One respondent kept hers on the dressing table in the bedroom and every time she passed by remembered to take a promise from the box. Another respondent kept hers in the bedroom drawer, 'next to my bed' and took a promise 'each morning' when she got up. One respondent who had moved from the UK to US, and had more than one example in the house, informed me, 'My guest room promise box I bought when we first came to this country and we had many family visitors who enjoyed discussing the promise they had read that morning.' One Salvationist couple who had been married for many years wrote to say that the Promise Box 'is kept on top of the television in full view so we do not forget to read a promise each day. My husband and I both take one and read it to each other... We keep it on top of the TV set, so that when we turn it off at night we remember to take a promise and we read them to each other before we go to bed.'

When there had been a tradition of using the Promise Box whenever guests had shared a meal in the family home (see further below), it was customary for the box still to be placed in the dining room. Many respondents recalled how the Promise Box in their family home when they were young was kept in a special place within the dining area. For example, a respondent recorded that 'The Promise box was kept in the china cabinet in the dining room and only used sometimes when we were having a special meal at the dining room table, usually if we had guests at the table'.

Attitudes to Promises Drawn from Promise Boxes

The majority of the respondents spoke positively about their experiences of using Promise Boxes, as one would expect if use had continued over a period of time. Promises were felt to speak directly and be apposite, offering advice, encouragement and comfort, or just reminding the user of verses in the Bible that communicate God's word. A Seventh Day Adventist respondent stated that 'Using the promises was always as if it was just written for me at that time...' A Salvationist also shared this experience and replied to the question about whether promises addressed their situation, with, 'Yes! They encourage me and it feels like God is speaking directly to me'. This view was echoed by others including the respondent who wrote, 'yes, they all have a message for me. Usually for the situation at any particular time'.

Not all experiences were positive, however, and respondents observed that some 'promises' were hard to understand. Respondents answered the question, 'does the promise always speak to you?', with replies such as: 'No. I have to say that I find some promises do not "speak to me"'; or, 'Not always. Some are harder to understand from just one verse.' Such experiences, though, did not discourage individuals from continuing to use Promise Boxes. For example, one respondent observed that whilst, 'I do not find that promises always speak to me...there are and have been many times in my life when they have given me an answer to a question or certain situations.'

The questionnaire also asked whether respondents would recommend using Promise Boxes. Mrs H answered: 'Yes, I would recommend them because sometimes when you are feeling low or anxious, that is when the Lord usually speaks to you through His word, in the Promise Boxes.' Mrs A replied that she found them 'always appropriate for the situation... Very encouraging especially in times of despondency.' Again, Mrs F wrote that using the Promise Box helped her 'to focus' and gave her 'courage to face the day ahead'. A similar view is conveyed in another reply which observed that using the box 'keeps you aware of God's Promises all through the day'.

In letters a number of participants described an occasion, often in the distant past, where a biblical verse had proved to be amazingly apposite to the situation. The event had remained fixed in their memories and had played a role not only in their continued use of and faith in Promise Boxes but also in keeping them in their Christian belief. For reasons of space just one example must suffice. It is written by a male respondent in his late seventies and records an incident during the Second World War at the time of the London Blitz, in 1940.

> At this time I was six years old and living with my mother in our home in Southend on Sea. My father had been called up into the navy and my brother had been evacuated into the country. It was during one night when the air-raid warning had sounded and the sound of enemy bombers could be heard overhead. The guns began to fire at the enemy aircraft and it was not long before several bombs began to fall onto the town. We had an air-raid shelter in our garden and we were trying to make up our minds whether to take shelter in it or stay indoors. It was at this time that my mother said to me let us take a promise from the promise box which had been in our family ever since I could remember. The promise which we took at random was the verse from Psalm 91 which read: 'Thou shalt not be afraid for the terror by night nor for the arrow that flieth by day' (KJV). How true this promise was because as a family we all survived those dangerous war years and as a life long Christian since those days I have lived to prove that the promises of God are sure.

A respondent from Australia conveys through her letter how promises recently taken from a Promise Box worked to address a deeply felt anxiety about the spiritual welfare of members of her family. She candidly wrote,

> I bought my Promise Box when I was a teenager more than 50 years ago. No words of mine could ever express how precious my promise box is to me, it has been the means of having a closer walk with God, a way of God guiding, instructing and comforting me all through my life. My recent comfort from my Promise Box came the very day I received three *Salvationists* (in one of which was the call for research participants). That evening I was praying for family members who once served the Lord and no longer attend a place of worship. After my prayer I went to my Promise Box asking the Lord to guide my hand to words He had for me at that time. The promise that came into my hand read, 'I give unto them eternal life, and they shall never perish, neither shall any man pluck them out of my hand' (John 10.28). I could not have more assurance that God still had his hand upon the lives of my loved ones guiding and directing them back to Himself. What comforting words they were for me, now in faith I wait for the Lord's timing.

Promise Boxes, the Bible and Hymns

One expected that a respect for the Word of God in Promise Boxes would extend, and indeed be derived from, a respect for the Word of God in the Bible. I was interested in discovering how far the Bible had been replaced by the Promise Box – providing a more bite-size and convenient exposure to the Bible suited to contemporary living or religiosity; I was also interested to ascertain whether the practice of using Promise Boxes followed any particular routines. The range of replies generally indicated that there was not a set ritual that respondents would use, but praying in relation to the promise was common. Many respondents showed themselves well informed about the relation between a text drawn from a Promise Box and the Bible from which it had come and understood principles of context – hence there was never a total 'eclipse of biblical narrative'.[9] The majority of respondents also read the Bible but not always regularly, but also made high use of Daily Bible Reading Guides. For many, the promises led to the Bible rather than away from it, and this notion accounted for the willingness to share promises with others who were in need, from their perspective, of spiritual support or 'bringing to the word'.

For example, a respondent recalled, 'Promises also taught us about the Bible. We could read a whole chapter later, and so put the promises into

---

9   See Hans Frei, *The Eclipse of Biblical Narrative: A Study in Eighteenth and Nineteenth Century Hermeneutics* (New Haven: Yale University Press, 1974).

context...sometimes it is good to find where the promise is from, to read the whole chapter, and put the promise into context.' Another respondent expressed: 'I believe a Promise Box should lead to a thirst for the truth in the Bible and an interpretation for each individual by guidance of The Holy Spirit.' Again, it was stated that 'I would recommend other Christians to read their Bibles, but I believe "The Word of God" is in a promise box, and is very valuable, and anything in all kinds of forms should be around for people to see when it is the Word of God.' Another respondent opined that Promise Box use 'can be very encouraging and give an appetite for further Bible reading and study'.

It should also be noted that for Salvationists, with the emphasis they place on band music and singing as a means of outreach and of worship, many valuable phrases and biblical motifs are remembered from songs and hymns. In times of despair it is the hymns and their particular turns of poetic phrase, learnt by heart over a long period of time, that provide comfort and support and often replace the use of a Promise Box or the searching out of verses in the Bible itself.

The Promise Box and the Sociology of Modernity

'A promise box is good when you have little time'

Biblical scholars have investigated the fate of the Bible in the modern world[10] but have not yet made use of sociological theories of modernity. Some sociologists characterize contemporary society as a mobile society.[11] This is a far more profound understanding of the 'great transition' from traditional to modern societies and processes of social and geographical mobility than that found in classical sociology.[12] Contemporary mobilities are far more intense and far-reaching. All things are on the move, constantly – people, ideas, information, material objects – in a variety of rhythms and complex journeys. It is difficult, if not impossible, to trace people and ideas back to their origin and their home – people, ideas,

10   See, for example, the work of James Barr, *The Bible in the Modern World* (London: SCM Press, 1973); Henning Graf Reventlow, *The Authority of the Bible and the Rise of the Modern World* (London: SCM Press, 1984); David J. A. Clines, *The Bible and the Modern World* (Sheffield: Sheffield Academic Press, 1997).

11   John Urry, *Sociology Beyond Societies: Mobilities for the Twenty-first Century* (London: Routledge, 2000); John Urry, *Mobilities* (Oxford: Polity, 2007).

12   The 'great transition from traditional to modern societies' is classically treated by Ferdinand Toennies, *Community and Association* (London: Routledge, 1955; originally published in German, 1887); Durkheim, *Division of Labour*; Talcott Parsons, *Societies: Evolutionary and Comparative Perspectives* (Indianapolis: Bobbs Merrill, 1966).

styles, symbols, technologies become almost free-floating, 'disembedded'[13] from their original contexts which are soon irrelevant to their meaning. The mobile phone is perhaps one of the best known devices that symbolize a life on the move as well as being a technology that aids and abets contemporary lifestyles: people still connect and communicate, but they communicate 'on the move' and the language is clipped and coded.[14] The Bible in modernity is not free from the implications of these processes, and the significance of the Promise Box may well hover here. The Promise Box partakes of disembedding processes, promotes them, and is a mobile and portable Bible for a mobile society. Yet its users know that its origins are firmly rooted in the parent. The artifact that is the Promise Box is still a *biblical* artifact and it survives on account of its connection with the greater text from which its promises are taken.

The relation between the Bible and mobility no doubt has a long history that has largely yet to be written. As the Bible moved into modernity it became mobile in new ways. The Bible has often had its content reduced in size and complexity as readers attempt to grapple with its bulk. Through the memorization of particular passages or texts, the Bible is personalized and the ideas are 'carried' in the head. The mobility of the Bible's contents also inheres in the manner in which various texts can be differently understood and applied: all attempts to fix the meaning of the biblical text fail in the light of actual use. Promises from a Bible Promise Box can be applied over and over again by individuals to new circumstances and the same text can take on different meanings depending on events.[15]

In this connection the physical size of an edition of the Bible and the form of its abbreviation are a key variable.[16] One way that the Bible was 'packaged' to suit a developing mobile society was the Gideon Bible and its placement in hotel rooms for the use of the weary and alienated traveller.[17] The Gideon Bible also had user-friendly contents pages that provided ready-made references to specific issues the reader might want

13   Conceptualization of 'disembedding' can be found in Anthony Giddens, *The Consequences of Modernity* (Oxford: Polity, 1990) and *idem*, *Modernity and Self-Identity: Self and Society in the Late Modern Age* (Oxford: Polity, 1991). Most recently, in Jock Young, *The Vertigo of Late Modernity* (London: Sage, 2007).

14   For further theorization of the sociology of mobile phone technology, see Urry, *Mobilities*, pp. 171–80.

15   An excellent introduction to this theme can be found in J. W. Rogerson, *According to the Scriptures: The Use of the Bible in Social, Moral and Political Questions* (London: Equinox, 2007).

16   Christopher de Hamel, *The Book: A History of the Bible* (London: Phaidon, 2001).

17   Robert Carroll, 'Lower Case Bibles: Commodity Culture and the Bible', in C. Exum and S. D. Moore (eds), *Biblical Studies/Cultural Studies: The Third Sheffield Colloquium* (Sheffield: Sheffield Academic Press, 1988), pp. 46–69.

addressing with some urgency. The shift from scrolls to codices in ancient times, and the production of small size Bibles in the Middle Ages, are surely also part of this process, as is the export of the Bible to colonial territories based on the mobility provided by Empire, capitalism and translation.[18] But the Bible moves in mysterious ways. For example, in the thirteenth century, miniature Bibles and giant Bibles occupied producers equally. As processes of industrialization and modernization quickened their advance, the physical form of the Bible was subject to what seems like a counter-tendency. Whilst some Bibles became pocket-size, another form which became dominant was the heavy, large and stationary Victorian family Bible, anchored in family tradition and social stability. This form paradoxically sought to stem the flow of modernizing tendencies, whilst caught in the matrices of capitalist marketing.

The Bible Promise Box partakes of this modernizing process and in some ways may be the example par excellence. The Promise Box and the scrolls within it are transportable. The biblical text is reduced to choice and palatable morsels. The biblical verse is instantly personal. The bite-size presentation of biblical verses suits a lifestyle of rapid movement and fleeting encounters: if one wants to share biblical ideas with others, what is shared has to be swiftly communicated and to the point. Promise Boxes have moved with their owners as they are posted within the UK or abroad. Rituals of use have developed which attempt to maintain some connection with people met during ministries in far flung places. Yet the Promise Box has also moved out of public space into the private realm, even into the privacy of the bedroom where the box is kept inside a bedroom drawer: it does not leave the house, it is no longer shared. When this occurs the Promise Box seems to retreat into the darker recesses of the house much like Jonah continually travelled further down into the bowels of the ship and then the depths of the sea itself. In the face of mobility and change, a Promise Box, though sharing features of modernity's drive for abbreviation and consumption, connects the user with the timeless traditions of God's promises. The Promise Box partakes of disembedding processes whilst users utilize it to remain embedded in the Christian faith and the Bible.

The metaphor of mobility also applies to the feeling of movement and change in values and relationships – that 'all that is solid melts into air', as Berman reminds us of Marx[19]; what Bauman calls a 'liquid modernity'.[20]

---

18   See, for a full analysis, R. S. Sugirtharajah, *The Bible and the Third World: Precolonial, Colonial and Postcolonial Encounters* (Cambridge: Cambridge University Press, 2001).

19   Marshall Berman, *All That is Solid Melts into Air: The Experience of Modernity* (New York: Simon and Schuster, 1982).

20   Zygmunt Bauman, *Liquid Modernity* (Oxford: Polity, 2000).

Modern persons sense these instabilities in the context of rapid social transformations. During periods when normal day-to-day living is under threat from external forces such as natural disasters or total war, these transformations fully force themselves on the attention, but social change impacts on the mundane level too. Bryan Wilson speaks of processes of 'societalization', where the basis for social organization shifts from the local community to the nation state and beyond. The implications for religion are profound since religion 'may be said to have its source, and draw its strength from the community'.[21] When the wider community is made up of individuals who share very little, how much harder is it to share spirituality in the community of the faithful? As we have seen, sharing a Promise Box publicly requires a degree of mutual social understanding.

Anthony Giddens' concept of 'disembedding' draws out even further contemporary social changes. Giddens defines disembedding – which, as we have seen already, is closely associated with mobilities – as 'the lifting out of social relationships from local contexts and their reconstruction across indefinite time/space distances'.[22] Related to this process is the development of relevant types of symbolic media of interchange. What types of symbols can circulate with meaning between individuals and groups whose relationships are so mobile and disembedded? The media of interchange that Giddens uses to illustrate is that of money.[23] It is helpful to think of the Bible as a medium for the interchange and exchange of ideas and values in society. The Bible no longer functions as a shared discourse between persons.[24] A promise from a Promise Box has more opportunity to work as a medium of interchange and exchange in a contemporary mobile society in a fashion similar to the way in which coin money functions so much more effectively and efficiently than an economic exchange reliant on a barrow-load of goods for barter. Yet, as I have argued, the Promise Box retains its connection with the Bible: for users this explains its retention of aura; for non-users, a reason for avoiding it.

Respondents expressed in their own terms a sense of social instability. For example, a Salvationist wrote, 'Personally living in a changing world, I feel that the only unchanging truth in which we can trust is found in the Bible, and I completely trust the Promises of God.' Day-to-day living can

---

21   Bryan Wilson, *Religion in Sociological Perspective* (Oxford: Oxford University Press, 1982), p. 154.

22   Giddens, *Modernity and Self-Identity*, p. 252.

23   Giddens, *Consequences of Modernity*.

24   This state of affairs, and its consequences for politics, emerges clearly in the following studies: Clines, *The Bible*; Jacques Berlinerblau, *The Secular Bible: Why Non-Believers Must Take Religion Seriously* (Cambridge: Cambridge University Press, 2005); and Roland Boer, *Rescuing the Bible* (Oxford: Blackwell, 2007).

also of course be seen as a difficult enterprise on a personal level, especially when people have to confront personal tragedies, injustice, ill health of self and loved ones, death and bereavement, and the need to make important choices at key stages of the life cycle. Giddens speaks of the general human need to feel a sense of 'ontological security'. He defines this as 'a sense of continuity and order in events'.[25] The lack of ontological security people may feel in their everyday lives is of course related to the wider social changes we have described. One dimension of ontological security is that individuals are asked to invest a large degree of trust in expert systems which direct the various departments of modern life, in educational, welfare, health, financial and political systems. These institutions are operated by professionals with levels of knowledge and expertise that render the client dependent. To a certain extent, reading the Bible, especially through the guidance of 'corporate others', is also to depend on an expert system, though the expert system of liberal biblical scholarship is hardly trusted. The experience of expert systems, in general, however is that whilst they seem an essential and inescapable part of life in modernity, they may not always be reliable and are subject to error, corruption or, in the event, leave the individual with so much information apparently necessary for informed decision-making that making choices is not simple but rather involves the weighing of varying degrees of risk. It is on this account that sociologists speak, following Beck, of a risk society. Contemporary societies are in fact more risky than traditional societies, because there is more consciousness of risk and some personal responsibility to understanding and controlling it.

An example from health care would be those occasions when a decision needs to be made about whether to undergo certain tests during pregnancy which may harm either mother and baby or both. The individual or couple are presented with probabilities of outcome, and the decision is left to them. Individuals then must draw on principles, often of a moral basis, which in effect have no relation to the medical advice and expert knowledge they were offered. One respondent who had sadly lost a baby through miscarriage found comfort, she told me, not in the expert medical system, but in her Promise Box, when the text drawn at random was Isaiah 43.2.

The use of Promise Boxes in the contemporary world takes place in these contexts of modernity: as C. W. Mills pointed out many years ago, the sociological imagination operates to make the connections between private troubles and public issues.[26] Many of the memories of Promise Box use relay experiences from periods of high anxiety, for example, during war time, when the promises served to support individuals in times

---

25   Giddens, *Modernity and Self-Identity*, p. 243.
26   C. W. Mills, *The Sociological Imagination* (Harmondsworth: Penguin, 1959).

of trial, in the face of failure of the expert system of the State to avoid war and protect its citizens from violence. These were periods where gaining 'basic trust' in God's promises had a significant personal evidential basis. Further, Promise Box use was important in what Giddens[27] refers to as 'fateful moments': those modal points in the life course when the individual is faced with making an essential and consequential choice.

The main point is that in a context of societalization, disembedding, risk and ontological insecurity, and where it is not possible, because of these social changes, to rely on the expert systems or depend on the sociability of others, the promises of God as contained within the Promise Box stand out in stark contrast for the user. As respondents constantly underlined, but in the words of one: 'God never fails, He keeps his word. I ask God to put my name on the promise before claiming same and trust he will (and he does!) answer in His Time.' Again, a different respondent observed, 'Personally living in a changing world, I feel that the only unchanging truth, in which we can trust is found in the Bible, and I completely trust the Promises of God.'

When respondents spoke using concepts of mobility, trust and risk, they did so, not in relation to expert systems but rather in terms of being let down by people they knew; or they spoke about general worrying processes in society encapsulated in notions of a busy, hectic, time-short modern lifestyle. One respondent, recalling the promise from Deut. 31.6, 'Be strong and of good courage... He will not fail thee', mentions that 'This verse has helped me through some very dark and depressed days, when people fail and have hurt me'. For another respondent the use of a Promise Box might be a way of encouraging people to, as it were, 'slow down' and find time to think more deeply: stemming the onward rush of modernity. She wrote that, 'in fact I've considered reviving the tradition because I think life is so hurried and it is but a tool to draw people's thoughts toward God'.

Concluding Remarks

In such personal circumstances within the midst of modernity, a Promise Box for those who continue the practice provides access to the Word of God which can provide direction, comfort, encouragement and instruction to its users. Promise Box use is based on a belief in a personal God: a God who can 'direct the hand' to find a promise that is appropriate, even if the full meaning and implication of that promise might not be immediately apparent. Users trust in God and this provides ontological security and the context for interpretation. A Promise Box is a more

---

27   Giddens, *Modernity and Self-Identity*.

reliable source of needed biblical words of wisdom than the Bible considered as a whole. However, Promise Box use is more often than not followed up by further Bible reading. Particularly in a busy world, and in times of witnessing, the Promise Box provides a valuable way, it is held, to access and spread the Word of God.

The Promise Box is treasured on this account, but it is also a special and sacred object, because of its association with positive circumstances and personal connections. It is these dimensions that help explain the survival of the Promise Box and its use by various individuals in contemporary society, albeit in ever decreasing social circles and numbers. These connections, gathered from the data, include fond childhood memories of family security and shared times, of being special and being given access to a box that retained its sense of aura; inheriting something of sentimental value from a loved relative or parent; and, as often was the case, receiving a box as a gift from a respected member of the Salvation Army itself. In short, the Promise Box, through being seen as the Word of God, and being related to the ontological securities of childhood and the security provided by being a member of a religious movement, survives within modernity: it both suits aspects of the organization and lifestyle of modernity and provides means for personal survival in modernity for those who are of the frame of mind that can benefit from its use. However, the numbers of people who are of the frame of mind that makes them sympathetic to such artifacts has decreased dramatically on account of modernity, and the Promise Box, even as the Bible before it, no longer serves as a symbolic medium of interchange that eases communication and the creation of sociability throughout the social system.

For some, the Promise Box is a private affair that provides a way of accessing God's word on a regular basis; whilst for others, it is a means of sharing God's word. For those who do not believe in a personal God or mistrust the ability of a text to speak directly to them, or to be meaningful when taken out of context, the Promise Box is a curious artifact, akin to a Chinese cookie, a Christmas cracker, or even a horoscope column in a less than quality daily newspaper. Even so, all readers when faced with such texts that carry some 'supernatural aura' search for their own story and can discover, in a process that feels most uncanny to them, some connection with their own lives.

From a sociological interest in the role of the Bible in culture and society it is important to understand the meanings and practices associated with Promise Box use, to chart its history, and to provide some explanation for the survival, and the mode of survival, of this biblical artifact in contemporary culture. I hope that the above makes some contribution to that sociological goal.

THE BIBLE AS ICON: MYTHS OF THE DIVINE ORIGINS OF SCRIPTURE

Dorina Miller Parmenter

The book has been one of the most powerful tools in Christian history. Undoubtedly the preeminent Western book, the Christian Bible, has influenced more people than any other book in world history. But the foundations and legitimizations of actions, morals, and beliefs that are derived from this book are not only about the messages gleaned from the text, but also the power and authority that have been accorded to the Bible as a sacred object.[1] The Bible as both text and physical entity has been and continues to function as an icon: an image that mediates between the material and spiritual world and thus is a locus of religious power. While most people would readily agree that the Bible is an iconic book, an immediately recognizable symbol with connotations of admiration or veneration,[2] my argument is that a more careful and detailed examination of the Bible as an icon that is seen to function as a mediator will contribute to an understanding of the power and status given to this book. Looking at the Bible as an icon also helps us to understand the place of the book as a signifying material object, because often the materiality of books, and Bibles in particular, is overlooked by an exclusive focus on the signifying properties of the text.

1 See Brian Malley, *How the Bible Works: An Anthropological Study of Evangelical Biblicism* (Walnut Creek, CA: Alta Mira Press, 2004), pp. 70–72.

2 Annabel Wharton, 'Icon, Idol, Totem and Fetish', in *Icon and Word: The Power of Images in Byzantium* (ed. A. Eastmond and L. James; Aldershot: Ashgate, 2003), pp. 4, 6. The most recent entry for 'icon' in the *Oxford English Dictionary* demonstrates the dematerialization of the icon as: 'A person or thing regarded as a representative symbol, esp. of a culture or movement; a person, institution, etc. considered worthy of admiration or respect. Freq. with modifying word.' 'Icon', *OED Online*, draft additions 2001. n.p. Online: http://dictionary.oed.com [accessed 5 Feb. 2008]. In contemporary American culture, most people are familiar with symbolic icons in the sense of 'pop culture icons' such as Oprah, Superman, and Elvis, the top three American pop culture icons, according to VH1 television and *People* magazine. See *Newsweek*, '200 Greatest Pop Culture Icons List: The Folks that Have Impacted American Society' (27 October 2003). n.p. Online: http://www.azreporter.com/entertainment/television/news/200popicons.shtml [accessed 28 Feb. 2006].

Christian portrait icons, such as those debated during the iconoclastic controversies of the eighth and ninth centuries and still used in Orthodox Christian rituals today, can be examined either from a general theoretical perspective of how images work (that is, the process of visual representation), or icons can be examined more specifically with regard to shared social understandings of how particular images come to exist.[3] Hans Belting has called these explanations 'legends of veracity' or 'testimony by tradition'; they offer reasons why some images are efficacious representatives of spiritual beings and powers and others are not. He states, '[a]s applied to images of Christ the legends of veracity either asserted that a given image had a supernatural origin – in effect, that it had fallen from heaven, or affirmed that Jesus' living body had left an enduring physical impression'.[4] According to Belting, these testimonies were 'otherwise invoked by Christianity only to prove the authenticity of *texts* of revelation'.[5]

This paper will examine similar legends of veracity, or underlying myths,[6] which support the idea that the Bible functions as an icon. By classifying the Bible as an icon I mean that the Bible is often treated as a material object that facilitates access to its transcendent prototype – in this case, a heavenly book – through likeness and resemblance.[7] The Christian Bible, like other sacred texts originating in Mesopotamia and the Mediterranean, participates in a long-standing mythology of prototypical

---

3   Hans Belting, *Likeness and Presence: A History of the Image before the Era of Art* (trans. E. Jephcott; Chicago: University of Chicago Press, 1994), pp. xxi, 3–4; see also p. 7: 'For the Jews, Yahweh was visibly present only in the written word.... His icon was Holy Scripture, which is why Torah scrolls are venerated like cult images.'

4   Examples include the traditions associated with the first icon *acheiropoiētos* 'not made by human hands', the imprint of Christ's face on a cloth, or the Virgin *Hodegetria*, 'who points the way' to the Christ child on her lap, painted by the evangelist Luke. See Belting, Chapter 4, 'Heavenly Images and Earthly Portraits: St. Luke's Picture and "Unpainted" Originals in Rome and the Eastern Empire', in *Likeness and Presence*, pp. 47–77.

5   Belting, *Likeness and Presence*, p. 4, italics original.

6   Here I am using the term *myth* without recourse to judgments of truth or historicity, but primarily in reference to a shared cultural narrative, following Howard Schwartz: 'Myth refers to a people's sacred stories about origins, deities, ancestors, and heroes. Within a culture, myths serve as the divine charter, and myth and ritual are inextricably bound.' Howard Schwartz, *Tree of Souls: The Mythology of Judaism* (Oxford: Oxford University Press, 2004), p. xliv, italics omitted. Multiple stories and images comprise a myth; main sources for myths are canonized religious scriptures, but also related are oral traditions and/or non-scriptural literary traditions, and the narratives that can be gleaned from visual art. When combined together, these sources contribute to the construction of shared (yet often unconscious) understandings of how the world does (or should) work.

7   Antony Eastmond, 'Between Icon and Idol: The Uncertainty of Imperial Images', in *Icon and Word: The Power of Images in Byzantium* (ed. A. Eastmond and L. James; Aldershot: Ashgate, 2003), p. 74; David Rice and Tamara Talbot Rice, *Icons and their History* (Woodstock: The Overlook Press, 1974), p. 10.

heavenly books whose copies are revealed to humans. Another important component of icons, and of the Bible as an icon, is its ritual use, which I have addressed in another study.[8] For present purposes, I assume that myth and ritual mutually reinforce one another, not necessarily directly or even consciously, but insofar as both myths and rituals promote the idea that the book of the Bible is a manifestation of Christ and its material substance acts as a mediator between the human and divine. That is, the image of the Bible, like other icons, supports an incarnational theology.

Since Christian views of the origins of the Bible build on a common mythological pattern that can be seen throughout religions of the ancient Near East and Western monotheistic religions, this paper will briefly survey that tradition before concentrating on its Christian variants.

Heavenly Books in the Ancient Near East

The earliest images of heavenly writings that aid creation and record destinies, thus conferring power on those who access or possess them, are articulated in various ancient writings preserved on clay tablets from Mesopotamia. These heavenly books are given many names in the ancient myths: the Tablets of Wisdom, the Law of Earth and Heaven, the Tablets of the Gods, the Bag with the Mystery of Heaven and Earth, and the Tablet of Destinies,[9] which is the name that I shall use in this study, specifically with regard to particular myths, but also as synecdoche for the Mesopotamian concept of heavenly books. Sumerian literary images from the third millennium BCE describe the scribal goddess and fertility figure, Nisaba, as the heavens itself, and the stars as her writing. In the Hymn to Nisaba she is a 'Lady coloured like the stars of heaven, holding a lapis-lazuli tablet ... the holy tablet of the heavenly stars'.[10] Later myths concern battles among the gods to possess this tablet, frequently scaled down to a lapis lazuli amulet, contained in a bag and worn on the body, but nevertheless inscribed with the destiny of the universe and thus endowed with supreme power.

The Tablet of Destinies is the focal point of the Akkadian Epic of Anzu and its Sumerian counterparts from the second millennium BCE. Anzu is a

---

8   Dorina Miller Parmenter, 'The Iconic Book: The Image of the Bible in Early Christian Rituals', *Postscripts: The Journal of Sacred Texts and Contemporary Worlds* 2.2-3 (2006): 160–89.

9   Geo Widengren, *The Ascension of the Apostle and the Heavenly Book* (Uppsala: Uppsala University Press, 1950), p. 11.

10   Jeremy Black, Graham Cunningham, Eleanor Robson and Gábor Zólyomi, *The Literature of Ancient Sumer* (Oxford: Oxford University Press, 2004), pp. 292–3. Lapis lazuli (Heb. *sappîr*/sapphire), with gold-like specks embedded in deep blue stone was commonly associated with the stars and firmament. See 'lapis lazuli', *Encyclopædia Britannica Online*.: http://www.search.eb.com/eb/article-9047165 [accessed 31 Jan. 2008].

monstrous bird who is appointed guard of the god Enlil's chamber, where he constantly sees (and covets) Enlil's 'trappings of supremacy' – his crown, his clothing, and the Tablet of Destinies that he wears around his neck. Anzu gives in to his temptation and snatches the Tablet when Enlil removes it to bathe. Without the Tablet, Enlil is powerless, chaos ensues among the gods, and a warrior is sought to fight Anzu and retrieve the Tablet. Finally Ninurta battles Anzu, slays the beast, and takes control of the Tablet of Destinies. But rather than returning it to Enlil, Ninurta keeps the Tablet himself, thereby becoming the king of the gods.[11]

The same idea that the Tablet confers power on its possessor is found in the Babylonian Epic of Creation, where Marduk battles Tiamat after she wages war on the gods. When Marduk is victorious, he takes on the Tablet, and becomes the supreme god, creating the heavens, earth, and humans, who will serve the gods while they establish destinies and sit in judgment in Babylon.[12] This image of the Tablet of Destinies figured prominently in ancient Mesopotamian New Year rituals that persisted into the Roman period. After pageantry and procession, the Epic of Creation was recited and apparently reenacted, with the king defeating the power of chaos, followed by the gods fixing the destinies for the coming year, by 'writing on the Tablet of Destinies and sealing [it] with the Seal of Destinies'.[13] It was imagined that the original Tablet remained in the heavens, guarded by the seven gods of destinies,[14] but, according to Stephanie Dalley, '[w]hat the gods wrote *upon* that tablet was sometimes divulged to mankind through the markings on the liver and lungs of sacrificial animals, so that a liver upon which omens were read was referred to as the "tablet of the gods" '.[15]

In summary, there are three aspects of the recurring pattern of the ancient Near Eastern heavenly tablet:

1   There is a divine record that resides with and is under the control of the god(s), endowing the god(s) with creative power, and producing cosmic order.
2   This heavenly book is guarded and sealed, but in some aspects it can also be altered.[16]
3   The contents of the heavenly book can be revealed to humans, with

11   Epic of Anzu in Benjamin R. Foster, *From Distant Days: Myths, Tales and Poetry of Ancient Mesopotamia* (Bethesda, MD: CDL Press, 1995), pp. 115–31.
12   Epic of Creation, in Foster, *From Distant Days*, pp. 9–51.
13   Stephanie Dalley, *The Legacy of Mesopotamia* (Oxford: Oxford University Press, 1998), pp. 77, 163.
14   Epic of Creation 6.81 in Foster, *From Distant Days*, p. 41.
15   Dalley, *The Legacy of Mesopotamia*, p. 166.
16   Dalley writes that 'the gods did not inscribe every event for every individual for all time'; therefore, apotropaic rituals and penitential acts were still necessary, for '[t]he gods might make a new decision at any time' (*The Legacy of Mesopotamia*, p. 164).

the intention of allowing human participation in the ordering of the world.

This pattern of the Tablet of Destinies is found in 'Religions of the Book' and is inherent in this Qur'anic classification of Judaism and Christianity with Islam.[17] The divine book that is given from heaven figures prominently in the founding myths of each religion, resulting in the earthly books of the Torah, New Testament, and Qur'an. Also in each tradition, there are references to other divine books associated with judgment at the end of time – either a predetermined eschatological favor, like the Book of Life, or ongoing records of good and bad deeds that shall be weighed at the apocalypse. The remainder of this paper will focus on the image of heavenly books in the Christian tradition, building on Jewish images of the Torah, although there is much more that could be said about similar images in Islam as well.[18]

Heavenly Books in Ancient Israelite Traditions

In traditions from ancient Israel, Moses is both a scribe, who writes the covenant, dictated by God (Exod. 24.4-7; 4.28),[19] and he is the direct recipient of the Tablets of the Law, written by God (Exod. 24.12; 32.16; 34.1). The Mishnah suggests further details about the divine origins of these writings, claiming that 'the Text, the Writing, and the Tables' were 'created on the eve of the [first] Sabbath at twilight'.[20] The Mishnah also associates the Torah with Wisdom: the book given to humans is 'the desirable instrument wherewith the world had been created',[21] further elucidated in Proverbs chapter 8.[22] The apocryphal book of Baruch also

---

17 Qur'an 5.65, 29.46; 'Religions of the Book' also includes the religion of the Sabians, whose book was revealed to Abraham; see Qur'an surahs 2.61 and 22.17 and Geo Widengren, *Muhammad, The Apostle of God, and His Ascension* (Uppsala: Almquist & Wiksells, 1955), pp. 133–36. In *The Ascension of the Apostle*, Widengren claims that this pattern of ascent to heaven to retrieve a heavenly book 'evidently reshaped also the traditions about Zarathustra and Mani, both of whom, according to Arabic authors, are said to have brought from heaven a holy Book' (p. 85). For Wilfred Cantwell Smith, it is this transcendent dimension that defines scripture: see W. C. Smith, *What is Scripture? A Comparative Approach* (Minneapolis: Fortress, 1993), esp. ch. 10.

18 See Widengren, *Muhammad*, and *The Ascension of the Apostle*.

19 See *B. Bat.* 15a. Talmud references are from Isidore Epstein (ed.), *Hebrew-English Edition of the Babylonian Talmud* (London: The Soncino Press, 1988).

20 *Abot* 5.6.

21 *Abot* 3.14; see also *Gen. Rab.* 1.1.

22 Prov. 8.22-31 RSV: 'The LORD created me at the beginning of his work, the first of his acts of old. Ages ago I was set up, at the first, before the beginning of the earth.... When he established the heavens, I was there ... when he marked out the foundations of the earth, then I was beside him, like a master workman; and I was daily his delight, rejoicing before

includes this image of Wisdom, again described as a book, consulted by God for creation, and then obtained by humans from its home in heaven. Baruch chapter 3 states:

> Who has gone up into heaven, and taken her, and brought her down from the clouds? ... No one knows the way to her, ... [but] she appeared upon earth, and lived among men. *She is the book of the commandments of God*, and the law that endures for ever. All who hold her fast will live, and those who forsake her will die. (Bar. 3.29-4.1 RSV)[23]

Each of these images reinforces the idea that the heavenly book is no longer remote, but has been made apparent. In Deuteronomy, Moses states that the book of the law 'is *not* in heaven, that you should say, "Who will go up to heaven for us, and get it for us so that we may hear it and observe it?"... [But instead it] is very near to you, it is in your mouth and in your heart for you to observe' (Deut. 30.10, 11, 14 NSRV).[24] This reflects back upon the Exodus narrative of Sinai and Moses' ascent to receive the heavenly book from God and bring it to God's people (Exod. 19.3; 19.20; cf. Exod. 24.13; 24.15). Various writings in the Talmud imagine that Moses rode on a cloud to the gate of heaven, where he was rebuked by the angels who questioned God's transfer of the Torah and threatened to attack Moses for taking it.[25] The resistance of the angels to

---

him always, rejoicing in his inhabited world and delighting in the sons of men'. Imagining Torah/Wisdom as the first of God's creation raises further questions that are addressed in Jewish commentaries. If the Torah were created before the creation of the world (as in Prov. 8.22, above), what did it look like? How does God write, and on what? Howard Schwartz synthesizes several answers in *Tree of Souls: The Mythology of Judaism*: 'God wrote the Torah while seated on the Throne of Glory, high in the firmament above the heads of the celestial creatures. The Garden of Eden was at God's right hand, and Gehenna was at His left. The heavenly sanctuary was set up in front of Him, with the name of the Messiah engraved [on a precious stone set] upon the altar. There, as the Torah rested on His knees, God wrote the letters in black fire on white fire. Later, it was tied to the arm of God, as it is said, *Lightning flashing at them from His right* (Deut 33.2). Others say that the Torah was written on the arm of God, while still others say it was carved in fire on God's crown... And God took the Torah and placed it before Him and gazed at it, and read it from beginning to end. And as He read those words, they came to pass' (Schwartz, pp. 248 and 74, following *Midrash Tehillim* 90.12, *Eliyahu Rabbah* 31.160, *Midrash Mishlei* 8; *Midrash Konen* in *Beit ha-Midrash* 2.24-39; *Avot de-Rabbi Natan* 31, *Alpha Beta de-Rabbi Akiva* in *Otzar Midrashim* 424; and Schwartz, p. 252, following *Aseret ha-Dibrot* in *Beit ha-Midrash* 1.62 and *Merkavah Rabbah*). See also Schwartz's entries on Torah/Wisdom as *Shekhinah* and bride, pp. 45–66.

23   Italics added. Other references to heavenly books that are revealed to humans can be found in *Jubilees, 4 Ezra* 14, 1 Chron. 28.19, and Ezek. 2.9-10.

24   Italics added.

25   Schwartz, p. 261, following *B. Shabbat* 88b-89a; *B. Menahot* 29b; *B. Sukkah* 5a; *B. Yoma* 4a; *Exodus Rabbah* 28; *Pesikta Rabbati* 20.4; *Mekhilta de-Rabbi Ishmael, ba-Hodesh* 4.55-58; *Ma'ayan Hokhmah in Beit ha-Midrash* 1.60-61; *Otzrot Hayim*; *Memar Markah* 5.3.

the release of the Torah from heaven explicitly links the heavenly Torah and the earthly Torah. When the angels discovered God's plan to give the Torah to Israel, they argued that its priority over the rest of creation also meant that the Torah's place was in heaven with them. Howard Schwartz synthesizes several Talmudic images when he identifies God's reply to the angels as, 'Are you the ones who will fulfill the Torah? The Torah cannot remain with you. It would not be appropriate for it to remain in a realm of creatures who have eternal life'.[26] The written law was then dictated to Moses during the day, and the oral law was explained to him at night, revealing 'the seventy meanings of every word of the Torah, like the many facets of a perfect jewel'.[27]

Just as divine books are imagined to guide the beginning of God's creation and the beginning of the covenant with the Israelites, other divine books (or perhaps unrevealed parts of the one divine book[28]) are imagined to play a role at the end – either the end of one's life, or the end of the world and the day of judgment. Early biblical references to being recorded in the 'book of the living' seem to be about one's present earthly condition; if one is in the book, then one is alive and in God's favor, and the opposite is the case if one is 'blotted out' from the book (Ps. 51.1; 69.28; Exod. 32.33).[29] As God's rewards for the faithful are projected into the future, seen in the later writings of the Hebrew scriptures, the books become associated with a future judgment of the dead. In the vision of Daniel he sees the apocalypse and the final courtroom, where the books of judgment are opened, and those who are found written in the book of life are delivered from destruction (Dan. 7.10; 12.1). In other examples of books of judgment, you *do not* want to make it into the book that records your sins and then is referenced in order to determine your ultimate fate (Isa. 65.6-7). These eschatological books seem to be imagined as ongoing and changeable, for when they are invoked as threats of judgment or lamentations of wrongdoings, they usually refer to the hope of altering the written records (Ps. 51.1).[30] These images come together in a vision of judgment from the first-century *Testament of Abraham*, where Abraham

26   Schwartz, p. 258, following *B. Sanhedrin* 109a, *Genesis Rabbah* 188.6, and *Pesikta Rabbati* 25.2.

27   Schwartz, p. 262; see references in n. 25.

28   See Geo Widengren, 'Holy Book and Holy Tradition in Islam', in *Holy Book and Holy Tradition* (ed. F. F. Bruce and E. G. Rupp; Manchester: Manchester University Press, 1968), pp. 214–15; and Eric Jager, *The Book of the Heart* (Chicago: University of Chicago Press, 2000).

29   See Samuel George Frederick Brandon, *The Judgment of the Dead* (New York: Charles Scribner's Sons, 1967), p. 65.

30   This combination of books that seal your fate and books that are changeable records also relates to how the Babylonian Tablet of Destinies was imagined. See n. 16.

witnesses the judgment process that includes an enormous book[31] that holds the records of human deeds, and scribal angels who record the judgment based on the reading of the book. One soul up for judgment is found to be 'balanced' between sin and righteousness and thus in limbo, but is eventually recorded among the favored and sent to Paradise with the help of Abraham's prayers (*T. Ab.* 7–14).

Heavenly Books in Christian Traditions

Christian writings imagine heavenly books in much the same way as already described – as instrumental for creation in the past, made accessible to humans in the present to reveal the will of God, and pivotal in one's future fate. But in each case Christ takes on the functions of the books, because he is associated with Wisdom, Word, and Judge. Thus the heavenly text becomes more abstract and allegorical; but, as shall be shown, the earthly book maintains its prominence as an iconic connection to the original.

In the well-known prologue of the Gospel of John, Logos is the eternal creative force of God, the Word through which all things came into being. The Word that dwelled with God in heaven became accessible to humans, according to the Fourth Gospel, appearing in the flesh and living among us (Jn 1.1-14). An eleventh-century ivory carving of the narrative of Doubting Thomas – also from the Gospel of John (20.24-29) – visually links Christ's body to the heavenly book given to Moses. One panel of this manuscript cover depicts Moses reaching upward to receive a tablet from the hand of God – standard iconography for Moses receiving the law. This image is paralleled by another panel with Thomas reaching up to touch the wounds of Christ, whose head and hand have replaced the position of the hand of God.[32] As the hand of God is common iconography for the divine voice,[33] and the story of Doubting Thomas emphasizes seeing and touching, this artist is clearly demonstrating the Christian claim that God's Word, available to the Jews in speech and writing, has been made visible in the body of Christ.[34]

Several non-canonical early Christian writings continue this connection between the body of Christ and the heavenly book of God quite explicitly. In his *Letter to the Philadelphians*, Ignatius makes a supersessionist claim

---

31 'whose thickness was six cubits, while its breadth was ten cubits', *T. Ab.* 12.7.

32 See Herbert Kessler, 'The Book as Icon' , in *In the Beginning: Bibles Before the Year 1000* (ed. M. P. Brown; Washington: Smithsonian Institution, 2006), p. 97, fig. 16.

33 Herbert Kessler, *Spiritual Seeing: Picturing God's Invisibility in Medieval Art* (Philadelphia: University of Pennsylvania Press, 2000), pp. 3–4.

34 Kessler, 'Book as Icon', pp. 95–103.

against those who will only believe those points on which the 'original documents' – the revealed Torah – agree with the gospel. Ignatius writes that 'it is Jesus Christ who is the original documents. The inviolable archives are his cross and death and his resurrection and the faith that came by him' (Ign. *Phld.* 8.2).[35] In the *Gospel of Truth*,

> the living book of the living was manifest, [the book] which was written in the thought and in the mind [of the] Father ... [The book] which no one found possible to take, since it was reserved for him who will take it and be slain. . . For this reason Jesus appeared. He took that book as his own. He was nailed to a cross. He affixed the edict of the Father to the cross. (*Gos. Truth* 19–20)[36]

Christian images of books associated with sin and judgment also become attached to Christ as the savior who controls the records of transgressions and Christ as the judge who opens the books. The author of the letter to the Colossians writes that 'God made you alive together with him ... erasing the record that stood against us, with its legal demands. He set this aside, nailing it to the cross' (Col. 2.13-14 NRSV). The Revelation to John also associates Christ with the preexistent book of life. In chapter 13, those who worship the beast from the sea are 'everyone whose name has *not* been written from the foundation of the world in the book of life of the Lamb that was slaughtered' (Rev. 13.8 NSRV, italics added; cf. 21.27).[37]

The book as representative of Christ as Word, Redeemer, and Judge comes together brilliantly in a mosaic image of the Last Judgment from Torcello.[38] In this mosaic, angels, cherubim, and two kneeling figures flank a throne, occupied by a jeweled codex. This image is part of an entire Last Judgment wall, where Christ is portrayed in his different roles. At the very top one sees the crucifixion. Looking down the wall, one sees the descent of Christ to unlock the gates of Hades followed by Christ in a mandorla, surrounded by the Virgin Mary, John the Baptist, and the twelve apostles. The scene with the book and the throne are part of the resurrection register, and below that are the saved and the damned, who roast in the flames. In the scene of resurrection – the time of judgment –

35   From Cyril C. Richardson (ed. and trans.), *Early Christian Fathers LCC* 1.110.

36   From Robert M. Grant (ed.), *Gnosticism* (New York: Harper & Brothers, 1961), pp. 148–49.

37   For artistic depictions of lambs, books, and altar/thrones, see Kessler, 'Book as Icon'; Kessler, *Spiritual Seeing*; and Vladimir Baranov, 'The Theology of Early Iconoclasm as found in St. John of Damascus' *Apologies*,' Христианский Восток [*Khristianskii Vostok*] 4 (2002): 23–55. Online: http://www.nsu.ru/classics/Baranov/earlyiconoclasm.htm. Accessed 2 Sept. 2006.

38   See Ernest T. DeWald, *Italian Painting: 1200–1600* (New York: Holt, Rinehart & Winston, 1961), pp. 20–21, fig. 1.12.

two figures, perhaps Adam and Eve, kneel before the enthroned book in supplication.[39] Instead of repeating the image of Christ in human form as in other parts of the mosaic wall, here he is the heavenly book – the divine Word is also the Book of Life.

Unlike the myths of the revelations of the Torah to Moses and the Qur'an to Muhammad, Christian scripture does not portray Christ as literally inscribing, dictating, or delivering the written text of the New Testament. The earliest Christians maintained that the revelation was the gospel, with Christ as both message and messenger, and not a written text.[40] But by necessity – to evangelize and combat perceived heresy – the message had to be written and canonized. Without Christ in the flesh, the heavenly Word became known through the book. By the fourth century, in an increasingly bookish and now Christian Roman Empire, Christians were generally unified by their canonized scripture, bound in a codex, even though the content of that scripture, the gospel message of who Christ is, was still highly debated and divisive. Despite the early (and anti-Jewish) arguments against revelation as a book, visual traditions of this more bookish era of Late Antiquity and the early Middle Ages did show Christ as the distributor of heavenly books to Moses, the apostles, and the evangelists.[41] Anthropomorphic images of Christ handing over books not only demonstrated that Christ was a divine being (as the Christ image was substituted for the hand of God), but also exemplified that 'Christ is both the source and the fulfillment of scripture'.[42] Similarly, iconography of the evangelists receiving heavenly books from their corresponding cherubim demonstrated the divine inspiration or dictation of the Gospels; some images were more direct, showing Christ handing a book to each evangelist.[43]

As the Word became a book, the written words were not always the focus. Representations of the Christian scriptures in portraits where the person is holding a book, adorned with jewels, act as symbols of piety and

39   Brandon, *The Judgment of the Dead*, p. 119.

40   Hans von Campenhausen, *The Formation of the Christian Bible* (trans. J. A. Baker; (Philadelphia: Fortress Press, 1972), pp. 1, 62–63.

41   For Christ presenting the Gospels to Peter and Paul, see Vatican Psalter gr. 342, fol. 134r, in Robert S. Nelson, 'Discourse of Icons, Then and Now', *Art History* 12.2 (June 1989): 144–57. For images of Christ delivering the law to Moses, Peter, and Paul, see the mosaics of the Apsidal Chapel of the Ambulatory in John Beckwith, *Early Christian Byzantine Art: The Pelican History of Art* (Harmondsworth: Penguin Books, 1970), plates 12, 13.

42   Kessler 'The Book as Icon', p. 90.

43   For example of books from cherubim, see the evangelist pages of the Lindisfarne Gospels (British Library, Cotton ms Nero D.iv; fd. 25b, 137b, 137b, fd. 209b), in Michelle P. Brown, *The Lindisfarne Gospels: Society, Spirituality and the Scribe* (London: British Library, 2003), pp. 346–70, plates 8, 14, 18, 22. For Christ handing a book to each evangelist, see the illuminations in *The Beatus of Saint-Sever* (Bibliothèque Nationale de France, lat. 8878), easily accessible online: http://beatus.saint-sever.fr/frameset/index.htm.

authority. But the fact that scriptures were actually covered in this way,[44] and used as ritual objects in the church liturgy and otherwise, emphasizes the books' function as icons. Art historian Hanns Swarzenski has pointed out that 'gold and jewels embody and convey . . . a supernatural . . . power. And it is due to this quality that they were used in Christian art to enshrine and emphasize the transcendental revelations of the [Church]'.[45] Precious metals, jewels, and pearls, all aspects of the transparency and radiance of Heavenly Jerusalem in the Revelation of John (21.11-21), were used as 'transmitters of divine light . . . which enabled the supernatural to become operative in [the] world'.[46] Similarly, icons are material objects that transmit their transcendent prototypes, thus channeling spiritual power.[47] The adorned ritual Bible downplays the anthropomorphic image of the Word (although certainly the image of Jesus Christ often is retained on the cover art) and harkens back to a prototypical heavenly book.

In practice, icons function both for private religious contemplation and as usable cult objects capable of miraculous power. As previously mentioned, the complementary side of this study of the Bible as an icon is a survey of rituals that manipulate the book, including rituals of procession, touching, and kissing, which are abundant in Christian history, as are stories of the book's protective powers, such as when books are worn as amulets.[48] One of many examples of the ritual use of the Book attested from the fourth century onward is placing a copy of the Gospels on a throne during courtroom proceedings or in Church councils. This is

---

44   Ornamented as early as the fourth century, according to Eusebius, who reported that one of the first acts of Constantine was to order 'fifty volumes with ornamental leather bindings, easily legible and convenient for portable use, to be copied by skilled calligraphists well trained in the art, copies that is of the Divine Scriptures, the provision and use of which you well know to be necessary for reading in church'. Eusebius, *Life of Constantine*, IV.36 (trans. A. Cameron and S. G. Hall; Oxford: Oxford University Press, 1999), p. 79.

45   Hanns Swarzenski, *Monuments of Romanesque Art: The Art of Church Treasures in North-Western Europe* (Chicago: University of Chicago Press, 2nd edn, 1967), p. 13.

46   Patrik Reutersward, *The Forgotten Symbols of God* (Stockholm: Almqvist & Wiksell Tryckeri, 1982), p. 111.

47   H. P. Gerhard, *The World of Icons* (New York: Harper and Row, 1971), p. 40, and Karel van der Toorn, 'The Iconic Book: Analogies between the Babylonian Cult of Images and the Veneration of the Torah', in *The Image and the Book: Iconic Cults, Aniconism, and the Rise of Book Religion in Israel and the Ancient Near East* (Leuven: Peeters, 1997), pp. 242–44.

48   Such as F. Maltomini (trans.), 'Letter of Agbar to Jesus', *P.Oxy.* vol. 65, no. 4469 (London: The British Academy, 1998), pp. 122–29. See also Kim Haines-Eitzen, 'Miniature Books and Rituals of Private Reading in Late Antiquity' (paper presented at the AAR-SBL Annual Meeting, Philadelphia, Nov. 2005); John Chrysostom, *Homily on the Statues* 19.14 (*NPNF*[1] 9.470); *Canons of the Synod of Laodicea* 36 (*NPNF*[2] 14.151).

illustrated in a representation of the Council of Constantinople of 381,[49] and there is documentation of this practice in various other conciliar and legal records.[50] In examples such as this it is clear that the Gospels were not present to use as a textual reference, but to assure that Christ was present in the room and in any decisions that were made. The Gospel used in this way was not symbolic or commemorative, but, according to Caroline Humfress, was an 'avenue of invocation'.[51]

The underlying mythos of the Christian Bible, rooted in images of revealed divine texts, contributes to its function as an icon, an object that is perceived to mediate between the material and the spiritual world, generating power through its image and physical form rather than solely a reading of its scriptural contents. This reverence for the Bible as both text (or Word) and object (or Book) can also be found in rituals that treat the Book as if it were the divine presence itself. I contend that these rituals and myths linger in formal liturgical rituals such as Gospel processions, and also in low-church Protestant displays of the Bible. These material practices then affect contemporary Christian attitudes about how the Bible should be read and what its place should be in society.[52] A careful and critical use of the term icon, applied to the status and function of the Bible in many different Christian contexts, will show that the interplay between the material icon and scriptural text has enhanced the spiritual power attributed to the Bible much more than generally has been acknowledged.

49   See the Manuscript of Gregory of Nazianzus (Bibliotheque Nationale Ms. Gr. 510, f. 355) in D. V. Aïnalov, *The Hellenistic Origins of Byzantine Art* (New Brunswick: Rutgers University Press, 1961), fig. 100.

50   Christopher Walter, *L'Iconographie des conciles dans la tradition Byzantine* (Paris: Institut français d'études Byzantines, 1970), p. 147, fig. 46; cf. fig. 44; Caroline Humfress, 'Judging By the Book: Christian Codices and Late Antique Legal Culture', in *The Early Christian Book* (ed. William E. Klingshirn and Linda Safran; Washington: Catholic University of America Press, 2007), p. 151.

51   Humfress, 'Judging By the Book', p. 158. See also Spiro K. Kostof, *The Orthodox Baptistery of Ravenna* (New Haven: Yale University Press, 1965), p. 80.

52   For an example of an analysis of iconic texts, see James Watts, 'Ten Commandments Monuments and the Rivalry of Iconic Texts', *Journal of Religion and Society* 6 (2004), n.p. Online: http://moses.creighton.edu/JRS/2004/2004–13.html [accessed 4 Feb. 2008].

APPENDIX

Round letters: angular letters
ε θ o σ

                                  δ α λ

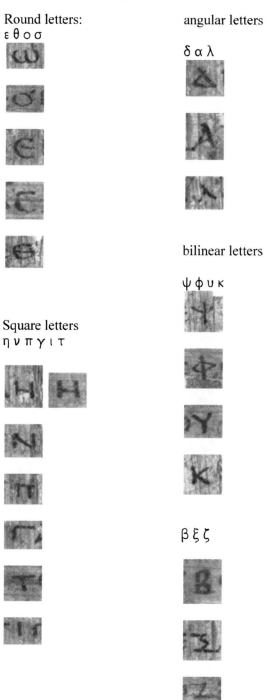

Square letters
η ν π γ ι τ

bilinear letters

ψ φ υ κ

β ξ ζ

Fig. 14 Paleography of Karanis

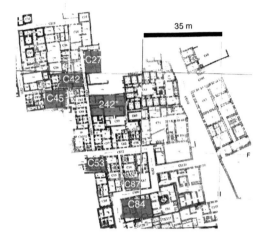

Fig. 15 Map of NORTHERN SECTOR of THE EASTERN KÔM, KARANIS
after Husselman, Topography and Architecture of Karanis (Ann Arbor 1979), Maps 11-12.
C27 P.Mich. IX 573 (Aur. Isidorus)
C42 Christian African Red Slipware (20977); wooden cross (7562)
C45 Crux ansata wall painting (Husselman, pl. 25)
242* Dump: fever amulet (P.Mich.Koenen 768)
C53 Christian African Red Slipware (7147, 7149, 20024, 20067, 7167)
C87 Karanis Psalter fr.
C84 Christian African Red Slipware (7145)

Fig. 17 fr. 1 Verso
Ps. 33:9-13 (LXX)

Fig. 16 Fr.1-2 Recto
Ps. 32:11-18 (LXX)

Fig. 18 Karanis Psalter fragment
P.Mich. inv. 5474 c

U. OF M. MUS. OF ARCHAEOLOGY

SCRIPTURE INDEX

10:25-45   210, 211, 216
10:52-54   210
10:56   211
11:30-37   211, 216
11:57   211
12   216
12:1-4   211
12:6-18   216
12:6-23   210, 211
12:16-17   211
13:36-40   211
14:18   211
14:20-23   211, 215
14:24   212
15:2-9   211
15:16-21   212

2 Maccabees
10:1-8   212
10:11   212
11:1   212
11:15   213
11:17-21   212
11:23-26   213
11:27-33   213
11:29   213
11:34-38   213

3 Maccabees
3:12-29   210
7:1-9   210
1 Esdras
2:16-24   214
2:25   214
6:27-31   214
6:34   214
8:9-24   214

Baruch
3:29-4:1   303

Pseudepigrapha

Letter of Aristeas   88
28–32   215
35–40   215
41–46   215

Testament of Abraham
7–14   305
12.7   305

Classical Writings

Aristophanes
The Knights
109–143   37
110–234   39
118–143   40
190–212   39
195–210   37
960–1096   37
960–1150   38
1000–1010   37
1003–1004   37
1035–1050   38

The Birds
957–991   41
957–995   41

Aristotle
Politics 1
1253b.1–14   234

Callimachus
Aetia book 1 (C87 K
   item A)   122

Demosthenes
In Aristocratem (C87 K
   item A)   122

Didymus Alexandrinus
Expositio in Ecclesiastes
9.9a   262

Harleanus
5635   238

Hegemonius
Acta Archelai
LXIV, 4–6   267
LXV, 2–6   267

Herodotus
7.6   32
8.20   36
8.77   35, 36
8.90-91   36
8.96   35, 36
9.43   36

Homer
Iliad
2   194

7.44-53   29

Odyssey
10.494-95   29
11.90-151   30
11.297   30
13.172   30

Libanius Ep.
1253   262

Musonius Rufus
Or. III   233
Or. IV   233

Palladius
Historia Lausiaca 37.8
   262

Pausanias
Description
I.7   33
I.22   33
1.34.4   29
8.5   33
8.31   33
8.37   33
9.35   33
9.5   33

Plato
Laws
6.780E-781D   233
7.804E-806C   233
8.838A-839B   233

Republic
364A-365A   42, 43
451C-461E   233

Pseudo-Apollodorus
Library
1.4.1   31
1.9.11   31
3.6.7   30, 31
3.10.2   31
3.12.5   31
3.12.6   31

Quintilian
Institutions
10.19   242
10.20   241

CPSIA information can be obtained at www.ICGtesting.com
Printed in the USA
BVOW010742270312

286114BV00002B/17/P